THE STUDIA PHILONICA ANNUAL
Studies in Hellenistic Judaism

Society of Biblical Literature

THE STUDIA PHILONICA ANNUAL
Studies in Hellenistic Judaism

Editors
David T. Runia
Gregory E. Sterling

THE STUDIA PHILONICA ANNUAL
Studies in Hellenistic Judaism

Volume XXV

2013

EDITORS
David T. Runia
Gregory E. Sterling

ASSOCIATE EDITOR
Sarah J. K. Pearce

BOOK REVIEW EDITOR
Ronald Cox

Society of Biblical Literature
Atlanta

THE STUDIA PHILONICA ANNUAL
Studies in Hellenistic Judaism

The financial support of

C. J. de Vogel Foundation, Utrecht
Queen's College, University of Melbourne
Yale University
Pepperdine University

is gratefully acknowledged

ISBN: 978-1-58983-937-3 (hardcover: alk. paper)
ISBN: 978-1-58983-938-0 (electronic book)
ISSN : 1052-4533

The cover photo, *Ezra Reads the Law*, is from a wall painting in the Dura Europos synagogue and used with permission from Zev Radovan (www.BibleLandPictures.com).

Printed on acid-free, recycled paper conforming to ANSI/NISO Z39.48-1992 (R1997) and ISO 9706:1994 standards for paper permanence.

∞

THE STUDIA PHILONICA ANNUAL
STUDIES IN HELLENISTIC JUDAISM

Contributions should be sent to the Editor, Prof. G. E. Sterling, 409 Prospect Street, New Haven, CT 06511, USA; email: gregory.sterling@yale.edu. Please send books for review to the Book Review Editor, Prof. Ronald Cox, Religion Division, Pepperdine University, 24255 Pacific Coast Highway, Malibu, CA 90263-4352; email: rcox@pepperdine.edu.

Contributors are requested to observe the "Instructions to Contributors" located at the end of the volume. These can also be consulted on the Annual's website: http://www.nd.edu/~philojud. Articles which do not conform to these instructions cannot be accepted for inclusion.

The Studia Philonica Monograph series accepts monographs in the area of Hellenistic Judaism, with special emphasis on Philo and his *Umwelt*. Proposals for books in this series should be sent to the Editor, Prof. Thomas H. Tobin, S.J., Theology Department, Loyola University Chicago, 1032 West Sheridan Road, Chicago, IL 60660-1537, U.S.A.; email: ttobin@luc.edu.

CONTENTS

NOTE. The editors wish to thank the typesetter Gonni Runia once again for her tireless
work on this volume. They wish to express their thanks to Kyle Conrau-Lewis (Melbourne) for his assistance with the bibliography, and also to Sister Lisa Marie Belz OSU,
and Najeeb Haddad, for meticulously proof-reading the final manuscript. As in previous
years we are deeply grateful to our publisher, The Society of Biblical Literature, and to
Leigh Andersen and Kathie Klein, for making the publication of the Annual possible.

The Studia Philonica Annual
Silver Anniversary 1989–2013

With the publication of this volume, the *Studia Philonica Annual* celebrates twenty-five years of existence. The first volume was published in 1989 by Scholars Press as volume 185 of Brown Judaic Series. It was a continuation of the earlier journal *Studia Philonica*, of which six issues were published in the years 1971–1980. In the past quarter of a century the Annual has served as a valued vehicle and instrument for research on Philo and Hellenistic Judaism. Through its articles, special sections, bibliographical section and book reviews, it has provided scholars with up-to-date information on developments in studies on Philo and his wider context, and in so doing has made a huge contribution to Philo studies world-wide. The cumulative statistics are impressive: in twenty-five years 220 articles have been published, 2549 bibliographical items have been summarized and 222 books have been reviewed. And we should also not overlook three Festschrifts (Hilgert 1991, Winston 1997, Hay 2001) and the 12 specific instruments of research that have been made available to scholars over the years in the Instrumenta section.

It is comparatively rare to have a journal devoted primarily to the research of a single ancient author. That this venture has now flourished for a quarter of a century has been made possible through the assistance of many institutions and individuals. We thank our publishers, first from 1989–2005 Scholars Press and Brown Judaic Studies, and now since 2006 the Society of Biblical Literature. For 25 years they have unfailingly underwritten a modest scholarly enterprise which without that support would not have been able to survive. Our thanks also go to the De Vogel Foundation (Amsterdam and Utrecht) which has offered an annual subsidy to the journal since 1993, as well as to a number of universities and colleges with which we have been associated. The number of individuals whom we need to thank is larger that we can list in full, but we especially acknowledge the contributions of (in rough chronological order) Robert Hamerton-Kelly† (on whom see further p. 249), Burton Mack, Earle Hilgert, Jacob Neusner, Jonathan Smith, Birger Pearson, David Hay†, David Winston, Alan Mendelson, Kenneth Fox, Shaye Cohen, Ross Kraemer, Hindy Najman, Leigh Andersen, Bob Buller, Kathie Klein, Tom Tobin and our ever faithful typesetter Gonni Runia.

May the Annual long continue to flourish, as it serves the dedicated band of Philo scholars spread over five continents of our globe.

The editors, September 2013

ABBREVIATIONS

The abbreviations used for the citation of ancient texts and modern scholarly literature generally follow the guidelines of the Society of Biblical Literature as published in *The SBL Handbook of Style* (Hendrickson: Peabody Mass. 1999) §8.4. In addition to the abbreviations listed in the Notes to contributors at the back of the volume, please note the following:

NTTSD	New Testament Tools, Studies and Documents
PCG	*Poetae Comici Graeci*
PRSt	*Perspectives in Religious Studies*
SH	*Supplementum Hellenisticum*
TAPA	*Transactions of the American Philological Association*
TLZ	*Theologische Literaturzeitung*
TrGF	*Tragicorum Graecorum Fragmenta*
TSK	*Theologische Studien und Kritiken*

The Studia Philonica Annual 25 (2013) 1–16

ENIGMATIC DREAMS AND ONIROCRITICAL SKILL
IN *DE SOMNIIS* 2

M. JASON REDDOCH[*]

Philo categorizes and interprets various dreams from Genesis in *De somniis* 1–2. At the beginning of the treatises, Philo refers to a three–fold dream classification system that he used to organize the dreams and explains that he devoted one treatise to each category.[1] The treatise that included his exegesis of the first class of dreams is no longer extant. The treatise now referred to as *De somniis* 1 deals exclusively with the second class of dreams and includes the two dreams of Jacob. *De somniis* 2 deals with the third class of dreams and includes the two dreams of Joseph as well as the dreams of the butler, the baker, and Pharaoh. Philo's classification system most resembles one attributed to Posidonius by Cicero (*Div.* 1.64), and although the details of influence are uncertain, Philo was most likely directly or indirectly influenced by the Posidonian tradition.[2] Aside from source criticism, Philo's tripartite classification system has not received a

[*] This article was adapted from my 2010 dissertation (*Dream Narratives and their Philosophical Orientation in Philo of Alexandria*) in the classics department at the University of Cincinnati. I wish to express my sincere gratitude to my dissertation advisers Prof. Peter van Minnen (UC) and Prof. Adam Kamesar (HUC, Cincinnati). I also wish to thank Prof. Daniel Marković (UC) and Prof. Susan Prince (UC) for valuable feedback.
[1] Philo, *Somn.* 1.1–2; 2.1–4. According to Eusebius (*Hist. eccl.* 2.18.4), there were originally five books on dreams. Louis Massebieau, "Le Classement des oeuvres de Philon." *Bibliothèque de l'École des Hautes Études: Sciences Religieuses* 1 (1889): 1–91, esp. 30, speculated that the two additional books must have presented a general overview of Greek philosophical attitudes to dreams (cf. PCW 3.xix–xx).
[2] PCW 3.204; PLCL 5.593–594; Émile Bréhier, *Les idées religieuses et philosophiques de Philon d' Alexandrie* (3rd ed.; Paris: Vrin, 1950), 179–196, esp. 186; Harry Austryn Wolfson, *Philo: Foundations of Religious Philosophy in Judaism, Christianity, and Islam* (2 vols.; Cambridge, MA: Harvard University Press, 1947), 2.57; Claes Blum, *Studies in the Dream Book of Artemidorus* (Uppsala: Almqvist & Wiksells, 1936), 52–71, esp. 65–71; A. H. M. Kessels, "Ancient Systems of Dream Classification." *Mnemosyne* 22 (1969): 389–424, esp. 396; Friedrich Pfeffer, *Studien zur Mantik in der Philosophie der Antike* (Meisenheim am Glan: Hain, 1976), 80–81.

great deal of scholarly attention.[3] However, the function of the classification system in relation to the exegesis has been criticized since the dreams seem to be placed in their categories arbitrarily.[4] In what follows, I shall focus on Philo's treatment of Joseph's dreams in *De somniis* 2 in order to point out an important relationship between the characteristics that Philo applies to the classification system and the dreams that fall in each category. As I shall show, Joseph's dreams are placed in the enigmatic third category because Joseph is considered a follower of the Peripatetic good, who, as a result of his misguided ethical values, was unable to understand his dreams clearly and thus required the assistance of men wise in onirocritical skill (i.e. the skill of dream interpretation).

Philo's Criteria for the Three Categories of Dreams

Philo describes all three categories as godsent (θεόπεμπτος) dreams that reveal either predictive information or information otherwise unknown to the dreamer. The first category is considered the most clear and to have been sent directly from God, and the second somewhat less clear and mediated through the World Soul. The third category is the most enigmatic and mediated by the soul of the dreamer. Aside from the mechanisms that bring about the dreams (i.e. God, World Soul, soul), the most important way Philo distinguishes between the three classes of dreams is that each is characterized by a different grade of clarity. The following is the most detailed passage in which Philo describes the importance of clarity for distinguishing between the dreams:

> διὸ ὁ ἱεροφάντης τὰς μὲν κατὰ τὸ πρῶτον σημαινόμενον φαντασίας τρανῶς πάνυ καὶ ἀριδήλως ἐμήνυσεν, ἅτε τοῦ θεοῦ χρησμοῖς σαφέσιν ἐοικότα διὰ τῶν ὀνείρων ὑποβάλλοντος, τὰς δὲ κατὰ τὸ δεύτερον οὔτε σφόδρα τηλαυγῶς οὔτε σκοτίως ἄγαν· ὧν ὑπόδειγμα ἡ ἐπὶ τῆς οὐρανοῦ κλίμακος φανεῖσα ὄψις. αὕτη γὰρ αἰνιγματώδης μὲν ἦν, τὸ δὲ αἴνιγμα οὐ λίαν τοῖς ὀξὺ καθορᾶν δυναμένοις ἀπεκρύπτετο. αἱ δὲ κατὰ τὸ τρίτον εἶδος φαντασίαι μᾶλλον τῶν προτέρων ἀδηλούμεναι διὰ τὸ βαθὺ καὶ κατακορὲς ἔχειν τὸ αἴνιγμα ἐδεήθησαν καὶ τῆς ὀνειροκριτικῆς ἐπιστήμης. πάντες γοῦν οἱ κατ᾽ αὐτὸ ἀναγραφέντες ὄνειροι τῷ νομοθέτῃ διακρίνονται πρὸς σοφῶν τὴν λεχθεῖσαν τέχνην ἀνδρῶν. (*Somn.* 2.3–4)

---

[3] For a summary of past scholarship on *Somn.* 1–2, see Earle Hilgert, "A Survey of Previous Scholarship on Philo's *De somniis* 1–2." *SBLSPS* 26 (1987): 394–402.

[4] PAPM 19.11 (cf. Hilgert, "A Survey of Previous Scholarship on Philo's *De somniis* 1–2," 397, who discusses criticism of Savinel's introduction); Madeleine Petit, "Les songes dans l'œuvre de Philon d'Alexandrie," in *Mélanges d'histoire des religions offerts à H. C. Puech* (ed. Suzanne Lassier; Paris: Presses Universitaires de France, 1974), 151–59, esp. 156; David M. Hay, "Politics and Exegesis in Philo's Treatise on Dreams." *SBLSPS* 26 (1987): 429–38, esp. 430–31.

Therefore, the hierophant revealed very clearly and conspicuously the images indicated in accordance with the first class, since God sends forth through dreams things similar to clear oracles, but those in the second class are neither very clear nor very obscure. An example of the second is the vision appearing upon the heavenly ladder. For it was enigmatic, but the enigma was not obscured too much for those who have keen vision. And the images in the third class, being more unclear than those in the first on account of having a deep and profound enigma are in need of onirocritical knowledge. For all the dreams recorded in it by the lawgiver are interpreted by men wise in the afore-mentioned skill.[5]

Here the dreams in the third category are said to be particularly enigmatic and require interpretation by someone with the appropriate onirocritical skill. The question is: how does Philo determine which dreams are enigmatic and in need of skillful interpretation? After all, the dreams in the third category that Philo labels enigmatic seem to the modern reader relatively easy to interpret, and the dreams in the second category that Philo labels moderately enigmatic seem extremely complicated.[6] In the case of the dreams of the butler, the baker, and Pharaoh, the answer is more obvious since Joseph explicitly plays the role of their dream interpreter. In other words, the biblical narrative makes it very clear that the Egyptians needed help to understand their dreams. This question is more difficult with regard to Joseph's own dreams since he does not seek out dream interpreters, and virtually everyone in the biblical narrative seems to understand the meaning of his dreams from the very beginning. A close analysis of Philo's treatment of Joseph's dreams and passages where the biblical characters respond to his dreams reveals that Philo considered Joseph's dreams to fit the same model as that of the Egyptians. When Philo describes the enigmatic nature of the third category of dreams, he is referring to the inability of the dreamer himself to make sense of his dream. When Philo describes the need for skill in dream interpretation, he is referring to the fact that some dreamers in the biblical narrative require assistance to understand their dreams because they did not perceive them clearly. Joseph's dreams are placed in the third category because Philo thought Joseph was unable to understand his dreams and was thus in need of his father and brothers to apply the appropriate onirocritical skill.

---

[5] All translations are my own.

[6] Petit, "Les songes dans l'œuvre de Philon d'Alexandrie," 156, is critical of Philo for placing the dreams of the Egyptians in the third category since their meaning seems relatively clear. Hay, "Politics and Exegesis in Philo's Treatise on Dreams," 430–31, is critical of Philo for putting Jacob's dreams in the second category since they seem very complex.

Joseph's Enigmatic Dreams

There are several passages that show that Philo's reference to the relative obscurity or clarity of a dream has to do with the experience of the dreamer. Notice that in the passage cited above, Philo explains that Jacob's dream of the ladder "...was not obscured too much for those who have keen vision" (*Somn.* 2.3). In other words, those who dream in the second category are able to understand their dreams if they have keen perception. In contrast, Philo explicitly points out that Joseph revealed uncertainty and lack of understanding when he described his dream of the sheaves to his brothers. Consider the following passage in which Philo examines the significance of the way Joseph describes his first dream:

> "ᾤμην" φησίν "ἡμᾶς δεσμεύειν δράγματα" (Gen 37.7). τὸ μὲν "ᾤμην" εὐθέως ἀδηλοῦντος καὶ ἐνδοιάζοντος καὶ ἀμυδρῶς ὑπολαμβάνοντος, οὐ παγίως καὶ τηλαυγῶς ὁρῶντος, ἀνάφθεγμά ἐστι ... ἀλλ'οὐχ ὁ ἀσκητὴς Ἰακωβ "ᾤμην" ἐρεῖ... (*Somn.* 2.17–18)

> "I thought," says Joseph, "that we were binding sheaves" (Gen 37.7). "I thought," for example, is an utterance of one who lacks clarity, is in doubt, and perceives faintly, not one who sees with strength and clarity ... By contrast, the practitioner Jacob does not say, "I thought."

Thus the difference between Jacob and Joseph is that Jacob is clear and certain about his dream while Joseph lacks these qualities, and this corresponds directly to the criterion of clarity that Philo applies to the second and third categories of dreams. In this way, the question of the enigmatic nature of a dream depends on a close reading of evidence in the narrative that suggests the dreamer's perceptual and intellectual experience was insufficient rather than on an evaluation of the complexity of the dream symbols on their own terms.

Onirocritical Skill

The idea that Joseph needed help to understand his dreams seems unlikely at first glance since Joseph, like the biblical Daniel, is generally thought of as a dream interpreter par excellence. However, Philo's presentation of Joseph being unable to interpret his own dreams in *De somniis* 2 should be understood within the larger context of Philo's seemingly contradictory treatments of Joseph in *De Josepho* and *De somniis* 2. In the former, Joseph is presented positively as a dream interpreter and a leader. In the latter, Joseph is presented negatively in association with vices such as vainglory. Using the language of mystery religion, Philo shows his awareness of this twofold aspect of Joseph when he refers to him simultaneously as both an initiate (μύστης) and initiator (μυσταγωγός) of dreams.[7] In other words, the initiate is the one who needs his dreams explained to him, and the initiator is the one who can interpret dreams for others. Although Philo never addresses this point in detail, he does suggest that at some point between Joseph's experiences as a dreamer and a dream interpreter Joseph underwent a major transformation from a life of vice to a life of virtue.[8] Thus Philo often uses dreaming and dream interpreting as metaphors for one who is ignorant/delusional and one who is knowledgeable and thus capable of dispelling the delusions/ignorance of others.[9] Whereas Joseph lacked insight as a young man dreaming of vain ambition and did not understand his dreams, Joseph was able to guide others with his insight later in life and even interpret their dreams. As I will show below, Joseph's inability to interpret his dreams in *De somniis* 2 is closely tied to his association with the Peripatetic view of the good. Thus it may be that Joseph's transformation should be understood as a movement away from Peripatetic values.

Regardless of how Philo conceived of Joseph's inability to interpret his own dreams, a close analysis of Philo's treatment of Joseph's brothers throughout his corpus and his corresponding onirocritical vocabulary demonstrates that he considers Joseph's family dream interpreters when they respond to his descriptions of his dreams.[10] In *De Iosepho*, Philo specifically says that Joseph's brothers were good at interpreting symbols.[11] Moreover, this perspective is not unique to Philo in this period since Josephus explicitly describes Joseph's brothers as dream interpreters in the *Antiquitates judaicae*.[12] In doing this, Josephus uses the noun κρίσις or the verb κρίνω, the same words he uses when he refers to Joseph and Daniel as dream interpreters in other passages.[13] Philo's vocabulary for dream interpretation is very similar, but he adds the prefix δια–, using the noun διάκρισις or the verb διακρίνω to refer to Joseph's activity as a dream

---

[7] Philo, *Somn.* 2.78.

[8] Philo, *Somn.* 2.105–108.

[9] M. Jason Reddoch, "Philo of Alexandria's Use of Sleep and Dreaming as Epistemological Metaphors in Relation to Joseph." *The International Journal of the Platonic Tradition* 5.2 (2011): 283–302, esp. 295–99.

[10] For a broad survey of Philo's onirocritical vocabulary, see Petit, "Les songes dans l'œuvre de Philon d' Alexandrie," 151–59. However, Petit does not touch on the issues discussed in this article.

[11] Philo, *Ios.* 7.

[12] Josephus, *A.J.* 2.11–17.

[13] Josephus, *A.J.* 2.64–86, 10.195–210; cf. *B.J.* 3.351–353, where Josephus uses the same vocabulary to refer to himself as a dream interpreter in relation to his own dreams.

interpreter in *De Iosepho* and *De Migratione Abrahami*.[14] Similarly, Philo also uses διακρίνω in *De somniis* 2 when referring to the need for onirocritical skill in relation to the third category of dreams.[15] The most basic meaning of this word is to separate, and thus it can mean to discern, judge, or examine.[16] The use of the word to refer specifically to dream interpretation is relatively rare outside of Philo, but as I have pointed out, he is fairly consistent in using it this way throughout his corpus.[17] Philo may also sometimes use διαστέλλω interchangeably with διακρίνω/διάκρισις.[18] I will discuss an important example of this below.

The terminology is important because Philo characterizes the response of Joseph's brothers to his dream in *De somniis* 2 using the same oniro-critical vocabulary. In the following passage Philo describes the indignant response by Joseph's brothers to his dream as a διάκρισις:

διάκρισις δὲ τοῦ μὲν προτέρου μετὰ σφοδρᾶς ἐπανατάσεως τοιαύτη· "μὴ βασιλεύων βασιλεύσεις ἐφ᾽ ἡμῖν; ἢ κυριεύων κυριεύσεις ἡμῶν;" (*Somn.* 2.7)

And the interpretation of the first [dream] with vehement threatening was this: "Will you really be a king over us? Or will you really be a lord over us?"

The explicit meaning of this passage based on the onirocritical vocabulary (i.e. the brothers are providing an actual interpretation of Joseph's dream) has been obscured for the modern reader by the seemingly straightforward symbolic content of the dream: the sheaves of the brothers bow down to the sheaf of Joseph, and thus the dream clearly points to a time when Joseph will have power over his family. The brothers seem to be asking a question about a dream, the meaning of which is apparent to everyone. However, from the perspective of Philo, the offended brothers essentially use a rhetorical question to offer an interpretation of the dream. Philo's treatment of the brothers' indignant response as dream interpretation perhaps also seems strange because they do not explicitly decode the dream symbol by symbol. On the other hand, their response does indicate the prophetic value of the dream while at this point in the narrative it has not been made

---

[14] Philo, *Ios.* 93, 98, 110; *Migr.* 19 (διαστέλλω is also used interchangeably here with διακρίνω).

[15] As in the first passage cited above (*Somn.* 2.4).

[16] Philo, *Somn.* 2.21–30 discusses harvesting as a metaphor for διάκρισις in the more general sense of "discernment."

[17] Also cf. Pausanias, *Descr.* 1.34.5, where διάκρισις may be used to refer to the interpretation of dreams. It may also be used in a medical context to refer to a diagnosis (e.g. Soranus 2.23).

[18] Philo, *Migr.* 19; *Somn.* 2.110.

explicit, and there is no suggestion that Joseph himself understands the dream.

There is also explicit evidence that Philo regarded Joseph's second dream of the celestial objects in exactly the same way. The passage below occurs as Philo moves from Joseph's first dream to his second dream. Having finished with his allegorical interpretation of the first, he writes the following:

> ἡ μὲν οὖν ἐπὶ τῶν δραγμάτων φανεῖσα ὄψις ἀπὸ γῆς καὶ διάκρισις εἴρηται· τὴν δὲ ἑτέραν καιρὸς ἤδη σκοπεῖν, καὶ ὡς ὀνειροκριτικῇ τέχνῃ διαστέλλεται. (*Somn.* 2.110)

> Therefore, the vision that appeared regarding the sheaves from the earth and the interpretation [of this vision] have been described. Now it is time to examine the other [vision] and how it is interpreted by onirocritical skill.

At first glance, Philo's reference here to διάκρισις might seem to refer to the allegorical interpretation that he has just finished in the previous section. If this were the case, then one would be inclined to read the following reference to ὀνειροκριτικὴ τέχνη as the skill that Philo himself will apply to the next dream as it is interpreted (διαστέλλεται).[19] However, there is an alternative reading of this passage that is more consistent with Philo's onirocritical vocabulary, which I described earlier. When Philo refers to the interpretation (διάκρισις) of the vision (ὄψις), he is not referring to his exegesis of the whole dream narrative; rather, he is referring to two categories of biblical passages, both of which are the object of his exegesis.[20] The vision (ὄψις) is Joseph's actual description of what he saw, and the interpretation (διάκρισις) is the interpretive response made by Joseph's brothers. As Philo then looks forward to his exegesis of Joseph's second dream, he basically restates the same idea in different words. By ἕτερα, he means the ὄψις of the next dream. When he refers to the interpretation (διαστέλλεται) that will be accompanied by onirocritical skill, he means the response to Joseph's second dream by his father, which also in effect interprets Joseph's dream for him. This reading of the passage is confirmed by what immediately follows—that is, an account of Joseph's description of the sun, moon, and stars bowing down to him as well as a disgruntled objection by his father at the implication of the dream. This passage also

---

[19] Cf. *Migr.* 19 where διαστέλλω and διακρίνω are used interchangeably to refer to Joseph's activity as a dream interpreter.

[20] In contrast to διαστέλλω and διακρίνω / διάκρισις, which refer to the interpretation of dreams in terms of their prophetic content, Philo uses ἀκριβόω more often to refer to his allegorical interpretation of the dream narrative. See esp. *Somn.* 1.4, 2.17, 2.155. In *Somn.* 2.197, ἀκριβόω refers to the dreamer discerning the dream in his mind's eye.

highlights the point that Philo himself is not practicing practical dream interpretation.[21] His interpretive activity in *De somniis* 1–2 is better described as a classification and exegesis of biblical dreams in their narrative contexts.

Joseph as a Representative of the Peripatetic Good

Thus far I have shown that Philo's characterization of the third category of dreams as enigmatic and in need of onirocritical skill corresponds directly to his treatment of the biblical narrative about Joseph's dreams. In the remainder of this article, I shall analyze the relationship between the third category of dreams and the ethical associations of the individual dreamers. Joseph's inability to understand his dreams is presented by Philo as a direct product of his association with the Peripatetic good, which, for Philo, corresponds to the lowest level of virtue.[22]

After Philo has reviewed the three categories of dreams and their basic characteristics at the beginning of *De somniis* 2, he explains that before he goes on to examine the dreams he must make some prefatory remarks. In this brief section (*Somn.* 2.8–16), Philo contrasts those who think that the good is three–fold and thus mixed with those who think it is singular and thus pure. The idea that the good is mixed and consists not only of virtue but also of physical well–being and external goods is a reference to the Peripatetic position, which he commonly associates with Joseph.[23] The singular and pure good is a reference to the Stoic position which asserts that only the morally good is truly good and is often expressed in the well

---

[21] Philo shows almost no interest in the predictive or prophetic value of the dreams, and there is no evidence that Philo is presenting his exegesis in *De somniis* 1–2 as a form of popular dream interpretation. Only Robert M. Berchman, "Arcana Mundi: Magic and Divination in the *De Somniis* of Philo of Alexandria," *SBLSPS* 26 (1987): 403–28, has argued for a direct relationship between Philo and popular dream interpretation such as Artemidorus. Unfortunately, Berchman often cites passages that do not support his claims and relies on a misuse of Philo's onirocritical terminology. For criticism of Berchman, see Derek S. Dodson, "Philo's *De Somniis* in the Context of Ancient Dream Theories and Classifications," *PRSt* 30 (2003): 308–309. Also note that in the introduction to his article, Berchman misquotes Wolfson, *Philo*, 2.55. By leaving out one word ("these"), the meaning of the quote is totally changed.

[22] Although Philo upholds the superiority of the Stoic view, he is at times much more accepting of the Peripatetic view; see *Her.* 285–86 and John Dillon, *The Middle Platonists* (2nd ed.; Ithaca, NY: Cornell University Press, 1996), 147–48.

[23] Other passages in which Philo associates Joseph with the Peripatetic idea of the three–fold good include the following: *Det.* 7; *Sobr.* 13; *Migr.* 22, 203.

known Greek phrase μόνον τὸ καλὸν ἀγαθόν.[24] Philo specifically contrasts Joseph as a representative of the Peripatetic good with Isaac as a representative of the Stoic good. In contrast to the austerity and vigor with which those who think that the good is pure are characterized, those who, like Joseph, think it is mixed are considered soft and prone to excess. Philo does not explain why he is making this digression, but as the treatise progresses, the relevance of this for Joseph as a dreamer becomes apparent.

As I have already shown, Philo contrasts Joseph's lack of clarity with Jacob's certainty about his dream (*Somn.* 2.17–18). As Philo goes on to elaborate, he explains that a dreamer's clarity is directly tied to his notion of virtue and corresponding actions. Still referring to Joseph's uncertainty in recounting his dream, Philo makes the following claim:

τῶν γὰρ τὸ καλὸν δι᾽ ἑαυτὸ αἱρετὸν νομιζόντων καὶ τὰς ἐν τοῖς ὕπνοις φαντασίας εἰλικρινεστέρας καὶ καθαρωτέρας ἐξ ἀνάγκης εἶναι συμβέβηκεν, ὥσπερ καὶ τὰς μεθ᾽ ἡμέραν δοκιμωτέρας πράξεις. (*Somn.* 2.20)

The images during sleep are necessarily clearer and purer for those who consider moral virtue desirable on its own, just as their daytime actions are more worthy of praise.

The reference here to "those who consider moral virtue desirable on its own" is to the Stoic idea of the singular good. Joseph's inability to understand his own dream is a product of his incorrect philosophical view, which, in turn, also causes his actions to be less virtuous. Thus Philo's criterion of clarity for his three categories of dreams is presented in terms of the Hellenistic debate between the Stoic and Peripatetic goods.[25]

The close connection that Philo draws between the Peripatetic good and Joseph as a dreamer who lacks virtue also makes sense in terms of Philo's allegorical interpretation of him throughout *De somniis* 2. Joseph and his dreams are primarily interpreted in terms of κενὴ δόξα, or vainglory, as it is commonly translated, and in this sense, the allegorical interpretation of Joseph is based on the metaphorical notion of a confused dreamer who

[24] This phrase occurs in Philo at *Det.* 9. Also see *Post.* 133 (= *SVF* 3.31).

[25] The idea that virtue alone is good and all that is needed to be happy is explicitly attested as far back as Zeno: *SVF* 1, fr. 187 (= Diogenes Laertius 7.127). Antiochus of Ascalon embraced the Peripatetic good; see Dillon, *The Middle Platonists*, 70–75, 123. The two students of Panaetius were said to have maintained the Stoic good: on Posidonius, see Ludwig Edelstein and Ian G. Kidd, *Posidonius: The Fragments* (3 vols.; Cambridge: Cambridge University Press, 1988–1999), T 38, = Cicero, *Tusc.* 2.61 (cf. Edelstein–Kidd, *Posidonius*, fr. 171–73); on Hekaton, see *SVF* 3, fr. 30, = Diogenes Laertius 7.101. Both positions are represented in Alexandria around the time of Philo: on Eudorus, who upheld the Stoic good, see Dillon, *The Middle Platonists*, 123–26; on Potamon, who upheld the Peripatetic good, see Diogenes Laertius *proem* 21 and Dillon, *The Middle Platonists*, 138, 147.

does not understand what he sees.[26] Joseph's lack of knowledge causes him to entertain grand fantasies, and he is treated as the embodiment of arrogance and worldly power since he suffers from vain aspirations of lording over his family. In other words, he is obsessed with external goods.[27] The dreams of the Egyptians also have the same type of associations with the Peripatetic good. As a symbol of the body, Egypt is associated with the negative values of physical and external goods, and Philo actually interprets the dreams of the butler and the baker as allegories of drunkenness and gluttony.[28] Unfortunately, *De somniis* 2 abruptly cuts off in the middle of Philo's interpretation of Pharaoh's first dream, but in the extant portion, Philo emphasizes his role as leader of the pleasures of the butler and baker.[29] Thus the Egyptians and their dreams collectively embody the physical pleasures, and all the dreamers in the third category have close associations with negative values corresponding to what Philo dislikes about the Peripatetic three-fold good.

There is no evidence of anyone else drawing a connection between various classes of dreams and the Hellenistic debate regarding the nature of the good, and it is unclear exactly how systematic Philo might have intended this to be. The connection between Jacob and the Stoic good also occurs in *Quod Deterius*, where Joseph, because of his variegated coat, is described as a representative of the Peripatetic good. According to Philo, Jacob is capable of instructing Joseph in Stoic ethics, but the brothers will do it because they are more gentle teachers.[30] The fact that Philo connects their ability to understand their dreams with their levels of virtue suggests that Philo's classification system is arranged from the first to the third class in terms of descending levels of virtue. If this is the case, then the first category of dreams should have included the most virtuous dreamer(s).

The traditional view established by Louis Massebieau in 1889 has been that Abimelech and/or Laban must have been the subject of the no longer extant first treatise.[31] The possible connection between the categories of dreams and different levels of virtue calls this into question. I have no

---

[26] See n. 9 above.

[27] See esp. Philo, *Somn.* 2.31–67, 110–116, 123–138.

[28] See esp. Philo, *Somn.* 2.155–163, 205–214.

[29] See esp. Philo, *Somn.* 2.215.

[30] *Det.* 6–9; cf. Dillon, *The Middle Platonists*, 146–148.

[31] Massebieau, "Le Classement des oeuvres de Philon," 30; PCH 3.163–164; PAPM 19.11; Clara Kraus Reggiani, *Filone di Alessandri: L'uomo e Dio. Il connubio con gli studi preliminari, La fuga e il ritrovamento, Il mutamento dei nomi, I songi sono mandati da Dio* (Milan: Rusconi, 1986), 51–52; Wolfson, *Philo*, 2.57–58; PLCL 5.593; James Royse, "The Works of Philo," in *The Cambridge Companion to Philo* (ed. Adam Kamesar; Cambridge: Cambridge University Press, 2009), 44–45; SHJP 3.2, 840.

intention of resolving this issue in the present article, but I would like to point out the importance of considering Isaac as a possible candidate. Sofía Torallas Tovar was the first to take this option seriously,[32] and I believe that the evidence presented in this article further supports her position. As a representative of the Stoic good, Isaac is specifically contrasted with Joseph at the beginning of *De somniis* 2.[33] Since Philo contrasts Jacob and Joseph in terms of this ethical debate and Jacob was the subject of the second class of dreams, the contrast between Isaac and Joseph under similar terms suggests that he also appeared in one of the lost treatises.

The location of Philo's treatises on dreams within the Allegorical Commentary as a whole also has some bearing on the question of which dreamer(s) Philo included in the first class of dreams. At the beginning of *De somniis* 1, Philo explains that the preceding treatise dealt with the first class of dreams.[34] *De somniis* 1 begins with Gen 28:10, and since the extant portions of *De somniis* 1–2 maintain a linear progression, it stands to reason that the first class of dreams focused on dreams/dreamers prior to Gen 28:10.

There is a large gap in the Allegorical Commentary prior to *De somniis* 1, and the last known treatise before it is the fragmentary *De Deo*, which went at least as far as Gen 18:2.[35] Thus assuming that Philo maintained the linear progression prior to *De somniis* 1, the missing treatise that dealt with the first class of dreams probably covered dreams somewhere between Gen 18:2 and 28:10. Since Laban's dream (Gen 31:24) actually falls after Gen 28:10, it seems unlikely that he would have been an important focus.[36] Abimelech's dream (Gen 20:3–7) falls within the expected boundaries and thus is certainly a possible candidate. The only question is whether or not Philo could have considered him virtuous enough to be included in the first

---

[32] Sofía Torallas Tovar, *El De Somniis de Filón de Alejandría* (Universidad Complutense de Madrid Ph.D., 1995), 306–62, esp. 352–62; eadem, *Filón de Alejandría: Sobre los sueños; Sobre José, introducción, traducción y notas* (Biblioteca Clásica Gredos 235; Madrid: Gredos, 1997), 32–35; eadem, "Philo Alexandrinus' *De Somniis*: An Attempt at Reconstruction," (Resource Pages for Biblical Studies 5, 1997), www.torreys.org/bible/mariaart.htm; eadem, "Sobre la clasificación de los sueños de Filón de Alejandría y sus implicaciones posteriores," *Cuadernos de filología clásics* 9 (1999): 191–212, esp. 191; eadem, "Philo of Alexandria on Sleep," in *Sleep*, (ed. Thomas Widemann and Ken Dowden; Nottingham Classical Literature Studies, vol. 8; Bari: Levante, 2003), 41–52, esp. 42–44.

[33] Philo, *Somn.* 2.10.

[34] Philo, *Somn.* 1.1.

[35] Royse, "The Works of Philo," 43–44.

[36] There is no extant reference by Philo to Laban's dream.

category.[37] It does not seem impossible that Abimelech was included in a discussion of the first class of dreams, but it is very difficult to imagine Philo making him the sole focus of a treatise about dreamers characterized by the highest level of virtue. Thus at the very least he was probably paired with another dreamer. If Isaac was included in the first category, then it was because of his nighttime vision at the Well of the Oath (Gen 26:24). The reason most scholars have not focused on Isaac as a possibility is probably because his vision is not explicitly described as a dream in the biblical narrative. However, considering the connection Philo draws between dreaming and virtue and the location of Isaac's vision within Gen 18:2 and 28:10, he should at least be considered.[38] The idea that Philo included Isaac along with Abimelech in the first class of dreams similarly to the way he included Joseph along with the Egyptians in the third class of dreams is compelling.

Virtue and Dreaming in Philosophical Context

Philo's application of different levels of virtue to different categories of dreams can be understood in terms of developments taking place in the philosophical tradition. From early to late antiquity, a number of authors related the efficacy of prophetic dreaming to virtue or the condition of the soul. Although the connection between virtue and prophetic dreaming may have connections to Orphic religion,[39] it appears prominently in Platonic and Stoic contexts. Book 9 of Plato's *Republic* seems to be an important point of inspiration for the later tradition as it relates to Philo.[40] In this passage, Socrates explains the process of prophetic dreaming in terms of

[37] When Philo refers to Abimelech's dream in *QG* 4.62, he describes him as a fool who lives in a daze. If the highest level of virtue was required for someone to dream in the first class, then this Armenian fragment suggests that Abimelech could not have been included in this category.

[38] The only extant passage where Philo mentions Isaac's vision is in *QG* 4.3* preserved in Latin (= Françoise Petit, ed., *L'ancienne version latine des Questions sur la genèse de Philon d'Alexandrie* [2 vols.; Berlin: Akademie Verlag, 1973], 1:68.). Philo does not say in this passage whether he considers Isaac's vision a dream, but he does emphasize Isaac's peaceful and virtuous demeanor during this prophetic experience.

[39] Sofía Torallas Tovar, "Orphic Hymn 86 'To Dream': On Orphic Sleep and Philo," in *Tracing Orpheus: Studies of Orphic Fragments* (ed. Herrero de Jáuregui et al.; Berlin: De Gruyter, 2011), 405–11.

[40] Plato, *Resp.* 9.571c–572b. This passage and a number of others that I discuss below have been analyzed in a similar context in relation to Medea's dream in Apollonius' *Argonautica* by M. Jason Reddoch, "Conflict and Emotion in Medea's 'Irrational' Dream (A.R. 3.616–35)," *Acta Classica* 53 (2010): 49–67, esp. 58–63.

the tripartite soul. One who stimulates the irrational parts of the soul before sleep is more likely to have shameful dreams and less likely to have prophetic dreams. In contrast to Philo who says that lack of virtue simply makes prophetic dreams more difficult to understand, this passage simply says that lack of virtue makes dreams less likely to be prophetic. Despite this distinction, they both share the basic notion that virtue has a positive effect on one's ability to have prophetic dreams.

That this passage from Plato's *Republic* is relevant for Philo is evident since it recurs in later authors where there are various other connections to Philo. First of all, a Latin paraphrase of this passage appears in Cicero's treatise on divination (*Div.* 1.60–61). This is particularly important because it occurs only a few sections before Cicero attributes a tripartite classification system to Posidonius that most closely resembles the one used by Philo (*Div.* 1.64). Exactly where Cicero's Posidonian sources begin and end in this treatise is difficult to determine, and thus it is possible but uncertain if a connection between the classification system and the passage from Plato's *Republic* was already made by Posidonius.[41]

Regardless whether Posidonius specifically applied this passage to his tripartite dream classification or not, there is another fragment in the dialogue that confirms that Posidonius thought there was an important connection between virtue and divination in general:

> ut igitur qui se tradidit quieti praeparato animo cum bonis cogitationibus tum rebus ad tranquillitatem adcommodatis, certa et vera cernit in som nis, sic castus animus purusque vigilantis et ad astrorum et ad avium reliquorumque signorum et ad extorum veritatem est paratior. (Cicero, *Div.* 1.121)[42]

> Therefore just as one who has given himself over to quietude when his soul is furnished with both good thoughts and matters beneficial for tranquility discerns definite and true things in dreams, so the innocent and pure soul of the one who is awake is more prepared for the truth of stars, birds and the remaining signs and of animal entrails.

Thus the ability to have prophetic dreams and the efficacy of other forms of divination require a virtuous person with a well–conditioned soul. The idea that the soul needs to be characterized by peace and tranquility in order to prophesy effectively suggests, like book 9 of the *Republic*, that the passions

[41] On Cicero's use of Posidonius and other sources in *De Divinatione*, see the following: David Wardle, *De Divinatione: Book I* (Oxford: Clarendon Press, 2006), 28–36; Pfeffer, *Studien zur Mantik in der Philosophie der Antike*, 74–81; Stanley Pease, *De Divinatione. Liber Primus, Liber Secundus* (2 vols; Urbana, IL: University of Illinois Press, 1920–1923), 1:18–28.

[42] Cicero, *Div.* 1.121 is considered a Posidonian fragment by Willy Theiler, *Die Fragmente* (2 vols.; Berlin: de Gruyter, 1982), fr. 376, but not by Edelstein–Kidd, *Posidonius*.

inhibit divination through dreams. However, it is unclear whether the Posidonian fragment is saying that the passions totally prevent prophetic dreams (like Plato) or that the passions only distort prophetic dreams and make them hard to understand (like Philo). The fact that there are a number of variations on these basic ideas in both Stoic and Platonic contexts suggests that book 9 of the *Republic* directly or indirectly inspired an array of possibilities from which Philo could have drawn.[43]

The passage from Plato's *Republic* also appears in the later Neoplatonic tradition. Calcidius, the Christian Neoplatonist, translates into Latin the passage from book 9 of the *Republic* in his commentary on Plato's *Timaeus*.[44] The passages preceding Calcidius' discussion of dreams certainly contain at least one fragment from the Old Stoa and have been labeled Posidonian.[45] After citing the passage from the *Republic*, Calcidius goes on to discuss Socrates in the following two sections (§§254–255) and explains that his ability to dream prophetically is a product of his purity of body and soul. He explains that some dreams come about in conjunction with the rational part of the soul and some are the product of disturbance when the soul is overwhelmed by the passions.[46] Perhaps most interestingly, Calcidius goes on to claim that Plato's theory of dreaming is consistent with Hebrew philosophy (*Hebraica philosophia*). The source of Calcidius's knowledge of Hebrew philosophy here is uncertain, but some have argued that it is a

---

[43] Variations on the idea that virtue affects prophetic dreaming appear in the following: Artemidorus, *Onir.* 4.proem (= Pack, p. 239, lines 14–19); Iamblichus, *Myst.* 3.3; Synesius, *Insomn.* 15. Reflecting a Stoic taxonomy of the passions, Artemidorus specifically says that hope and fear prohibit predictive dreams since they make the soul turbid (cf. Reddoch, "Conflict and Emotion in Medea's 'Irrational' Dream," 61–63). Iamblichus describes three types of dreams that are experienced on a sliding scale of purity depending on their origin. There is a direct connection between the classification systems of Posidonius and Iamblichus according to Pfeffer, *Studien zur Mantik in der Philosophie der Antike*, 81–82, 137–142. Theiler, *Fragmente*, includes *Myst.* 3.3 among the fragments of Posidonius. According to Synesius, all dreams are prophetic but differ in terms of their depth of enigma and need for onirocritical skill. He specifically says that those who are virtuous are more likely to have prophetic dreams with obvious meaning. On *Insomn.* 15, see M. Andrew Holowchak, "Synesius' Mantike Techne: A Neoplatonic Paean to Prophecy Through Dreams," *Journal of Neoplatonic Studies* 8 (1999–2000): 1–22.

[44] Calcidius, *Comm. in Ti.* 253.

[45] Calcidius, *Comm. in Ti.* 251 = *SVF* 2, fr. 1198; *Comm. in Ti.* 248–253 is strongly Posidonian according to Blum, *Studies in the Dream Book of Artemidorus*, 58.

[46] *Multiformis ergo est ratio somniorum, siquidem sunt quae velut percussa grauius verberataque mente vestigiis doloris penitus insignitis per quietem refouent imagines praeteritae consternationis, sunt item quae iuxta cogitationes rationabilis animae partis vel purae atque immunis a perturbatione vel in passionibus positae oboriuntur, nihiloque minus quae divinis potestatibus consulentibus praemonstrantur vel etiam poenae loco ob delictum aliquod formata in atrocem et horridam faciem* (Calcidius, *Comm. in Ti.* 256).

veiled reference to Philo.[47] Considering the emphasis Philo put on the connection between virtue and prophetic dreaming, I believe this to be all the more likely. Interestingly, the categories of dreams that Calcidius attributes to Plato seem to be an artificial formulation gleaned from various passages in the Platonic corpus, and they do not match Philo's three categories of dreams in an exact way. Thus there is no reason to think that Calcidius was engaged in a close reading of primary sources; rather, he was the heir of an interpretive tradition in which Jewish and Platonic sources had already been assimilated through a Stoic channel.[48] Philo's use of the Posidonian classification system and the close connection between the passage from Plato's *Republic* and various Posidonian contexts suggests that Plato's influence affected the later tradition indirectly through Stoic sources, which may have elaborated on or reformulated the basic idea that virtue affects prophetic dreaming. Philo's classification system and his emphasis on virtue and its relationship to prophetic dreaming are a product of this development.

Conclusion

The placement of Joseph's dreams in the most enigmatic third category can be explained by an emphasis Philo places on Joseph's inability to understand his dreams and the help he gets from his family who are able to play the role of dream interpreters. Thus Philo's description of the third class of dreams being enigmatic and requiring onirocritical skill corresponds to the placement of Joseph's dreams in the third category. The reason for Joseph's inability to understand his dreams is presented by Philo as a product of Joseph's lack of virtue and association with the Peripatetic three–fold good. This link between virtue and prophetic dreaming shows that Philo's treatment of dreams was influenced by a popular notion inspired by Plato's *Republic* that one who is virtuous is better able to prophesy through

[47] Jan Hendrik Waszink, "Die sogenannte Fünfteilung der Träume bei Chalcidius und ihre Quellen." *Mnemosyne* 9 (1941): 65–85. Waszink thinks that Calcidius got his classification system from Porphyry and Porphyry got it from Philo via Numenius. Cf. Pfeffer, *Studien zur Mantik in der Philosophie der Antike*, 83–84; Kessels, "Ancient Systems of Dream Classification," 406–07; Claudio Moreschini, *Calcidio. Commentario al "Timeo" di Platone* (Milan: Bompiani, 2003), 753–754, n. 645; Blum, *Studies in the Dream Book of Artemidorus*, 59; Torallas Tovar, "Sobre la clasificación de los sueños de Filón de Alejandría y sus implicaciones posteriores," 205–9.

[48] Strabo (*Geogr.* 16.2.35–39, = Theiler, *Fragmente*, fr. 133) preserves another Posidonian fragment in which the notion that virtue affects prophetic dreaming is attributed to Moses.

dreams. The importance Philo places on virtue in relation to prophetic dreaming suggests that each of Philo's three categories of dreams corresponds to a different level of virtue. This relationship provides some basis for speculating on the content of the lost treatise that preceded *De somniis* 1, in which Philo dealt with the first class of dreams. Considering the connection between virtue and prophetic dreaming, the first class of dreams probably included some biblical dreamers that Philo considered particularly virtuous, and thus Isaac emerges as an important contender.

Colorado Mesa University

The Studia Philonica Annual 25 (2013) 17–39

"AFTER THE WAYS OF WOMEN": THE AGED VIRGIN IN PHILO'S TRANSFORMATION OF THE PHILOSOPHICAL SOUL

NICOLE L. TILFORD

Since Richard Baer's 1970 monograph on Philo's usage of "male" and "female" categories, scholars have attempted to comprehend Philo's portrayal of women and his usage of masculine and feminine terminology to represent the intellectual and sensual faculties of the human soul. Particularly troubling in this regard has been Philo's descriptions of "spiritual childbearing"—that process by which the male philosopher allegorically assumes the role of a "virgin" woman in order to produce the spiritual offspring (i.e., wisdom) of God—for the image contains a positive adoption of feminine imagery that seems somewhat at odds with the overwhelming negative portrayal of women found elsewhere in Philo's writings.

Perhaps most perplexing in this regard is Philo's adoption of the biblical matriarch Sarah as the preeminent example of the soul's progression towards wisdom. Sarah, a woman barren for the greater part of her life, miraculously produces an offspring for her husband Abraham, despite being ninety years old and post-menopausal. This miraculous event occurs only after it has "ceased to be with [Sarah] after the ways of women" (Gen 18:11), a phrase which Philo interprets to mean that Sarah has returned to a virgin state. While such a miracle could be interpreted as proof of God's divine power, Philo presents Sarah's transformation as a natural phenomenon and a necessary prerequisite for all philosophers wishing to achieve intellectual perfection. There seems to be little doubt in his mind that the contemporary male philosopher would have trouble fathoming an event that might seem at first glance a biological impossibility.

Here, I will argue that Philo's perception of the spiritual child-bearer, particularly his depiction of the aged woman-turned-virgin that is embodied in Sarah, is heavily influenced by the Hellenistic medical understandings of reproduction and aging of his day. As I shall show, the medical literature with which Philo would have been familiar suggests that virginity is not a state limited to an adolescent, unmarried female; rather, virginity is something that can be lost or regained throughout the woman's lifecycle, particularly as she approaches old age. If this is the understanding of virginity under which Philo operated, then the "virgin soul" of the spiritual child-bearer that Philo envisions through Sarah is not that of a callow youth, unacquainted with the pleasures of the flesh, but rather an experienced sage who, like an older woman, has suffered through the bearing of fleshly children (in this case, encyclical knowledge), has cast off his "feminine ways" (sense-perception), and has now returned to a virginal *masculine* state, dry and ready to bear spiritual children (wisdom). This image, although feminine on the surface, reinforces the maleness of the perfect philosophical soul and therefore stands in harmony with the negative portrayal of women found elsewhere in Philo's writings.

A Platonic Worldview

Following the teachings of Plato, Philo ascribes to a view of reality in which two spheres of existence operated concurrently. On the one hand, there is the intelligible world, an immaterial and incorporeal realm in which the "Ideas," or divine Forms, of the corporeal world exist in a pure, unadulterated state. It is here, in this intelligible realm, that a unified, indivisible divine being (known to Philo as the Jewish God of Genesis) operates, and it is here that the Logos (the rational divine plan) takes form in order to provide a blueprint for all subsequent creation.[1] This blueprint of creation includes a model for the ἄνθρωπος, that rational faculty of humanity upon which its physical counterparts are based. As Philo states, this ἄνθρωπος, as exemplified by the first creation account in Gen 1:26–27, is "an idea or type or seal, an object of thought only, incorporeal, neither male nor female, by nature incorruptible" (*Opif.* 134).[2] This model, being fully united with the divine, is neither male nor female, but rather asexual in nature, incapable of change or sexual differentiation.

Corresponding to the intelligible realm is the corporeal world, the realm of matter and sensation in which humanity operated. This corporeal realm is merely a copy of the divine image in the intelligible realm, and because it is an imperfect copy, certain distinctions occur. For instance, unlike the idea of the ἄνθρωπος, the bodies of human individuals are created with specific

---

[1] Walter Wilson, "Sin as Sex and Sex with Sin: The Anthropology of James 1:12–15," *HThR* (2002): 147–68 (149); Richard Baer, *Philo's Use of the Categories Male and Female* (Leiden: Brill, 1970), 16–17.

[2] Baer, *Philo's Use of the Categories Male and Female*, 19, 65. Unless otherwise noted, all biblical citations follow the NRSV and all translations of Philo come from F. H. Colson et al., eds. and trans., *Philo* (12 vols.; LCL; New York: Harvard University Press, 1929–1953)

genders, male or female. As proof of this, Philo points to the second creation account of Gen 2 in which God fashions a man out of clay, breathes life into him, and later creates a female to be his helper (e.g., *Opif.* 134–156). More importantly, it is in this act of creation that the rational and irrational elements of the human soul separate and become engendered. Whereas in the intelligible realm the rational faculty of humanity is unified and asexual, in the corporeal realm the faculties of each soul are split between the rational and irrational and are subsequently engendered, the rational aspect of the mind (νοῦς) becoming male and the irrational sense-perception (αἴσθησις) female.[3]

According to Philo, the philosopher's ultimate goal is to escape the irrational, tomb-like existence of the body. To do so, the philosopher must abandon αἴσθησις in favor of the more masculine, rational faculties of νοῦς: "the passions are by nature feminine, and we must practice the quitting of these for the masculine traits that mark the noble affections" (*Det.* 28). By abandoning αἴσθησις, the philosopher will bring about the triumph of the male faculties of his soul, become unified in mind and body, and participate in the asexuality of the divine. This expulsion of αἴσθησις is not an easy task, but it should still, according to Philo, be the life-long goal of any intelligent philosopher. Through study and contemplation, the philosopher is to transcend the male-female dichotomy, cleanse himself of the feminine aspects of sense-perception, and thereby unite with the unadulterated and pure divine realm.

The Woman and The Virgin

Although Philo describes this philosophical purging in various ways, the most intriguing image Philo uses is that of the philosopher "becoming virgin," that is, rejecting his debased feminine nature (represented by γυνή) in favor of a virgin (παρθένος) state.[4] Yet, just as his worldview draws heavily from the Greek philosopher Plato, Philo's perception of femininity is heavily influenced by the prevailing cultural perceptions of womanhood.

---

[3] Baer, *Philo's Use of the Categories Male and Female*, 65. For more on the subtle nuances of Philo's use of male and female imagery, see Sharon Mattila, "Wisdom, Sense Perception, Nature, and Philo's Gender Gradient," *HTR* 89 (1996): 103–29.

[4] Other images Philo utilizes in this male-female dichotomy are that of the philosopher "becoming male" or "becoming one." These three phrases—"becoming male," "becoming one," and "becoming virgin"—are not the exact ways in which Philo describes his metaphors. Rather, they are Baer's terminology for the process (*Philo's Use of the Categories Male and Female*, 45–53).

Thus, in order to understand how this Jewish philosopher utilizes his image of the γυνή and the παρθένος, it is necessary to determine how the larger Hellenistic culture interpreted these words.

Here, the medical literature with which Philo would have been familiar is especially useful, for it provides a clear picture of the greater cultural context in which Philo and his audience would have operated. As an educated man living in first century B.C.E. Alexandria, Philo had access to a plethora of medical theories, yet none were as important as those of the Hippocratic Corpus. Although a collection of writings compiled in Alexandria some two hundred years prior to Philo and probably composed even earlier, the Hippocratic Corpus remained highly influential during Philo's lifetime. The figure of Hippocrates dominated as the doctor *par excellence*, and the works ascribed to him, while modified and expanded by such later theorists as Aristotle and Galen, continued to be the dominant explanatory model for understanding the human body.[5] Although writing primarily for a Jewish audience and engaging mostly in a philosophical exposition of the Jewish Scriptures, Philo was clearly conversant with contemporary medical theories on the human body. His writings contain numerous references to Hippocrates (e.g., *Opif.* 105, 124–125; *Contemp.* 17), Hippocratic medical terminology (e.g., μελαγχολία, "melancholy," in *Cher.* 69, 116; ῥῖγος, "chilled fever," in *Praem.* 136, 143), and other Hellenistic biological concepts (e.g., Aristotle's conceptions of reproduction in *QG* 3.47), and these theories influenced the ways that Philo explained the world and Jewish tradition (see, for example, *Spec.* 4.19, where Philo explains the Mosaic dietary laws via Hellenistic disease theories).[6] By examining Hellenistic medical theories about the γυνή and the παρθένος, one can gain a clearer understanding of how Philo interpreted, utilized, and transformed these terms.

---

[5] Vivian Nutton, *Ancient Medicine* (London: Routledge, 2004), 156. For more on the philosophical use of medical literature at this time, see Philip van der Eijk, *Medicine and Philosophy in Classical Antiquity: Doctors and Philosophers on Nature, Soul, Health, and Disease* (Cambridge: Cambridge University Press, 2005), 1–42. Unless otherwise noted, the Greek text and translation of Hippocratic medical texts follow W. H. S. Jones et al, eds. and trans., *Hippocrates* (9 vols.; LCL; New York: Harvard University Press, 1923–2010). That of Aristotle follow H. Rackham et al., eds. and trans., *Aristotle* (23 vols., LCL; Cambridge, Mass: Harvard University Press, 1926–2011).

[6] For more on Philo's use of medical literature, see Larry Hogan, *Healing in the Second Temple Period* (Ph.D. diss., Universitätsverlag Freiburg Schweiz, 1992), 191–206. In his chapter on Philo, Hogan argues that Philo himself was a physician and therefore had first-hand knowledge of human anatomy. While this is unlikely, Philo's frequent reference to Hellenistic medical theories makes it clear he, like most Hellenistic philosophers, was well-versed in the medical literature of his day.

1. The γυνή

The Hellenistic culture in which Philo lived defined womanhood as a specific period of a female's life characterized by menstruation and childbearing. Menstruation, the most obvious sign of womanhood, theoretically began around age thirteen or fourteen (see Aristotle, *Hist. an.* 581a–581b)[7] and was thought to be only the first stage of a female's journey toward becoming a fully mature woman, a γυνή. Yet, because menstruation was so characteristically feminine, it also became an apt explanatory tool for explaining the social and biological distinctions between males and females. As Lesley Dean-Jones argues, "the deeply implanted cultural belief that men and women are radically different can condition the interpretation of empirical evidence so that science, in turn, supports the belief that perceived differences between men and women are the result of biology rather than social conditioning."[8] In the case of the Hippocratic Corpus, these early medical theorists interpreted menstruation in such a way as to reaffirm the a priori assumption that dominated Greek culture, namely, the idea that the male was superior to the female.

For instance, the Hippocratic authors believed menstruation to be a natural by-product of the human digestive system. According to their theory, food consumed by the human body was converted into blood when it entered the stomach. For males, this blood coursed through the body, but was quickly used up, either due to the male's natural heat or the heat that he generated through physical activity. This was especially true when the male was young, for his growing body created a surplus of heat that allowed him to quickly use up the excess blood.[9] Moreover, "because a man has more solid flesh than a woman, he is never so totally overfilled with blood that pain results if some of his blood does not exit each month" (*Mul.* 1.1).[10] Due to his heat and natural solidity, the male body of any age quickly

---

[7] As Lesley Dean-Jones points out, due to a lack of proper nutrition, it is unlikely that many girls in ancient Greece actually began to menstruate as early as thirteen or fourteen years old. Yet, any delay in the appearance of menstruation was not taken as a sign that the girl remained physically immature, but rather that the menstrual blood was trapped in the body and needed medical intervention to be expelled. Lesley Dean-Jones, *Women's Bodies in Classical Greek Science* (Oxford: Clarendon, 1994), 47–48.

[8] Dean-Jones, *Women's Bodies in Classical Greek Science*, 42.

[9] As one Hippocratic author stated, "Growing creatures have most innate heat, and it is for this reason that they need most food, deprived of which their bodies pine away" (*Aph.* 14).

[10] This passage continues on to say, "He draws whatever quantity of blood is needed for his body's nourishment; since his body is not soft, it does not become overstrained nor is it heated up by fullness, as in the case of a woman. The fact that a man works harder

used up his nutriment and was prevented from retaining any great amount of blood on a regular basis.

Women, on the other hand, were thought to be naturally moister than men (*Nat. puer.* 15.7). When young, a woman's body presumably used up all the nourishment in her growth process, much the same way as her male counterpart did. Upon reaching puberty, however, that growth slowed, and her moist body began to act as a sponge, soaking up the surplus blood into her flesh.[11] Being colder and less physically active than a man, the woman's body was less capable of using up this excess blood. Therefore, each month, this spongy flesh was, in a sense, wrung dry, so that the blood ultimately spilled over into the woman's womb and was eventually evacuated from her body through menstruation (*Mul.* 1.1).[12]

Should a woman fail to discharge enough blood during a given month, the Hippocratics believed that the menstrual blood could move throughout the body, becoming a dangerous "pus" or "pathological agent" that caused various illnesses in the woman, including headaches, fevers, suffocation, and eventually even death (see *Diseases of virgins; Mul.* 1.2; *Superf.* 34.7).[13]

---

than a woman contributes greatly to this; for hard work draws off some of the fluid" (*Mul.* 1.1). For a translation of this text, see Ann Hanson, "Hippocrates: Diseases of Women 1," *Signs* 1 (1975): 567–84.

[11] Thus, *Mul.* 1.1 specifically compares the female body to a sheet of wool: "I say that a woman's flesh is more sponge-like and softer than a man's: since this is so, the woman's body draws moisture both with more speed and in greater quantity from the belly than does the body of a man. For if anyone should set clean wool and a piece of cloth which is clean, thickly-woven, and equal in weight to the wool, over water or on top of a damp place for two days and two nights, when he takes them off and weighs them, he will discover that the wool is much heavier than the cloth. The reason this happens is that water in a wide-mouthed jar always escapes in an upward direction. Now the wool, on the one hand, because it is both porous and soft, receives more of the escaping water, while the cloth, because it is solid and thickly woven, will be filled up, although it does not take on much of the escaping water. It is in this way, then, that a woman, because she is more porous, draws more moisture and draws it with greater speed from her belly to her body than does a man."

[12] Dean-Jones, *Women's Bodies in Classical Greek Science*, 48.

[13] Ibid., 30–31, 226. When the woman was actually pregnant, the menstrual blood was no longer deemed an unnecessary and dangerous agent, but rather an essential component to the health and growth of the fetus. According to the Hippocratics, the excess (menstrual) blood supplied the food/nourishment necessary for the growing fetus, a logical conclusion given that the Hippocratics believed that blood was converted food to begin with (153–76). Aristotle expanded this theory, arguing that the woman's menstrual blood not only provided nourishment for the fetus, but was actually the female seed from which that fetus was formed. Because the woman was an "imperfect male," this seed did not have enough "heat" to provide the "faculties of the human soul" itself (that came from the male); but, it could provide the "matter" for the male seed to "ensoul" (184–85, 190). At any rate, whether food for the fetus or the matter from which it grew, the woman's menstrual blood

Regular intercourse was thought to alleviate this danger by loosening both the στόμα ("mouth") of the womb and the veins throughout her body, thereby allowing the blood to flow more freely. Intercourse also allowed the woman to receive the male seed, which had the benefit of not only producing an offspring but of stretching out the passage of her uterus and allowing her to expel more blood on a regular monthly basis thereafter (*Diseases of virgins; Mul.* 1.1, 2; *Nat. puer.* 4).[14]

In this way, the "empirical observation of menstruation" created "a biological construct [that women are porous, etc.] which upheld the cultural characterization of a woman as inherently weaker, softer, and less stable [i.e., more prone to illness] than a man."[15] She was less capable of taking care of herself and needed a man in order to remain healthy and survive. More importantly, her moist nature was thought to incline her toward the natural, animalistic world, making her more emotional and more sexually voracious (*Vict.* 1.36; Aristotle, *Hist. an.* 608a–609a; *Metaph.* 986a–b).[16]

Although the first occurrence of menstruation began a female's journey towards womanhood, she did not become a γυνή until she married and bore her first child. This, according to Greek custom, should be done as soon as the woman's body was able, preferably around age thirteen or fourteen, lest she become prone to the aforementioned diseases.[17] After the birth of her first child, however, the woman became a full γυνή, a status she continued to hold throughout her reproductive years as long as she continued to menstruate, have intercourse, and bear children. This γυνή status, while more socially acceptable than an unwed youth, continued to carry with it the negative connotations of her female menstrual nature.[18]

---

became a productive component of the reproductive process. For a translation of *Disease of Virgins*, see Rebecca Flemming and Ann Hanson, "Hippocrates' 'Peri Parteniôn' (Diseases of Young Girls): Text and Translation," *Early Science and Medicine* 3 (1998): 241–52.

[14] For more on the healing effect of intercourse in ancient Greek medical literature, see Giula Sissa, "Maidenhood without Maidenhead: The Female Body in Ancient Greece," in *Before Sexuality: The Construction of Erotic Experience in the Ancient Greek World* (ed. David Halperin et al.; Princeton: Princeton University Press, 1990), 339–64 (348–52); Dean-Jones, *Women's Bodies in Classical Greek Science*, 51, 126.

[15] Dean-Jones, *Women's Bodies in Classical Greek Science*, 58.

[16] See Dean-Jones, *Women's Bodies in Classical Greek Science*, 56–58; Helen King, *Hippocrates' Woman: Reading the Female Body in Ancient Greece* (London: Routledge, 1998), 28.

[17] King, *Hippocrates' Woman*, 23.

[18] Ibid., 76–77. According to King, children were considered to be "wild." Unmarried maidens, in particular, were thought to be "untamed" and thus a danger to society. Only by marriage could she be brought "inside" the society and made socially acceptable.

Thus, the γυνή became associated with the most negative aspects of Greek thought: passivity, plurality, left-handedness, wickedness, et cetera.[19]

Philo's perception of women builds upon this larger cultural definition. In doing so, he transforms the idea of a γυνή as a negative, inferior, menstrual creature into a symbol for the irrational, beastly portion of the human soul, the αἴσθησις. For instance, in describing why an Essene does not take a wife, Philo states that a female is

> a selfish creature, excessively jealous and an adept in beguiling the morals of her husband and seducing him by her continued impostures...she first ensnares the sight and hearing, and when these subjects have as it were been duped she cajoles the sovereign mind...casting off all shame she compels him to commit actions which are all hostile to the life of fellowship. (*Hypoth.* 11.14–17)

Likewise, in *Legum allegoriae*, the female is called "incomplete, diseased, enslaved...[and] full of disabilities" (2.97; see also *Post.* 166; *Migr.* 205–206).[20] Whether or not these passages reflect some personal animosity toward women by Philo himself as some scholars suggest, these passages clearly illustrate the dangerous nature that Philo attributes to women throughout his writings, an image that stands in continuity with the larger cultural perceptions of women.[21] Like his Hellenistic counterparts, Philo believes that a γυνή, by nature, is a selfish creature, one that distracts her mate from following a righteous path and brings disaster to those she meets.

In Philo's allegorization of the γυνή, these "natural" negative female qualities become equated with αἴσθησις, the irrational, sensual aspect of the human soul. Thus, in *De Opifico Mundi*, Philo states that in each human, "mind (νοῦς) corresponds to man (ἀνήρ), the senses (αἴσθησις) to woman (γυνή)" (§165; see also *Leg.* 2.38). As David Runia points out, this man-mind/woman-senses scheme should not be taken literally. For Philo, every man and woman consists of a masculine νόος and a feminine αἴσθησις.[22] Yet, modeled as it is upon the Hellenistic concept of the biological γυνή, the

---

[19] Dean-Jones, *Women's Bodies in Classical Greek Science*, 44. For more on Pythagorean views on woman in Philo, see Judith Romney Wegner, "Philo's Portrayal of Women: Hebraic or Hellenic?" in *"Women Like This": New Perspectives on Jewish Women in the Greco-World* (ed. Amy-Jill Levine; Atlanta: Scholars, 1991), 41–66 (51).

[20] Baer, *Philo's Use of the Categories Male and Female*, 42; Wegner, "Philo's Portrayal of Women," 54.

[21] Some scholars, for instance, speculate that the passage concerning the wife of an Essene reflects Philo's own experience of women and his own misogynistic attitude towards them. See Wegner, "Philo's Portrayal of Women," 61.

[22] David T. Runia, *Philo of Alexandria: On the Creation of the Cosmos according to Moses* (PACS 1; Leiden: Brill, 2001), 381–82; see also Baer, *Philo's Use of the Categories Male and Female*, 35–39.

feminine, irrational αἴσθησις of a person's soul remains extremely negative; it is a debased portion of the human being that hinders the soul from obtaining unity with the divine. Thus, in *Quaestiones et solutiones in Genesin*, Philo calls sense-perception the ruler over "death and everything vile" (1.37), "the beginning of evil" (1.45), and more generally the reason that the mind comes to destruction (1.43, 45, 46).[23] This, for Philo, is evident from an allegorical reading of such passages as Gen 3 (e.g., *Opif.* 165–166), in which Eve (αἴσθησις) eats the forbidden fruit and causes Adam (νόος) to be cast out of the Garden (the divine realm).[24] In this way, the γυνή becomes equated with the most debased portions of human life, the "illnesses of the soul" that keep the individual from uniting with the divine.

Given the connection between menstruation and illness in the medical literature, it is not surprising that Philo connects these negative characteristics, these "illnesses," to menstruation. Again, the biblical passages themselves give Philo the necessary tool by which to build his allegory. In describing the physical state of the biblical matriarch Sarah, LXX Gen 18:11 states that "it had ceased to be with Sarah τὰ γυναικεῖα."[25] Literally meaning "things pertaining to women," the LXX uses τὰ γυναικεῖα here euphemistically to refer to menstruation, a euphemism also suggested in the medical literature (e.g., *Aph.* 5.28).[26] Yet, as Maren Niehoff points out, in the Greek world, the adjective γυναικεῖα carries a wide range of connotations, including female sexual organs, medical disorders, garments, makeup, quarters, and even feminine/effeminate character traits.[27] Philo plays with this ambiguity, using the term and its many connotations to indicate the negative qualities of women. For instance, in *Quaestiones et solutiones in Genesin*, the "woman's quarter" of Sarah, probably ἡ γυναικεία or its equivalent in the original Greek, is the feminine parts of the human soul.[28]

---

[23] Baer, *Philo's Use of the Categories Male and Female*, 41.

[24] For more on the negative aspects of sense-perception, especially in the story of Adam and Eve, see Wilson, "Sin as Sex and Sex with Sin," 151–52.

[25] As a Jew living in first century B.C.E. Alexandria, Philo's primary access to Jewish scriptures would have been through the Greek Septuagint. It is unclear how much Hebrew, if any, he knew.

[26] In the Hippocratic text of *Aph.* 5.28, τὰ γυναικεῖα occurs in place of the typical καταμήνια (e.g., *Aph.* 5.36) for "menstruation." Maren Niehoff, "Mother and Maiden, Sister and Spouse: Sarah in Philonic Midrash," *HTR* 97 (2004): 413–44 (434 n. 60).

[27] King, *Hippocrates' Woman*, 23; Niehoff, "Mother and Maiden, Sister and Spouse," 434. As Niehoff points out, the use of τὰ γυναικεῖα in Gen 18:11 to mean menstruation is the sole occurrence of this meaning in the LXX.

[28] While *Quaestiones et solutiones in Genesin* is only preserved in Armenian, the context of the passage makes it fairly certain that the original Greek was ἡ γυναικεία or its equivalent (Niehoff, "Mother and Maiden, Sister and Spouse," 434).

It is "a place where womanly opinions go about and dwell, being followers of the female sex. And the female sex is irrational and akin to bestial passions, fear, sorrow, pleasure and desire, from which ensue incurable weaknesses and indescribable disease" (4.15). Elsewhere, τά γυναικεῖα represents "unmanly and feminine" ways (*Fug.* 128), "human ways of custom and mere reasoning" (*Fug.* 167), and most importantly, human passions (*Det.* 28; *Cher.* 8, 50; *Ebr.* 59–63). Thus, as in the medical literature, the "ways" or menstrual qualities of the γυνή become the sign of her debased nature. Equated with αἴσθησις, the γυνή and her "ways" become Philo's primary symbol of passion, weakness, imperfection, evil, and death.[29]

2. *The παρθένος*

As a counter to this negative portrayal of the γυνή, Philo advocates that the soul "become virgin," that is, that it cast off her most feminine of characteristics, αἴσθησις, and take on the role of a παρθένος. In the medical literature, a παρθένος typically signified an unmarried girl, less than thirteen or fourteen years old, who had not yet begun to menstruate, have intercourse, or bear children.[30] If this pre-pubescent girl is the παρθένος envisioned by Philo, then, medically speaking, it would be impossible for a γυνή to become a παρθένος again, for she would not be able to undo the biological processes that becoming a woman entailed.

Yet, this is exactly the situation that Philo describes. For instance, when explaining the allegorical meaning for the treatment of widows and orphans, Philo states that "when a man comes in contact with a woman, he marks the virgin as a woman. But when souls become divinely inspired, from (being) women they become virgins, throwing off the womanly corruptions which are (found) in sense-perception and passion" (*QE* 2.3).[31] Likewise, Philo states in *Cher.* 50, "when God consorts with the soul, He

[29] Baer, *Philo's Use of the Categories Male and Female,* 42. For more on Philo's link between menstruation and negative, female qualities, see Dorothy Sly, *Philo's Perception of Women* (Atlanta: Scholars, 1990), 74–89.

[30] Dean-Jones, *Women's Bodies in Classical Greek Science,* 53; Sissa, "Maidenhood without Maidenhead," 347–48. As Sissa points out, in ancient Greece, a young woman could have sex and still be considered a παρθένος if her sexual activity went unnoticed. The designation of a girl as a παρθένος was thus a societal construct based on observation, rather than a true biological fact, and the change in status from a παρθένος to γυνή occurred, as noted above, only after a woman was publically recognized as having born a child.

[31] Like *Quaestiones et solutiones in Genesin, Quaestiones et solutiones in Exodum* is only preserved in Armenian; yet, it is likely that the original Greek utilized that same terminology for "women" and the "virgins" here, that is, γυνή and παρθένος, as it does elsewhere.

makes what before was a woman (γυνή) into a virgin (παρθένος) again, for he takes away the degenerate and emasculate passions which made it womanish and plants instead the native growth of unpolluted virtues." By losing its corrupt feminine nature, the soul becomes pure again, undefiled by the sensual world. According to this latter example, this miraculous transformation requires divine intervention. Whereas a human man makes a παρθένος into a γυνή, the divine makes a γυνή into a παρθένος. Therefore, a simple, yet divine inversion seems to take place. The divine becomes the active, male agent, while the philosopher takes on the role of the passive female.[32]

At the same time, the virgin soul envisioned by Philo is almost always linked to some sort of spiritual child-bearing, a distinctly feminine γυνή image that seems contradictory to the status of an actual pre-pubescent, pre-menstrual παρθένος. But again, the divine makes this possible, taking the role of the active agent, here that of the husband, while the philosopher, as the virgin wife, becomes the passive (female) receptacle.[33] For instance, in *Cher.* 43–44, only a few lines earlier than the description of God's conversion of a γυνή into a παρθένος, Philo states:

> Man and Woman, male and female of the human race, in the course of nature come together to hold intercourse for the procreation of children. But virtues whose offspring are so many and so perfect may not have to do with a mortal man, yet if they receive not seed of generation from another they will never of themselves conceive. Who then is he that sows in them the good seed save the Father of all, that is, God unbegotten and begetter of all things? He then sows, but the fruit of His sowing, the fruit which is His own, He bestows as a gift. For God begets nothing for Himself, for He is in want of nothing, but all for him who needs to receive.

According to this and other such passages, the virgin state of the soul enables and even requires the soul to bear the spiritual offspring of God, namely, the virtue of divine wisdom. God becomes the divine father of a divine offspring, not out of any self-need for progeny, but rather as a gift to the human soul, so that it may gain the wisdom it desires.

It seems, then, that although an inversion in the female's status occurs, her ability to bear children does not diminish. Verna Harrison suggests that, in preserving the child-bearing capability of the γυνή-turned-παρθένος, Philo is insisting that the soul who wishes to become παρθένος must become female in its most complete and "best sense," that is, it must bear a

[32] Baer, *Philo's Use of the Categories Male and Female*, 61.
[33] Ibid., 55. See also Wilson, "Sin as Sex and Sex with Sin," 155–56.

child.[34] If so, then, the femininity of the image seems firmly, and even positively, entrenched.

3. *The Aged* παρθένος

Yet, if one reads Philo's virgin metaphor in light of medical theories about the aging γυνή, rather than that of the adolescent παρθένος, a different interpretation emerges, one in which the virgin soul, even in its child-bearing capacity, is more male than female. As Helen King states, "to be a woman is to menstruate"; any lack of menstruation results in a subsequent lack of womanhood.[35] This, according to the Hippocratic Corpus, could happen at any age. For example, fearing that a lack of menstruation for even one month might cause the γυνή to "slip" back into the category of the "non-bleeding, non-productive" παρθένος, the Hippocratics carefully observed their female patients and prescribed extensive, often excruciating, treatments (vapor baths, drugs, fastings, lead probes, etc.) to "cure" the woman should she cease to menstruate (*Mul.* 1.10–11).[36] Yet, even all the treatments in the world could not stop the fact that eventually, if a γυνή lived long enough, she stopped menstruating. In this way, an aged γυνή naturally lost the most essential characteristic of being female; she had lost her ability to menstruate, her feminine nature, and consequently her classification as a true γυνή.

This loss of γυνή status in an aging woman resulted in a corresponding process in which her body became more male-like. Although little is said directly about menopause within the Hippocratic literature, passages about male aging suggests that aging, for both males and females, was the natural result of a drying out and cooling of the human body, one that began at birth and culminated in the death of the individual. If so, then, the moist, spongy feminine body became drier and more "male" the further it progressed in age.

For instance, in a lengthy description of male aging, *Vict.* 1.33 connected the stages of a man's life to the risings and fallings of his heat levels and its

---

[34] Verna Harrison, "The Allegorization of Gender: Plato and Philo on Spiritual Childbearing," in *Asceticism* (eds. Vincent Wimbush and Richard Valantasis; Oxford: Oxford University Press, 1998), 520–34 (530).

[35] King, *Hippocrates' Woman*, 76.

[36] These treatments could only be postponed if a woman could prove that she was pregnant, which often only involved her stating that she could feel a child growing within her or that she could remember the moment of conception (King, *Hippocrates' Woman*, 254 n. 2). See also ibid., "Women's Health and Recovery in the Hippocratic Corpus," in *Health in Antiquity* (ed. Helen King; London: Routledge, 2005), 150–61 (158).

subsequent drying effects. According to this Hippocratic text, a child's body was the moistest, for it retained many of the moist, watery compounds of its mother's womb. Being the most like its mother, the child was the most "feminine."[37] As the child grew, however, that initial moisture dried out and was replaced by warm, fiery elements. At full maturity, a man became completely dry, and his body cooled, since the fire which helped him grow was no longer prevalent or needed. For this author, then, aging was a process of drying out that culminated in the fully mature male individual. After that, old age set in, at which point, the individual's "fire retreats and there is an onset of water; the dry elements have gone and the moist have established themselves" (*Vict.* 1.33). A man ended his days as a cold and moist body, much as it began.[38]

Aristotle, although agreeing with the Hippocratics that the human body became colder and drier as it aged, did not support the notion that the human body became moist again in its final state. He argued that over the course of an individual's life, a man experienced a gradual diminishing of his innate heat, that element within a man which normally provided the animating principle to the heart, organs, and limbs. This heat, according to him, did not simply disappear, but was slowly breathed away, leaving the body and its organs weakened. Unlike the Hippocratics, Aristotle argued that the body continued to dry even as it cooled. For example, the lungs, which were supposed to help regulate the innate heat, gradually dried up over time, becoming "hard" and "earthy" and incapable of movement. Because "the source of life fails its possessors when the heat which is associated with it is not moderated by cooling" (*Resp.* 479a), the failure of the lungs to regulate the innate heat of an individual resulted in a cooling

[37] Elsewhere in the Hippocratic Corpus, there are indications that, prior to the onset of puberty, males and females were essentially of one nature. Although sexual differentiation itself was thought to have occurred as early as conception, both the Hippocratic Corpus and the writings of Aristotle reflect the opinion that this difference did not become fully realized until puberty. Because the Hippocratic Corpus does not distinguish between the gender of children, Dean-Jones concludes that, at least prior to the onset of puberty/ menstruation, male and female children were medically treated the same. Likewise, Aristotle argued that although the genital organs developed by the time an infant was born, the generative properties themselves—that is, the ability to produce either seed (males) or menstrual blood (females)—did not develop until puberty, and it was only at that point that a boy ceased to appear as a woman (*Gen. an.* 728a, 728b). Prior to puberty, both males and females were thought to have the same "moist" nature of a female (Dean-Jones, *Women's Bodies in Classical Greek Science*, 45–47).

[38] Another Hippocratic author concurs, stating that "the body is hot which grows and progresses with force; but when the body begins to decay with an easy decline it grows cooler. It is on account of this that a man, growing most on his first day, is proportionally hotter then; on his last day, decaying the most, he is proportionately cooler" (*Nat. hom.* 30).

and drying out of the rest of the body.[39] Thus, the process of the body drying continued well beyond maturity until the body became a dry, cold corpse (*Long. brev.* 466b).

Galen, some two hundred years after Philo, expressed similar sentiments. According to him, the heating process began in the womb, where a slow drying of the wet substances of blood and semen produced the embryo. This heating/drying continued throughout a man's life until all growth ceased and the innate heat of the individual diminished. From there, the older one became, the drier one's tissue and internal organs became until, with wrinkled dry skin, one reached old age (*San. Tuenda* 5.1.2).[40] Thus, while heating and cooling continued to be a major explanatory language for aging, by the late Hellenistic and early Roman eras, the drying of a human body had slowly developed into a primary component for explaining the aging process.

The few references to older women within this medical literature seem to imply that a similar process occurred within the γυνή. Aristotle and Galen, for instance, made no distinction between male and female bodies, which suggests that they believed that all humans, male and female, dry as they age.[41] Even the Hippocratics, who argued that males became moist in their final years, agreed that the woman continued to dry the further she progressed in age. For instance, the Hippocratic gynecological texts (e.g., *Nat. mul.* 2. 6; *Mul.* 2. 3) supported the idea that "older women are dry and have less blood than younger women."[42] Menopause, then, was perceived as "that natural process of 'drying out' which transforms even a wet and spongy female body into something that does not need to bleed."[43] The older a γυνή became, the less she appeared like the moist child of *Vict.* 1.33 and the more she became like the fully mature, dry male.

According to these medical writers, this drying of women due to old age resulted in the subsequent acquisition of male characteristics. Dean-Jones, for instance, notes two cases recorded in the Hippocratic treatise *Epidemiae* in which women began growing facial hair and developed deeper voices after the cessation of their menses (6.356). Likewise, in the *Historia*

---

[39] Karen Cokayne, *Experiencing Old Age in Ancient Rome* (London: Routledge, 2003), 35. Aristotle notes that, in addition to this gradual drying out, excessive sexual intercourse can speed up the drying process, for the moist residue of the seed cannot be replaced (*Hist. an.* 7.582a). See also Robert Garland, *The Greek Way of Life: From Conception to Old Age* (Ithaca, N.Y.: Cornell University Press, 1990), 248.

[40] Cokayne, *Experiencing Old Age in Ancient Rome*, 36.

[41] Dean-Jones, *Women's Bodies in Classical Greek Science*, 106–07.

[42] Ibid., 106.

[43] King, *Hippocrates' Woman*, 76.

animalium, Aristotle remarked that some women grew facial hair when they ceased to menstruate (3.518a).[44] Aristotle also noted that "masculine-looking women are produced in whom the menstrual discharges do not occur" (*Gen. an.* 747a). As Dean-Jones argues, the "cessation of menstruation" at menopause "without dire effects was empirical evidence that a woman's body had become physiologically more like a man's."[45] Because her body and her behavior posed less of a danger to her family, the aged γυνή gained a new independence and freedom unlike any before in her life. She lost her status as a γυνή, was no longer defined by and confined to the domestic sphere, and could now participate in the freedom of movement normally reserved for males.[46] In essence, without menstruation, her body regained the virginal nature of her youth, and she became, in all but name, a παρθένος again.

If this is the understanding of virginity with which Philo operated, then the παρθένος that Philo envisions is most likely not that of a moist youth, unacquainted with the pleasures of the flesh. Rather, she is an older γυνή, who has suffered through the bearing of fleshly children and has now returned to a virgin, male-like state, dry and ready to bear spiritual children. As Dorothy Sly notes, virginity for Philo was a state that could occur either "before puberty" or "after menopause," and it seems that Philo has the latter in mind when describing the transformation of the soul into a παρθένος.[47] Admittedly, the medical literature never refers to the aged γυνή as a παρθένος. Yet, Philo himself seems to make this connection, either by specifically linking the παρθένος to a physically aged γυνή, by describing the παρθένος allegorically as a post-menopausal woman, or by depicting the state of the spiritual παρθένος as one that occurs after the bearing of children.

Sarah, the paradigm of Philo's vision of spiritual transformation, exemplifies this very process. As a biblical matriarch, Sarah represented for the Jewish people of Philo's time the ideal wife who stood by Abraham through all of his travails. While preserving this literal nature of Sarah (e.g., *Abr.* 93, 245–246), Philo also allegorizes her, transforming her character into an important component of the spiritual journey of the philosopher, one that exemplifies his attainment of virtue and divine wisdom (e.g., *Fug.* 128; *Ebr.* 59–61; *Det.* 28). Yet, such an accomplishment, this "spiritual childbirth," did not occur for Sarah until she became a παρθένος, and that only

---

44 Dean-Jones, *Women's Bodies in Classical Greek Science,* 134.
45 Ibid., 107.
46 Ibid., 108.
47 Sly, *Philo's Perception of Women,* 72.

happened after she had aged, "bore" a child via Hagar, and ceased to menstruate.

For instance, in the book of Genesis, Sarah is largely portrayed as an older woman, who, by the time of her death, has lived more than one hundred years with her husband Abraham (Gen 23:1). Throughout his writings, Philo preserves this literal age of Sarah, referring to her frequently as "advanced in age" (e.g., *QG* 3.14) and "old" (e.g., *QG* 3.16, 17; see also γῆρας in *Abr.* 111). Moreover, by the time she conceives her son Isaac, she has already lived ninety years (*QG* 3.56) and has produced a corporeal heir, Ishmael, for her husband (*Abr.* 253). Ishmael, of course, was not Sarah's physical offspring. As Genesis relates, the barren Sarah, knowing that she was too old to produce children, gave her servant Hagar to Abraham so that she could "obtain children by her" (Gen 16:2). Yet, like many early interpreters of this passage, Philo reads this as confirmation that Sarah was legally Ishmael's mother.[48] In fact, he stresses this very point, making it clear in his obituary of the matriarch that the child, although physically born of Hagar, legally belongs to Sarah. He states, for example, through Sarah's mouth, "if our prayers for the birth of children are answered, the offspring will be yours in full parenthood, but surely also mine by adoption" (*Abr.* 248–50). This adoption, according to Philo, does not show any impropriety but rather stands as the epitome of Sarah's virtue. Because this matriarch has such esteem for the biblical command to have children (*Abr.* 248//Gen 1:28) and "values [her husband's] gain more than her own standing," she ensures that he will have a child before he dies (*QG* 3.20). In Philo's eyes, then, Sarah has truly produced a child, not through physical birth but through her love of Abraham and her prudent counsel. As Niehoff states, "her motherhood, even if only legal and not biological, is crucial. She will be the mother of Abraham's child even if she has not given birth to it."[49]

---

[48] E.g., Josephus *A.J.* 1.2215. Some rabbinic texts (*Gen Rab.* 48.16, *Targum Psuedo-Jonathon,* and *Targum Neofiti*) contain a similar interpretation. Commenting on Gen 18:10, they read the phrase והוא אחריו ("and he was behind him") as evidence that Ishmael was in the tent with Sarah when the angels of God announced the birth of Isaac to her. According to Carol Bakhos, since Jewish law stipulated that a female could not be left alone in a tent with males not related to her, Ishmael's presence indicates that the rabbis viewed him as Sarah's son or at least a part of her extended family unit. Carol Bakhos, *Ishmael on the Border: Rabbinic Portrayals of the First Arab* (Albany: State University of New York Press, 2006), 39.

[49] Niehoff, "Mother and Maiden, Sister and Spouse," 422. For more on the allegorical reading of Hagar as encyclical studies, see Sarah Pearce, *The Land of the Body: Studies in Philo's Representation of Egypt* (WUNT 208; Tübingen: Mohr Siebeck, 2007), 167–77.

Allegorically, this production of children via Hagar takes on a more important meaning. The maidservant becomes for Philo the symbol of Hellenistic encyclical learning (grammar, astronomy, etc.) that a soul must engage in prior to obtaining divine wisdom. As Philo states, "those who are unable by virtue to beget fine and praiseworthy deeds ought to pursue intermediate education, and in a sense produce children from school studies" (*QG* 3.20; see also *Congr.* 11ff). In this way, the soul will not be "resigned to being childless," but will prepare itself for spiritual children by cultivating a "milder and gentler teaching" (*QG* 3.20). This is in keeping with statements throughout Philo's writings, in which he implies that the soul often does and indeed must bear earthly children before becoming a spiritual παρθένος. For instance, in *De praemiis et poenis*, Philo states that "When the soul is 'many,' full that is of passions and vices with her children, pleasures, desires, folly, incontinence, injustice, gathered around her, she is feeble and sick and dangerously near to death. But when she has become barren and ceases to produce these children or indeed has cast them out bodily she is transformed into a pure virgin (παρθένος)" (158–160).[50] Although negatively portrayed, the bearing of these sensual children is a necessary preparatory step, without which the soul would not be able to recognize the pure children of divine wisdom. At some point, then, the γυνή soul (Sarah) must produce the feminine, bastard children of the sensual world (Hagar) before returning to a pure, παρθένος state.

Finally, in addition to being identified as an aged γυνή and a woman who has already produced a child, Philo portrays the παρθένος Sarah as one who has ceased to menstruate. As noted above, Genesis portrays Sarah's conception of Isaac as occurring after "it had ceased to be with [her] after τά γυναικεῖα" (Gen 18:11). As already noted, τά γυναικεῖα carried a wide range of connotations in Greek culture, and Philo plays with these nuances when interpreting the figure of Sarah. On the one hand, he allows the biblical phrase to stand as an indication that the biblical matriarch has become old and has ceased to menstruate before she gives birth to her son Isaac (e.g., *Abr.* 110–113). Allegorically, however, he interprets τά γυναικεῖα to mean that Sarah (the soul) has abandoned the allures of the "ways" of women, the αἴσθησις, in favor of bearing the virtue of wisdom (e.g., *Fug.* 128; *Ebr.* 59–61; *Det.* 28).[51] In this way, then, the abandonment of the αἴσθησις

---

[50] Here, Philo is building on Isa 54:1, which states that "for more are the children of the desolate than the children of one who has a husband" (see Baer, *Philo's Use of the Categories Male and Female*, 53).

[51] Niehoff, "Mother and Maiden, Sister and Spouse," 434; Wegner, "Philo's Portrayal of Women," 56.

becomes analogous to the physical drying out of Sarah's aging body. As Sly notes, virginity "entails freedom from passion, since passion arises at puberty and dies at menopause."[52] Just as the drying of Sarah's menstrual blood serves as preparation for her conception of Isaac, the drying of the soul's sensual, passionate nature acts as the preparatory step for completing her transformation into a spiritual παρθένος.

It is only after abandoning τά γυναικεῖα that this aged, post child-bearing, postmenopausal Sarah is specifically identified as a παρθένος. For instance, following the description of the γυνή-turned-παρθένος in *Cher*. 50, Philo states that the παρθένος is Sarah, whom God does not talk to "till she has ceased from all that is after the manner of women and is ranked once more as a pure virgin (παρθένος)." Sarah, then, exemplifies both the biological process of aging in the cessation of menstruation and the intellectual process of aging that enables spiritual childbirth. As a matriarch in Jewish history, Sarah has ceased to menstruate. As a soul, she has ceased to follow αἴσθησις. Either way, she casts off a previous γυνή nature, bears base corporeal children (via Hagar/encyclical studies), and through time and experience, becomes an aged παρθένος capable of bearing a divine offspring.

Such a reading of Sarah may be supported by a similar reading of Philo's description of the Therapeutae, a contemporary group of ascetics whose numbers included actual women who spent all day in prayer and in reflection on the Torah and who therefore served as exemplary models for Philo's spiritual program.[53] According to Philo, these women were "mostly

---

[52] Sly, *Philo's Perception of Women*, 72.

[53] Because there is no external evidence for the existence of the Therapeutae and because the group fits too closely with Philo's view of the ideal community, many scholars debate the historicity of this community. Compare, for instance, Ross Kraemer, "Monastic Women in Greco-Roman Egypt: Philo Judaeus on the Therapeutrides," *Signs* 14 (1989): 342–70; Troels Engberg-Pedersen, "Philo's *De Vita Contemplativa* as a Philosopher's Dream," *JSJ* 30 (1999): 40–64; Joan Taylor, "Virgin Mothers: Philo on the Women Therapeutae," *JSP* 12 (2001): 37–63 (38–40); idem, *Jewish Women and Greek Philosophers of First-Century Alexandria: Philo's 'Therapeutae' Reconsidered* (Oxford: Oxford University Press, 2003); Mary Ann Beavis, "Philo's Therapeutae: Philosopher's Dream or Utopian Construction?" *JSP* 14 (2004): 30–42; and Shari Golberg, "The Two Choruses Become One: The Absence/Presence of Women in Philo's On the Contemplative Life," *JSJ* 39 (2008): 459–70. Based on its formal characteristics, Engberg-Pedersen argues that Philo's account of the Therapeutae is, like Plato's *Timaeus*, a "utopian fantasy done for a serious purpose" (43). Kraemer, Beavis, and Taylor, however, argue that there was, in fact, a small community of philosophers living not far from Philo's hometown of Alexandria upon which his philosophical treatise, however stylized, was based. Finally, Golberg argues that the historicity of this group is largely irrelevant, since Philo uses the example of these women primarily as an allegory for spiritual virtue. On the one hand, it is true that Philo probably exaggerates

aged virgins" (πλεῖσται γηραιαί παρθένοι), who, "eager to have [wisdom] for their life mate...have spurned the pleasures of the body and desire no mortal offspring but those immortal children which only the soul that is dear to God can bring to birth unaided because the Father has sown in her spiritual rays enabling her to behold the verities of wisdom" (*Contempl.* 68). These women, desiring to contemplate God, abandoned the normal life of Jewish women and withdrew into the desert to be spouses of God.

According to Joan Taylor, Philo's use of πλεῖσται ("mostly") with γηραιαὶ παρθένοι implies that not all of these women were old or had been married. Additionally, Philo's notation that these women "desired no mortal offspring" suggests to her that these ascetics were actually perpetual virgins, women who had never become married and had thus never held a γυνή status. This leads Taylor to argue that Philo would not have seen the actual παρθένος as an aged γυνή, for it is unlikely that he would have thought that "real women could become virgins again in terms of their actual social or physical status."[54] Instead, Taylor suggests that Philo uses the image of the γηραιαὶ παρθένοι to shock his reader and to stress how different the spiritual world was from the corporeal. More importantly, according to Taylor, Philo's use of the παρθένος image here is simply a "smokescreen" to avoid discussing the possible celibacy of these women.[55]

---

when describing this community. On the other hand, because Philo provides such exact descriptions of their location and its topography and because this location was not far from Alexandria where Philo lived (*Contemp.* 22–23), it is also probable that this group actually existed in some form, for otherwise Philo's readers would have known that Philo was not being truthful and would not have attended to his message.

[54] Taylor, "Virgin Mothers," 55; idem, *Jewish Women and Greek Philosophers*, 249–51. See also Kraemer ("Monastic Jewish Women," 351–53), who argues that these women either never married or waited until their husbands were deceased before joining the monastic community. As evidence, Kraemer points to *Contemp.* 18, where Philo states that the members of this community leave behind their γυναῖκες when joining the community. According to Kraemer, the use of the fem. pl. term here ("wives") rather than the more gender neutral term σύμβιες ("spouses") suggests that only the men of the community had previously been married. Yet, given the androcentric perspective of Philo's writings and the fact that γυνή was a much more common term in Hellenistic writings than σύμβιος, the male orientation of this passage is hardly surprising and cannot be used as definitive evidence of the (non)marital status of the female Therapeutae.

[55] Taylor ("Virgin Mothers," 56–57; *Jewish Women and Greek Philosophers*, 253) argues, for instance, that whereas the male ascetics of this group were "good" for leaving "their wives" behind in order to enter the community (*Contempl.* 17), the women in Philo's world could not be considered "good" for leaving their husbands and children behind. Thus, he focuses on their virginity instead in order to "sidestep" the issue of their celibacy. He also emphasizes their role as "spiritual mothers" of the community in order to provide them with a modicum of respect (*Jewish Women and Greek Philosophers*, 246–48).

While Taylor is correct to emphasize the powerful nature of Philo's imagery, she overemphasizes the celibate nature of this group and underemphasizes their aged state. Because Philo describes them as γηραιαί, a term that in Greek culture signaled women past the age of bearing children, it is clear that he envisions these female ascetics as older, post-menopausal women.[56] Moreover, as noted above, the medical literature, although not explicitly identifying the aged γυνή as a παρθένος, does imply that virginity—that dry, male-like state which lacks menstruation and the ability to bear children—could be regained at any time during a woman's life, especially at old age. Finally, because Philo and his Jewish contemporaries placed such a strong emphasis on the divine command to bear children, it is unlikely that these women would have remained celibate their entire life prior to joining the Therapeutae.[57] Rather, it seems more likely that these aged παρθένοι have been married and have already borne earthly children. Like Sarah, it is only after leaving behind their "womanly" ways (i.e., have become too old to menstruate) that they fled to the desert, bore divine children, and become spiritual "mothers" to the members of their community (*Contempl.* 72). Thus, contra Taylor, it is reasonable to assume that Philo saw the aged γυνή as a παρθένος.

As with the biologically aged γυνή, this spiritual aging and drying process is accompanied by a masculinization of the soul. Because "becoming virgin" entails an elimination of the most feminine aspect (αἴσθησις) of the soul, the end product of this transformation is like a dry male body, free from feminine menstrual qualities of the senses and dominated by the male νοῦς. Indeed, as *QE* 1.8 states, spiritual "progress is nothing else than the giving up of the female gender by changing into the male, since the female gender is material, passive, corporeal and sense-perceptible, while the male is active, rational, incorporeal and more akin to mind and thought." Thus, throughout Philo's writings, Sarah as a παρθένος increasingly becomes

---

[56] As Garland (*The Greek Way of Life*, 243–44) notes, γέρων and γραῖα were pejorative terms used to refer to older men and women (respectively), who were no longer able to serve in the military or bear children. The latter group, specifically, were older, post-menopausal women who, because they could no longer bear children, were deemed of "diminished" value by the Greek society. See also Sly (*Philo's Perception of Women*, 73), who states that time (i.e., old age) and asceticism has "rescued" these women from the sensual body and has made them virgins again.

[57] See *Abr.* 248; *Spec.* 1.112, 138, 3.113; Baer, *Philo's Use of the Categories Male and Female*, 94; Adele Reinhartz, "Parents and Children: A Philonic Perspective," in *The Jewish Family in Antiquity* (ed. Shaye Cohen; BJS 289; Atlanta: Scholars, 1993), 61–88 (70). Taylor herself acknowledges that the celibate state of these women would only have been possible if they had grown up in a household sympathetic to the philosophical ideals of the Therapeutae (*Jewish Women and Greek Philosophers*, 260).

characterized as male. As virtue incarnate, she actively "sows the seeds" of instruction which her "husband" (i.e., reason) receives (*Abr.* 99–102; see also *Her.* 62).[58] Although capable of bearing spiritual children, the aged Sarah-παρθένος is more male than female.[59] By actively striving to rid itself of the harmful, feminine distractions of αἴσθησις, the virgin soul brings about the triumph of the rational faculties and becomes male.

Conclusion: The Philosophical Journey

When read within the larger context of Philo's writings and his culture, the seemingly miraculous transformation of the γυνή into a παρθένος in *QE* 2.3 and *Cher.* 50 is not as miraculous or as feminine as it first appears. While the divine is certainly still involved in the spiritual process, especially in the bearing of spiritual children, the transformation from γυνή into παρθένος itself occurs as the result of a human process, one that involves an aging of the soul and the drying out of its sensations. This aged παρθένος has undergone the trials of corporeal life and has produced the offspring of the senses, but now it has abandoned that life in favor of becoming a spiritual child-bearer of the divine. This, as suggested by the medical literature, is not a preservation of the feminine nature of the soul, as Harrison would have it, but rather a triumph of the masculine νοῦς. Like the aged γυνή, the spiritually mature παρθένος has cast off its "womanly," bestial nature and embraced the rational νοῦς. In so doing, the soul has lost its status as a γυνή and has become male.

As with most of his writings, this aged state of the παρθένος that Philo lays out is not a literal age, but rather an allegorical one. Commentating on the advanced age of Sarah, Philo states "the foolish man is a child and a crude person, for even though he may be advanced in age, his folly produces childishness. But the wise man, even though he be in the prime of youthfulness, is old, and virtue is old and venerable, since it is worthy of old age and honour" (*QG* 4.14). Physical age can be deceiving, for it does not guarantee wisdom; but intellectual age, no matter the physicality of the individual, brings about spiritual maturity. While the image of the παρθένος is that of an aged γυνή, past her child-bearing years, the philosopher himself can be of any physical age, given that he has the intellectual age of the mature παρθένος.

---

[58] Niehoff, "Mother and Maiden, Sister and Spouse," 432.
[59] Mattila, "Wisdom, Sense Perception, Nature, and Philo's Gender Gradient," 106.

This understanding of the παρθένος as an aged γυνή has profound implications for the philosopher, for it suggests that, instead of being a state that one either has or does not have at birth, spiritual virginity was something that one could obtain at any point in one's life, given enough spiritual maturity. Unlike a maiden παρθένος, who is simply born into her state, this aged παρθένος requires an aged soul, one that has experienced the sensual world and risen above it. This requires the philosopher to work for his spiritual enlightenment. Although portrayed elsewhere as the passive receptacle of the divine seed, the philosophical soul is not transformed into a παρθένος by simply waiting for God to act. Rather, the philosopher must actively engage the spiritual process and be the catalyst for its production. Only then, will the divine act to change the γυνή philosopher into the ultimate παρθένος soul.

As noted above, the primary way by which the philosopher can achieve this intellectual age is by casting off his feminine, bestial nature and bearing corporeal children (e.g., *Det.* 28). Hagar, who represents encyclical learning, serves as a preparatory stage for the soul's mating with the divine, one that the young soul must pass through before being capable of receiving wisdom. According to Philo, philosophers "are not capable as yet of receiving the impregnation of virtue unless [they] have first mated with her handmaiden" (*Congr.* 9). This implies an active participation in the material world by the philosopher, not a detachment. It is only by engaging with the feminine learning of the senses—the cultural learning of geometry, astronomy, music, and the like—and bearing their "bastard children" (*Congr.* 6) that the philosopher can understand philosophical knowledge and reject the distractions of αἴσθησις. Like an aged Sarah, it is only after the intellectually mature philosopher has undergone the trials of the senses, borne the earthly children required of him, and advanced beyond them that he can become a dry παρθένος, ready for a union with the divine.

If this is so, then Philo's image of the παρθένος takes on new meaning. The παρθένος is not merely a description of the spiritually mature soul, one that has abandoned the base feminine nature of the sensual world and has obtained divine wisdom. Rather, the image of the παρθένος is an imperative, a command left by Philo in his writings to those of his Jewish-Hellenistic contemporaries who desired to follow a philosophical path. It is a guide by which they could heal their soul of its diseased corporeal nature and become fully united with the divine God of the Jewish people. This, according to Philo, is a process that should be taken up as soon as the philosopher was able. As Philo asks in *Cher.* 52, if a philosopher knows that he could gain a παρθένος soul by following Philo's allegorical readings, why should he delay? "Why then, O soul, since it is right for you to dwell as a virgin in the house of God, and to cleave to wisdom, do you stand aloof from these things and rather embrace the outward sense which effeminates and pollutes you?" Instead, the philosopher should begin the path of wisdom marked out by Philo, transform his γυνή soul into a pure, masculine παρθένος, and thereby bear the divine wisdom of God.

Georgia State University

ΔΟΡΥΦΟΡΕΙΝ, ΔΟΡΥΦΟΡΟΣ :
L'IMAGE DE LA «GARDE» CHEZ
PHILON D'ALEXANDRIE

OLIVIER MUNNICH[*]

En *Lois spéciales* 1.45, Philon d'Alexandrie présente les puissances divines comme δορυφόροι, « porte-lances », « escortes ». Dans la reformulation de l'Alexandrin, Moïse dit en effet à Dieu :

> ἱκετεύω δὲ τὴν γοῦν περὶ σὲ δόξαν θεάσασθαι· δόξαν δὲ σὴν εἶναι νομίζω τὰς περὶ σὲ δορυφορούσας δυνάμεις, ὧν διαφεύγουσα ἡ κατάληψις ἄχρι τοῦ παρόντος οὐ μικρὸν ἐνεργάζεταί μοι πόθον τῆς διαγνώσεως.

> « Je te supplie de me laisser au moins contempler la gloire qui t'entoure ; je tiens pour ta gloire les puissances qui font escorte autour de toi, dont la saisie, qui m'échappe jusqu'à présent, ne suscite pas en moi un mince désir de connaissance ».[1]

Ce thème de l'escorte divine est préparé par la reformulation du lemme biblique : δεῖξόν μοι τὴν σεαυτοῦ δόξαν, « montre-moi ta gloire » (Ex 33:18) devient ἱκετεύω δὲ τὴν γοῦν περὶ σὲ δόξαν θεάσασθαι, « je te supplie de me laisser contempler en tout cas la gloire *qui t'entoure* » ; en outre, Philon n'écrit pas que les puissances « escortent » Dieu—on aurait pu trouver une construction transitive—, mais, qu'elles « font escorte *autour de* toi » (περὶ σέ). L'auteur *spatialise* donc délibérément les puissances. Cela s'accorde avec le début de son développement consacré à la possibilité de connaître l'essence de Dieu :

> [37] τούτων γὰρ ὁ λογισμὸς ἀπὸ γῆς ἄνω μετέωρος ἀρθεὶς αἰθεροβατεῖ καὶ συμπεριπολῶν ἡλίῳ καὶ σελήνῃ καὶ τῷ σύμπαντι οὐρανῷ, τἀκεῖ πάντα γλιχόμενος ἰδεῖν, ἀμυδροτέραις χρῆται ταῖς προσβολαῖς, ἀκράτου καὶ πολλοῦ φέγγους ἐκχεομένου, ὡς τὸ τῆς ψυχῆς ὄμμα ταῖς μαρμαρυγαῖς σκοτοδινιᾶν.

---

[*] Cette étude a bénéficié des suggestions éclairantes de Françoise Frazier : qu'elle trouve ici l'expression de ma reconnaissance.

[1] Lorsque nous ne renvoyons pas à la traduction française des œuvres de Philon d'Alexandrie (PAPM, Éditions du Cerf), c'est que nous proposons notre propre traduction.

la pensée de ceux qui se sont rassasiés de philosophie « soulevée, en effet, au-dessus de la terre jusqu'en haut des nues, se meut dans l'éther et accompagne dans leurs révolutions le soleil, la lune et l'ensemble du ciel ; en dépit de son désir de voir tout ce qui est là-bas, elle a des perceptions confuses car une lumière si pure et abondante en émane que les éclats scintillants plongent l'œil de l'âme dans un tourbillon d'obscurité ».

En une représentation inspirée par l'analogie platonicienne entre le Bien et le soleil (*République* 6, 508b13–c2), Philon décrit la recherche de l'essence divine comme une contemplation—vouée à l'échec—de la lumière des astres ; à défaut de voir le soleil, il faut se contenter d'observer « l'éma-nation de ses rayons sur la terre » (τὴν φερομένην ἀπόρροιαν τῶν ἀκτίνων ἐπὶ γῆν, §40). Au §45, la mention du verbe δορυφορεῖν s'accorde bien avec un tel schéma argumentatif : il n'est pas possible, explique Philon, de contempler l'Être (le soleil), ni même les puissances (les astres satellites) mais seulement « le spectacle du monde et de ce qu'il contient » (τὴν τοῦ κόσμου καὶ τῶν ἐν αὐτῷ … θέαν, §49). On peut également expliquer le recours à cette représentation astrale comme une réponse monothéiste aux cultes astraux, critiqués au début du traité : les astres ne sont pas des magistrats *indépendants* (ἄρχοντας οὐκ αὐτεξουσίους, §14) mais des *lieutenants* du Père unique de toutes choses (ἑνὸς τοῦ πάντων πατρὸς ὑπάρχους, *ibid.*).

Un tel développement suppose connu de l'Alexandrin l'emploi de δορυφόρος au sens astronomique de « planète ». Grâce à l'excellente étude de S. Denningmann, on sait désormais que l'usage de cette image en astronomie n'est pas inspiré par un cérémonial de cour oriental, comme le pensait A. Bouché-Leclercq,[2] mais qu'il est déjà attesté aux IIe ou Ier siècles avant J.-C. par l'astronome Sarapion d'Alexandrie.[3] Ailleurs dans son oeuvre, l'Alexandrin signale même qu'il a entendu un enseignement sur la δορυφορία des astres.[4] Dans le texte des *Lois spéciales*, la représentation des

<hr />

[2] *L'astrologie grecque* (Paris: E. Ledoux, 1899), 252.

[3] Susanne Denningmann, *Die astrologische Lehre der Doryphorie. Eine soziomorphe Metapher in der antiken Planetenastrologie* (München: K. G. Saur, 2005), 48–62. Je remercie David T. Runia de m'avoir fait connaître cette étude.

[4] μέμνημαι δὲ καὶ πρότερόν τινος ἀκούσας ἀνδρὸς οὐκ ἀμελῶς οὐδὲ ῥαθύμως τῷ μαθήματι προσενεχθέντος, ὅτι οὐκ ἄνθρωποι μόνοι δοξομανοῦσιν, ἀλλὰ καὶ οἱ ἀστέρες καὶ περὶ πρωτείων ἀμιλλώμενοι δικαιοῦσιν οἱ μείζους ἀεὶ πρὸς τῶν ἐλαττόνων δορυφορεῖσθαι, « je me rappelle avoir autrefois entendu dire à quelqu'un qui s'était adonné à l'étude d'une façon qui n'avait rien de négligent ou de dilettante, qu'il n'y a pas que les hommes à être fous de gloire, mais que les astres aussi ont des rivalités de préséance et que les plus grands trouvent juste d'avoir toujours les plus petits pour les escorter », *Somn.* 2.114 trad. de Pierre Savinel (légèrement remaniée) (PAPM 19; Paris: Cerf, 1962), 177. Chez Plutarque, chronologiquement proche de Philon, on lit ceci à propos des variations de la course du soleil : Πλάτων Πυθαγόρας Ἀριστοτέλης παρὰ τὴν λόξωσιν τοῦ ζῳδιακοῦ κύκλου, δι' οὗ φέρεται λοξοπορῶν ὁ ἥλιος, καὶ κατὰ δορυφορίαν τῶν τροπικῶν κύκλων, « Selon Platon,

puissances comme *satellites* de Dieu s'accorde à la comparaison entre Dieu et le soleil qu'on lit juste auparavant (§40) et aux métaphores courantes chez l'Alexandrin.[5]

I. La δορυφορία *des sens*

Philon emploie fréquemment l'adjectif δορυφόρος dans des contextes différents. Il s'agit, le plus souvent, d'exprimer de façon imagée la garde que montent les sens autour de l'âme :

– δορυφόροι δὲ αἱ αἰσθήσεις τοῦ νοῦ περὶ κεφαλὴν οὖσαι, « les sens sont les gardes de l'intellect, qui se trouvent dans la tête », *Leg.* 3.115 ;

– οὐκ ὀφθαλμοὶ καὶ ὦτα καὶ ὁ τῶν ἄλλων χορὸς αἰσθήσεων ψυχῆς ὥσπερ τινὲς δορυφόροι καὶ φίλοι, « les yeux et les oreilles et le chœur des autres sens ne sont-ils pas comme les gardes et les amis de l'âme ? », *Det.* 33 ; τὰς δὲ νοῦ δορυφόρους αἰσθήσεις, « les sens qui forment la garde de l'intellect », *Det.* 85 ;

– ἄγγελοι διανοίας εἰσὶ … δορυφόροι ψυχῆς εἰσιν, les sens « sont des messagers pour la pensée …, ils sont la garde de l'âme », *Somn.* 1.27 ; κεφαλήν, περὶ ἣν καὶ αἱ αἰσθήσεις λοχῶσιν … οἷα μεγάλου βασιλέως ἐφεδρεύειν τοὺς δορυφόρους, « la tête autour de laquelle les sens sont aux aguets … comme veillent les gardes d'un Grand Roi », *Somn.* 1.32.

Dans un cas, la parole est qualifiée de la même façon : οἰκεῖον καὶ προσφυέστατον ἕξει δορυφόρον : avec elle, l'homme « aura un garde personnel entièrement dévoué », *Somn.* 1.103.

Comme l'écrit P. Boyancé, « il est très certain que l'origine de cette comparaison est encore dans le *Timée* » :[6] selon ce traité, l'âme mortelle comporte dans la poitrine humaine deux parties, l'une—supérieure—portée au courage, l'autre—inférieure—portée aux désirs ; entre les deux, les être divins « ont placé le cœur *au poste de garde* » (εἰς τὴν δορυφορικὴν οἴκησιν κατέστησαν, 70b 2) : en cas de conflit entre les instances de l'âme, le cœur, par tous ses vaisseaux, peut transmettre à la partie inférieure les recommandations de la raison. S'ils reprennent l'image du *Timée*, les exemples réunis plus haut attestent d'une inflexion stoïcienne de cette

---

Pythagore et Aristote, cela est dû à l'obliquité du cercle zodiacal qui lui imprime une courbe oblique, et aussi au fait que les cercles tropiques en sont les gardiens », *Opinions des philosophes*, *Œuvres morales*, t. 12[2] (éd. et trad. Guy Lachenaud ; Paris: Les Belles Lettres, 1993), 119.

[5] ὃς λαμπροτάτῳ φωτί, ἑαυτῷ, τὰ ὅλα αὐγάζει, (Dieu) « qui éclaire l'univers d'une lumière très éclatante, à savoir Lui-même », *Fug.* 136.

[6] « Études philoniennes », *REG* 76 (1963): 110.

représentation : à la différence de Platon, ce sont les sens que les Stoïciens définissent comme des *messagers* de l'âme : selon Chrysippe, cité par Calcidius, *totaque anima sensus, qui sunt eius officia … ex principali parte illa …, futuros eorum quae sentiunt nuntios, ipsa de iis quae nuntiaverint iudicat ut rex*, « l'âme entière répand hors de cette partie éminente les sens qui sont ses serviteurs, afin qu'ils soient les messagers de ce qu'ils perçoivent ; elle-même, elle juge, tel un roi, de ce qu'ils lui ont annoncé ».[7] Si l'on ne peut savoir quel terme grec se trouvait chez Chrysippe derrière *officia*, une formulation de Cicéron paraît lever l'incertitude : dans une phrase dont P. Boyancé,[8] puis A. Mosès[9] ont perçu, par rapport à la pensée de Philon, toute l'importance, Cicéron écrit : *ipsum autem hominem eadem natura non solum celeritate mentis ornavit sed <ei> et sensus tamquam satellites attribuit ac nuntios*, « c'est encore la même nature qui, non seulement a muni l'homme en sa propre personne d'un esprit doué de promptitude, mais de plus lui a assigné les sens comme *gardes* et messagers » :[10] derrière le terme *satellites* appliqué aux sens, il est difficile de ne pas voir le mot grec δορυφόρος ; en outre, on soulignera le lien entre le rapprochement chez Cicéron des mots *satellites ac nuntios* et la formulation de Philon dans le *De somniis* 1.27 : ἄγγελοι διανοίας εἰσί … δορυφόροι ψυχῆς εἰσιν, les sens « sont des messagers pour la pensée …, ils sont les gardiens de l'âme ». Au IIe siècle après J.-C., Galien dit que le cerveau est logé dans la tête comme le Grand Roi sur son acropole et il ajoute : καθάπερ τινὰς δορυφόρους ἔχει τὰς αἰσθήσεις περιῳκισμένας, « il dispose des sens, établis là comme des sortes de gardes ».[11] La représentation des sens comme δορυφόροι de l'âme est donc tradition-nelle ; ainsi que le suggère S. Denningmann, elle correspond à une réélabo-ration stoïcienne de l'image du *Timée*.[12] Contre la tripartition platonicienne de l'âme à l'intérieur de laquelle le cœur est placé au poste de garde » (τὴν

---

[7] Joannes von Arnim, ed., *Stoicorum Veterum Fragmenta* (4 vols.; Leipzig-Stuttgart: Teubner, 1903–1904), t. 2, fr. 879, 235, 34–37 ; cité par Susanne Denningmann, *Die astro-logische Lehre*.

[8] « Études philoniennes », 110.

[9] *Spec.* 3–4 (PAPM 25; Paris: Cerf, 1970), 130 n. 3.

[10] *De legibus* 1.26. Texte éd. et trad. par Georges de Plinval (Paris: Les Belles Lettres, 1959), 15; cf. aussi *sensus autem interpretes ac nuntii rerum in capite tamquam in arce … collocati sunt*, De natura deorum 2.140.

[11] *On the Doctrines of Hippocrates and Plato* 2.230. Texte éd., trad. et comm. par Phillip De Lacy (*CPM* 5.4.1.2, t. 1; Berlin: Akademie-Verlag, 1978), 120, l. 2–3.

[12] Influence inverse selon Werner W. Jaeger : « Diese ganze Übernahme aus der Psychologie des Timaios muß von Poseidonios stammen, denn er ersetzte den altstoischen Seelenbegriff durch den platonischen des Timaios », *Nemesios von Emesa. Quellen-forschungen zum Neuplatonismus und seinen Anfängen bei Poseidonios* (Berlin: Weidmann, 1914), 25. Cependant, l'auteur ne fournit pas d'appui textuel à cette assertion.

δορυφορικὴν οἴκησιν), les Stoïciens voient dans l'âme le composé de l'ἡγεμονικόν, des cinq sens et de l'aptitude à la parole et à la procréation. Par sa présentation des sens—mais aussi du langage[13]—comme δορυφόροι de la raison, Philon se révèle un fidèle témoin de la façon dont la psychologie du *Timée* a été ultérieurement interprétée.

De tels usages, conformes à la tradition philosophique, permettent de mieux apprécier, chez Philon, des emplois de cette image en un sens moins traditionnel. L'Alexandrin emploie parfois l'image en rapport avec la partie rationnelle de l'âme :

– πάντες οἱ δορυφόροι καὶ ὑπέρμαχοι ψυχῆς συμφρονήσουσι λογισμοί, « tous les raisonnements qui gardent l'âme et combattent en sa faveur s'accorderont entre eux », *De confusione linguarum* 55 ;

– ὡς μὴ πρὸς τῶν σοφίας δορυφόρων ποτὲ καθαιρεθεῖεν, les constructeurs de la Tour de Babel agissent « pour n'être jamais anéantis par les gardes de la sagesse », *De confusione linguarum* 101 ;

– ἀλλά σου τὰς ἐπανατάσεις καὶ τὰς ἀπειλὰς ἐφόδῳ μιᾷ καταδραμούμεθα σὺν τοῖς δορυφόροις καὶ ὑπασπισταῖς, φρονήσεως ἐγγόνοις, « mais tes intimidations et tes menaces, nous les repousserons d'une seule attaque avec les gardes et les écuyers—litt. les porte-lances et les porte-boucliers— que sont les enfants du bon sens » *De somniis* 2.96 ;

– ψυχῆς τελείως κεκαθαρμένης ... τὰ δὲ ἄλλα ὅσα νενόμισται ἐν δορυφόρων καὶ ὑπηκόων λόγῳ ταττούσης, « une âme parfaitement purifiée ... qui dispose tout ce qui est l'objet d'estime au rang de gardes et de serviteurs », *De Sobrietate* 62.

Dans ces différentes formulations, l'Alexandrin reste encore tributaire de la tradition philosophique et l'on rapprochera les exemples précédents de ce fragment de Chrysippe : ἔστι δὲ ὁ θυμὸς τὸ δορυφορικὸν τοῦ λογισμοῦ, « le coeur est le gardien du raisonnement » (fr. moral 416, J. von Arnim, *SVF* III, p. 102).

II. *La δορυφορία de Dieu*

En revanche, on s'explique plus difficilement l'emploi par Philon d'une telle image pour désigner l'escorte dont s'entoure Dieu, dans des contextes où, à la différence de *Lois spéciales* 1.45, l'image astrale ne semble plus présente. Les cinq lieux concernés sont les suivants :

– *De Sacrificiis* 59 ἡνίκα ὁ θεὸς δορυφορούμενος ὑπὸ δυεῖν τῶν ἀνωτάτω δυνάμεων ἀρχῆς τε αὖ καὶ ἀγαθότητος εἷς ὢν ὁ μέσος τριττὰς φαντασίας

---

[13] Cf. *Somn.* 1.103, cité *supra*.

ἐνειργάζετο τῇ ὁρατικῇ ψυχῇ, « quand Dieu, escorté par les deux puissances les plus élevées—la souveraineté et la bonté—et placé entre elles deux, Lui qui est un, offrait à la vue de son âme contemplative (celle d'Abraham) trois images … »;[14]

– *De Abrahamo* 122 δορυφορούμενος οὖν ὁ μέσος ὑφ' ἑκατέρας τῶν δυνάμεων παρέχει τῇ ὁρατικῇ διανοίᾳ τοτὲ μὲν ἑνὸς τοτὲ δὲ τριῶν φαντασίαν, « ainsi, au centre, escorté par chacune des deux puissances, il offre à la pensée qui en a la vision l'apparence tantôt d'un seul être, tantôt de trois » ;

– *Quod deus sit immutabilis* 109 παρατηρητέον δ' ὅτι τὸν μὲν Νῶέ φησιν εὐαρεστῆσαι ταῖς τοῦ ὄντος δυνάμεσι, κυρίῳ τε καὶ θεῷ, Μωυσῆν δὲ τῷ δορυφορουμένῳ πρὸς τῶν δυνάμεων καὶ δίχα αὐτῶν κατὰ τὸ εἶναι μόνον νοουμένῳ, « Il faut remarquer que si, selon l'Écriture, Noé a plu aux puissances de l'Être, c'est-à-dire au Seigneur et à Dieu, Moïse a plu à celui qu'escortent les puissances et qui sans elles n'est conçu que dans son existence » ;

– *De Deo* 4 : « Celui qui est au milieu d'eux s'appelle l'Étant … Parmi les deux qui l'escortent, l'un est Dieu, l'autre le Seigneur, le premier étant le symbole de la vertu créatrice et l'autre de la vertu impériale »;[15]

– *Legatio ad Gaium* 6 : οὐ γὰρ φθάνει προσαναβαίνειν ὁ λόγος ἐπὶ τὸν ἄψαυστον καὶ ἀναφῆ πάντη θεόν, ἀλλ' ὑπονοστεῖ καὶ ὑπορρεῖ κυρίοις ὀνόμασιν ἀδυνατῶν ἐπιβάθρᾳ χρῆσθαι πρὸς δήλωσιν, οὐ λέγω τοῦ ὄντος—οὐδὲ γὰρ ὁ σύμπας οὐρανὸς ἔναρθρος φωνὴ γενόμενος εὐθυβόλων καὶ εὐσκόπων εἰς τοῦτο ἂν εὐποροίη ῥημάτων—ἀλλὰ τῶν δορυφόρων αὐτοῦ δυνάμεων, « la raison, en effet, ne peut manquer de tenter l'ascension jusqu'au Dieu impalpable et absolument inaccessible, mais elle s'abîme et s'écroule dans son impuissance à employer des mots propres comme échelons pour désigner, je ne dis pas l'Être—car le ciel tout entier se transformerait-il en voix articulée qu'il ne saurait disposer d'expressions exactes et typiques à cette fin—mais les puissances qui l'escortent ».[16]

La perplexité naît ici de la constance avec laquelle l'Alexandrin associe cette tournure imagée au rapport qui unit Dieu à ses puissances. Les notes de l'édition française de Philon parle souvent de « l'image du souverain oriental qui n'a de rapport avec ses sujets que par l'intermédiaire de ses

---

[14] Trad. Annita Méasson (PAPM 4; Paris: Cerf, 1966), 123.

[15] Folker Siegert, « Le fragment philonien *De Deo*. Première traduction française avec commentaire et remarques sur le langage métaphorique de Philon ,» in *Philon d'Alexandrie et le langage de la philosophie* (éd. Carlos Lévy; Paris: Brepols, 1998), 188. L'auteur a très probablement raison de rétrovertir l'arménien par τῶν δορυφόρων.

[16] Trad. (légèrement modifiée) André Pelletier, *Legatio ad Caium* (PAPM 32; Paris: Cerf, 1972), 65.

hauts fonctionnaires »[17] sans donner plus d'explication sur le recours à cette image. Plus récemment, F. Siegert semble avoir mieux repéré le problème : « Cet usage de δορυφόρος pour parler cosmologie … présuppose le transfert du cérémoniel de cour perse (passé depuis plusieurs siècles, mais toujours présent dans la mémoire collective) aux sommets de la doctrine de Dieu. Philon est précédé par le *De Mundo* (398a10–35, b1ss.) : du « Roi des Rois », qui ne touche rien ni n'agit lui-même, mais qui par ses signes manifeste à ses Grands sa volonté, on passe *via eminentiae* au Dieu unique ».[18] En fait, on voit mal ce qu'est cette « mémoire collective » et l'on ne comprend pas l'emploi d'une telle image à propos d'un Dieu entouré de *deux* puissances et non de *toute* une cour céleste.

III. *Philon d'Alexandrie et le* De Mundo *du pseudo-Aristote*

À y réfléchir, le parallèle avec l'imagerie du souverain oriental et le rapprochement, souvent fait par la critique, avec le *De Mundo* du pseudo-Aristote suscitent des réserves : dans ce texte, il est question de δύναμις divine *et* de δορυφόροι, mais, maintes fois mentionnée, cette puissance par laquelle la divinité intervient dans le monde, l'est toujours au singulier :

– σωτὴρ μὲν γὰρ ὄντως ἁπάντων ἐστὶ καὶ γενέτωρ τῶν ὁπωσδήποτε κατὰ τόνδε τὸν κόσμον συντελουμένων ὁ θεός, οὐ μὴν αὐτουργοῦ καὶ ἐπιπόνου ζῴου κάματον ὑπομένων, ἀλλὰ δυνάμει χρώμενος ἀτρύτῳ, « car si Dieu est bien réellement le conservateur et le créateur de tout ce qui, de quelque façon que ce soit, est accompli dans ce monde visible, ce n'est pourtant pas qu'il endure la fatigue d'un travailleur manuel et d'une homme de peine ; non, il a à son service une puissance que rien n'use »;[19]

– μάλιστα δέ πως αὐτοῦ τῆς δυνάμεως ἀπολαύει τὸ πλησίον αὐτοῦ σῶμα, « les effets les plus vifs de sa puissance se communiquent d'abord, en quelque manière, au corps le plus rapproché de lui » (397b);[20]

---

[17] André Pelletier, *Legatio ad Caium*, 64, n. 7. Cf. aussi Suzanne Denningmann, « Ähnliche (i.e. par rapport à Philon) soziomorphe Vorstellugen als Leitmotiv des Weltverständnisses finden wir auch in der pseudoaristotelischen Werk *De Mundo* », *Die astrologische Lehre*, 138.

[18] « Le fragment philonien *De Deo* », 199.

[19] *De Mundo* 397b; trad. André-Jean Festugière, « Le traité pseudo-aristotélicien 'Du Monde' », in *La révélation d'Hermès Trismégiste. II Le Dieu cosmique* (Paris: Les Belles Lettres, 1949), 470. Cf. également σεμνότερον δὲ καὶ πρεπωδέστερον αὐτὸν μὲν ἐπὶ τῆς ἀνωτάτω χώρας ἱδρῦσθαι, τὴν δὲ δύναμιν διὰ τοῦ σύμπαντος κόσμου … κινεῖν, « Il est plus digne et convenable d'admettre que Dieu lui-même siège au sommet de l'univers tandis que sa puissance … circule à travers l'ensemble du monde » (*ibid.*, 398b).

[20] *Ibid.*

– κρεῖττον οὖν ὑπολαβεῖν, ὃ καὶ πρέπον ἐστὶ καὶ θεῷ μάλιστα ἁρμόζον, ὡς ἡ ἐν οὐρανῷ δύναμις ἱδρυμένη καὶ τοῖς πλεῖστον ἀφεστηκόσιν, ὡς ἔνι γε εἰπεῖν, καὶ σύμπασιν αἴτιος γίνεται σωτηρίας, « il est donc préférable—c'est d'ailleurs ce qui convient et qui s'accorde le plus à Dieu—de se représenter que la puissance qui siège au ciel est cause de leur conservation même pour les êtres les plus distants, d'un mot pour la totalité des êtres » (398a).[21]

Plus encore, l'auteur du traité insiste sur l'*unicité* du mouvement par laquelle *la* puissance divine introduit une impulsion qui se propage dans la totalité de l'univers,[22] tels les montreurs de marionnettes, ajoute-t-il, qui, d'une seule ficelle, meuvent plusieurs membres d'un pantin. Or, chez Philon,—sur la base d'un corpus restreint aux quatre livres des *Lois spéciales*—il nous a semblé qu'il existait un usage différencié de *la* puissance et *des* puissances de Dieu;[23] d'après cette oeuvre, l'action de Dieu sur l'univers est médiatisée pas *ses* puissances et, en aucune façon, par *sa* puissance.

Dans le *De Mundo*, il est question de δορυφόροι à la cour d'un Grand Roi, « invisible à tous » (παντὶ ἀόρατος) ; l'auteur du traité les décrit ainsi :

Ἔξω δὲ τούτων ἄνδρες οἱ πρῶτοι καὶ δοκιμώτατοι διεκεκόσμηντο, οἱ μὲν ἀμφ' αὐτὸν τὸν βασιλέα δορυφόροι τε καὶ θεράποντες, οἱ δὲ ἑκάστου περιβόλου φύλακες, πυλωροί τε καὶ ὠτακουσταὶ λεγόμενοι, ὡς ἂν ὁ βασιλεὺς αὐτός, δεσπότης καὶ θεὸς ὀνομαζόμενος, πάντα μὲν βλέποι, πάντα δὲ ἀκούοι.

« Outre cela, il y avait toute une hiérarchie des premiers et plus illustres personnages, les uns attachés à la personne même du roi comme gardes et serviteurs, les autres chargés de surveiller chaque enceinte, nommés gardiens des portes ou 'écouteurs', en sorte que le roi lui-même, qui était appelé souverain maître et dieu, vît et entendît tout ce qui se passait » (398a).

On perçoit, dans le *De mundo*, la distance entre le principe universel qu'est la δύναμις divine et de tels ministres qui, quelle que soit leur proximité avec le roi, n'en sont que les exécutants. Si, à la différence de Philon, il n'est pas

---

[21] *Ibid.*

[22] οὕτως οὖν καὶ ἡ θεία φύσις ἀπό τινος ἁπλῆς κινήσεως τοῦ πρώτου τὴν δύναμιν εἰς τὰ συνεχῆ δίδωσι καὶ ἀπ' ἐκείνων πάλιν εἰς τὰ πορρωτέρω, μέχρις ἂν διὰ τοῦ παντὸς διεξέλθῃ, « ainsi en va-t-il de l'être divin : il lui suffit d'un simple mouvement de ce qui lui est le plus proche pour communiquer sa puissance aux parties qui viennent immédiatement après, et de là encore aux plus éloignées, jusqu'à ce qu'elle se soit propagée d'un bout à l'autre du monde entier » (*ibid.*, 398b). Dans son ouvrage, Roberto Radice souligne, dans le *De Mundo*, l'unicité de la δύναμις θεοῦ, *La filosofia di Aristobulo e i suoi nessi con il « De mundo » attribuito ad Aristotele* (Milano: Vita e Pensiero, 1994), 29–41.

[23] Olivier Munnich, « Les puissances divines dans les *Lois spéciales* de Philon d'Alexandrie », in *Potere e potenze in Filone di Alessandria*. Actes du colloque de Milan (14-17 juin 2011), à paraître chez Brepols en 2014.

question, dans le *De mundo*, de δύναμις δορυφόρος, c'est qu'il existe, pour son auteur, un abîme entre la δύναμις et les δορυφόροι dont parle le traité.

En revanche, il est étonnant que les commentateurs de Philon n'aient pas repéré le lien qui existe—à un autre niveau—entre ce traité et l'œuvre de l'Alexandrin. En des termes apparentés à la description de la cour du Grand Roi entouré, dans le *De Mundo*, de ses δορυφόροι, Philon présente les sens comme les δορυφόροι du Grand Roi qu'est, le plus souvent, le νοῦς mais aussi, dans un cas, la raison :

– παρέχουσα ... τῷ δὲ νῷ καθάπερ μεγάλῳ βασιλεῖ τὰ μὲν διὰ τούτων ὡς ἂν δορυφόρων ὅσα αἰσθητά, (la Nature) « fournissant à l'esprit, tel à un Grand Roi, tout ce qui relève du sensible par l'intermédiaire des sens, comme par celui de gardiens », *Lois spéciales* 3.111 ;

– ὅπου ὁ βασιλεύς, ἐκεῖ καὶ οἱ δορυφόροι, δορυφόροι δὲ αἱ αἰσθήσεις τοῦ νοῦ περὶ κεφαλὴν οὖσαι, « là où est le roi, là aussi se trouvent les gardes ; or, les gardes ce sont les sensations qui, situées dans la tête, assurent la garde de l'intellect », *Allégories des lois* 3.115 ;

– τὸ πρόσωπον, ἔνθα αἱ δορυφόροι τοῦ νοῦ καθάπερ μεγάλου βασιλέως αἰσθήσεις παρίδρυνται, « le visage, où siègent les sens, ces gardes de l'intellect, tels d'un Grand Roi », *Lois spéciales* 4.123 ;

– λόγῳ μὲν ὡς ἡγεμόνι τὴν ἄκραν ἀπένειμαν οἰκειότατον ἐνδιαίτημα κεφαλήν, ἔνθα καὶ τῶν αἰσθήσεων αἱ τοῦ νοῦ καθάπερ βασιλέως δορυφόροι τάξεις παρίδρυνται, « à la raison, comme à un souverain, ils ont assigné, en guise de citadelle, une résidence tout à fait adéquate, la tête, où sont également installées les guérites des sens qui montent la garde autour de l'intellect comme autour d'un roi », *Lois spéciales* 4.92.[24]

On trouve la même formulation dans le *De somniis* 1.32 et en 1.27 avec une légère variante, puisqu'il est question, non du Grand Roi qu'est le νοῦς, mais de la maîtresse qu'est l'âme : δορυφόροι ψυχῆς εἰσιν, ὅσα ἂν ἴδωσιν ἢ ἀκούσωσι δηλοῦσαι κἂν εἴ τι βλαβερὸν ἔξωθεν ἐπίοι προορώμεναί τε καὶ φυλαττόμεναι, ὡς μὴ λάθρᾳ παρεισρευὲν αἴτιον ζημίας ἀνηκέστου τῇ δεσποίνῃ γένηται, les sens « sont les gardes de l'âme, lui révélant *tout ce qu'ils voient ou entendent*, apercevant de loin les dangers qui pourraient s'approcher du dehors et se tenant sur leurs gardes pour éviter qu'ils ne s'infiltrent sans être vus et ne causent à leur maîtresse un dommage irréparable » : on a là une représentation qui rappelle celle du *De mundo* où, grâce à ses δορυφόροι, le roi « voit tout, entend tout »—πάντα μὲν βλέποι, πάντα δὲ ἀκούοι—(cf. *supra*, 398a).

En somme, les « puissances doryphores » de Philon n'ont rien de commun avec les « Grands » de la cour orientale, évoqués par le *De Mundo* ;

---

[24] Trad. André Mosès (PAPM 25; Paris: Cerf, 1970), 255.

en revanche, la description philonienne des rapports entre le νοῦς et les sens fait songer à la forte hiérarchie de cour, présente dans ce traité (l'Alexandrin et l'auteur du *De Mundo* dépendant probablement d'une source qui leur serait commune).[25] Expliquer l'image philonienne des puissances escortant Dieu par le cérémonial de la cour orientale reviendrait à assimiler les puissances à des sens de Dieu : l'hypothèse aboutit à une impasse. Autant l'image de sens « doryphores » est donc bien attestée dans la tradition grecque, autant celle de « puissances doryphores » de Dieu semble, pour sa part, une particularité propre à Philon.

IV. Δορυφορεῖσθαι *dans la tradition philosophico-religieuse*

Pour comprendre cette expression, il convient d'examiner, tout autant que les lieux bibliques qui l'inspirent à l'Alexandrin, ceux qui, chez lui, ne la *suscitent pas*. Comme l'a noté D. T. Runia,[26] Philon évoque les puissances divines à propos de la triade formée par les chérubins et l'épée de feu de Gen 3:24 (*Cher.* 27 *et passim*) ou par les trois mesures de farine de Gen 18:6 (*Sacr.* 60 *et passim*), à propos de l'hexade formée par les villes de refuge (*Fug.* 95 *et passim*) ou les ailes des séraphins (*Deo* 9) et à propos de l'hebdomade dans la description de l'Arche d'alliance (*QE* 2.68) ou au sujet des filles du prêtre de Madiân (*Mut.* 110). Or, aucun de ces lieux scripturaires n'amène Philon à qualifier de doryphores les puissances divines. En revanche, quatre des cinq fois où il emploie « doryphores » à propos de Dieu flanqué de ses puissances, l'auteur fait allusion à l'apparition de Mambré (Gen 18). Il existe donc un lien étroit entre une telle image et cet épisode—central pour Philon—, au cours duquel Abraham accueille trois visiteurs angéliques qui, suggère le texte scripturaire, n'en font qu'un. Un élément formel rend ce lien plus étroit encore : quand il fait allusion à l'épisode de Mambré, Philon emploie le participe δορυφορούμενος (peut-être l'indicatif dans le *De deo* qu'on ne conserve qu'en traduction). Sensiblement différente des autres occurrences qui tournent toutes autour

[25] Dans le *De usu partium* 17, Galien écrit : τὰς αἰσθήσεις ἁπάσας ἔχειν ἐν αὐτῇ, καθάπερ τινὰς ὑπηρέτας τε καὶ δορυφόρους μεγάλου βασιλέως, « tous les sens se trouvent en elle (i.e. la tête) comme des serviteurs et gardiens d'un Grand Roi » (Karl G. Kühn, *Claudii Galeni opera omnia* [Leipzig, 1822; rééd. Hildesheim: G. Holms, 1964), 3:614. La représentation de l'ἡγεμονικόν de l'âme comme un Grand Roi appartient, selon Pierre Boyancé, à « une anthropologie qui vient selon toute vraisemblance d'Antiochus » (« Études philoniennes », 110).

[26] « Philo of Alexandria on the Human Consequences of Divine Power », communication au colloque *Potere et potenze in Filone di Alessandria*.

de l'apparition de Mambré, la *Legatio ad Gaium* 6 recourt, non au verbe δορυφορεῖσθαι mais à l'adjectif (τῶν δορυφόρων αὐτοῦ δυνάμεων) : Dieu n'est plus « escorté » par les puissances , mais ce sont les puissances qui l'escortent. Indifférent sur le plan sémantique, ce détail renforce le lien entre l'emploi du *verbe* δορυφορεῖσθαι et l'évocation de l'*épisode* de Mambré où Dieu est, selon l'Alexandrin, « escorté » par *deux* puissances. Comment comprendre le motif qui a conduit Philon à recourir à ce verbe imagé pour représenter « celui qui est » (ὁ ὤν) « flanked by his two chief powers », comme le dit D. T. Runia,[27] « escorté » par la puissance créatrice (ὁ θεός) et la puissance royale (ὁ κύριος) ? Touchant un point si central de la réflexion théologique, on ne peut imaginer chez l'Alexandrin un simple *trait de langue*.

L'ample documentation réunie par S. Denningmann fournit des éléments qui permettent, semble-t-il, de répondre à la question. En dehors de son sens propre et de son acception astronomique—« satellite »—, δορυφόρος se rencontre dans des textes philosophico-religieux, ainsi dans le *Corpus hermeticum* : lorsque l'âme entre dans le corps, elle est accompagnée par deux doryphores :

Εἰσὶ γὰρ ἄνωθεν οἱ δορυφόροι, <δύ'> ὄντες, τῆς καθόλου προνοίας, ὧν ὁ μὲν ψυχοταμίας, ὁ δὲ ψυχοπομπός· καὶ ὁ μὲν ψυχοταμίας ψυχῶν <...>, ὁ δὲ ψυχοπομπὸς ἀποστολεύς τε καὶ διατάκτης τῶν ἐνσωματουμένων ψυχῶν. καὶ ὁ μὲν τηρεῖ, ὁ δὲ προΐησι κατὰ γνώμην τοῦ θεοῦ.

« il y en effet, venus de là-haut, au nombre de deux, les gardiens de la providence universelle ; l'un est l'intendant de l'âme, l'autre son guide. Selon le projet du dieu, l'un la conserve, l'autre la fait avancer ».[28]

Ce couple de δορυφόροι fait songer aux deux puissances qui, chez Philon, escortent Dieu, mais le contexte est bien différent.

En revanche, on trouve δορυφορεῖν chez le néo-platonicien Proclus, bien postérieur à Philon (il écrit au 5è siècle), dans des contextes où les données astronomiques sont, comme chez Philon, prises dans une réflexion philosophique :

Εἰ δὲ δὴ κρατοίη τὸν μὲν ἥλιον ἐν τῷ μέσῳ τάττειν τῶν ἑπτά, καθάπερ οἱ θεουργικοὶ λόγοι καὶ θεοί φασιν, τὸν δὲ Ἑρμῆν ὑπὲρ σελήνην, σκόπει τὴν τάξιν, ὅπως ἐστὶ προσήκουσα τοῖς τῆς γενέσεως ὅλης προστάταις. ὁ μὲν γὰρ ὡς καὶ τῶν ὁρατῶν πάντων βασιλεὺς καὶ τὰς δημιουργικὰς δυνάμεις διὰ τῶν τοῦ φωτὸς ἀκτίνων ἀπομιμούμενος ὑπὸ πάντων δορυφορεῖται τῶν κοσμοκρατόρων, γενν[ῶν τε καὶ] ζωῆς πληρῶν <καὶ> ἀνανεάζων τὰς γενέσεις.

---

[27] *Ibid.*

[28] *Corpus hermeticum*, t. 4. *Fragments extraits de Stobée*, fr. 26, 3. Texte édité et traduit par André-Jean Festugière (Paris: Les Belles Lettres, 1954), 81 (trad. légèrement remaniée).

« Si donc la thèse l'emporte de placer le Soleil au milieu des sept, comme le disent les enseignements des Théurges et les Dieux, et, juste au-dessus de la Lune, Mercure, observe comme cet ordre a convenance avec les dieux qui président sur toute la création. Le Soleil en effet, comme Roi de tout le visible et reproduisant les forces du Démiurge par les rayons de sa lumière, a pour gardes du corps tous les Maîtres du monde, étant celui qui engendre, qui remplit de vie et qui renouvelle les générations ».[29]

Dans ce texte, Proclus déclare qu'il s'écarte de Platon et des astronomes de son temps, qui placent le Soleil en septième position à partir de la sphère des fixes ; il se réfère ici—comme Philon—à l'ordre chaldéen, reçu des théurges et des dieux, selon lequel le Soleil occupe une place centrale.

Conformément à la doctrine des *Oracles chaldaïques*, Proclus adopte une représentation fortement dualiste, opposant les mondes intelligible et sensible. Sur le premier règne le Père, sous forme de feu transcendant ou de premier νοῦς et sur le second, le Démiurge ou second νοῦς. Analogue du Démiurge, le Soleil assure par ses rayons le passage du feu intelligible au monde sensible. Il assure ses pouvoirs démiurgiques (τὰς δημιουργικὰς δυνάμεις) de création (γεννῶν) mais aussi de préservation de l'univers (ἀνανεάζων τὰς γενέσεις) grâce aux « maîtres du monde » (τῶν κοσμοκρα-τόρων), par qui il est escorté (δορυφορεῖται). La suite du texte montre claire-ment que ces dieux-astres participent à la création du Démiurge-Soleil : au-dessus de celui-ci, les trois astres mâles développent des « activités produc-trices » (δραστηρίους ποιήσεις) et, au dessous de lui, les trois autres, fémi-nins à l'exception de l'élément central, « reproduisent la force génératrice des Causes » (τὸ γόνιμον μιμοῦνται τῶν αἰτίων τοῦ κόσμου).[30] L'intérêt de ce texte tient au fait qu'il atteste l'emploi du verbe δορυφορεῖσθαι dans un contexte théosophique où il est question de l'intervention démiurgique d'un dieu-astre, escorté par *deux* groupes de dieux-astres qui, sur des plans complémentaires, lui portent assistance. Dès lors, l'emploi philonien de l'image apparaît comme une reformulation monothéiste et biblique d'une semblable représentation. Certes, l'Alexandrin écrit près de quatre siècles avant Proclus, mais, avec les *Oracles chaldaïques*, le philosophe néo-platonicien s'inspire de données réunies vers le IIème siècle et reposant sans doute, pour certaines formulations, sur des traditions antérieures.

Le témoignage de Proclus est, lui-même, corroboré par un poème au dieu-Soleil, conservé dans un papyrus magique que cite S. Denningmann :

---

[29] Wilhelm Kroll, *Procli Diadochi in Platonis rem publicam commentarii* (Leipzig: Teubner,1901), 2:221. XVIè Dissertation. Le Mythe d'Er, in *Commentaire sur la « Répu-blique »*, traduction et notes par André-Jean Festugière (Paris: Vrin, 1970), 3 :173.

[30] *Ibid*. Nous modifions l'accentuation de Wilhelm Kroll (αἰτίων) en fonction de la traduction d'André-Jean Festugière.

Ἀστέρες ἀέριοι, ἑῷοι περιδινοπλανῆται, αὐταῖς σαῖς βουλαῖς σοι δορυφοροῦσιν ἅπαντα, «des astres aériens, des planètes tournoyantes t'escortent en tout dans tes volontés».[31]

Exprimée avec le verbe δορυφορεῖν, on trouve ici encore l'idée, bien attestée dans les textes philosophiques, d'une collaboration des planètes à l'œuvre créatrice du Soleil.[32]

V. *Vénus et Mercure,* δορυφόροι *du Soleil*

Chez Proclus, l'image de l'escorte céleste se spécifie pour désigner deux planètes, Vénus et Mercure. La réflexion du philosophe se fonde sur un passage délicat du *Timée* (38 d2–6): décrivant la naissance du Temps, du Soleil, de la Lune et des cinq astres qu'on appelle errants, Timée expose comment le dieu les a placés dans les sept orbites que décrit la substance de l'Autre :

> après la Lune et le Soleil, «l'astre du matin et celui dont on dit qu'il est consacré à Hermès (ἑωσφόρον δὲ καὶ τὸν ἱερὸν Ἑρμοῦ λεγόμενον), de telle sorte qu'ils parcourent leurs cercles *avec une vitesse égale* à celle du Soleil (εἰς τὸν τάχει μὲν ἰσόδρομον ἡλίῳ κύκλον ἰόντας), mais qu'ils reçoivent une impulsion de direction contraire à la sienne. De là vient que le Soleil, l'astre du matin et celui d'Hermès *se rattrapent* tour à tour *et sont rattrapés* les uns par les autres, suivant une loi constante » (ὅθεν καταλαμβάνουσίν τε καὶ καταλαμβάνονται κατὰ ταὐτὰ ὑπ' ἀλλήλων ἥλιός τε καὶ ὁ τοῦ Ἑρμοῦ καὶ ἑωσφόρος).

Le commentaire de Proclus est le suivant :

> ὅ γέ τοι Πτολεμαῖος ἐν μὲν τῇ Συντάξει [9, 1] τῷ εὐλόγῳ καὶ τῷ πιθανῷ φησιν ἀκολουθοῦντας τίθεσθαι προσήκειν τῶν ἑπτὰ μέσον τὸν ἥλιον, ἵνα τῶν πέντε πλανωμένων πρὸ αὐτοῦ μὲν ὦσιν οἱ παντελῶς αὐτοῦ ἀφιστάμενοι, μετ' αὐτὸν δὲ οἱ συνόντες αὐτῷ καὶ προπομπεύοντες ἢ δορυφοροῦντες αὐτόν, « Ptolémée dit sans doute, dans la *Syntaxis* (9,1), que, si l'on suit le vraisemblable et le probable, il convient de placer le Soleil au milieu des sept, afin que, des cinq astres planétaires, il y ait avant lui ceux qui s'éloignent totalement de lui, après lui ceux qui l'accompagnent et l'escortent ou lui servent de *gardes du corps* ».[33]

Comme le note S. Denningmann, après la citation de Ptolémée, Proclus quitte le registre descriptif qui était celui de l'astronome et passe à un plan

---

[31] Karl Preisendanz, Albert Henrichs, *Papyri Graecae Magicae. Die griechischen Zauberpapyri* 3 (Stuttgart: Teubner, 1973–1974), 556 f.

[32] Nombreuses références chez Denningmann, *Die astrologische Lehre*, 152, n. 443.

[33] *Commentaire sur le Timée* 4, 258A. Texte Ernst Diehl, *Procli Diadochi in Platonis Timaeum commentaria* (Leipzig: Teubner, 1906), 3 :62, l. l. 17–22. Traduction André-Jean Festugière, *Commentaire sur le Timée* (Paris: Vrin, 1968), 4 :85.

plus « mystique » : chez le philosophe néo-platonicien, le verbe προπομ-πεύειν, note-t-elle, qualifie le plus souvent l'escorte des anges et des démons.[34] Dans son *Commentaire sur la République*, Proclus propose une description identique :

> « Et en effet, pour ce qui est des trois planètes au-dessus de lui (*i.e.* Saturne, Jupiter, Mars), les marches en avant et rétrogradations (αἱ προσθαφαιρέσεις) s'accomplissent selon les aspects trigones avec lui ... Quant aux trois planètes au-dessous de lui, deux (*i.e.* Vénus et Mercure) le flanquent comme *gardes du corps*, la troisième (la Lune) tourne autour de lui, étant mue à partir de lui et vers lui » (τῶν δὲ μετ᾿ αὐτὸν οἱ μὲν δορυφοροῦσιν αὐτόν, ἣ δὲ χορεύει περὶ αὐτόν, ἀπ᾿ αὐτοῦ κινουμένη καὶ ἐπ᾿ αὐτόν).[35]

Avec ces deux textes, on passe d'une conception où la *totalité* des astres « escortent » le dieu-Soleil[36] à une autre, où *seuls Vénus et Mercure* sont « doryphores ». Ailleurs, Proclus commente ce parallélisme entre ces deux astres et le Soleil :

> Ὑπὲρ δὲ ἥλιον Ἀφροδίτην καὶ Ἑρμῆν, ἡλιακοὺς ὄντας καὶ συνδημιουργοῦντας αὐτῷ καὶ πρὸς τὴν τελεσιουργίαν τῶν ὅλων αὐτῷ συντελοῦντας· διὸ καὶ ἰσόδρομοι τυγχάνουσιν ὄντες ἡλίῳ καὶ περὶ αὐτόν εἰσιν ὡς συγκοινωνοῦντες αὐτῷ τῆς ποιήσεως, « Vénus et Mercure sont au-dessus du Soleil, parce qu'ils sont « solaires », qu'ils collaborent à son action créatrice, qu'ils contribuent avec lui à l'achèvement de toutes choses ».[37]

Il reprend l'adjectif ἰσόδρομον, présent en *Timée* 38d2, en le commentant ainsi : ces deux dieux-astres contribuent à l'activité démiurgique du Soleil et participent avec lui à la création (on sera, dans la citation, sensible à la récurrence du préverbe συν-). À cet égard, le commentaire du *Timée* marque, chez le néo-platonicien, une inflexion sensible par rapport au texte platonicien, où la convergence du *mouvement* des astres n'implique nullement une similitude de leur *action*.

Les textes du néo-platonicien Proclus offrent des similitudes avec les données présentes chez Philon : dans l'oeuvre de l'Alexandrin, on trouve δορυφορεῖν employé des deux mêmes façons : tantôt, en un sens astronomique, les astres *dans leur ensemble* sont présentés comme *l'escorte* du Soleil, ainsi dans le *Quis Heres* : « chacune des planètes porte une lumière ; elles sont très brillantes et envoient jusqu'à la terre des rayons tout à fait

---

[34] *Die astrologische Lehre*, p. 154.

[35] *Commentaire sur la République*, XIIIè Dissertation, II, 58, 24–59, 2. Trad. Festugière, *Commentaire sur la « République »*, t. 22, 167.

[36] Ainsi dans le texte de la XVIème Dissertation, cité ci-dessus.

[37] *Commentaire sur le Timée* 4, 259A. Texte Ernst Diehl, *Procli Diadochi*, t. 3, 65, 22–26. Trad. Festugière, *Commentaire sur le Timée*, 4.90.

lumineux, mais celle qui est au milieu des sept, le Soleil, l'emporte sur toutes. Je l'appelle 'central', non seulement parce qu'il occupe la place centrale, comme l'ont estimé certains (ὡς ἠξίωσάν τινες),[38] mais parce qu'il est fondé à être tout particulièrement (δίκαιος ἄλλως ἐστί)[39] servi et *escorté*, de chaque côté, par des écuyers (καὶ θεραπεύεσθαι καὶ δορυφορεῖσθαι πρὸς ὑπασπιζόντων ἑκατέρωθεν), du fait de sa dignité, de sa grandeur et des services qu'il rend à toutes les régions terrestres »;[40] tantôt, en un sens théologique, l'image est employée pour les *deux* puissances qui escortent Dieu.

Commentant l'épisode de Mambré au cours duquel Abraham accueille trois visiteurs qui, selon le texte scripturaire, n'en forment qu'un, Philon fait, selon nous, un rapprochement avec le passage du *Timée* 38d2, où Vénus et Mercure accompagnent le Soleil en suivant un parcours égal (ἰσόδρομον ... κύκλον). Selon son degré de pureté, l'âme a la vision de l'Être, soit dans son unicité, soit de façon triple, c'est-à-dire « à travers ses réalisations comme créateur ou comme dirigeant » (τὸ ὂν ... διὰ τῶν δρωμένων, ἢ κτίζον ἢ ἄρχον, *De Abrahamo* 122). L'Alexandrin interprète l'apparition des visiteurs à Abraham (Gen 18) comme une allégorie de la pluralité des noms de Dieu : « celui qui est » (ὁ ὤν, dans l'épisode du Buisson ardent, Ex 3:14)—, ὁ θεός, « Dieu » comme « puissance créatrice » - ἡ μὲν ποιητική (δύναμις)—, ὁ κύριος, « le Seigneur » comme puissance royale—ἡ δ' αὖ βασιλική—(*De Abrahamo* 121). Chez l'Alexandrin, l'emploi réitéré de δορυφορεῖσθαι pour désigner le fait que Dieu est *flanqué* par ses puissances les plus proches[41] s'explique par le fait que Philon fonde sa représentation sur la cosmogonie du *Timée* et sur l'interprétation théologique qui en a été faite, sans doute bien avant le néo-platonisme : en une

[38] La remarque suppose connue de Philon le débat astrologique entre ordre chaldéen et « égyptien », selon la désignation de Pierre Boyancé, « La religion astrale de Platon à Cicéron », *REG* 38 (1952) : 346 n. 1. À cet égard, on ne suit pas le jugement de Susanne Denningmann : « Eine astrologische Lehre ist hinter dem Text Philons nicht zu erkennen », *Die astrologische Lehre*, 161.

[39] La formulation de Philon comporte une allusion subtile à l'étymologie du *Cratyle* 413 b : ὁ μὲν γὰρ τίς φησιν τοῦτο εἶναι δίκαιον, τὸν ἥλιον· τοῦτον γὰρ μόνον διαϊόντα καὶ κάοντα ἐπιτροπεύειν τὰ ὄντα, « Suivant l'un, en effet, le juste, c'est le soleil, car lui seul, en les *parcourant* (διαϊών) et en les *échauffant* (κάων), gouverne les êtres » : chez Philon, ἄλλως peut s'entendre au sens de « tout particulièrement » mais aussi de « autrement » (*i.e.* que ne le dit Platon).

[40] § 222–223 ; traduction (légèrement remaniée) de Marguerite Harl (PAPM 15; Paris: Cerf, 1966), 275.

[41] Cf. *supra*, II, « La δορυφορία de Dieu ».

perspective, non plus astronomique,[42] mais philosophico-religieuse—
« solartheologisch », écrit S. Denningmann,[43]— les planètes—et en particu-
lier les deux qui escortent le Soleil—y sont considérées comme associées à
l'activité démiurgique de celui-ci. Pour décrire la relation entre Dieu et ses
deux puissances principales, Philon a probablement songé à cette tradition
philosophique, issue du *Timée*, selon laquelle le Soleil et les deux planètes
intérieures forment ce que, pour Proclus, W. Saltzer nomme « eine heilige
Dreieinigkeit », « la sacralité d'une unité triadique ».[44]

Si une telle tradition est surtout attestée chez un auteur aussi tardif que
Proclus, elle n'en a pas moins une origine plus ancienne. Un texte attribué à
Antiochos, astronome athénien qu'on situe entre le 1er siècle avant et le 1er
siècle après J.-C., confère déjà à Vénus et à Mercure la fonction d'assister le
Soleil dans son activité créatrice, l'une sur le plan sensible, l'autre sur le
plan intelligible :

Καὶ ὡς βασιλέων μὲν ἐπέχουσιν λόγον Ἥλιος καὶ Σελήνη ἔπεται δὲ καὶ ὑπηρετεῖ
τῷ Ἡλίῳ μὲν Ἀφροδίτη καὶ Ἑρμῆς, ἡ μὲν ἀφῆς καὶ ὀρέξεως καὶ γονῆς, ὁ δὲ λόγου
καὶ φρονήσεως συνεργάται.

« Vénus et Mercure suivent le Soleil et lui *apportent assistance*, l'une en
collaborant sur le plan du contact, du désir et de l'engendrement, l'autre sur
celui de la raison et du raisonnement ».[45]

Les termes « porter assistance » et surtout « collaborer » impliquent déjà
une participation à l'activité créatrice du Soleil, comme la thématisera bien
plus tard Proclus. Ainsi que le note S. Denningmann, le thème de l'association de Vénus et de Mercure à l'œuvre du Soleil apparaît également chez
Cicéron dans le Songe de Scipion, en une formulation tributaire de celle du
Timée, *hunc (sc. Solem) ut comites consequuntur Veneris alter, alter Mercurii
cursus*, « tels des compagnons, les orbites respectives de Vénus et de Mercure le suivent » (*De Republica* 6.17) ou dans le *De Natura deorum* : *infraque
Martem duae Soli oboediant*, « et en dessous de Mars il y en a deux qui
obéissent au Soleil » (2.119).[46] Moins explicite que celui de l'astronome
Antiochos, le témoignage de Cicéron est probablement plus significatif en

[42] « Auch die Vorstellung, dass Venus und Merkur δορυφόροι der Sonne sind, ist in
den astrologischen Schriften nicht nachzuweisen », Denningmann, *Die astrologische Lehre*,
162.
[43] *Die astrologische Lehre*, 162 ; « Die Planeten sind gleichsam das 'Werkzeug' Gottes,
also ein Art Zwischenwesen, die auf Gottes Befehl handeln » (*ibid.*).
[44] « Zum Problem der innneren Planeten in der vorptolemäischen Theorie », *Sudhoffs
Archiv. Beihefte* 54 (1970): 155.
[45] *Epitome I 5 ex Antiochi Atheniensis Isagoga*, éd. Petrus Boudreaux, *Catalogus codicum
astrologorum Graecorum* 8.3 (Bruxelles: H. Lamertin, 1912), 113.
[46] Denningmann, *Die astrologische Lehre*, p. 158.

ce qu'il montre que l'idée d'une collaboration de Vénus et de Mercure aux œuvres du Soleil était, à l'époque de Philon, un *thème* diffusé en dehors des cercles de spécialistes. La formulation du commentaire philonien suggère que l'usage du *terme* δορυφορεῖσθαι pour désigner l'escorte céleste l'était également.

Au-delà des parallèles mentionnés ci-dessus, c'est dans le *De Abrahamo* 119 sq. l'*allure* même du commentaire philonien qui fournit le meilleur indice du fait que l'Alexandrin pense le lien entre Dieu et ses deux puissances à partir d'une tradition inspirée du *Timée* et de sa réception philosophique : toute l'interprétation philonienne repose sur la mention, dans le texte scripturaire, du mot « midi » (μεσημβρίας, Gen 18:1) qui chez l'Alexandrin devient le *soleil* de midi ; les modalités de l'apparition divine sont tout entières formulées à travers une imagerie solaire : « l'âme est illuminée en Dieu comme sous un soleil de midi (ἡ ψυχὴ καθάπερ ἐν μεσημβρίᾳ θεῷ περιλαμφθῇ, 119) ; « elle est comblée par les rayons qui se diffusent tout autour d'elle » (ἀναπλησθεῖσα ταῖς ἐν κύκλῳ κεχυμέναις αὐγαῖς, *ibid.*) : lisant dans l'Écriture une apparition angélique qui a lieu sous le soleil de midi, Philon l'a reformulée selon les conceptions, héritées de la réception du *Timée*, relatives au rôle démiurgique du Soleil et de ses acolytes astraux. Sur le plan littéraire, un détail de formulation surprend ici chez l'Alexandrin. Quand l'âme, comme au soleil de midi, est illuminée (περιλαμφθῇ) par Dieu, elle saisit une triple vision (φαντασία) de l'objet : l'objet lui-même comme réalité (τοῦ μὲν ὡς ὄντος) et « deux ombres qui, pour ainsi dire *rayonneraient* à partir de celui-ci » , τῶν δ' ἄλλων δυοῖν ὡς ἂν ἀπαυγαζομένων ἀπὸ τούτου σκιῶν (*De Abrahamo* 119). D'une façon remarquable, les deux ombres de l'objet *brillent elles-mêmes*, tout comme l'objet. N'y a-t-il pas, dans cette formulation si particulière, un souci, de la part de Philon, d'éviter une autonomie des puissances et l'idée d'une « unité triadique », pour reprendre l'expression citée ci-dessus ?

VI. *La fonction philosophique de la* δορυφορία *chez Philon*

Ni les emplois philoniens relatifs aux *sens* « doryphores », ni même l'emploi par l'Alexandrin de cette image pour qualifier Dieu « escorté » par ses puissances principales ne s'écartent donc d'éléments philosophiques tirés de la tradition grecque : là où nous croyions repérer un trait propre à l'œuvre philonienne, celle-ci ne manifeste, avec cette image, que les échos de réflexions, passées dans la *langue* scientifique ou philosophique, dont des textes grecs—parfois ultérieurs—offrent des parallèles. Il n'en reste pas moins que Philon recourt à cette image avec une fréquence bien supérieure à ce qu'on trouve chez tout autre philosophe ; concernant un auteur comme Philon, on hésite à attribuer cette récurrence à un simple *trait de style*.

Dans différents cas, l'auteur esquisse, autour du mot δορυφόρος, un parallélisme entre des plans différents : οὗτοι λέγουσι τὰς μὲν τυχηρὰς εὐπραγίας δορυφόρους εἶναι σώματος, ὑγείαν δὲ καὶ ἰσχὺν καὶ τὸ ὁλόκληρον καὶ ἀκρίβειαν αἰσθητηρίων καὶ ὅσα ὁμοιότροπα τῆς βασιλίδος ψυχῆς, « ces philosophes disent que les faveurs du sort sont les gardiens du corps et que la santé, la vigueur, l'intégrité et le fonctionnement rigoureux des organes des sens sont ceux de l'âme royale » (*Ebr.* 201) ; de même, dans le *De confusione linguarum*, il met en perspective les δορυφόροι σώματος (§18) et les δορυφόροι ψυχῆς (§19) ; dans le *De virtutibus*, il oppose implicitement la richesse, gardienne du corps (ὁ μὲν δὴ σώματος δορυφόρος πλοῦτος) aux vertus qui sont l'apanage et la garde des « hommes vénérables et inspirés par Dieu » (§8). Un passage du *Quis heres* souligne encore plus ce parallélisme entre les niveaux de l'être humain et évoque une triple δορυφορία : χρῄζει γὰρ ἕκαστον οἰκείων δορυφόρων· δορυφορεῖται δὲ σῶμα μὲν εὐδοξίᾳ καὶ περιουσίᾳ καὶ ἀφθονίᾳ πλούτου, ψυχὴ δὲ τῷ τοῦ σώματος ὁλοκλήρῳ καὶ κατὰ πάντα ὑγιεινῷ, ὁ δὲ νοῦς ὑπὸ τῶν ἐν ταῖς ἐπιστήμαις θεωρημάτων, « chacun réclame ses propres gardes : le corps est gardé par la gloire, la richesse et l'opulence de la fortune ; l'âme, par l'intégrité du corps et sa parfaite santé ; l'intellect, par les connaissances acquises dans les sciences » (§286).[47]

Or, dans ce même traité, Philon insiste sur le rapport de ressemblance qui existe entre le monde céleste, le chandelier du Temple et l'âme humaine : ἐπίγειον οὖν βουληθεὶς ἀρχετύπου τῆς κατ' οὐρανὸν σφαίρας ἑπταφεγγοῦς μίμημα παρ' ἡμῖν ὁ τεχνίτης γενέσθαι πάγκαλον ἔργον προσέταξε, τὴν λυχνίαν, δημιουργηθῆναι. δέδεικται δὲ καὶ ἡ πρὸς ψυχὴν ἐμφέρεια αὐτῆς· ψυχὴ γὰρ τριμερὴς μέν ἐστι, δίχα δὲ ἕκαστον τῶν μερῶν, ὡς ἐδείχθη, τέμνεται, μοιρῶν δὲ γενομένων ἐξ ἕβδομος εἰκότως τομεὺς ἦν ἁπάντων ὁ ἱερὸς καὶ θεῖος λόγος, « Voulant donc qu'il y ait chez nous un archétype terrestre à l'imitation de la sphère céleste aux sept lumières, l'artisan ordonna de fabriquer, à titre d'ouvrage entièrement beau, le chandelier. Or, nous avons montré la ressemblance qu'il a également avec l'âme : l'âme en effet a trois parties et chacune de ces parties est divisée en deux ; aux six parties ainsi constituées, s'ajoute en septième le Logos sacré et divin qui est naturellement le diviseur de toutes chose » (§225).[48] Philon élabore une philosophie

---

[47] Trad. (légèrement modifiée) de Harl, PAPM 15:311.

[48] Il ne paraît pas opportun d'adopter, comme Mangey la leçon du témoin le plus ancien contre le reste de la tradition manuscrite : ἀρχετύπου Pap. (Mangey) : ἀρχέτυπον *codd*.

où les « répliques » (ἀντίμιμα),[49] les « similitudes » (μιμήματα) entre les
niveaux de l'Être tiennent une place fondamentale:[50] la race issue de Noé
τὴν ἡγεμονίαν τῶν περιγείων ἅπαξ ἁπάντων ἔλαχεν ἀντίμιμον γεγονὸς θεοῦ
δυνάμεως, εἰκὼν τῆς ἀοράτου φύσεως ἐμφανής, ἀιδίου γενητή, « a reçu une
fois pour toutes la direction de tout ce qui se trouve sur terre, étant la
réplique d'une puissance divine, l'image visible et périssable de la nature
invisible et éternelle » (*De vita Mosis* 2.65) ; plus significatif encore est ce
texte du *Quis heres* 88 : βούλεται γὰρ ἀντίμιμον οὐρανοῦ, εἰ δὲ χρὴ καὶ
προσυπερβάλλοντα εἰπεῖν, οὐρανὸν ἐπίγειον ἀποφῆναι τὴν τοῦ σοφοῦ ψυχὴν
ἔχουσαν <ἐν ἑαυτῇ καθάπερ> ἐν αἰθέρι καθαρὰς φύσεις, τεταγμένας κινήσεις,
χορείας ἐμμελεῖς, θείας περιόδους, ἀρετῶν ἀστεροειδεστάτας καὶ περιλα-
μπεστάτας αὐγάς. Εἰ δ' ἀμήχανον αἰσθητῶν ἀστέρων ἀριθμὸν εὑρεῖν, πῶς οὐχὶ
μᾶλλον νοητῶν ; « Il veut signifier que l'âme du sage est une réplique du ciel
ou bien, s'il faut employer une expression hyperbolique, un ciel sur terre :
elle a en elle-même, comme en a l'éther, des natures pures, des
mouvements ordonnés, des chœurs harmonieux, des évolutions divines,
des vertus éclatantes tout à fait semblables à des astres et très brillantes. Et
s'il est impossible de trouver le nombre des étoiles sensibles, ne l'est-ce pas
à plus forte raison pour les étoiles intelligibles » ?[51]

Par la *plasticité* des emplois métaphoriques qu'attestent en grec les mots
de la famille de δορυφορεῖν, l'image offre à la conception philonienne d'une
analogie entre les niveaux de la réalité un *mode de formulation* : le corps a,
avec la gloire et la richesse ses doryphores, de même que l'âme avec les
sens ; à un stade plus rationnel, les raisonnements, les vertus ainsi que le
langage sont aussi pour elle des doryphores, comme le sont les sciences
pour l'intellect. Si l'on passe au plan de l'intelligible, ce sont les Idées qui
sont doryphores et, au niveau de l'Être divin lui-même, les puissances
tiennent ce rôle. Il est remarquable que tous ces usages philoniens du mot
possèdent, à l'exception peut-être des Idées doryphores, des parallèles dans
la tradition grecque : à partir du sens propre—les porte-lances du roi—, le
mot y acquiert une acception psychologique, philosophique, astrologique et
religieuse.

Se faisant l'héritier des ressources, non seulement de la langue, mais de
la tradition grecque, Philon les exploite pour exprimer, à sa façon, le thème

---

[49] Il est remarquable que, chez l'Alexandrin, le terme perde sa valeur négative
(« contrefaçon ») : la tunique du Grand prêtre est la réplique (ἀντίμιμον) de l'ensemble du
ciel (*Somn.* 1.215) ; le Nil est, pour les Égyptiens, une réplique du ciel (*Fug.* 179; *Mos.* 1.195).

[50] Sur ce point, cf. la belle étude de Françoise Frazier, dans laquelle elle montre
combien l'Alexandrin met à profit « l'analogie grecque entre ordre du cosmos, de la cité et
du monde », « Le principe d'égalité chez Philon », in *Ktèma* 31 (2006): 291–308.

[51] Trad. de Harl, PAPM 15:209.

selon lequel le sage doit reproduire l'ordre céleste et se régler sur l'intelligible : dans le *De migratione Abrahami*, le verset « Monte vers le Seigneur, toi, Aaron, Nadab, Abiud et soixante-dix du Conseil des Anciens d'Israël » (Ex 24:1) suscite, sur la base d'une interprétation allégorique des noms propres, la reformulation suivante : « Monte, âme, vers la vision de l'Être, monte dans un accord total, où il y ait le verbe, la liberté, l'absence de peur, l'affection, où il y ait aussi les chiffres sacrés de la perfection : dix fois le nombre sept » (§168–169) ; l'Alexandrin conclut ainsi : Αἵδ' εἰσὶν αἱ τοῦ βασιλεύειν ἀξίου νοῦ δορυφόροι δυνάμεις, ἃς συνέρχεσθαι τῷ βασιλεῖ παραπεμπούσας αὐτὸν θέμις, « Telles sont les puissances qui forment la garde de l'intellect bien digne de régner ; il est légitime qu'elles accompagnent le roi en faisant procession à ses côtés » (§170) : outre Dieu, le sage possède *aussi* de puissances « doryphores » qui, si elles diffèrent par essence des puissances divines, entretiennent néanmoins une relation d'ἀντίμιμον avec elles, de la même façon que, dans la littérature rabbinique, les attributs humains par rapport aux attributs divins, désignés les uns et les autres par le mot *middot*, « mesures ». Alors que les textes rabbiniques ont eu surtout recours à ce substantif pour définir le rapport entre le divin et l'humain, il semble que l'Alexandrin ait, pour le faire, massivement utilisé une épithète empruntée aux mots de la famille de δορυφορεῖν.

Un dernier élément peut, chez Philon, avoir joué dans le choix de ces mots pour exprimer le rapport entre des plans différents : aux livres 8–9 de la *République*, Socrate décrit les quatre formes de gouvernement et les âmes des hommes qui leur ressemblent. La force de l'exposé tient au rapport de *ressemblance* et d'*analogie* qu'il établit entre niveau politique *et* niveau psychique. De même que le tyran est entouré par des gardes qu'il nomme des « doryphores » (567e5), Socrate décrit, au livre suivant, l'âme tyrannique « escortée par la folie » (δορυφορεῖταί τε ὑπὸ μανίας 573a8).[52] Il est possible que Philon ait associé les *termes* δορυφόρος-δορυφορεῖσθαι, présents en *République* 8–9 au *thème* de l'analogie, du rapport entre niveaux de rang divers, qui soutient tout l'exposé platonicien.

---

[52] Au livre 9, on comprend rétrospectivement l'emploi de l'adjectif, au livre précédent : l'âme tyrannique est « poussée » —le verbe est celui qu'on emploie pour le cheval que l'on pousse— par ses désirs comme par des aiguillons » (τοὺς δ᾽ ὥσπερ ὑπὸ κέντρων ἐλαυνομένους, 573e5) : les porte-lances sont, au plan de l'âme, devenus des piqûres intérieures.

Conclusion

Avec les mots de la famille de δορυφορεῖν, les traités de Philon comportent une image dont la relative rareté dans les textes grecs éveille l'attention. J. Dillon parle d'une « favourite image of Philo's ».[53] Notre parti a été de ne pas y voir qu'un trait de style, mais de repérer chez un auteur si attentif aux termes qu'il utilise, la portée philosophique de cette expression. En outre, la récurrence de l'image nous a conduit à rechercher, dans ces emplois, une sorte de cohérence, une structuration du discours par une image faisant office d'outil, sinon de concept. Tous les emplois que l'Alexandrin fait de l'image possèdent des parallèles exacts dans les textes philosophiques et appartiennent donc à une langue technique. L'acception philosophico-religieuse—Dieu escorté de ses deux puissances principales—nous a paru directement inspirée du *Timée* 38d2–6, où le Soleil est escorté de Vénus et de Mercure. Un tel texte a donné lieu à une réélaboration philosophique faisant des deux astres les assistants du Soleil-démiurge dans son œuvre créatrice. Comme cela arrive pour d'autres notions (ainsi la théologie négative),[54] Philon nous semble ici le premier témoin de cette relecture du *Timée*, très présente chez Proclus mais dont on trouve déjà des indices chez des auteurs antérieurs à l'Alexandrin ou contemporains de celui-ci.

Il est remarquable que, pour réfléchir à l'épisode biblique de Mambré—lu allégoriquement par Philon comme la saisie de l'Être, accompagné ou non par ses deux puissances principales—, l'Alexandrin ait, si notre hypothèse est juste, eu recours à une réélaboration, directe ou indirecte, de la cosmogonie du *Timée*;[55] pour un point fondamental chez Philon, la philosophie grecque devient ici le langage et le cadre logique de l'exégèse. Philon ne réfléchit pas avec l'*appoint* qu'apporterait la philosophie grecque : c'est *à l'intérieur* de celle-ci qu'il conçoit le texte biblique. Nous nous demandions pourquoi l'Alexandrin n'employait pas le terme « doryphores » à propos des puissances, lorsqu'il les envisage comme triade, hexade ou hebdomade.

---

[53] *The Middle Platonists. A Study of Platonism 80 B.C. to A.D. 220* (Londres: G. Duckworth, 1977), 161.

[54] Cf. la remarque de John Dillon : « The question thus arises as whether Philon is responsible for introducing the notion of an 'unknowable' God into Greek thought … The alternative is that the influence of the First Hypothesis of the *Parmenides*, which is behind Albinus' negative theology was at work in Alexandrian Platonism, before Philo's time », *The Middle Platonists*, 155.

[55] À cet égard, le cas de δορυφορεῖν, non envisagé par David T. Runia, renforce la dépendance de Philon envers ce traité platonicien, minutieusement étudiée par ce critique, *Philo of Alexandria and the Timaeus of Plato* (PhilAnt 44; Leiden: Brill, 1986).

La réponse doit être cherchée dans l'influence qu'a exercée sur l'Alexandrin le texte du *Timée*, où le Soleil est escorté de *deux* acolytes ἰσόδρομοι.

En outre, la multiplicité des niveaux où les mots δορυφορεῖν / δορυφόρος sont employés en grec—garde exercée par le coeur dans le *Timée*, par les sens chez les stoïciens, astres satellites—a permis à l'Alexandrin d'exprimer sa conception d'une correspondance entre les plans divin, céleste, intellectuel, spirituel et sensible : ce qui était en grec une image est devenu chez l'Alexandrin un moyen de penser les analogies entre les réalités du monde.

Une telle représentation a peu été reprise par les Pères ; évoquant les puissances incorporelles des Hébreux et les astres qui en sont, selon eux, les symboles, Eusèbe de Césarée écrit que, d'après les « oracles des Hébreux », les puissances « escortent le Dieu, roi absolu de l'Univers … aussi les compare-t-on de façon normale aux luminaires du ciel » (τὸν παμβασιλέα πάντων δορυφορεῖν θεὸν … διὸ καὶ φωστῆρσι τοῖς κατ' οὐρανὸν εἰκότως παρα-βάλλεσθαι).[56] Les « Hébreux » dont parle Eusèbe désignent probablement Philon et si Eusèbe mentionne encore sa formulation, il n'y paraît déjà plus sensible. À partir du IVe siècle, il est souvent question, chez les auteurs chrétiens, de « l'escorte des anges », ainsi chez Éphrem le Syrien ou Sévé-rien ; Jean Chrysostome emploie fréquemment le mot, accompagné de τιμαί, pour désigner les soins et les honneurs qui entourent au ciel l'âme trouvée juste : avec ces emplois, on quitte la logique de l'Alexandrin. Enfin, la liturgie orthodoxe comporte une hymne attribuée à Basile de Césarée et à Jean Chrysostome :[57] Οἱ τὰ Χερουβεὶμ μυστικῶς εἰκονίζοντες καὶ τῇ Ζωοποιῷ Τριάδι τὸν Τρισάγιον ὕμνον προσᾴδοντες πᾶσαν τὴν βιωτικὴν ἀποθώμεθα μέριμναν ὡς τὸν βασιλέα τῶν ὅλων ὑποδεξόμενοι ταῖς ἀγγελικαῖς ἀοράτως δορυφορούμενον τάξεσιν· Ἀλληλούϊα, « Nous qui figurons mystiquement les chérubins et chantons à la Trinité vivifiante l'hymne trois fois sainte, écartons tout souci de ce monde pour recevoir le Roi de l'univers escorté invisiblement par les ordres angéliques. Alléluia » : le sens astronomique s'est ici imposé et l'image désigne l'ordre de la cour céleste. De tels emplois mettent, par contraste, en relief ce que l'on pourrait nommer le « moment philonien » de la δορυφορία : l'Alexandrin cherche à comprendre les images d'un texte—la Bible—avec les ressources d'une langue, celle de la philosophie grecque, qu'elle soit de tradition stoïcienne ou de tradition

---

[56] *Préparation évangélique* 7.16, 1, trad. de G. Schroeder, légèrement remaniée (SC 215; Paris: Cerf, 1975), 248–249.
[57] Elle est entrée dans l'*ordo* byzantin vers 574 (PG 121, 748, « Abrégé d'histoires » de Kedrinos). Elle serait attestée antérieurement dans d'autres liturgies (St Marc, St Jacques, liturgie arménienne).

platonicienne. De tels emplois mettent, par contraste, en relief ce que l'on pourrait nommer le « moment philonien » de la δορυφορία : l'Alexandrin cherche à comprendre les images d'un texte—la Bible—avec les ressources d'une langue, celle de la philosophie grecque, qu'elle soit de tradition stoïcienne ou de tradition platonicienne.[58]

Université Paris Sorbonne

---

[58] Ultime avatar du terme, il en est venu, pendant la Seconde guerre mondiale, à désigner les Allemands: cf. Boris Cyrulnik « C'est au cœur d'un village (peut-être Castillon) que j'ai vu pour la première fois des Allemands prisonniers … Ces soldats qui nous avaient vaincus, écrasés, dominés dans la vie quotidienne, les « doryphores », comme on les surnommait, paraissaient à leur tour hébétés par le malheur » (*Sauve-toi, la vie t'appelle*, [Paris: Odeile Jacob, 2012], p. 35). En note, l'auteur ajoute ceci : « Doryphore : insecte coléoptère aux élytres rayés de noir qui dévorait les feuilles de pommes de terre, comme les Allemands quand ils réquisitionnaient la récolte »

The Studia Philonica Annual 25 (2013) 65–68

AESCHYLUS IN PHILO, *ANIM.* 47 AND *QE* 2.6*

DAVID LINCICUM

In Philo's treatise *De Animalibus*, preserved only in Armenian, we find this quote at §47, presented here in the translation by Abraham Terian:[1]

As the poets say,

We're thought to be of seed divine
And of kinship closely akin.
But when enslaved by food and drink,
Such lowly things do make us fall
From heav'n above to earth beneath.[2]

Terian states that,

The verse, with its ascription to the "poets" (as also in *Quaes Ex* II 6) and subject matter as well, is reminiscent of the so-called Orphic poems. The concept of human devolution from the divine has its origin in Orphic theogony and cosmogony, where Zeus is said to have created man from the ashes of the Titans whom he had stricken with his thunderbolt because they have killed and eaten the divine infant Dionysus. Thus man came to occupy a middle position between gods and beasts, due to the mixture of the material from which he was created….The Orphics are alluded to in Pl. *Tim.* 40d as "descendents of gods."[3]

---

* The following abbreviations are used in this note: PCG: Rudolf Kassel and Colin Austin, eds., *Poetae Comici Graeci*, 8 vols. (Berlin: de Gruyter, 1983-); TrGF 2: Richard Kannicht and Bruno Snell, eds., *Tragicorum Graecorum Fragmenta Vol. 2: Fragmenta Adespota* (Göttingen: Vandenhoeck & Ruprecht, 1981); TrGF 3: Stefan Radt, ed., *Tragicorum Graecorum Fragmenta Vol. 3: Aeschylus* (Göttingen: Vandenhoeck & Ruprecht, 1985); SH: Hugh Lloyd-Jones and Peter Parsons, *Supplementum Hellenisticum* (Berlin: de Gruyter, 1983). Citations of Philo generally PLCL, though the translation is sometimes modified. For *De Providentia*, I follow Mireille Hadas-Lebel, *De Providentia I et II: Introduction, Traduction et Notes* (PAPM 35; Paris: Cerf, 1973).

[1] Abraham Terian, ed., *Philonis Alexandrini, De animalibus: The Armenian Text with an Introduction, Translation, and Commentary* (Studies in Hellenistic Judaism 1; Chico, CA: Scholars Press, 1981), 88.

[2] In Jean–Baptise Aucher's Latin translation of the Armenian: *Diis proximos factos fuisse semine, et propinquos generatione; verum a cibo exiguo potuque superati, humi jacemus, ab alto caelo cadentes*; cf. Aucher, *Philonis Judaei sermons tres hactenus inediti* (Venice, 1822), 148.

[3] Terian, *De animalibus* 159.

Derivation from an Orphic source is not impossible, though curiously, however, Philo nowhere else cites an Orphic poem. The few unidentified citations in Philo of non-biblical literature are as follows: *Contempl.* 43 (a comic poet; PCG 8: 475); *Prob.* 145 (TrGF 2: 318); *Prob.* 152 (TrGF 2: 327); *Aet.* 27 (TrGF 2: 327a); *Aet.* 41 (an unknown poet[4]); *Anim.* 28 (unknown ode); *Spec.* 4.20 (an unknown text); and *Aet.* 140 (SH 1134a). In none of these cases is an identification with an Orphic poem likely.[5]

When one turns to *QE* 2.6, one finds there: "As the poets say, rulers are closely akin and near in lineage to and of the same seed as the gods, for leaders and rulers are, as these say, able to do good or evil by virtue of their own power."[6] Marcus does not suggest a reference, and in Terian's edition of the *Quaestiones in Exodum* for the French series Les Oeuvres de Philon d'Alexandrie, he repeats his suggestion about the Orphic poem.[7] But this sounds remarkably like something else we encounter in Philo in a few places:

> *Opif.* 144: Conversing and consorting with these [spiritual and divinely inclined people] man could not but live in unalloyed bliss, and being of near kin to the Ruler (συγγενής τε καὶ ἀγχίσπορος ὢν τοῦ ἡγεμόνος), since the divine Spirit had flowed into him in full current, he earnestly endeavoured in all his words and actions to please the Father and King, following Him step by step in the highways cut out by virtues, since only for souls who regard it as their goal to be fully conformed to God who begat them is it lawful to draw nigh to him.

> *Mos.* 1.279: Who has made accurate discovery of how the sowing of their [i.e., the Jews'] generation was first made? Their bodies have been moulded from human seeds, but their souls are sprung from divine seeds, and therefore their stock is akin to God (τὰ μὲν σώματ' αὐτοῖς ἐξ ἀνθρωπίνων διεπλάσθη σπερμάτων, ἐκ δὲ θείων ἔφυσαν αἱ ψυχαί· διὸ καὶ γεγόνασιν ἀγχίσποροι θεοῦ).

> *Spec.* 4.14: But it is the lot of man, as we see, to occupy the place of highest excellence among living creatures because his stock is near akin to God, sprung from the same source in virtue of his participation in reason which gives him immortality (ἀγχίσπορος ὢν θεοῦ καὶ συγγενὴς κατὰ τὴν πρὸς λόγον κοινωνίαν), mortal though he seems to be.

---

[4] Xenophanes of Colophon? So Andrei Lebedev, "Xenophanes on the Immutability of God: A Neglected Fragment in Philo Alexandrinus," *Hermes* 128.4 (2000): 385–91.

[5] There are also a handful of short citations in Philo that are too brief to be identified: *Ebr.* 116; *Somn.* 1.22; *Abr.* 194 (cf. Libanius, *Orat.* 64.48.6); *Spec.* 2.77; *Spec.* 3.69; *Aet.* 66 (cf. *Mos.* 2.84; *Spec.* 3.33, 109; *Legat.* 56); *Anim.* 33 (cf. Arist., *HA* 611a26).

[6] Presented here in Ralph Marcus's PLCL translation of the Armenian, for which no Greek fragments are extant.

[7] Abraham Terian, *Quaestiones et solutiones in Exodum I et II e versione armeniaca et fragmenta graeca* (PAPM 34c; Paris: Cerf, 1992), 116 n. 3.

The rare word ἀγχίσπορος (near of kin) also occurs in *Spec.* 4.236 and *Virt.* 80. In fact the only pre-Philonic use of ἀγχίσπορος seems to be Plato, *Rep.* 3.391e, where he is apparently citing Aeschylus (though without explicit attribution, the same quotation is later attributed by Strabo to Aeschylus). On the passage in *Mos.* 1.279, Colson gives a note in reference to the fragment of Aeschylus's play, *Niobe* (TrGF 3: 162),[8] to which it seems likely that all these texts are in some way alluding:

οἱ θεῶν ἀγχίσποροι,
<οἱ> Ζηνὸς ἐγγύς, ὧν κατ᾽ Ἰδαῖον πάγον
Διὸς πατρῴου βωμός ἐστ᾽ ἐν αἰθέρι,
κοὔ πώ σφιν ἐξίτηλον αἷμα δαιμόνων.

That Philo in *QE* 2.6 and the first half of the citation in *Anim.* 47 is alluding to this passage from Aeschylus seems likely. But this judgment may appear problematic from two angles. First, the citation in both *QE* 2.6 and *Anim.* 47 is ascribed to "the poets" rather than to a named author. This fact, it will be recalled, plays into Terian's identification of the citation with the Orphic poems. In fact, however, while Philo often uses the plural "poets" to introduce generic poetic turns of phrase, he sometimes also uses it to introduce short phrases of Homer or, in one instance, Sophocles: *Agr.* 24 (citing Hom., *Il.* 5.487); *Ebr.* 103 (Hom. *Il.* 2.489); *Fug.* 31 (Hom., *Od.* 21.294); *Somn.* 2.275 (Hom. *Il.* 2.246); *Spec.* 1.74 (Hom. *Il.* 18.104; *Od.* 20.379); *Prob.* 42 (Soph., *OC* 1293); *Aet.* 127 (Hom. *Il.* 28.397); *Prov.* 2.13 (Hom. *Il.* 13.599). What is more, Philo explicitly classes Aeschylus among the poets in *Prob.* 143. Therefore, if Philo has intended to cite Aeschylus in this way, it does not fall outside the realm of his normal citation practices.

But secondly, and perhaps more significantly, is the fact that the citation in *Anim.* 47 seems to extend beyond what we might cull from the Aeschylus fragment adduced above—a fact that presumably also contributed to Terian's identification of the citation as Orphic in nature. But if we here compare another fragment of Aeschylus (TrGF 3: 159) ascribed to the same play, found in Plutarch (*de Exil.* 10. 603a), we find the following:

οὑμὸς δὲ πότμος οὐρανῷ κυρῶν ἄνω
ἔραζε πίπτει καί με προσφωνεῖ τάδε·
γίνωσκε τἀνθρώπεια μὴ σέβειν ἄγαν;

Might it be that Philo has alluded to two fragments of Aeschylus's play and interspersed his own comments between them? If so, then *Anim.* 47 might be punctuated roughly as follows:

---

[8] A suggestion he apparently took over from Isaac Heinemann in PCH 2.252 n. 1.

As the poets say, we're thought to be "of seed divine and of kinship closely akin" (fr. 162). But when enslaved by food and drink, such lowly things do make us "fall from heaven above to earth beneath" (fr. 159).[9]

The interspersed comments about food and drink cohere with what we find elsewhere in Philo. It is unsurprising that food (βρῶσις) and drink (πόσις) are often linked together in Philo, as regularly elsewhere. But while we occasionally find them referred to positively or neutrally (*Opif.* 38; *Ios.* 154), it is significant that more often he views them negatively as distracting or pernicious (*Congr.* 29; *Somn.* 2.155; 2.215; *Spec.* 1.150; cf. *Leg.* 2.29). For example, he writes,

> While they were engaged in such lamentations, Moses again addressed his supplications to God, that, knowing the weakness of His creatures, and particularly of mankind, and the necessities of the body, which depends on food, and is tied to those stern mistresses, food and drink (τὰς τοῦ σώματος ἀνάγκας ἐκ τροφῆς ἠρτημένου καὶ δεσποίναις χαλεπαῖς συνεζευγμένου, βρώσει καὶ πόσει) He should pardon the despondent and also satisfy the needs of all (*Mos.* 1.184).

Thus, the interspersed comments cohere entirely with Philo's views on food and drink elsewhere in his corpus. Moreover, for Philo to introduce two brief snippets of Aeschylus with the attribution to the plural "poets" is similar to Philo's practice of citing snippets of Homer ascribed to "poets" mentioned above; nowhere does Philo adduce a single, extended quote and ascribe this to "poets."

In sum, then, especially given the fact that Philo does have a certain penchant for Aeschylus,[10] in contrast to his total lack of clear reference to Orphic poetry, and in light of his citation practices elsewhere and the verbal similarities between Philo and the tragedian, it seems best to conclude that in both *QE* 2.6 and *Anim.* 47, Philo is alluding to Aeschylus.[11]

Mansfield College, Oxford

---

[9] I leave the reconstruction of a Greek *Vorlage* to those familiar with the translation techniques of the Armenian translator.

[10] In addition to the references to TrGF 3:162 above, note *Aet.* 49 (TrGF 3:139); 139 (TrGF 3:402); *Prov.* 2.8 (TrGF 3:344); 2.90 (TrGF 3:345). On the Armenian of the citations in *Prov.* 2.8 and 2.90, see Moreno Morani, "Due frammenti di Eschilo e la traduzione Armena del *De Providentia* di Filone Giudeo," *Istituto Lombardo (Rend. Lett.)* 113 (1979): 489–95.

[11] Whether the continuation of *QE* 2.6 ("for leaders and rulers are, as these say, able to do good or evil by virtue of their own power") is also Aeschylean is very difficult to say on the basis of the available evidence.

The Studia Philonica Annual 25 (2013) 69–73

SPECIAL SECTION

PHILO'S ANCIENT READERS

INTRODUCTION

GREGORY E. STERLING

The extent of Philo's influence on the development of thought has ranged from those who considered him an isolated elite who moved within a very limited circle[1] to those who have thought that he was an architect for the basic structure of Western thought in the medieval period.[2] Neither extreme has support among contemporary Philonic specialists who have worked to situate him in a broader context.

The efforts have taken three different approaches. The Alexandrian Jewish exegete's three series of commentaries preserve the largest single corpus of Jewish exegesis from the Second Temple period. One approach has been to explore the extent to which the exegetical traditions attested by Philo represent exegetical traditions from a wider circle. Some have attempted to work out a pattern of exegetical traditions within Alexandria,[3]

---

[1] E.g., Samuel Sandmel, "Philo's Place in Judaism: A Study of the Conceptions of Abraham in Jewish Literature," *HUCA* 25 (1954): 209–37; 26 (1955): 151–332; reprinted as *Philo's Place in Judaism: A Study of the Conceptions of Abraham in Jewish Literature* (New York: Ktav, 1971); and Fausto Parente, "La 'Lettera di Aristea' come fonte per la storia del giudaismo alessandrino durante la prima metà del I secolo a.C.," *Annali della Scuola Normale Superiore di Pisa, Classe di Lettere e Filosofia* 2 (1972): 177–23, 517–67, esp. 545.

[2] E.g., Harry A. Wolfson, *Philo: Foundations of Religious Philosophy in Judaism, Christianity, and Islam* (2 vols.; Cambridge: Harvard University Press, 1947).

[3] This was the impetus behind the launching of the Philo Institute and the original publication of the *Studia Philonica*. See the programmatic essays of Robert G. Hamerton-Kelly, "Sources and Traditions in Philo Judaeus: Prolegomena to an Analysis of His Writings," *SPh* 1 (1972): 3–26; Burton L. Mack, "Exegetical Traditions in Alexandrian Judaism: A Program for the Analysis of the Philonic Corpus," *SPh* 3 (1974–75): 71–112; idem, "Philo Judaeus and Exegetical Traditions in Alexandria," *ANRW* II.21.1: 227–71. The major works that have attempted to do this–even though they were not part of the project–are: Thomas H. Tobin, *The Creation of Man: Philo and the History of Interpretation* (CBQMS 14;

while others have worked comparatively and analyzed Philo's interpretations with treatments of the same text by other authors without positing direct influence one way or another.[4] This approach does not raise the question of Philo's direct influence on other writers, but whether Philo is a witness either to an extensive Alexandrian exegetical movement or to widespread Jewish exegetical traditions. In either case, the presence of exegetical traditions in Philo suggests that he inherited a body of work and should not be set aside as an elite maverick. It also suggests that Philo's works may have been read by others who participated in the exegetical enterprise.

A second approach has been the effort to distinguish among the implied audiences of Philo's commentary series. Apart from the comments of Erwin R. Goodenough on the audience of Philo's *De vita Moysis* and the Exposition of the Law,[5] there has not been a great deal of work on Philo's audiences until recently.[6] While there are some significant differences about specifics, it is widely recognized that the Exposition of the Law assumes a broader audience than the *Quaestiones et Solutiones* or the Allegorical Commentary. This does not constitute proof that Philo's works were read more broadly but does suggest that at least one set of commentaries was intended for an audience beyond a group of intellectual elites.[7]

A third approach is much more direct. It asks the pointed question: who read Philo? There have been some attempts to address this question, but

---

Washington, D.C.: The Catholic Biblical Association of America, 1983), who argued for an elaborate stratigraphy of exegetical traditions prior to Philo, and Robert Goulet, *La philosophie de Moïse: Essai de reconstitution d'un commentaire philosophique préphilonien de Pentateuque* (Histoire des Doctrines de l'Antiquité Classique 11; Paris: J. Vrin, 1987), who argued that Philo corrupted a superior full commentary on the Pentateuch.

[4] E.g., Peder Borgen, *Bread from Heaven: An Exegetical Study of the Concept of Manna in the Gospel of John and the Writings of Philo* (NovTSup 10; Leiden: E. J. Brill, 1965, 1981[2]); idem, *Philo, John, and Paul: New Perspectives on Judaism and Early Christianity* (BJS 131; Atlanta: Scholars Press, 1987); and idem, *Philo, An Exegete for His Time* (NovTSup 86; Leiden: E. J. Brill, 1997). I have also attempted to do this in a number of articles.

[5] Erwin R. Goodenough, "Philo's Exposition of the Law and His *De vita Mosis*," *HThR* 26 (1933): 109–25, who argued that *Mos.* and the Exposition had far more of the character of propaganda in them than earlier scholars had recognized.

[6] Ellen Birnbaum, *The Place of Judaism in Philo's Thought: Israel, Jews, and Proselytes* (BJS 290; Atlanta: Scholars Press, 1996), esp. 17–21; my cursory comments in "General Introduction" to *Philo of Alexandria, On the Creation of the Cosmos according to Moses: Introduction, Translation and Commentary*, by David T. Runia (PACS 1; Leiden: E. J. Brill, 2001), x–xiii; and Maren Niehoff, *Jewish Exegesis and Homeric Scholarship in Alexandria* (Cambridge: Cambridge University Press, 2011), 134–39, 153–58, 170–77.

[7] I am setting aside consideration of the implied audience of the apologetic treatises that may have had a non-Jewish audience in mind for their delivery.

not in a systematic or sustained way.[8] We should consider three groups as potential readers: Jewish readers, Christian readers, and pagan readers. It is well known that there is little evidence for Philo's influence on subsequent Judaism. He was not explicitly cited by a Jewish author until Azariah dei Rossi in the sixteenth century.[9] The most likely ancient candidate is Josephus who mentioned Philo when he described the Alexandrian Jewish embassy to Gaius.[10] There are, however, other possibilities. 2 *Enoch* may have drawn from *De opifico mundi* when relating the creation of the world. If the author did not know Philo's treatise, the author certainly knew some of the same traditions.[11] The same should be said for Rabbi Hoshaya who also appears to know Philo's *De opificio mundi*, even though his knowledge may have been indirect.[12] There are also some striking similarities between Philo and the Hellenistic Synagogue Prayers, although it is not always certain what is Jewish underlay and what is Christian overlay in these prayers.[13] The other obvious place to look is within the Jewish tradition is the later mystical tradition. We attempted to do this at a special session of the Philo of Alexandria Group of the Society of Biblical Literature in 1995; the revised papers were published in the *SPhA*. However, the results of

---

[8] I have tried to do so on two occasions: "*Magister* or Maverick? Philo and Alexandrian Judaism," (paper presented at the annual meeting of the *Studiorum Novi Testamenti Societas*, Edinburgh, Scotland, August 1993) and "Recherché or Representative? What is the Relationship between Philo's Treatises and Greek-Speaking Judaism?" *SPhA* 11 (1999): 1–30. David T. Runia treated some of the evidence in *Philo in Early Christian Literature: A Survey* (CRINT 3.3; Assen: Van Gorcum / /Minneapolis: Fortress, 1993), 8–12 (for pagan authors) and 12–16 (for Jewish authors).

[9] On Azariah dei Rossi's use of Philo see Ralph Marcus, "A 16th Century Hebrew Critique of Philo (Azariah di Rossi's *Meor Eynayim*, Pt. I, cc. 3–6)," *HUCA* 21 (1948): 29–71.

[10] Josephus, *AJ* 18.259–60.

[11] See my "'Day One': Platonizing Exegetical Traditions of Genesis 1:1–5 in John and Jewish Authors," *SPhA* 15 (2005): 118–40, esp. 135–37.

[12] *Gen Rab.* 1:1. There has been a debate about whether Rabbi Hoshaya knew Philo. Ephraim E. Urbach, *The Sages: Their Concepts and Beliefs* (2 vols.; Jerusalem: Magnes Press, 1987), 1:198–202, minimized the possible connection. David T. Runia, on the other hand, argued that Rabbi Hoshaya knew Philo's view via Origen: "Polis and Megalopolis: Philo and the Founding of Alexandria," *Mnemosyne* 42 (1989): 410–12; idem, *Philo in Early Christian Literature*, 14; and idem, *Philo of Alexandria*, On the Creation of the Cosmos, 154–55. See also R. P. D. Barthélemy, 'Est-ce Hoshaya Rabba qui censura le "Commentaire allégorique"? A partir des retouches faites auz citations bibliques, étude sur la tradition textuelle du Commentaire Allégorique de Philon,' in *Philon d'Alexandrie: Lyon 11–15 Septembre 1966* (Paris: Éditions du Centre National de la Recherche Scientifique, 1967), 45–78.

[13] See my "Recherché or Representative," 16–18.

these explorations were largely negative.[14] While there is not much evidence, there is a need to continue to explore possible points of contact.

The Christian readers are the best attested and have been the most widely studied.[15] Philo had significant influence on a number of Christian authors including Clement, Origen, Eusebius, Gregory of Nyssa, Ambrose, Jerome, and Augustine (via Ambrose and Jerome). Yet even in the case of Christian readers there are still a number of questions that need to be addressed. We are not sure—and may never be certain—about the possible influence on some authors, including Justin Martyr, Athenagoras, and Theophilus of Antioch. In other cases, there are ambiguities about specific *testimonia* or potential borrowings. And in some areas, there has not been enough work, e.g., the Armenian translation of Philo.[16]

The area that needs the most attention in my opinion is the reception of Philo among pagan readers. There is enough evidence to warrant a full study that would encompass a number of authors.[17] These should include: Plutarch, Numenius, Celsus, Plotinus, and Calcidius—assuming that he was not a Christian—in the philosophical tradition. There is some evidence that literary figures knew some of Philo's works: the author of *De sublimitate* may have known *De ebrietate*,[18] while the novelist Heliodorus cited *De vita Moysis* in his novel.[19] While the evidence for these authors is limited, it needs to be more thoroughly explored.

The need to address some of these questions led the Society of Biblical Literature Philo of Alexandria Group to devote a special session to the question of Philo's ancient readers at the 2012 annual meeting in Chicago,

---

[14] See *SPhA* 8 (1996): 73–106. The section includes: Gregory E. Sterling, "Philo and Mysticism," 73; David Winston, "Philo's Mysticism," 74–82; Brian E. Daley, S. J., "'Bright Darkness' and Christian Transformation: Gregory of Nyssa on the Dynamics of Mystical Union," 83–98; and Elliot R. Wolfson, "Traces of Philonic Doctrine in Medieval Mysticism: A Preliminary Note," 99–106.

[15] The most important treatment is Runia's *Philo in Early Christian Literature*. There is a large bibliography that deals with specific authors. This literature is best identified through the standard bibliographies on Philo and the annual updates in this journal: Roberto Radice and David Runia, et al., eds., *Philo of Alexandria: An Annotated Bibliography (1937–1986)* (VCSup 8; Leiden: E. J. Brill, 1988); David T. Runia, et al., *Philo of Alexandria: An Annotated Bibliography, 1987–1996: With addenda for 1937–1986* (VCSup 57; Leiden: E. J. Brill, 2000); and idem, *Philo of Alexandria: An Annotated Bibliography, 1997–2006: With addenda for 1987–1996* (VCSup 109; Leiden: E. J. Brill, 2012).

[16] Although now see the essays in Sara Mancini Lombardi and Paolo Pontani, eds., *Studies on the Ancient Armenian Version of Philo's Works* (Studies in Philo of Alexandria 6; Leiden/Boston: Brill, 2011).

[17] See my "Recherché or Representative," for a summary of the evidence.

[18] Philo, *Ebr.* 198 and Pseudo-Longinus, *Subl.* 44.1–5.

[19] Philo, *Mos.* 2.195 and Heliodorus, *Aethiopica* 9.9.

IL. Three of the four papers that were presented at that session follow. James Royse tackles one of the most important presuppositions raised by the question. He asks whether Philo published his works and answers in the negative. He is much less sanguine than I am about the possible use of Philo in some early authors. In my own article, I tried to work through the basic evidence for Josephus as a Jewish representative and made the case that Josephus knew Philo's *De opificio mundi* and *De vita Moysis*. Jennifer Otto tackled the enigmatic statement of Clement of Alexandria that Philo was a Pythagorean. She argues, in contrast to David Runia, that Clement did not situate Philo within the Jewish-Christian tradition. Clement deliberately called him a Pythagorean to situate him among the wise, but not among the Jews who rejected Jesus Christ.

We offer these three essays with the realization that they do not resolve or exhaust the issues; rather, we offer them with the hope that they will demonstrate the complexities of the limited evidence and serve as a stimulus for others to pursue work in these areas with these complexities in mind.

Yale Divinity School

The Studia Philonica Annual 25 (2013) 75–100

DID PHILO PUBLISH HIS WORKS?*

JAMES R. ROYSE

The short answer to the question posed in the title is, I suggest, "no." But of course such an answer requires justification, and it is to that justification that this paper is devoted. But let me be clear that I hesitate to present this answer and its justification as anything more than suggestions. The life and literary activity of Philo of Alexandria are for the most part hidden in mystery, and the means by which his works survived in the first and second centuries C.E. are unknown. It would thus be foolhardy to be confident about much that will be said here. Nevertheless, the importance of Philo's work invites investigation into these matters, and the obscurity in which we move has not deterred others and will not deter me.

My presentation here, which will be very limited at all points, consists of three parts. First, I consider what we may call the external evidence for the early publication of Philo's works, namely the alleged citations of his works during or shortly after his lifetime.[1] Second, I look at the cross-references within Philo's works for evidence concerning the sequencing and chronology of his works. And third, I consider what the status of Philo's works as unpublished (by him) may tell us about the origin and use of those works.

But before turning to those three items, let me dispose of two preliminaries. It hardly makes sense to discuss our topic without having at least some notion of what it meant in antiquity to publish a work. There has, of course, been much discussion of this topic.[2] Essentially, publication, for

---

* This is a revised version of a paper presented to the Philo of Alexandria section at the annual meeting of the Society of Biblical Literature in Chicago, November 18, 2012.

[1] Naturally, there is no doubt that Philo's works were eventually published; the issue is whether he published them.

[2] See, e.g., B. A. van Groningen, " Ἔκδοσις," *Mnem*, 4th series, 16 (1963): 1–17; Raymond J. Starr, "The Circulation of Literary Texts in the Roman World," *CQ* 37 (1987): 213–23; and Harry Y. Gamble, *Books and Readers in the Early Church: A History of Early Christian Texts* (New Haven: Yale University Press, 1995), 82–93, in particular 83–84: "Authors who wished to make their work public had several ways to do so. They might make or have made, at their own expense, several copies of an initial draft, which they would then

which the Greek term is ἔκδοσις (related to the verb ἐκδίδωμι),[3] occurred when the author made (or had scribes make) copies of a work to be distributed beyond the author's control. This distribution could be to friends, a wealthy patron or some other influential person, or to a bookseller, or perhaps to a library. These recipients might, or might not, make further copies, but any further copies would not be copied by the author or under the author's control. Inevitably the copies would have errors, and thus would begin the diversity of readings that we find in manuscript traditions. It would even be possible that a copy of the work would be altered in some more substantial way by a reader or in the copying process (e.g., folios lost or misplaced), and the title or name of the author could be lost or changed. In contrast, of course, before publication an author would be free to make whatever revisions he or she desired. The difference from publication is that the work remained under the control of the author, who could still make changes to the work.[4]

The crucial point in publishing a work is thus that the work left the control of the author, and copies were made available to anyone who wanted to pay the amount required to copy the work. As is true now, many stages of writing, revision, and copying could proceed the actual publication; but these earlier stages were done by the author or at least were controlled by the author. Once the work was published, though, the author was no longer able to make revisions, except (of course) within a separate edition. While second editions are known in antiquity (Josephus's *Jewish War* is an example), they are not all that common, and since there seems to be no evidence that Philo's works appeared in more than one edition, I will simplify our discussion by ignoring such possibilities here. So I will

---

distribute to friends. This alone did not amount to publication but constituted what we might think of as a referee procedure: the author expected a private reading and response from the recipients, with a view to revising and improving the work. Alternatively, they might invite a small group of friends to a reading (*recitatio*), at which the work, or parts of it, would be read by the author and discussed by the gathered company. In these ways an author made his work known, but only to a small and sympathetic circle of acquaintances. The work remained essentially private, under the author's direct control, and was still subject to revision.

Only after the author had tentatively proffered a composition and then revised it would he or she make it available to a larger audience."

[3] The noun does not occur in Philo, but the verb does, although not in the sense of "to publish."

[4] There could also be some intermediate forms of circulation. For example, Kim Haines-Eitzen, *Guardians of Letters* (New York: Oxford University Press, 2000), 104, states that during the second and third centuries, "transmission of Christian literature ... appears to have proceeded along the personal channels of friendships and acquaintances."

proceed from the view that once someone published his or her work, that work circulated (to whatever extent it did) free from the control of the author.

Note that a potential complication is that "unpublished" does not necessarily mean "unknown." A work circulated privately would still be known to the small circle of friends. But knowledge of the work could then go beyond these friends. It was even possible for a work somehow to get into circulation against the author's wishes, and among the ancient authors who complained about the unauthorized publication of their works were Galen, Arrian, Cicero, and Tertullian. For example, as Mansfeld observes, Galen, in his *De ordine librorum*, "explains that (most of) his writings were never intended for the public at large but only for his friends and pupils. Copies came into the hands of others against his will (ἄκοντος ἐμοῦ), and were used by these others. Today we would speak of pirated editions."[5] Mansfeld cites similar comments by Arrian, Cicero, and Tertullian.[6] Here we have works that were unpublished by their authors, but nevertheless known to a wider audience.

For a modern example of writings that were unpublished but known generally, consider the teachings of Ludwig Wittgenstein. His *Tractatus Logico-Philosophicus* was published in German in 1921, and there he discusses the notion of a tautology at some length.[7] Yet Bertrand Russell in his *Introduction to Mathematical Philosophy*, published in 1919 (i.e., two years earlier), discusses the notion of a tautology as a "characteristic of logical propositions." From the dates of the published works we might think that Russell influenced Wittgenstein, but in fact Russell tells us: "The importance of 'tautology' for a definition of mathematics was pointed out to me by my former pupil Ludwig Wittgenstein, who was working on the

[5] Jaap Mansfeld, *Prolegomena: Questions to Be Settled Before the Study of an Author, or a Text* (PhilAnt 61; Leiden: Brill, 1994), 118–19. See also 118, n. 208 (–119): "Though Galen's story may to some degree be true, I believe it is in the first place a variety of the *modus modestiae* based on this *topos*, which is already instanced at Plato, *Parm.* 128d. But his account at any rate takes the distinction between private or limited circulation and regular publication for granted."

The text is: Galen, *De ordine librorum suorum ad Eugenianum* (*Claudii Galeni Pergameni scripta minora* 2, [ed. Ivan Mueller Leipzig: B. G. Teubner, 1891], 81 [19.51K.]): οὐκ ὠρέχθην οὐδεπώποτε τῶν ἐμῶν ὑπομνημάτων οὐδὲν ἐν τοῖς ἀνθρώποις εἶναι· διαδοθέντων δ' εἰς πολλοὺς αὐτῶν ἄκοντος ἐμου, καθάπερ οἶσθα, πρὸς τὸ διδόναι τι τοῦ λοιποῦ τοῖς φίλοις ὑπόμνημα λίαν ὀκνηρῶς ἔσχον.

[6] *Prolegomena*, 110, n. 187, citing Arrian (Epistle to Lucius Gellius), Cicero (*De or.* 1.94), and Tertullian (*Adversus Marcionem* 1.1).

[7] *Tractatus Logico-Philosophicus*, German text and English translation by D. F. Pears and B. F. McGuiness (London: Routledge and Kegan Paul, 1961), 4.3–4.4661.

problem."[8] Here the (at that time) unpublished work of Wittgenstein influenced Russell's published work. Similarly, Wittgenstein's later philosophical works were all published after his death in 1951, beginning with his *Philosophical Investigations* in 1953. Yet his views were well known much earlier among his students and colleagues at Cambridge, as well as within wider circles.[9] Fortunately, we have the detailed publication history of the relevant works, as well as biographical information about Wittgenstein, to guide us in these matters. But we can imagine the mistaken conclusions that future scholars might draw if they had only a few fragments of this literature to work with.

The second preliminary point that I would make is that, of course, Philo could have published some but not all of his works. Since the early history of his works is so obscure, it seems unlikely that we could somehow distinguish his published works from his unpublished works. But perhaps it is not impossible to say something about such matters, and I will return very briefly to this issue later on. However, for the most part I will simplify the discussion and consider the fate of Philo's works as a whole.

1. *The Alleged Early Citations of Philo's Works*

The relevant material here has been collected and studied at length. Direct citations of Philo's works within early writers are not as frequent as one might think. The first explicit references to works of Philo in another writer are found in Clement of Alexandria (ca. 150–215).[10] In his survey of Christian uses of Philo, Runia begins his chapter on Clement by stating: "After all the 'ifs,' 'maybes,' and 'probablys' of the previous chapters it is a great relief to reach an author of whom we may be absolutely certain that he knew about Philo, had read his writings, and even had some of them, as

---

[8] *Introduction to Mathematical Philosophy* (London: George Allen and Unwin, 1919), 205 n. 1.

[9] See, for example, Keld Stehr Nielsen, *The Evolution of the Private Language Argument* (Aldershot: Ashgate, 2008), 2: "his [Wittgenstein's] presence is detectable, as I show in Chapter 2, in pre-1950s discussions between Rudolf Carnap and Otto Neurath."

[10] See the "testimonia" in PCW 1:lxxxxv–lxxxxvi, as well as, for example, Annewies van den Hoek, *Clement of Alexandria and His Use of Philo in the "Stromateis"* (VCSup 3; Leiden: E. J. Brill, 1988), 210–11 (summary of conclusions). A very useful survey may be found in David T. Runia, "References to Philo from Josephus up to 1000 AD," *SPhA* 6 (1994): 111–21, where the only citation from Josephus is *A.J.* 18.257–60 (to be discussed shortly), and the next ones are from Clement.

it were, on his desk."[11] As evidence of Clement's knowledge we have several perfectly clear examples. At *Strom.* 1.153.2 he gives a close paraphrase of *Mos.* 1.23 with the attribution: "as Philo says in the Life of Moses" (ᾗ φησι Φίλων ἐν τῷ Μωυσέως βίῳ).[12] At *Strom.* 1.31.1 and 5.8.5 he cites as Philonic the etymologies found at *Leg.* 3.244 and *Cher.* 4. At *Strom.* 5.35.6 he states that the term "Cherubim" means ἐπίγνωσιν πολλήν, which seems to be taken from *QE* 2.62.[13] And, as Wendland showed, in book 2 of the *Stromateis* Clement makes extensive use of *De virtutibus*, and cites the four extant sections in the order found in PCW.[14]

What the testimony of Clement and of (the later) Origen shows is that the works of Philo were known to what is called the Catechetical School at Alexandria. But this evidence is no earlier than the latter part of the second century. All we can infer from the testimony is what we knew already: all of Philo's works were written by the second century.[15]

An excellent survey of some (alleged) very early uses of Philo has been made by Gregory E. Sterling, who writes:

> There is evidence to suggest that some of Philo's treatises began circulating in Egypt, Syria, and Rome within Jewish and pagan circles during the first and second centuries C.E.[16]

Sterling is guarded in how he phrases this, but it seems to me that this suggestion of circulation (i.e., as it seems, of publication) is not persuasive. Let us take a brief look at some of the cited evidence.

---

[11] Runia, *Philo in Early Christian Literature: A Survey* (CRINT 3.3; Assen: Van Gorcum; Minneapolis, Fortress, 1993), 132; this is the opening of the extended discussion at 132–56.

[12] See van den Hoek, *Clement*, 54.

[13] See my "Philo of Alexandria, *Quaestiones in Exodum* 2.62–68: Critical Edition," *SPhA* 24 (2012): 42.

[14] "Philo und Clemens Alexandrinus," *Hermes* 31 (1896): 443–56 (see the summary statement at 456). See also Runia, "Underneath Cohn and Colson: The Text of Philo's *De virtutibus*," *SBLSPS* 1991 (Atlanta: Scholars Press, 1991), reprinted in his *Philo and the Church Fathers* (Leiden: E. J. Brill, 1995), 81. See my further comments and references in "The Text of Philo's *De virtutibus*," *SPhA* 18 (2006): 80–81.

[15] However, note that the testimony of Clement and Origen does not prove that Philo's works were published even then, since the Catechetical School could have come into possession of the scrolls of Philo's works that derived from Philo himself or from his own circle of students and colleagues. See my "The Text of Philo's *De virtutibus*," 80 n. 30, where I suggested that Clement had access to Philo's autographs.

[16] "Recluse or Representative? Philo and Greek-Speaking Judaism Beyond Alexandria," *SBLSP* (1995): 595–616, here 615. A later version of this paper was published as "Recherché or Representative? What Is the Relationship between Philo's Treatises and Greek-Speaking Judaism?" *SPhA* 11 (1999): 1–30.

One example is from Pseudo-Longinus, the anonymous first-century C.E. writer who famously cites (*De sublimitate* 9.9) Gen 1:3 and paraphrases Gen 1:9 as follows:

ὁ τῶν Ἰουδαίων θεσμοθέτης ... εὐθὺς ἐν τῇ εἰσβολῇ γράψας τῶν νόμων "εἶπεν ὁ θεός" φησί, — τί; "γενέσθω φῶς, καὶ ἐγένετο· γενέσθω γῆ, καὶ ἐγένετο."

Observe the nature of this remark. We are told that this is from the beginning of the laws (presumably οἱ νόμοι). And we have an almost literal quotation from Gen 1:3: εἶπεν ὁ θεός γενεθήτω φῶς, καὶ ἐγένετο φῶς. Only the final φῶς is not repeated and the imperative is shifted from passive to middle (as one also finds in Philo).[17] Of course, the further words are only an allusion to Gen 1:9, where γενέσθω, or γενεθήτω, γῆ does not occur at all.

This, of course, is not a use of Philo, although some have suggested Philo as the intermediate source of the citation from Genesis.[18] But Sterling, like others, cites a section from Pseudo-Longinus that "closely parallels a statement from Philo's *De ebrietate*."[19] Here are the words involved:

Ἐγὼ δ᾽ οὐ <u>τεθαύμακα</u>	<u>θαυμά μ᾽</u> ἔχει (44.1)
εἰ πεφορημένος καὶ μιγὰς ὄχλος,	Cf. the many (44.1)
<u>ἐθῶν</u> καὶ νόμων τῶν ὁπωσοῦν	οἱ δὲ νῦν ἐοίκαμεν ἔφη παιδομαθεῖς
εἰσηγμένων ἀκλεὴς <u>δοῦλος</u>,	εἶναι <u>δουλείας</u> δικαίας,
ἀπ᾽ αὐτῶν ἔτι <u>σπαργάνων</u> ὑπακούειν	τοῖς αὐτῆς <u>ἔθεσι</u> καὶ ἐπιτηδεύμασιν
ὡς ἂν δεσποτῶν ἢ τυράννων <u>ἐκμαθών</u>,	ἐξ ἁπαλῶν ἔτι φρονημάτων
κατα<u>κεκονδυλισμένος</u> τὴν ψυχήν ...	μόνοι οὐκ <u>ἐνεσπαργανωμένοι</u> (44.3)
	ὑπὸ συνηθείας ἀεὶ <u>κεκονδυλισμένον</u> (44.4)

Sterling makes three points:

---

[17] See my discussion of this point in "Some Observations on the Biblical Text in Philo's *De Agricultura*," *SPhA* 22 (2010): 115–21, especially 118–19 on Longinus.

[18] In contrast to the author's intimate acquaintance with the works of Plato and Demosthenes, let us say, he here shows that he has at most picked up a line or two from the LXX. Such knowledge could have easily come from some indirect channels, although of course it remains an intriguing mystery exactly what the source might have been. But it need hardly have been a scroll of Philo's *De opificio*. However, note that the attribution could be taken as an echo of the opening words of *Mos.* 1.1: Μωυσέως τοῦ ... νομοθέτου τῶν Ἰουδαίων.

[19] "Recluse," 612. I reproduce Sterling's underlining.

First, every line of Philo's has a parallel in Pseudo-Longinus. Second, the lines are in sequence in both texts. Third, there are a number of verbal echoes, most significantly the allusion to "swaddling clothes" and "being knuckled under."[20]

However, the contrast with the genuine citation from Gen 1:3 is clear. With this latter passage we find not a reference to a literary work but rather the ascription to "some philosopher," and we find no *identity* of words at all (except for καί and other common words). I grant that the sequence of *similar* words is intriguing.[21] Various hypotheses have been proposed, such as that Pseudo-Longinus met Philo on Philo's visit to Rome or on Pseudo-Longinus's visit to Alexandria. Eduard Norden hypothesized that this citation comes either from a work of Philo or even from Philo himself during his visit to Rome on the embassy.[22] Alternatively, Goold states that Pseudo-Longinus could have visited Alexandria around 12 C.E. and there come into contact with Philo, but ends up approving the idea that the unnamed philosopher is Pseudo-Longinus himself.[23] As for the parallels with Philo's writings here (and some other places), Goold cites with approval Sedgwick's suggestion that Pseudo-Longinus was himself a Jew.[24] But, of course, that still leaves open how exactly the similarities between Philo and Pseudo-Longinus are to be explained.

But it seems to me that Sterling, like others, goes beyond the evidence when he concludes: "The literary critic [i.e. Pseudo-Longinus] either knows some of Philo's treatises or works very similar to them. On the balance I am inclined to the former."[25] However, how can we judge the odds here? If enough Greeks write enough treatises using a finite (even if fairly large) vocabulary, on occasion we may get some verbal parallels. But apart from chance, why is the hypothesis that both Pseudo-Longinus and Philo are drawing ultimately from some common source rejected? We may not know of such a source, but much of ancient literature has been lost. I would suggest that what we have here is an interesting parallel. But if this is the best we have, we don't have all that much.

---

[20] Ibid.

[21] The words κονδυλίζω and κατακονδυλίζω are comparatively unusual (69 and 29 instances in the TLG), although both occur in the LXX.

[22] See my *The Spurious Texts of Philo of Alexandria: A Study of Textual Transmission and Corruption with Indexes to the Major Collections of Greek Fragments* (ALGHJ 22; Leiden: E. J. Brill, 1991), 143, for discussion and some further references.

[23] G. P. Goold, "A Greek Professorial Circle at Rome," *TAPA* 92 (1961): 174–78.

[24] W. B. Sedgwick, "Sappho in 'Longinus' (X, 2, Line 13)," *AJPh* 69 (1948): 198–99.

[25] "Recluse," 613. See the revised discussion by Sterling, "Recherché or Representative?," 25–26.

A second example is Josephus. Naturally, the relationships between Philo and Josephus have been much studied, and scholars have often held the view that Josephus knew (at least some of) Philo's writings.[26] For example, Cohn says that Josephus "tacite multas sententias et expositiones eius in usum suum convertit." But Cohn also concedes: "textus Philonis e Iosephi locis nullum fere fructum percipit, quoniam is non verba sed sententias tantum nostri scriptoris adhibuit."[27] Indeed, Cohn's comments elicited sharp criticism by Heinrici, who argues that the resemblances are of the sort, "dass eine *literarische* Beziehung mit Sicherheit nicht erkannt werden kann."[28]

Sterling tells us that "there is now a consensus that Josephus used Philo's treatises" and that "we are virtually certain that Philo's works were in Rome in the first century C.E."[29] Such facts would (we may think) presuppose publication of (at least some of) Philo's works at a relatively early date. The one example that Sterling cites is that of *A.J.* 1.21–24 and *Opif.* 1–3.[30] These texts are cited in English translation, but the lack of close verbal correspondence is clear. Indeed, Sterling states: "The issue is not whether Josephus quoted Philo, but whether he paraphrased him. I am convinced that he did."[31] Here Josephus makes no suggestion that he is citing or alluding to anyone (except Moses and his account of creation). And the similarities can be, I suggest, readily explained as the results of the efforts of two Hellenistic Jews of the first century to present God's activity in creation and to extol the account given by Moses. It would be surprising if

---

[26] Among many comments consider Emil Schürer, *Geschichte des jüdischen Volkes im Zeitalter Jesu Christi* (3rd and 4th ed.; Leipzig: J. C. Hinrichs, 1901), 1:81 ("Auch der Einfluss Philo's ist mehrfach bemerkbar" [on *A.J.*]), *SHJP* 1:49, and Runia, *Philo in Early Christian Literature*, 13.

[27] PCW 4:xxv–xxvi.

[28] Georg Heinrici, Review of PCW 4, *TLZ* 28 (1903): 80–81.

[29] "Recluse," 613.

[30] The resemblance here is also noted by Louis H. Feldman, "Use, Authority and Exegesis of Mikra in the Writings of Josephus," in *Mikra: Text, Translation, Reading & Interpretation of the Hebrew Bible in Ancient Judaism & Early Christianity* (ed. Martin Jan Mulder and Harry Sysling; Peabody, Mass.: Hendrickson, 2004 [originally published 1988]), 461, who observes that "in his paraphrase of the creation chapter" Josephus "closely follows Philo's *On the Creation.*" Similarly, Folker Siegert, "Early Jewish Interpretation in a Hellenistic Style," in *Hebrew Bible / Old Testament: The History of Its Interpretation* 1.1 (ed. Magne Sæbø; Göttingen: Vandenhoeck and Ruprecht, 1996), 187, says that Josephus "seems to have read his *De opificio mundi.*" See also Thomas W. Franxman, *Genesis and the "Jewish Antiquities" of Flavius Josephus* (BibOr 35; Rome: Biblical Institute Press, 1979), who points out many parallels but does not seem to make any assertions regarding dependence. (But cf. the comment by Feldman, *Josephus and Modern Scholarship (1937–1980)* (Berlin: de Gruyter, 1984), 936–37.)

[31] "Recluse," 614.

there were not some common features in any such efforts, whereas the similarities between Philo and Pseudo-Longinus are unexpected. But even where there is agreement, there is also substantial difference. Consider, for example, the allusion to harmony in both writers; Philo speaks of the harmony between the cosmos and the law, whereas Josephus speaks of the harmony that everything has with the nature of the universe. Apart from the general notion of harmony, for which we might readily find a common source, the details are quite different.

So, here too we have perhaps at best an intriguing parallel, although one that seems to me to be plausibly explained. But in any case, we have something much less than a clear citation by Josephus of one of Philo's works. And, of course, we can readily find places where Josephus does explicitly cite a work by someone other than Philo.[32] But not Philo.

There are also correspondences between *Contra Apionem* and *Hypothetica*. Here we certainly seem to have some kind of literary connection.[33] But it is far from clear that the connection consists in Josephus's use of Philo. Of course, Philo's use of Josephus is ruled out because of the dates involved, but the hypothesis that both draw upon one or more common sources has often been supported, and most recently defended in detail by Carras.[34]

Of course, it would be beyond the scope of this article to attempt a comprehensive comparison of Philo and Josephus; rather, I will simply state that the alleged parallels between certain passages of Josephus and passages of Philo all seem to me to be more or less speculative, and if some literary relationship is implied, it can more plausibly be explained by

---

[32] E.g., we find references to Plato's works at *C. Ap.* 2.168, 223, 224, 225, 256, 257, and references to Aristotle's works at *C. Ap.* 1.176, 176, 176, 178, 182. Gustav Hölscher lists Josephus's citations of sources in "Josephus," PW 9:1964–65 (for *A.J.*) and 9:1996 (for *C. Ap.*).

[33] See, e.g., Colson's comment at PLCL 9:409 n. a.

[34] George P. Carras, "Dependence or Common Tradition in Philo *Hypothetica* viii 6.10–7.20 and Josephus *Contra Apionem* 2.190–219," *SPhA* 5 (1993): 24–47, especially the summary at 44–47. Carras's view is endorsed by Peder Borgen, "Philo of Alexandria: Reviewing and Rewriting Biblical Material," *SPhA* 9 (1997): 47–50. Even those who maintain that Josephus used Philo often note that the use of common sources would explain the similarities. See, e.g., Samuel Belkin, "The Alexandrian Source for Contra Apionem II," *JQR*, n.s. 27 (1936–1937): 31: "The evidence discussed indicates clearly that in *Contra Apionem*, II, Josephus is either directly dependent on the *Hypothetica* of Philo or on one of its sources, more probably the former." In fact, it seems that Belkin does not present any evidence that would make the former more probable. And a few years later Belkin (*Philo and the Oral Law* [Cambridge: Harvard University Press, 1940], 194) refers to a "common origin" of remarks found in Philo and Josephus, and even states explicitly (ibid., 42): "Josephus, in my opinion, never saw the works of Philo."

supposing that the two authors drew upon common sources.[35] Nowhere do we find either the explicit attribution of a text to Philo or the substantial verbal identity with a Philonic passage that would show that Josephus was in fact familiar with some work of Philo.[36]

Now, what I just said may well be seen as simply an *argumentum e silentio*. We are not, of course, likely to find an explicit statement by someone to the effect that he has *not* seen or read a book by Philo, or an explicit statement that Philo did *not* publish a book of a certain sort. As with all arguments from silence, the question is whether we fail to find citations where we could reasonably expect to find them, or references of a sort that we could reasonably expect to find if the person is in fact making a citation. In this context, we may find it useful to reflect on the most famous argument from silence in history (I suppose), that of Sherlock Holmes in "Silver Blaze," where we find a reference to the argument's crucial point in the following dialogue between Inspector Gregory and Holmes:

> "Is there any other point to which you would wish to draw my attention?"
> "To the curious incident of the dog in the night-time."
> "The dog did nothing in the night-time."
> "That was the curious incident," remarked Sherlock Holmes.

Although I cannot be expected to have anything to say that is so logically decisive and witty as Sherlock Holmes's final sentence, the point is that we fail to find behavior that we would expect. The problem with transferring this point to our discussion of Philo is that the range of behavior of authors is not nearly so limited as that of a good watchdog at night.

Nevertheless, the final curious incident that I would note here is the behavior of Josephus, who gives no report on Philo's works, but makes his one reference to Philo in connection with the disturbances in Alexandria

---

[35] See, for example, the parallel cited by Marcus at *QE* 2.73 (PLCL Supp 2:122 n. e), who refers to *A.J.* 3.182 and *B.J.* 5.217. Summaries of many discussions of this issue are conveniently found in Feldman, *Josephus and Modern Scholarship*, 410–18.

[36] Note, of course, that piling up parallels between Philo and Josephus does not tend to prove that Josephus used Philo. This sort of argument can be found in Schürer, Review of Heinrich Bloch, *Die Quellen des Josephus in seiner Archäologie, TLZ* 4 (1879): 568: "Denn die Parallelen zwischen Philo und Josephus sind so stark und zahlreich, dass sie die an sich naheliegende Benützung Philo's durch Josephus zu einem hohen Grad von Wahrschein-lichkeit erheben." The *non sequitur* here can be appreciated by considering, say, the parallels between Matthew and Luke, which are numerous and far more literal than anything that we find in Philo and Josephus. While it is abstractly possible that Luke used Matthew or that Matthew used Luke, most scholars think that the parallels are adequately explained by the use of common sources (i.e., Mark and Q).

and the consequent embassy to Gaius. Josephus describes Philo's leading role in that embassy (*A.J.* 18.259–60), introducing him as follows:

Φίλων ὁ προεστὼς τῶν Ἰουδαίων τῆς πρεσβείας, ἀνὴρ τὰ πάντα ἔνδοξος, Ἀλεξ-άνδρου τε τοῦ ἀλαβάρχου ἀδελφὸς ὢν καὶ φιλοσοφίας οὐκ ἄπειρος, οἷός τε ἦν ἐπ᾽ ἀπολογίᾳ χωρεῖν τῶν κατηγορημένων.[37]

Now, Josephus does not state that Philo did *not* write books, nor does he say that he (Josephus) did *not* have a substantial collection of Philo's books in his personal library, nor does he report that many of Philo's works were *not* readily available at the local book dealer in Rome. We could hardly expect such statements. But we might reasonably expect (I believe) some allusion to Philo's literary activity if Josephus had in fact known of Philo's works. For all that Josephus says here, Philo might well have been like Socrates, devoted to philosophy but not a writer. Indeed, I wonder if the modest description of Philo as "not unskillful in philosophy"[38] would be appropriate if Josephus had known of Philo's extensive commentaries on Genesis and Exodus. Of course, in the context of the mission to Gaius, Josephus might have considered an excursus into Philo's allegorical works irrelevant and distracting; but then perhaps we might all the more expect some allusion to Philo's discussion in *Flaccus* of Alexandrian politics or to Philo's description of the embassy itself in *Legatio ad Gaium*. Such considerations are, in any case, far from conclusive, and this is probably inevitable unless we are Sherlock Holmes. But I still find Josephus's silence to be a curious incident.

In fact, in the same context Josephus says that three ambassadors were sent from the Jews and three from the Greeks (*A.J.* 18.257), while Philo (*Legat.* 370) says that the Jews sent five. Mangey inferred from the discrepancy that one should read πάντως (with A) instead of πέντε.[39] On the other hand, Whiston concludes from this inconsistency that, "if there be no mistake in the copies," Josephus had not read Philo's account.[40] This is not, of course, an argument from silence; however, it seems to ignore the possibility that Josephus knew Philo's report but simply made an over-

---

[37] *A.J.* 18.259: "But Philo, the principal of the Jewish embassage, a man eminent on all accounts, brother to Alexander the alabarch, and one not unskillful in philosophy, was ready to betake himself to make his defense against those accusations." (Translation by William Whiston, *The Works of Josephus* [original edition 1736; repr.: Peabody, Mass.: Hendrickson, 1987], 494).

[38] (Whiston) or "no novice in philosophy" (Feldman).

[39] *Opera* 2:600 n. f.; PCW apparatus ad loc.

[40] Note to *A.J.* 18.257 (*The Works of Josephus*, 493 n. a).

sight.[41] There are as well other discrepancies between Josephus's account of the embassy and Philo's own report, which might be explained in various ways.[42] However, I suggest that a plausible conclusion from all this is that Josephus was not aware of Philo's works.

As a curiosity, I will mention very briefly that in 1841 Kirschbaum appealed to Josephus as part of his argument that the works attributed to Philo are all Christian forgeries.[43] In fact, according to Kirschbaum, at least two forgers were involved, creating the works in two groups, the first consisting of what we call the Exposition of the Law, and the second consisting of what we call the Allegorical Commentary; and we can tell that there were these two different forgers since, as is obvious, the author of the books of the Allegorical Commentary could hardly be the author of the books of the Exposition.[44] Naturally, I disassociate myself from any such thesis. But along the way Kirschbaum asserts that Josephus's silence about Philo's works at *A.J.* 18.259 and the discrepancies between Josephus's account of the embassy and what we find in Philo's *Legatio* show that Philo's works did not yet exist when Josephus was writing.[45] The possibility that the works existed but were unavailable to Josephus is simply dismissed. It is remarkable that a few years later Grossmann gives sustained attention to Kirschbaum's work in his own insightful study of the works of Philo.[46] Grossmann appeals to the principle that silence implies consent, and accordingly argues that Josephus's silence concerning the *Legatio* should be

---

[41] For further discussion see P. J. Sijpestein, "The Legationes ad Gaium," *JJS* 15 (1964): 87–96.

[42] Consider, for example, the discrepancy about the time of year between *A.J.* 18.272 and *Legat.* 249, as noted by Feldman (LCL *A.J.* ad loc.). Of course, there are also discrepancies between Josephus's accounts in *A.J.* and *B.J.*, as Feldman also notes from time to time.

[43] Eliezer Simon Kirschbaum, *Der jüdische Alexandrinismus eine Erfindung christlicher Lehrer. Oder: Beiträge zur Kritik jüdischer Geschichte und Litteratur*, Book 1: *Jüdisch-griechische Originale, vorzüglich Philo und Sirach* (Leipzig: C. L. Fritzsche, 1841), 23–25.

[44] Ibid., 14–22.

[45] See especially ibid., 23 ("Ich setze voraus, daß Josephus … um die Arbeiten eines so bedeutenden, und auch von ihm geachteten Mannes seines Volkes, … gewußt haben müßte, wenn welche zu seiner Zeit existirt hätten, und daß er ihrer … zu erwähnen nicht ermangelt haben würde, wenn kein besonderer Grund ihn davon abgehalten.") and 24–25 ("Wie konnte aber Josephus … bei der Achtung, die er gegen Philo an den Tag legt, demselben in Dingen widersprechen, wo er als Augenzeuge dasteht? Muß man nicht vielmehr annehmen, daß Josephus diese Berichte gar nicht gekannt? Wenn er sie aber nicht gekannt, können sie da auch existirt haben?").

[46] C. G. L. Grossmann, *De Philonis Iudaei operum continua serie et ordine chronologico commentatio* 1–2 (Leipzig: Wilhelm Staritz, 1841–1842), 1:4–21 (especially 19). This was a preliminary study to Grossmann's planned edition of Philo's works, designed to supersede Mangey's edition.

interpreted as meaning that Josephus consented to the common position that Philo wrote the *Legatio*. That this was the common position at the time seems not to be discussed by Grossmann. In any case, I would think that my suggestion that Philo's works were written but unpublished is superior to the theses of Kirschbaum and Grossmann; but that is admittedly not saying much.

As a third example of the alleged early use of the works of Philo, let us consider briefly the New Testament book of Hebrews. Much has been written on the similarities between the thought of Philo and the thought of the author of Hebrews.[47] Such discussions seem to remain inconclusive. However, there are a few places where some precise verbal connection seems to occur.[48] A striking example is Heb 13:5b, where the author quotes as a saying of God: Οὐ μή σε ἀνῶ οὐδ' οὐ μή σε ἐγκαταλίπω. At *Conf.* 166 Philo quotes exactly the same words as an oracle of God. Although these exact words are not found in the LXX, Mangey referred the citation in Philo to Jos 1:5, and he is followed by later editors and indices.[49] Williamson discusses this issue at some length, noting the divergent uses that the two writers make of the quotation, and concludes that there is no reason to suppose that the author of Hebrews is here quoting Philo; rather they are both citing some written source (perhaps a form of the LXX) found in Alexandria.[50] Earlier, however, Peter Katz concluded that the form found in Philo derives from Gen 28:15 (οὐ μή σε ἐγκαταλίπω), which has been expanded from Deut 31:6 and 31:8 (where we find οὐ μή σε ἀνῇ; the third person thus needed to be shifted to the first).[51] And in a subsequent article Katz discusses Heb 13:5b, arguing that both Philo and the author of Hebrews are quoting Gen 28:15 in "a text current in Egypt in the first century A.D."[52] Katz further notes that at Gen 28:15 the minuscule f (53)

---

[47] See Runia, *Philo in Early Christian Literature*, 74–78.

[48] Runia, ibid., 76, cites four texts where "coincidence must be ruled out," and then in n. 69 calls special attention to Heb 13:5b. As a further example, Scott D. Mackie, "Early Christian Eschatological Experience in the Warnings and Exhortations of the Epistle to the Hebrews," *TynBul* 63 (2012): 111 n. 44, has recently called attention to the fact that Philo, *Congr.* 163–80, and Heb 12:1–17 both quote Prov 3:11–12, and share "a number of terms and motifs."

[49] But Kahn (PAPM 13:136 n. 2) notes the differences (but not the identity with Heb 13:5b), and concludes: "on peut se demander si c'est bien notre Bible grecque que l'auteur avait sous les yeux."

[50] Ronald Williamson, *Philo and the Epistle to the Hebrews* (ALGHJ 4; Leiden: E. J. Brill, 1970), 570–73 (conclusion at 573). See also Kenneth L. Schenk, "Philo and the Epistle to the Hebrews: Ronald Williamson's Study after Thirty Years," *SPhA* 14 (2002): 128.

[51] *Philo's Bible* (Cambridge: Cambridge University Press, 1950), 72 n. 2.

[52] "Οὐ μή σε ἀνῶ, οὐδ' οὐ μή σε ἐγκαταλίπω Hebr. xiii 5. The Biblical Source of the Quotation," *Bib* 33 (1952): 523–25, here 524. Katz further discusses these texts in his review

shows the text with the supplement as found in Philo and Hebrews.[53] Katz then notes that many readings from the New Testament have been introduced into the manuscripts of the LXX, and wonders whether the text of 53 is "a mere reflex of" Heb 13:5, i.e., has been assimilated to the New Testament passage.[54] But then perhaps we should be prepared to think that it is possible that the reading in Philo's manuscripts has also been influenced by Heb 13:5.[55] Thus, instead of the influence of Philo on Hebrews or (Katz's position) a common source for Philo and Hebrews, we would have the influence of Hebrews on (the manuscripts of) Philo. In any case, it seems that this striking agreement between Philo and Hebrews does not indicate that the author of Hebrews knew of Philo's work.

2. *The Cross-References within Philo's Works*

Let me turn next to the quite different issue of the chronological sequence of Philo's works. One important sort of evidence that has been cited to establish such a sequence is the cross-references (i.e., Philo's references to his own works) to be found within his writings. The principle utilized here is, of course, straightforward: If book B refers to book A, then book A must have been written before book B. If we can find a sufficient number of such cross-references, then we might hope to construct a more or less complete sequence, i.e., a relative chronology of the works.

Good examples of very clear cross-references are furnished by Josephus, who refers four times in the *Antiquitates* to a specific book of the *Bellum Judaicum*.[56] We can thus deduce that the *Bellum* was written before the *Antiquitates*. Of course, we would know this already from the explicit

---

of Bleddyn J. Roberts, *The Old Testament Text and Versions*, TLZ 76 (1951): 536–37, and in his "The Quotations from Deuteronomy in Hebrews," ZNW 49 (1958): 220–21. For some further comments see my *Scribal Habits in Early Greek New Testament Papyri* (NTTSD 36; Leiden: Brill, 2008), 759–60 (Supplementary Note 13). Naomi G. Cohen, *Philo's Scriptures: Citations from the Prophets and Writings* (JSJSup 123; Leiden: Brill, 2007), 105–7, argues that at *Conf.* 166 Philo is quoting Deut 31:6, but does not refer to Heb 13:5b or to the literature on this issue.

[53] The Göttingen LXX adds 664^mg in support of 53.

[54] "Οὐ μή σε ἀνῶ," 524–25.

[55] Similarly, at *Somn.* 1.219 the manuscripts GFHP contain the addition τῆς ὁμολογίας, which is taken from Heb 3:1; see my "Philo, Κύριος, and the Tetragrammaton," SPhA 3 (1991): 173. Naturally, the scribes of the LXX and of the works of Philo were Christians, to whom the wording of the New Testament would have been very familiar.

[56] See my "Philo's Division of His Works into Books," SPhA 13 (2001): 67 n. 51. Josephus also sometimes refers to specific books of other writers; see ibid., n. 52.

mention of the *Bellum* at the beginning of the *Antiquitates* (1.6). But, in any case, this is the sort of cross-reference that enables us to establish a relative chronology.

Looking at Philo's cross-references, we find that they are of two types.[57] The first type is the reference at (or near) the beginning of one book to the previous book within a given series.[58] Now, we have quite a few such references in the Allegorical Commentary, fixing the order of the books, and on occasion indicating that books are missing. Thus, we can be sure that the order of these books agrees with the order of the biblical text. And we have several such references in the Exposition. These again fix the order of the books. There are, regrettably, no such references in the *Quaestiones*, whose format hardly provides an opportunity for such. But the nature of these cross-references means that they are useless for deciding the relative chronology among the three series mentioned.

The second type of cross-reference is a reference in the course of one discussion to a discussion elsewhere in the Philonic corpus, and from now on I will discuss these exclusively.[59] But here we find a pervasive difficulty: these cross-references are, without exception, completely vague. As just noted, Josephus sometimes makes his cross-references quite precise (at least within the context of ancient writing where references to particular pages, for example, would be pointless, since each manuscript copy had a unique page layout). But Philo never, I believe, gives us the precision in these cross-references that would allow us to identify the text beyond doubt.

Related to this imprecision is the general problem that Philo is curiously reticent about referring to his own books by name.[60] The only possible reference by name to any of his extant works seems to be *Abr.* 258; but Colson translates this as "and it came, as was shown in the story of creation, from God," where it seems that κοσμοποιΐα is not taken as a title. On the other hand, Philo does refer seven times to the lost *De numeris*, but leaves it unclear whether it consisted of one or more books.[61] Other references to lost works at least indicate the contents; see *Her.* 1 where the (lost) preceding

---

[57] On this topic generally see ibid., 61–67. See also Sterling, 'Prolific in Expression and Broad in Thought: Internal References to Philo's Allegorical Commentary and Exposition of the Law,' *Euphrosyne: Revista de filologia clássica* 40 (2012): 55–76.

[58] Similar references are found in Polybius and Josephus (ibid., 60).

[59] A very useful summary of these issues may be found in Jenny Morris, "The Jewish Philosopher Philo," *SHJP* 3.2:841–44, with further references. Naturally, I am not attempting here a complete survey of the material and literature.

[60] He is also not all that forthcoming about the names of other persons' books; see, e.g., the comments by Runia, *Philo of Alexandria and the Timaeus of Plato* (PhilAnt 44; Leiden: E. J. Brill, 1986), 366–69, regarding Philo's citations from Plato.

[61] See my "Philo's Division of his Works into Books," 64–65.

book is said to have discussed "the question of rewards" (τὰ περὶ μισθῶν), and *Mut.* 53, where two books are said to have discussed "the whole subject of the covenants" (τὸν περὶ διαθηκῶν σύμπαντα λόγον); and perhaps περὶ παθῶν (to be discussed later). I have no explanation for why Philo's references to his works that provide names are all (apart perhaps from *Abr.* 258) to works that have been lost.

As an example of the problems that we encounter, let us consider *Spec.* 1.269, where Philo says of the offering of the heifer (as found in Num 19:1–9): "What these things symbolically indicate has been described in full elsewhere where we have expounded the allegory." Where is this "elsewhere" (δι' ἑτέρων)? Cohn thought that this must be a reference to the lost *Questions and Answers on Numbers*, confirming other indications that the *Quaestiones* extended beyond Genesis and Exodus.[62] Many years ago I expressed doubts that the *Quaestiones* ever went beyond the first two biblical books, and said: "Philo could have brought in a discussion of Num 19:1–9 at various places in the missing sections of the allegorical exposition, since his ability to connect texts and topics of the most disparate sorts is well known."[63] Abraham Terian, though, states that *Spec.* 1.269 is not necessarily a reference to a discussion of Num 19:1–9, but rather to the symbolism involved. And he accordingly suggests that Philo is in fact referring to *Her.* 100–236, where Philo allegorizes on Abraham's offering a heifer. Another possibility that Terian mentions is that Philo is referring to the discussion at *QG* 3.3–8 of Abraham's offering. But Terian thinks that "the lengthier discussion in the *Allegoriae* is more in keeping with the inherent meaning of the text."[64]

While I am now very much inclined to agree with Terian's analysis, note the varying possibilities here. Is Philo referring to a discussion in the lost *Questions and Answers on Numbers*, to a lost portion of the Allegorical Commentary, to *QG* 3.3–8, or to *Her.* 100–236? Philo's vagueness with "elsewhere" (which perhaps reflects a vagueness in his thought about the reference) means that the answer to that question may be elusive. And, of course, the fact that a considerable portion of the Philonic corpus is lost gives room for scholarly creativity in finding sources. Indeed, any such

[62] Leopold Cohn, "Einteilung und Chronologie der Schriften Philos," *Phlgs, Supplementband* 7 (1899): 403 (separately published with original pagination: Leipzig: Dieterich, 1899).

[63] "The Original Structure of Philo's *Quaestiones*," *SPh* 4 (1976–77): 43.

[64] "The Priority of the *Quaestiones* among Philo's Exegetical Commentaries," in *Both Literal and Allegorical: Studies in Philo of Alexandria's "Questions and Answers on Genesis and Exodus"* (ed. David M. Hay; BJS 232; Atlanta: Scholars Press, 1991), 44–45. See also his discussion in chapter 2 of his translation of *QE* (PAPM 34C:48–50).

reference can be to some lost text; for even if we find a suitable passage in the extant works, it is always possible that what Philo *really* had in mind was another passage in a work that is now lost.

Nevertheless, it would be perverse to ignore the clues that are furnished by the cross-references that Philo scatters about his works.[65] The most thorough discussion of them is by Abraham Terian, who bases his analysis on an improved understanding of the Armenian of the *Quaestiones* at several places.[66] Terian examines quite a few of Philo's cross-references, and concludes that "the *Quaestiones* are the earliest of Philo's exegetical commentaries,"[67] i.e., earlier than the Allegorical Commentary and the Exposition. The cornerstone of Terian's argument is that three passages in the Allegorical Commentary refer to the *Quaestiones*.

Terian considers *Leg.* 3.139, where Philo (in the Loeb translation) refers to "a treatise (λόγος) specially devoted to" the passions.[68] Terian argues that this mistranslates λόγος, which more likely refers simply to a discussion.[69] And Philo could be referring to such a discussion in earlier parts of the Allegorical Commentary (*Leg.* 2.8, 2.102; 3.113) or to one of the many discussions in the *Quaestiones*, for which Terian gives a dozen references. Indeed, Terian thinks that *Leg.* 3.139 is "a likely allusion to the *Quaestiones*."[70]

Similarly, and (it seems to me) more convincingly, Terian cites *Sobr.* 52: "We have said before that Shem bears a name which means 'good.'" Adler suggested that the reference was to a lost book of the Allegorical

---

[65] One interesting feature about the cross-references is that they often involve verbs of saying or speaking. Wilhelm Oncken, *Die Staatslehre des Aristoteles in historischen-politischen Umrissen*, Part 1 (Leipzig: Wilhelm Engelmann, 1870), 57–62, calls attention to various features in the *Nicomachean Ethics* and *Politics* that suggest that these works were actually lecture-notes, and among these features is the use of verbs of speaking, including in cross-references (see 60 n. 2). However, as Eduard Zeller observes (*Die Philosophie der Griechen in ihrer geschichtlichen Entwicklung dargestellt* 2.2: *Aristoteles und die alten Peripatetiker* [3rd ed.; Leipzig: Fues, 1879], 135 n. 3 [–136]), it is common for writers at all times to use such verbs. Oncken, *Staatslehre*, 60 n. 2, even refers to *Pol.* 1318b7: καθάπερ ἐν τοῖς πρὸ τούτων ἐλέχθη λόγοις, which seems to be a reference to the discussion at 1291b22–1293a10. But surely the use of λόγος for a writing is well-established; for its use by Philo see my "Philo's Division of his Works into Books," 68.

[66] See his "Priority" and "La place des *Quaestiones* dans l'oeuvre de Philon," which is chapter 2 of his translation of *QE* (PAPM 34C:27–51).

[67] "Priority," 46; see also PAPM 34C:51.

[68] Colson and Whitaker (PLCL 1:394 n. d) state: "This treatise was never written or is lost." See the similar translation and comment by Mondésert (PAPM 2:251 and 250 n. 1).

[69] Already Mangey glosses it with "Stoicorum disciplina." See also the translation by Heinemann (PCH 3:130 [and n. 1]).

[70] "Priority," 37–38; PAPM 34C:39–40.

Commentary that dealt with Gen 9:23,[71] and he was followed by Colson and Gorez.[72] Massebieau thinks that the reference is to a lost book or lost part of a book on Gen 4:26–5:32.[73] But Terian more plausibly asserts that Philo is referring to his interpretation of the name Shem in *QG* 1.88 and 2.79.[74]

The remaining example is the reference at *Sacr.* 51. Here Philo is discussing Abel and Cain, and in connection with Gen 4:2 states that "what is meant by a tiller of the soil I have shown in earlier books." What are these earlier books? The translators into German, English, and French refer to the *later* discussion (assuming that Philo wrote the books of the Allegorical Commentary in the order of our editions, which is the order of the biblical text) in *Agr.* 21–25.[75] Of course, taking the reference to "earlier books" to be to a later book (assuming that *Agr.* is indeed later) is clearly not desirable. Terian, however, argues that Philo is referring to *QG* 1.59, *QG* 2.66,[76] and *QE* 1.6,[77] where the three references in different books of the *Quaestiones* fit well with Philo's use of the plural "books."[78] This all seems quite reasonable. However, Runia notes that "the cross-reference does seem very far away." He then observes that Gen 3:23 also mentions "tilling the soil," and that this verse would have been discussed in the lost fourth book of

---

[71] PCH 5:93 n. 4.

[72] PLCL 3:471 n. c; PAPM 11–12:150 n. 4.

[73] "Le classement des oeuvres de Philon," *Bibliothèque de l'École des Hautes Études*, Section des Sciences religieuses 1 (1889): 22 n. 1 (separately published with original pagination: Paris: Ernest Leroux, 1899). In fact, Massebieau takes the lost portion to be the beginning of *De gigantibus* (see 21–23), although he cites the verses covered as 4:26–6:32, which is an obvious error, since he immediately says that *De gigantibus* begins with 6:1b. (But Wendland, PCW 2:xxii, repeats the error.) Since Gen 5 is mostly names, we may doubt that Philo gave much if any attention to that chapter, but we might expect some discussion of 5:32, in which Seth is mentioned. (*De posteritate Caini* ends with 4:25.) On the other hand, perhaps Philo decided just to skip all this genealogical material.

[74] "Priority," 40–41; PAPM 34C:42–44. Already Grossmann, *Serie* 2:15, asserted that *Sobr.* 52 is referring to these two passages. Massebieau ("Le classement," 22 n. 1) refers to Grossmann (but miscites the references) and says: "Mais on ne doit supposer un renvoi aussi vague à un ouvrage différent, qu'en désespoir de cause, et ce n'est pas ici le cas." Of course, Grossmann's and Terian's view has the advantage of finding actual passages, rather than a hypothesized one.

[75] As Terian cites: PCH 3:235 n. 4; PLCL 2:490–91; PAPM 4:117 n. 3. Grossmann, *Serie* 1:22, takes the reference to be to *Agr.* 3–25; but see the following note.

[76] Already Grossmann, *Serie* 2:14–15, states that this passage is being referred to by *Sacr.* 51; but see the preceding note.

[77] However, the theme of tilling the soil is found at *QE* 1.6 only in the Armenian, but not in the Greek fragment; see my "Philo's *Quaestiones in Exodum* 1.6," in *Both Literal and Allegorical*, 18–19 (Greek text) and 21–22 (where I judge the Armenian "tilling the soil" to be a corruption).

[78] "Priority," 38–40; PAPM 34C:40–42.

Legum Allegoriae, which discussed Gen 3:20–23.[79] Runia accordingly suggests that a more plausible source for Philo's reference at *Sacr.* 51 was this
lost fourth book of *Legum Allegoriae.*[80] Dähne, Massebieau, Cohn, and
Schürer had earlier made the same proposal.[81] Again we find conflicting
interpretations.

Now, the differences so far discussed do not, in fact, necessarily affect
Terian's major point, namely that the *Quaestiones* are earlier than the
Allegorical Commentary. But that point has not always been accepted. In
his detailed analysis of issues of the structure and chronology of Philo's
works, Cohn, the learned editor of Philo, states: "In the entire question of
the chronology of the Philonic writings indeed nothing is as certain as that
the *Quaestiones* were written later than the great allegorical Commentary on
Genesis."[82] How could Cohn have been so confident about a conclusion
that is diametrically opposed to Terian's view?

Cohn looks at only a few passages, but evidently finds them adequate
and decisive. One is *QE* 2.34, which states (in Marcus's translation):
"Concerning the divine covenant we have already spoken in detail." Cohn
(relying on Aucher's Latin) sees here a reference to the lost books "on the
covenants," which were a portion of the Allegorical Commentary.[83] Terian
analyzes this text at length, and argues that it is more plausible that with
the singular "covenant" Philo is referring to a discussion in the *Quaestiones,*

[79] Runia says "3:19–23," but the end of 3:19 has already been discussed in *Leg.* 3.253.
See further my "The Text of Philo's *Legum Allegoriae,*" *SPhA* 12 (2000): 2–3.

[80] "Secondary Texts in Philo's *Quaestiones,*" in *Both Literal and Allegorical,* 71–72. Some
skepticism about Terian's overall chronology is expressed by Runia, *On the Creation of the
Cosmos according to Moses* (PACS 1; Leiden: Brill, 2001), 4. By the way, already Mangey said
on the passage: "Quae verò dixerat Philo de terrae culturâ perierunt, ut rectè videtur Viro
Clarissimo Benzelio." Grossmann, *Serie* 1:22, considers this "liber *de terrae cultura*" to be
spurious, and states that the reference is neither to *Leg.* 1.96 nor to *QG* 1.56, but rather to
Agr. 3–25; and he later, *Serie* 2:14–15, adds *QG* 2.66.

[81] August Ferdinand Dähne, "Einige Bemerkungen über die Schriften des Juden
Philo," *TSK* 6 (1833): 1015; Massebieau, "Le classement," 19; Cohn, "Einteilung und
Chronologie," 430; Schürer, *Geschichte des jüdischen Volkes im Zeitalter Jesu Christi* (3rd ed.;
Leipzig: J. C. Hinrichs, 1898): 3:503 n. 44; Jenny Morris, *SHJP* 3.2:833 n. 65. At "Le classement," 19 n. 1, Massebieau says: "Il est naturel de penser que Philon renvoie à un livre
précédent du *Commentaire,*" and cites half a dozen similar phrases. But those phrases are
all at the beginning of one book where Philo is referring to the immediately preceding
book (in the singular), and thus are not really parallel to the reference to books (in the
plural) in *Sacr.* 51, which does not refer to the immediately preceding book (*De Cherubim*).

[82] "Einteilung und Chronologie," 431: "In der ganzen Frage über die Chronologie der
Philonischen Schriften ist gerade Nichts so sicher, wie daß die *Quaestiones* später verfaßt
sind als der große allegorische Commentar zur Genesis."

[83] "Einteilung und Chronologie," 431, as already suggested by Grossmann, *Serie* 2:16,
and Massebieau, "Le classement," 23 n. 2 (see Wendland, PCW 2:xxii).

such as the lost portion on Exod 6:4–5 or *QG* 3.40–60 on the covenant between God and Abraham. Terian buttresses these points with an argument from silence: if the Allegorical Commentary had already existed when Philo wrote the *Quaestiones*, one would expect that he would have referred in *QG* 3.40–60 to the lost books "on the covenants" or to *Mut.* itself, where God's covenant with Abraham, as related in Gen 17, is treated.[84] However, given the relative paucity of cross-references in Philo's works, such an argument perhaps is not all that weighty.

A further passage that Cohn cites is *QE* 2.100, where Philo says: " … the number seventy-five is produced, concerning which something has been said before." Cohn takes this to refer to *Migr.* 198–99.[85] While this seems possible, one wonders whether a discussion of a number might more plausibly be found in the lost *De numeris*, as suggested by Marcus.[86] Terian, who does not mention Cohn's view, suggests either a missing portion of the *Quaestiones in Exodum* or the *De numeris*.[87] Here Cohn's position at least has the merit of finding an extant source for the reference.

Cohn also cites *Her.* 215, where Philo says of the principle that "opposites together form a single whole" (213), which was stated by Heraclitus but actually discovered by Moses: "This point will be discussed in detail elsewhere." Cohn asserts that the promised discussion is found in *QG* 3.5, and that the future tense (ἀκριβώσομεν) shows that the *Quaestiones* were yet to be written.[88]

Finally, one very interesting piece of evidence that would appear to show that the *Quaestiones* are later than the Allegorical Commentary was located already by Aucher, and then utilized by Dähne, Grossmann, and Cohn.[89] At *QG* 1.55 Philo says: "For the highest principles, as I have often said,[90] are two: one, that God is not like man; and the other, that just as a

---

[84] "Priority," 33–34; PAPM 34C:33–35.

[85] "Einteilung und Chronologie," 431.

[86] However, Marcus bases this suggestion on his assertion that there is no reference to the number seventy-five to be found in Philo's extant works, thus overlooking *Migr.* 198–99.

[87] PAPM 34C:238 n. 1.

[88] Cited also by Grossmann, *Serie* 2:15. The German, English, and French translations make no comment on this phrase.

[89] The Greek fragment (from the *Sacra parallela*) was edited by Mangey, *Opera*, 2:669, and then located by Aucher, *Paralipomena*, 37 n. 2; Dähne, "Einige Bemerkungen," 1037 n. a; Grossmann, *Serie* 2:15; Cohn, "Einteilung und Chronologie," 431 (refers to *Deus* 53 and *Somn.* 1.237).

[90] The Armenian has simply *orpēs asac'i*, which Marcus translates as "as I have said." But the Greek fragment has ὡς πολλάκις ἔφην, which I consider original; see Petit, PAPM 33:54. The usual Armenian rendering of πολλάκις would be *bazum angam* (Marcus cites "5 exx." in his "Index," and there are five examples in *Prov.*), and there seems to be no reason

man disciplines his son, so the Lord God disciplines you." Here we have references to Num 23:19 and Deut 8:5, and indeed besides *QG* 1.55 Philo relates these two verses at *QG* 2.54, *Sacr.* 94 and 101, *Deus* 53–54 and 69, *Somn.* 1.237, and in a fragment attributed to the fourth book of *Legum Allegoriae*.[91] Of all these passages, only at *QG* 1.55 does Philo say that he has made this point elsewhere. Now, assuming that we take the reference in *QG* 1.55 to be to an "earlier" discussion (and not, for example, to *QG* 2.54), there is no such discussion in *QG* 1.1–54, and no reason to suspect the existence of any lacuna. So it would seem that we should conclude that in *QG* 1.55 Philo is referring to a passage written prior to the *Quaestiones*. And rather than postulating lost sources, it would seem reasonable to suppose that Philo was thinking of the several extant passages in the Allegorical Commentary. The plurality of such passages would certainly fit with what the Greek fragment has: "as I have *often* said."

In fact, Philo's comment at *QG* 1.55 has been perhaps the most important text brought forward to prove that the *Quaestiones* are later than the Allegorical Commentary. Its earliest use seems to be by Dähne, who describes the *Quaestiones* as written "wahrscheinlich später" than the Allegorical Commentary, and gives as the sole support this Greek fragment of

---

for omission in the Armenian; but then there also seems to be no reason that πολλάκις would be added in the Greek. (I was able to examine three Armenian manuscripts that contain this passage: Erevan 1500, Jerusalem 333, and Venice 1040. All three read exactly as does Aucher's text.) I have found two close parallels in Philo to such a phrase. First, at *Conf.* 135 he says that, "as I have often said elsewhere" (ὡς πολλάκις ἐν ἑτέροις εἶπον), Moses is applying human terms to God who is not human. This is, of course, the point for which Num 23:19 is often cited; indeed, Kahn (PAPM 13:114 n. 2) refers at this phrase to his note on *Conf.* 98, and in that text Philo quotes Num 23:19. And second, at *Deo* 12 (extant only in Armenian) we find *orpēs aha asac'i bazum angam*, which Aucher translates as "ut jam dixi saepius." Siegert, *Philon von Alexandrien, Über die Gottesbezeichnung "wohltätig verzehrendes Feuer" ("De Deo"): Rückübersetzung des Fragments aus dem Armenischen, deutsche Übersetzung und Kommentar* (WUNT 46; Tübingen: J. C. B. Mohr, 1988), 31 ll. 149–50, retroverts the Armenian as: ὥσπερ δὴ ἔλεγον πολλάκις. However, instead of δή I would prefer ἤδη for *aha*, as at *Prov.* 2.103 (but see Siegert, ibid., n. 128).

[91] See *The Spurious Texts*, 9, and also Petit, PAPM 33:54 n. d. Mangey (*Opera* 2:669 n. a) had already said of this fragment: "Confer cum lib. de Dei Immut. p. 301." This is actually a reference to *Deus* 53–54, which appears at *Opera* 1:280–81, but is, as seen from Mangey's margin, on p. 301 of the Paris edition.

QG 1.55.[92] Then it was utilized for the same purpose by Grossmann and Cohn.[93]

On the other hand, after discussing both the Allegorical Commentary and the Exposition, Ewald argues that the *Quaestiones* must have preceded the Allegorical Commentary: "dieser versuch den höheren sinn nach seiner eigenthümlichen auffassung nur erst überall zu begründen bezeichnet das werk als ein anfangswerk der ganzen großen Allegorischen kunstbemühung Philon's." Then, in a note, he cites this Greek fragment of *QG* 1.55 and comments: "so kann er damit sehr wohl auf jetzt verloren gegangene stellen zu anfange dieses selben werkes zurückweisen, doch fehlt das πολλάκις in der Arm. Uebersezung Auch. II. p. 37 ganz. Jedenfalls also braucht dieser ausdruck nicht auf ein verschiedenes früheres werk zurückzuweisen."[94] However, as already noted, there appear to be no lacunae in the *Quaestiones* prior to *QG* 1.55, and (whether or not we read "often") it seems gratuitous to postulate lacunae (or even earlier works) when we have at least five (and perhaps six) appropriate passages in the Allegorical Commentary.

So, what are we to make of all this? The cross-references examined here are not very numerous and are not at all precise. But perhaps—in order to make a decision—we can say that *Sobr.* 52 does refer to *QG* 1.88 and 2.79, and that *QG* 1.55 does refer to the half-dozen places in the Allegorical Commentary where Num 23:19 and Deut 8:5 are discussed. This is a meager result, but it leaves us with a puzzle: How can the *Quaestiones* refer to the Allegorical Commentary and the Allegorical Commentary refer to the *Quaestiones*?

The answer is simple: Philo did not publish his works, but kept them as his own notes to which he on occasion added cross-references.[95] Naturally,

---

[92] Dähne, "Einige Bemerkungen," 1037 and n. a, where Dähne notes that Philo has "noch nicht" discussed these matters in the *Quaestiones*, but discusses them "sehr oft" in the Allegorical Commentary, citing *Deus* and *Migr.* 113 (where though only Num 23:19 is cited).

[93] Grossmann, *Serie* 2:15 n. 70, which is actually a reference to n. 69 at 2:26; Cohn, "Einteilung und Chronologie," 431.

[94] Heinrich Ewald, *Geschichte des Volkes Israel*, vol. 6: *Geschichte des apostolischen Zeitalters bis zur Zerstörung Jerusalem's* (3rd ed.; Göttingen: Dieterich, 1868), 295 and n. 1. (I have retained Ewald's German orthography.)

[95] At least, this is *one* answer, and it is the answer that seems most attractive to me. However, there are (of course) other possibilities. Let us note a pervasive presupposition in much of the literature on these cross-references. Frequently it seems to be taken for granted that if a book from one series refers to a book of another series, the entire first series must be later than the entire second series. Thus, for example, if one book from the Allegory refers to one book of the *Quaestiones*, the entire Allegory must be later than the entire *Quaestiones*. One has only to make this principle explicit to see that the inference is unfounded. Indeed, such a view is questioned by Sze-kar Wan in his review (*SPhA* 5

he would have written the works sequentially. (We can leave it open here exactly what the sequence was.) But they were never, as it were, "finished" and sent to be published. So the possibility remained to revise them in various ways. And among the revisions were some cross-references.

The model, of course, for this sort of activity is found in the works of Aristotle. Now, Aristotle's cross-references are more frequent and more precise than are Philo's,[96] and indeed it is perfectly clear that we have circular cross-references. As a small sample, consider that *Top.* 162a11 refers to the *Analytics*, while *An. pr.* 24b12 cites the *Topics*; and that *Poet.* 1456a34–35 refers to the *Rhetoric*, while *Rhet.* 1404a38–39 refers to the *Poetics*.[97] There are in fact many cross-references, so that there can be little doubt that they are genuinely in the text of the works.[98]

The usual explanation for these cross-references is that Aristotle's works were not published in some order or another,[99] but are in fact works

---

[1993]: 226) of *Both Literal and Allegorical*, in which he discusses Terian's arguments there (in "Priority"), and observes: "In any case, it may be methodologically unwise to assume that such enormous works as the *Allegoriae* or the *Quaestiones* would be composed in an absolute sequence with no time overlap." Similarly, Siegert, "Early Jewish Interpretation in a Hellenistic Style," 166 n. 174, observes: "Nothing justifies the assumption that Philo finished one *genre* of writing before using another. It rather seems that Philo worked on more than one of these series at the same time." Indeed, Cohn had already mentioned that it was possible that the Allegory and the Exposition had been written in parallel, although he in fact thought that the Allegory preceded the Exposition (see "Einteilung und Chronologie," 435 and 433). Already Schürer (*Geschichte* [3rd ed., 1898], 3:500–501) says that the writing of the *Quaestiones* was "theils früher theils später" than that of the Allegorical Commentary, as the reciprocal cross-references show. On this point he appeals to Ewald (the *Quaestiones* are earlier) and Dähne (the Allegorical Commentary is earlier). And then he refers to Grossmann, *Serie* 2:14–17. In fact, there is also hardly any requirement that one book would have to be completed before another was begun. If Philo worked on two books during the same period, he could have supplied them with cross-references to each other.

[96] Aristotle also has quite precise references to the works of Plato. Among the listing of references in Hermann Bonitz, *Index Aristotelicus* (Berlin: Georg Reimer, 1870), 598–99, see those marked with "(a)."

[97] Zeller, *Aristoteles*, 127–29, gives many examples. See the citations in Bonitz, *Index Aristotelicus*, 95–105. This curious feature of the Aristotelian corpus is well known and much discussed; see, for example, Jonathan Barnes, "Life and Work," in idem, ed., *The Cambridge Companion to Aristotle* (Cambridge: Cambridge University Press, 1995), 19.

[98] Barnes, ibid., says of the cross-references: "the vast majority of them are readily detachable from their contexts: they look for all the world like later additions to the text, inserted either by Aristotle himself or by a later editor." Of course, it would seem to be the nature of a cross-reference that it is basically parenthetical. Barnes's point is that one cannot use the cross-references to date the texts.

[99] See, e.g., Zeller, *Aristoteles*, 132.

meant for study by Aristotle and his pupils during Aristotle's life.[100]
Keeping these notes under his own control meant that he could insert a
reference to work A within work B and also insert a reference to work B
within work A, and all copies could be so updated.[101]

Consequently, establishing a relative chronology of Aristotle's works on
the basis of these cross-references is impossible.[102] Now, this does not
mean, of course, that all the works were written simultaneously. Whatever
revisions and insertions of cross-references Aristotle may have made, we
must suppose that he wrote certain works, or at least substantial portions of
certain works, before other works (or portions thereof). And, of course,
scholars have attempted to judge that some Aristotelian works are earlier
and some are later. But this is done by an examination of something other
than the cross-references, such as style or, more usually, subject matter or
thought to be found in the various works.[103]

By the way, it is curious that Aristotle's published works have been lost
(except for a few fragments), while his unpublished works have survived
(except for occasional lacunae or missing portions). Of course, the circular
cross-references are found in the works for which Aristotle is known, i.e.,
the unpublished works.[104]

Now, my suggestion (tentatively expressed, with a recognition that
there is much uncertainty) is that Philo's works also were unpublished by
him, and somehow survived the vicissitudes of first and second century
c.e. Alexandria to be recovered by the Alexandrian Catechetical School. At

---

[100] Sometimes it is said that the works correspond to lecture notes; see Barnes, "Life
and Works," 12–14, who surveys the notion, but prefers the notion that the works "were,
by and large, working drafts." Zeller, *Aristoteles*, 133–35, presents strong objections to the
view that the treatises were designed for Aristotle alone. Mary Louise Gill, *Aristotle on
Substance: The Paradox of Unity* (Princeton: Princeton University Press, 1989), 10, says that
"it is widely agreed that the extant treatises were not written and published for popular
consumption but were tools used for teaching in the Lyceum." See Zeller, *Aristoteles*, 110:
"fast alle diese Schriften, so weit sie für ächt gehalten werden können, sind mit einander …
durch ausdrückliche Verweisungen in einer Weise verknüpft, wie diess nur dann möglich
war, wenn sie als zusammengehörige und sich gegenseitig erläuternde Theile Eines
Ganzen für denselben Leserkreis bestimmt waren."

[101] As Starr, "Circulation," 219, notes: "Since private copies were usually made in
small numbers, an author could revise his work at any time." Starr cites some examples
from Cicero.

[102] See Barnes, "Life and Works," 21.

[103] See, for example, Werner Jaeger, *Aristotle: Fundamentals of the History of his Development* (2nd ed.; London: Oxford University Press, 1948), who briefly (294–95) dismisses the
use of the cross-references as a "chronological criterion."

[104] Aristotle himself refers to his "published works" from time to time, as at *Poet.*
1454b17–18: εἴρηται δὲ περὶ αὐτῶν ἐν τοῖς ἐκδεδομένοις λόγοις ἱκανῶς. (Note the verb
ἐκδίδωμι.) See in general Zeller, *Aristoteles*, 112–24.

that point, they began to be published, and we have some very early evidence of their circulation (i.e., as it seems, their publication) in the two third-century papyri from Coptos and Oxyrhynchus.

3. *The Use and Origin of Philo's Works as Unpublished*

But if Philo did not publish his works, what purpose did he have in writing them? The hypothesis that seems to me to be most plausible is that of Sterling, who suggested some time ago that Philo was the leader of a school devoted to the study of Scripture.[105] On this occasion I will not be able to discuss Sterling's position in detail, and so a few citations will have to suffice.

Sterling's basic proposal is that "Philo had a private school in his home or personally owned structure for advanced students which was similar to schools of higher education run by individuals throughout the Greco-Roman world."[106] Sterling sees the main function of this school to be the study of Scripture, and the *Quaestiones* and the Allegorical Commentary would most clearly fit into such a curriculum. At one point, he suggests that the *Quaestiones* were designed for "beginning students," while the Allegorical Commentary would be for "advanced" students, who would form a "sophisticated audience who know the biblical text exceptionally well and are capable of appreciating extended philosophical expositions of it."[107] And Sterling further suggests that it would be appropriate for such a school to have a library in which Philo's works would be the core, but in which other Jewish writings were represented. And somehow this library eventually fell into the hands of the Christian community, at least by the time of Clement.[108] Now, Sterling does not, I believe, comment on the publication history of Philo's works. But I would extend his thought in the direction of suggesting that Philo's works were the private, unpublished books of this school. They thus would have had the same status as did Aristotle's (non-popular, unpublished) books for his philosophical school.

Let me make a final observation and disclaimer. Philo wrote books that are of different genres and that seem to be addressing different audiences.

---

[105] "'The School of Sacred Laws': The Social Setting of Philo's Treatises," *VC* 53 (1999): 148–64.

[106] Ibid., 150.

[107] Ibid., 159–60.

[108] Ibid., 160–63.

Most of his works deal with the interpretation of Scripture, particularly Genesis and Exodus, although even there we can distinguish the different styles of the *Quaestiones*, the Allegorical Commentary, and the Exposition. It is thus reasonable to think that these three series were intended for different groups of readers.[109] But others (e.g. *Aet.*, *Prov.* 1–2 and *Anim.*) deal with traditional philosophical issues, others (*Flacc.* and *Legat.*) deal with contemporary political events, and others (e.g. *Mos.* 1–2 and *Contempl.*) seem to have broadly apologetic purposes. Is it plausible that he would have written all of these diverse books for the private use of himself and his circle of students and colleagues? In this paper I have concentrated, of course, on the exegetical works, and in particular on the *Quaestiones* and the Allegorical Commentary and the cross-references among them, and in principle it is completely possible that Philo kept those books unpublished while publishing others, say *Flacc.* and *Legat.* Nevertheless, my first general point (the argument from silence, for whatever it is worth) applies to all of the works. Perhaps, indeed, it is even more applicable to the historical and apologetic works; we might expect such works to generate some comment or response. Naturally, it is possible that they did, but that the responses have been lost. It also might be expected (or hoped) that there would be some distinction in the manuscript tradition between published and unpublished works. (For Aristotle the distinction is clear; the published works are preserved as fragments in citations, while the unpublished works are preserved, for the most part, in numerous manuscript copies and translations.) Now, there are plenty of vagaries and complications in the transmission of Philo's works, but I don't see that any of them would somehow be clarified by distinguishing between published and unpublished works. Again, we are left, I regret, with something much less than clarity and certainty.

---

[109] Philo's intended audience is often discussed. See, for example, Maren R. Niehoff, *Jewish Exegesis and Homeric Scholarship in Alexandria* (Cambridge: Cambridge University Press, 2011), 133–85 (summary at 185), who indeed finds that Philo had three quite different audiences for the three series of the *Quaestiones*, the Allegorical Commentary, and the Exposition.

The Studia Philonica Annual 25 (2013) 101–113

"A MAN OF THE HIGHEST REPUTE":
DID JOSEPHUS KNOW THE WRITINGS OF PHILO?

GREGORY E. STERLING

There is a curious phenomenon in the writings of the two most prolific Jewish authors of the first century C.E.: both Philo and Josephus openly cited non-Jewish sources but failed to name Jewish predecessors. We know that they had Jewish predecessors and used them. Philo was not only indebted to some known Jewish authors such as Ezekiel the Tragedian but to a tradition of exegesis that included allegorists and literalists. Yet he never named any of his Jewish predecessors or contemporaries. On the other hand, he cited a range of Greek literary authors[1] by name such as Homer,[2] Aeschyhlus,[3] Sophocles,[4] and Euripides,[5] as well as philosophical writers, most notably Heraclitus[6] and Plato.[7] Similarly, Josephus openly attributed citations to non-Jewish authors, but failed to credit Jewish colleagues. So, for example, in the retelling of the Pentateuch in his *Jewish Antiquities*, he explicitly cited or referred to at least fifteen authors.[8] While two of these may have been Jewish—Cleodamus Malchus (?) and the author of the 3rd *Sibylline Oracle*—Josephus cited them as pagan sources. Yet we know that he used Jewish predecessors whom he probably knew

---

[1] We now have a very helpful summary of this evidence in David Lincicum, "An Index to Philo's Non-Biblical Citations and Allusions," elsewhere in this year's *SPhA*.

[2] Philo, *Conf.* 4; *Abr.* 10; *Prob.* 31; *Contempl.* 17; *Legat.* 80.

[3] Philo, *Prob.* 143.

[4] Philo, *Prob.* 19.

[5] Philo, *Prob.* 99, 116, 141.

[6] Philo used his proper name 5x (*Leg.* 1.108; *Her.* 214; *Aet.* 111; *Prov.* 2.67; *QG* 2.5a), and the adjectival form of his name once (*Leg.* 3.7).

[7] Philo, *Opif.* 119, 133; *Prob.* 13; *Contempl.* 57; *Aet.* 13, 14, 16, 27, 38, 52, 141.

[8] All of these are in *AJ* 1: Alexander Polyhistor in *AJ* 1. 240; Acusilaus in *AJ* 1.108; Berossus in *AJ* 1.93, 107, 158; Cleodamus Malchus in *AJ* 1.240–41; Ephorus in *AJ* 1.108; Hecataeus of Abdera in *AJ* 1.108, 119, 159; Hellanicus in *AJ* 1.108; Hesiod in *AJ* 1.108; Hestiaeus in *AJ* 1.107; Hieronymus in *AJ* 1.94, 107; Manetho in *AJ* 1.107; Mochus in *AJ* 1.107; Mnaseas in *AJ* 1.94; Nicolaus of Damascus in 194, 108, 159; and *Sib. Or.* 3.97–104 in *AJ* 1.118.

through Alexander Polyhistor.[9] When he mentioned two of them by name in *Against Apion*, Demetrius and Eupolemus, he implied that they were Greeks by identifying Demetrius as Demetrius Phalerus and apologizing for their inability to follow the Jewish Scriptures accurately.[10] When he had referred to the same group of writers in the *Jewish War*, he called them Greeks.[11] He did the same thing when he introduced the legend of the LXX in the *Jewish Antiquities*: he treated the figure of Aristeas as a real pagan and not as a *nom de plume* for a Jewish author.[12] Josephus's refusal to name his compatriots may have been a result of knowing them through Polyhistor's *Concerning the Jews*, but it probably also reflects a mindset: Josephus did not want to acknowledge any Jewish predecessors apart from the LXX.

Josephus's refusal to acknowledge his Jewish predecessors means that we can only determine his indebtedness to a Jewish author by comparing texts; we have no attributions. One of the most important potential sources was Philo of Alexandria. While the question whether Josephus knew the works of Philo has been asked with some frequency, there is not a satisfactory study on their relationship.[13] The purpose of this article is to indicate the basic areas that require investigation and to offer some tentative conclusions.

The Story of Israel

The first area that requires investigation is the way that the two retold the story of Israel. There are two places in Josephus's *Jewish Antiquities* where his retelling of the biblical text has clusters of similarities to the accounts that we find in Philo. The first is his account of creation.[14] While Josephus's treatment is brief, it recalls Philo's treatment in *On the creation of the cosmos*

---

[9] For an analysis see Gregory E. Sterling, *Historiography & Self-definition: Josephos, Luke-Acts, and Apologetic Historiography* (NovTSup 64; Leiden: Brill, 1992), 263–284.

[10] Josephus, *CA* 1.218. For details see John M. G. Barclay, *Against Apion: Translation and Commentary* (Flavius Josephus Translation and Commentary 10; Leiden: Brill, 2007), 124–125.

[11] Josephus, *BJ* 1.17.

[12] Josephus, *AJ* 12.17. For Josephus's use of the *Letter of Aristeas* see André Pelletier, *Flavius Josèphe, Adaptateur de la Lettre d'Aristée: Une reaction atticisante contre la Koiné* (Paris: C. Kincksieck, 1962).

[13] The most important summary of older works is Louis H. Feldman, *Josephus and Modern Scholarship (1937–1980)* (Berlin: de Gruyter, 1984), 410–18.

[14] This is a significant expansion of Gregory E. Sterling, "Recherché or Representative? What is the Relationship between Philo's Treatises and Greek-Speaking Judaism?" *SPhA* 11 (1999): 1–30, esp. 27–29.

in striking ways. They both have similar prefaces to the creation account: they contrasted Moses with other legislators who had used myths to construct their creation accounts[15] and argued that the function of the creation story was to demonstrate the harmony of the law with the cosmos.[16] The accounts themselves also have some telling agreements. Philo made a great deal out of the use of the cardinal number "one" (μία) versus the ordinal numbers "second, third, fourth, fifth, sixth, and seventh." This was one of the lines of demarcation between the intelligible and sense-perceptible worlds in his commentary.[17] Josephus was aware of the distinction but refused to discuss its significance: "This would be the first day (πρώτη ἡμέρα), but Moses called it one (μία). I could provide an explanation now, but since I promised to set out the bases of all things by writing a separate work, I defer the interpretation of this point until then."[18] Although Josephus repeatedly referred to this planned work, he apparently never completed it.[19] The only hint of Josephus' understanding of "day one" is the general description of the planned work given just lines above the reference we cited. Josephus wrote: "For those, however, who want to explore the rationale for each point, the investigation would be profound and very philosophical." He then made his first reference to the proposed work: "I am going to defer it for the moment, but if God gives me time, I will attempt to write a work after this one."[20] The hint is that this matter is profound and very philosophical. While this is not the same as saying that

---

[15] Philo, *Opif.* 1–2 // Josephus, *AJ* 1.22–24. Note that Philo draws the contrast with two types: those who set out a bare lawcode and those who "conceal the truth with mythical fabrications" (οἱ δέ ... μυθικοῖς πλάσμασι τὴν ἀλήθειαν ἐπικρύψαντες); Josephus only makes the latter comparison (οἱ μὲν γὰρ ἄλλοι νομοθέται τοῖς μύθοις ἐξακολουθήσαντες).

[16] Philo, *Opif.* 3 // Josephus, *AJ* 1.24.

[17] On this see my treatment in "'Day One': Platonizing Exegetical Traditions of Genesis 1:1–5 in John and Jewish Authors," *SPhA* 17 (2005): 118–140, esp. 130–135, for discussion and bibliography.

[18] Josephus, *AJ* 1.29.

[19] Josephus, *AJ* 1.25, 29, 192, 214; 3.94, 143, 205, 230, 257, 259, 264; 4.198; 20.268.

[20] Josephus, *AJ* 1.25. There has been a debate over whether Josephus wrote this proposed work or not. Some think that it is included in *CA* (e.g., Hans Petersen, "Real and Alleged Projects of Josephus," *AJP* 79 [1958]: 263–65) or possibly in CA 2.145ff. (Christine Gerber, *Ein Bild des Judentums für Nichtjuden von Flavius Josephus: Untersuchungen zu seiner Schrift Contra Apionem* [AGAJU 40; Leiden/New York/Köln: E. J. Brill, 1997], 64–65, who pointed out that this could not be the full realization of the promised work but might have made it superfluous) or in a revised edition of *AJ* (e.g., David Altshuler, "The Treatise ΠΕΡΙ ΕΘΩΝ ΚΑΙ ΑΙΤΙΩΝ 'On Customs and Causes' by Flavius Josephus," *JQR* 69 [1978]: 226–232). Others argue that Josephus never wrote it (e.g., Geza Vermes, "A Summary of the Law by Flavius Josephus," *NovT* 24 [1982]: 290).

day one referred to the intelligible world, it is a statement that is compatible with this position.[21]

The compatibility is stronger than broad similarities. Philo and Josephus both used the verb "adorn" (διακοσμεῖν) to describe God's adornment of the heavens on the fourth day.[22] Since the days of Anaxagoras, the verb and noun had become important terms in Greek philosophy to describe the order of the cosmos.[23] The verb does not appear in the LXX's account of creation, although the noun κόσμος meaning "adornment" does in Genesis 2:1. While Josephus could have made the connection between God's adornment of the cosmos on the fourth day and the summary in Gen 2:1, it is far more likely that he was drawing on a source that had greater philosophical sophistication than he did and already used it on the fourth day.

Similarly, Josephus used the verb "create" (δημιουργεῖν) to describe God's work on the sixth day.[24] The verb does not occur in the LXX's account, but is common in Philo's version that drew upon Plato's famous metaphor of the creator as Demiurge in the *Timaeus*.[25]

Finally, as Josephus began to discuss Genesis 2 he said: "And here after the seventh day, Moses began to philosophize (φυσιολογεῖν) speaking about the formation of humans in this way."[26] What does he mean by "to philosophize"?[27] Unfortunately he only provided a literal retelling of the narrative. I wonder, however, if he meant to use it as a means of demarcating the first and the second creation accounts in Genesis in much the same way that Philo had when he used the two accounts as a means of drawing a second line between the intelligible and the sense-perceptible worlds.[28] While the evidence does not permit certainty, it seems to be not only possible but probable that Josephus had read Philo's *On the creation of the cosmos* and drew from it as he paraphrased Genesis 1.

---

[21] The tradition is attested beyond Philo in John 1:1–5 and 2 *Enoch* 24.2–26.3. See Sterling, "'Day One'," 118–40.

[22] Philo, *Opif.* 45, 47, 53, 62 (see also §§ 40, 62 for the third day); Josephus, *AJ* 1.31.

[23] Anaxagoras, Frg 59; Plato, *Tim.* 37d; Pseudo-Aristotle, *Mund.* 392b.

[24] Josephus, *AJ* 1.31.

[25] Philo, *Opif.* 10, 13, 16, 21, 52, 55, 63, 76, 88, 131, 140, 142 (for the verb) and 10, 18, 36, 68, 72, 138, 139, 146, 171 (for the noun). See Plato, *Tim.* 28b. Philo used the noun δημιουργός in § 36 and elsewhere to refer to God. Josephus later claimed that Abraham was the first to declare that God as the δημιουργός was one (*AJ* 1.155), a statement that echoes Philo's credo (*Opif.* 171). On the Platonic background of this imagery see David T. Runia, *Philo of Alexandria and the* Timaeus *of Plato* (PhilAnt 44; Leiden: Brill, 1986), 107–11.

[26] Josephus, *AJ* 1.34.

[27] On the term see Steven di Mattei, "Moses *Physiologia* and the Meaning and Use of *Physikos* in Philo of Alexandria's Exegetical Method," *SPhA* 18 (2006): 3–32.

[28] Philo, *Opif.* 129–30.

The second place where there is a significant cluster of agreements is in the cosmological interpretation of the tabernacle.[29] Philo's accounts are much fuller than Josephus's summary.[30] While the two differ in numerous aspects, there are some striking similarities. They both have a cosmological understanding of the tabernacle in general and in specific details:[31] they both argue that the twelve loaves represent the twelve months of the year,[32] the seven branches of the candelabrum represent the seven planets,[33] and the four materials of the tapestries are symbols of the four elements of the cosmos.[34] They are even closer in their agreements when they interpreted the cosmological significance of the high priest's apparel. I say closer in the sense that the account in Josephus follows closely—although not precisely —the interpretation in Philo's *The Life of Moses*. Philo's account in the *Questions and Answers on Exodus* gives moral interpretations as well as cosmological interpretations and is not as close. Both Philo and Josephus understood that the high priest's tunic contained symbols for the four elements, although they differ in their precise identifications.[35] They both argued that the two stones on the shoulders were the sun and the moon[36] and that the twelve stones on the breastplate represented the zodiac.[37] In short, there is enough agreement to suggest that they knew a common tradition. Is there enough evidence to suggest literary dependence? We will return to the question below.

In addition to these two major locations there are a significant number of examples where the two agree in providing details not in the biblical text. For example, they both characterized the Egyptian oppression of the Jews in Egypt with the same cognates, cognates not found in the LXX. They

[29] For general treatments see Jean Danielou, "La symbolique du temple de Jérusalem chez Philon et Josèphe," in *Le symbolisme cosmique des monuments religieux: Actes de la conférence international qui a eu lieu sous les auspices de l'Is. M.E.O. à Rome. Avril-Mai 1955* (Série orientale 14; Rome: Istituto italiano per il medio ed estremo oriente, 1957), 83–90 and Ursula Früchtel, *Die kosmologischen Vorstellungen bei Philo von Alexandrien: Ein Beitrag zur Geschichte der Genesisexegese* (Leiden: Brill, 1968), 98–100.

[30] Philo, *Mos.* 2.71–140; *QE* 2.51–124; Josephus, *AJ* 3.180–187.

[31] Philo *QE* 2.83; *Spec.* 1.66; and *Mos.* 2.89 (the tabernacle as a temple); Josephus, *AJ* 3.180; cf. also *BJ* 5.212–214.

[32] Philo, *Spec.* 1.172; Josephus, *AJ* 3.182; cf. also *BJ* 5.217.

[33] Philo, *Mos.* 2.103; *QE* 2.75; *Her.* 221; Josephus, *AJ* 3.183; cf. also *BJ* 2.517.

[34] Philo, *QE* 2.85; *Mos.* 2.88 (a slightly different order); Josephus, *AJ* 3.184.

[35] Philo, *Mos.* 2.117–118, violet=air, flowers=earth, pomegranates=water, bells=harmony between earth and water; Josephus, *AJ* 3.184, linen=earth, violet=heaven, pomegranates=lightning, bells=thunder.

[36] Philo, *Mos.* 2.122; *QE* 2.109; Josephus, *AJ* 3.185.

[37] Philo, *Mos.* 1.124; *QE* 2.112; *Spec.* 1.87; Josephus, *AJ* 3.186.

both described the oppression as "acts of insolence" (ὕβρεις).[38] While the biblical text does not make a distinction between the Egyptian and the Israelites until the fourth plague,[39] Philo and Josephus claimed that a distinction was made with the very first plague when the Nile turned to blood for the Egyptians but not for the Israelites,[40] a tradition that is later attested in *Deuteronomy Rabbah*.[41] This list could be expanded at great length; however, the evidence that this type of material offers only proves that they knew common traditions.

The Law

The second large area of similarity deals with their presentations of the Jewish law. There are three areas that require comment. First, Philo and Josephus provided a common panegyric for the law: Philo gave his as an introduction to the story of the translation of the LXX in his *Life of Moses*;[42] Josephus gave his as a summary of the law code in *Against Apion*.[43] The two made the same arguments in the same sequence with some of the same details. They opened with a claim that the law had not changed in contrast to the codes of other peoples. Philo wrote: "The laws of Moses alone are firm, unshakeable, immovable, stamped as it were with the seals of nature herself and remain secure from the day they were written until the present and our hope is that they will remain for all future ages, as if immortal (ἀθάνατα), as long as the sun, and moon, and the entire heaven and cosmos exist."[44] Josephus expressed it more simply as "our law remains immortal (ἀθάνατος)."[45] The second stage of their argument is to point out that other people have come to admire the Jewish law code and embraced Jewish practices including Sabbath observance[46] and fasts on holy days inspired by the fast of Yom Kippur.[47] The common twofold argument and the specific

---

[38] Philo, *Mos.* 1.72; Josephus, *AJ* 2.268; 4.242 (Josephus uses the singular). Cf. also 2.202 for the verb.

[39] Exod 8:22.

[40] Philo, *Mos.* 1.144; Josephus, *AJ* 2.295.

[41] *Deut. Rab.* 3:8.

[42] Philo, *Mos.* 2.12–24.

[43] Josephus, *CA* 2.276–286.

[44] Philo, *Mos.* 2.14. See §§ 12–16 for the full argument.

[45] Josephus, *CA* 2.277. See §§ 276–279 for the full argument.

[46] Philo, *Mos.* 2.21–22 (see §§ 17–24 for the full argument) and Josephus, *CA* 2.282 (see §§ 280–286 for the full argument).

[47] Philo, *Mos.* 2.23–24 and Josephus, *CA* 2.282. See also *AJ* 3.240 and Strabo in *AJ* 14.66. It is possible that Josephus had Sabbath fastings in mind since he goes on to mention the

thematic similarities are so striking that, in combination with the similarities in the treatment of the high priest's apparel, it appears to me probable that Josephus had read Philo's *Life of Moses*.[48]

The second set of texts that we need to examine is the summaries of the Mosaic law code. Eusebius, the bishop of Caesarea who early in his life helped to catalogue Philo's works in the library at Caesarea, noted the striking agreements between the summary of the law in Philo's *Hypothetica* and Josephus's *Against Apion*.[49] After he gave Philo's account, he introduced Josephus's treatment with these words: "Philo wrote the preceding. Josephus narrated an account similar to his in the second book of his work *Concerning the Antiquity of the Jews*."[50] Modern scholars have added a third similar account, Pseudo-Phocylides' sapiential hexameters.[51]

The arrangement of the laws among the three is different: Philo[52] and Josephus[53] both used editorial headings to set out five groups of laws. While Philo did not offer themes in his headings, Josephus did. They

---

lighting of lamps. There is some evidence that Jews may have fasted on Sabbath; at least there was a widespread perception that they did (Pompeius Trogus in Justin, *Epitome* 36.2.14 [Menahem Stern, *Greek and Latin Authors on Jews and Judaism* {3 vols.; Jerusalem: The Israel Academy of Sciences and Humanities, 1974}, 1:335, 337 {hereafter *GLAJJ*}]; Petronius, Frg 37 [*GLAJJ* 1:444]; Martial 4.4 [*GLAJJ* 1:523–524]; and Suetonius, *Aug.* 76.2 [*GLAJJ* 2:110]. Cf. also Strabo in Josephus, AJ 14.66 [*GLAJJ* 1:276–277], who appears to have confused the Sabbath with Yom Kippur on the basis of the common link of fasting). For details see Margaret H. Williams, "Being a Jew in Rome: Sabbath Fasting as an Expression of Romano-Jewish Identity," in *Negotiating Diaspora: Jewish Strategies in the Roman Empire* (ed. John M. G. Barclay; Library of Second Temple Studies 45; London/New York: T&T Clark, 2004), 8–18.

[48] So also Barclay, *Against Apion*, 359.

[49] For full details on this section see Gregory E. Sterling, "Universalizing the Particular: Natural Law in Second Temple Jewish Ethics," *SPhA* 15 (2003): 64–80.

[50] Eusebius, *Praep. ev.* 8.7.21.

[51] For major recent treatments see James E. Crouch, *The Origin and Intention of the Colossian Haustafel* (Göttingen: Vandenhoeck & Ruprecht, 1972); Max Küchler, *Frühjüdische Weisheitstraditionen: Zum Fortgang weisheitlichen Denkens im Bereich des frühjüdischen Jahweglaubens* (OBO 26; Freiburg/Göttingen; Vandenhoeck & Ruprecht, 1979); Karl-Wilhelm Niebuhr, *Gesetz und Paränese: Katechismusartige Weisungsreihen in der frühjüdischen Literatur* (WUNT 2.28; Tübingen: Mohr Siebeck, 1987), 6–72, esp. 31–72; George P. Carras, "Dependence or Common Tradition in Philo *Hypothetica* viii 6.10–7.20 and Josephus *Contra Apionem* 2.190–219," *SPhA* 5 (1993): 24–47; Christine Gerber, *Ein Bild des Judentums für Nichtjuden von Flavius Josephus: Untersuchungen zu seiner Schrift Contra Apionem* (AGJU 40; Leiden: Brill 1997), 100–118; Katell Berthelot, *Philanthropia judaica: Le débat autour de la 'misanthropie' des lois juives dans l'Antiquité* (JSJSup 76; Leiden: Brill 2003), 368–374; and Barclay, *Against Apion*, 353–361.

[52] Philo, *Hypoth.* 8.7.1, 3, 6, 8, 9.

[53] Josephus, *CA* 2.190, 199, 209, 211, 215.

appear to be echoing the structure of the Pentateuch.[54] Pseudo-Phocylides arranged his material thematically but did not offer headings.[55] Within these literary arrangements, the three have at least twenty-six laws in common, although only thirteen occur among all three. Philo and Josephus have twenty-one laws in common. They also both make many of these capital offenses,[56] even though the same violations are not capital offenses in the biblical text or elsewhere in their own writings. There have been a number of explanations offered to account for these agreements, including that Josephus knew and used Philo. While this is possible, it does not explain the material held in common with Pseudo-Phocylides.

I have noticed that the specific laws tend to come in thematic clusters. By a cluster I mean a group of laws that deal with a common topic. There are two criteria for a cluster: the laws must be in close textual proximity within a work and they must be in close proximity in at least two of the three authors. If we apply these criteria we discover that there are nine clusters: the first deals with sexuality: homosexuality,[57] adultery,[58] and rape to be specific.[59] The second focuses on violations of a person or a person's property: the abuse of a slave,[60] theft,[61] and irreverence towards a higher authority.[62] Philo and Josephus have particularly close connections in these two clusters, although they have some variations in sequence. The third cluster is the household code: the husband-wife relationship,[63] parent-child relationship,[64] and the place of elders.[65] All three texts connect honoring

---

[54] See also the Psalter (1–41, 42–72, 73–89. 90–106, 107–150), the *Megillot* (Ruth, Song, Eccl, Lam, Esther), Ethiopic *1 Enoch* (1–36, 37–71, 72–82, 83–90, 91–107), Matthew's discourses (5:1–7:28; 10:5–42; 13:1–52; 18:1–35; 23:1–25:46 or 24:1–25:46), and *Pirqe 'Aboth* 1, 2, 3, 4, 5 [chapter 6=*Kallah* 8 and was added to fit the liturgical needs of having a chapter for each Sabbath during the Omer period]).

[55] On the structure of Pseudo-Phocylides see Walter T. Wilson, *The Mysteries of Righteousness: The Literary Composition and Genre of the Sentences of Pseudo-Phocylides* (TSAJ 40; Tübingen: Mohr Siebeck, 1994). I do not see the same formal structure that he does, but prefer the following clusters: 9–21, justice; 22–30, generosity; 42–47, money; 38–50, integrity; 59–69b, moderation; 70–75, envy; 97–121, death; 122–131, speech; 132–152, avoidance of evil; 153–174, work; 175–206, marriage; 207–217, children, 218–227, the family.

[56] Philo, *Hypoth.* 8.7.1, 9, for the frames. Philo grouped capital offenses in the first two of his groups of laws and mentioned the death penalty again in the third. Josephus, *CA* 2.215, makes a simple statement.

[57] Philo, *Hypoth.* 8.7.1; Josephus, *CA* 2.199, 201, 216; Pseudo-Phocylides 3, 190–192.

[58] Philo, *Hypoth.* 8.7.1; Josephus, *CA* 2.199, 201, 215; Pseudo-Phocylides 3, 177–183.

[59] Philo, *Hypoth.* 8.7.1; Josephus, *CA* 2.200, 215; Pseudo-Phocylides 198.

[60] Philo, *Hypoth.* 8.7.2; Josephus, *CA* 2.215; Pseudo-Phocylides 225–226.

[61] Philo, *Hypoth.* 8.7.2; Josephus, *CA* 2.216; Pseudo-Phocylides 6.

[62] Philo, *Hypoth.* 8.7.2; Josephus, *CA* 2.217.

[63] Philo, *Hypoth.* 8.7.3; Josephus, *CA* 2.201.

[64] Philo, *Hypoth.* 8.7.3; Josephus, *CA* 2.206; Pseudo-Phocylides 207–209, cf. also 8.

parents with honoring God. The fourth cluster deals with property rights: deposits[66] and theft.[67] The fifth and sixth clusters combine three of the four laws of Buzyges, the Athenian hero who pronounced curses on those who failed to provide fire, water, directions, or burial.[68] The fifth cluster prohibits the denial of fire and water[69] and commands Jews to give food to those in need.[70] The sixth expands Buzyges' curse against denying burial[71] to include a prohibition not to disturb a grave.[72] The seventh sets out laws on human reproduction: sterilization,[73] abortion,[74] infanticide,[75] and inter- course with a pregnant wife.[76] The eighth addresses financial transactions: the problems of scales and measurements. [77] The last consists of an argu- ment *a minore ad majus* by requiring kind treatment of animals:[78] do not empty a nest[79] or reject the pleas of an animal.[80] How do we explain these clusters of laws? They are not all due to common clusterings in the biblical text; in some cases the biblical laws are widely scattered. I suggest that they reflect synagogue instruction on ethical topics. Philo and Josephus suggest this by associating their presentations with the Sabbath when instruction was given.[81] I do not therefore find this as evidence that Josephus knew and used Philo's *Hypothetica*.

The third pair of texts is the sequence of the laws treated by Philo in his *On the virtues* and by Josephus in his summaries in *Jewish Antiquities* 3 and 4

---

[65] Josephus, *CA* 2.206; Pseudo-Phocylides 220–222.

[66] Philo, *Hypoth.* 8.7.6; Josephus, *CA* 2.208; cf. also 2.216.

[67] Philo, *Hypoth.* 8.7.6; Josephus, *CA* 2.208 (cf. also 2.216); Pseudo-Phocylides 18.

[68] On Buzyges see Jacob Bernays, "Philon's Hypothetika und die Verwunschungen des Buzyges in Athen," *Monatsberichte des Kgl. Akademie der Wissenschaften zu Berlin* (1876): 589–609; reprinted in *Gesammelte Abhandlungen von Jacob Bernays* (ed. Hermann Usener; Berlin: W. Hertz, 1885), 1:262–282, esp. 277–282. Philo mentioned Buzyges in *Hypoth.* 8.7.8.

[69] Philo, *Hypoth.* 8.7.6; Josephus, *CA* 2.211.

[70] Philo, *Hypoth.* 8.7.6; Josephus, *CA* 2.211; Pseudo-Phocylides 22–30, 109.

[71] Philo, *Hypoth.* 8.7.7; Josephus, *CA* 2.211; Pseudo-Phocylides 99.

[72] Philo, *Hypoth.* 8.7.7; Pseudo-Phocylides 100–101.

[73] Philo, *Hypoth.* 8.7.7; Pseudo-Phocylides 187.

[74] Philo, *Hypoth.* 8.7.7; Josephus, *CA* 2.202; Pseudo-Phocylides 184.

[75] Josephus, *CA* 2202.; Pseudo-Phocylides 185.

[76] Josephus, *CA* 2.202; Pseudo-Phocylides 186 (?).

[77] Philo, *Hypoth.* 8.7.8; Josephus, *CA* 2.216; Pseudo-Phocylides 14–15. They use different terms.

[78] On this argument see Abraham Terian, "Some Stock Arguments for the Magnani- mity of the Law in Hellenistic Jewish Apologetics," in *Jewish Law Association Studies 1: The Touro Conference Volume* (ed. Bernard S. Jackson; Chico: Scholars Press, 1985), 141–49.

[79] Philo, *Hypoth.* 8.7.9; Josephus, *CA* 2.213; Pseudo-Phocylides 84–85.

[80] Philo, *Hypoth.* 8.7.9; Josephus, *CA* 2.213.

[81] Philo, *Hypoth.* 8.7.10–20; Josephus, *CA* 2.171–178.

and in *Against Apion* 2.[82] The question is whether Josephus used Philo's work in setting up the sequence of laws that he treated.[83] If we begin by comparing the laws in Philo's *On the virtues* with Josephus's summary in *Against Apion*, there are some common clusters. Philo has a series of laws that deal with foreigners, a cluster that matches the third group in Josephus.[84] Philo next explored the treatment of enemies who are included in the fourth group of laws in Josephus's summary.[85] Both dealt specifically with the treatment of women captives, although Josephus only mentioned them in a list while Philo has an extensive discussion. Philo then turned to the treatment of the animals of enemies. Josephus also mentioned the treatment of animals in this section, but dealt with the treatment of animals more broadly, not specifically with the treatment of the animals of enemies.[86] The two shared a common understanding of the function of all these laws: they taught φιλανθρωπία.[87] If we compared the summaries of laws in *Jewish Antiquities* 3 and 4, we would have similar results. It seems to me that the evidence again points in the direction of common instruction about the laws in synagogues, although I think that there is still work to do in this area.

Historical Figures and Events

The final area that needs at least a nod is the historical. There are several examples of overlap between Philo and Josephus as they described major events and figures. One example will need to suffice. The event about which we have a little detail in Philo's life was his role in the embassy to Gaius. Philo described this at length in a treatise devoted to it.[88] Josephus provided a brief account in the *Jewish Antiquities* 18.[89] The two accounts are in basic agreement, but differ in details. The most important difference is

---

[82] Philo, *Virt.* 82–160 and Josephus, *AJ* 3.90–286 and 34.196–302; *CA* 2.190–214.

[83] Berthelot, *Philanthropia Judaica*, 374–76, argues that he did on the basis of thematic comparisons between Philo, *Virt.* 82–160 and Josephus, *CA* 2.190–214; Barclay, *Against Apion*, 359–60, cautiously follows Berthelot; Walter T. Wilson, *On Virtues: Introduction, Translation, and Commentary* (PACS 3; Leiden: Brill, 2011), 37–39, argues that both knew a common tradition although he does not consider *CA* 2.190–214.

[84] Philo, *Virt.* 102–108 and Josephus, *CA* 2.209–210.

[85] Philo, *Virt.* 109–119 and Josephus, *CA* 2.211–214.

[86] Philo, *Virt.* 116–119 and Josephus, *CA* 2.213–214.

[87] This is the virtue under consideration in Philo, *Virt.* 51–174. Philo uses the term in §§ 51, 66, 76, 80, 88, 95, 99, 105, 121, 140. Josephus used it in *CA* 2.213.

[88] Philo, *Legat.*

[89] Josephus, *AJ* 18.257–260.

that Josephus collapsed the two meetings the Jewish delegation had with Gaius into one.[90] The two authors varied in the personnel and their roles. Philo stated that the Jewish delegation had five members; Josephus stated that the delegations consisted of three.[91] It is unlikely that the Alexandrian delegation consisted of fewer representatives than the Jewish delegation. It may be that Josephus knew names of the three Alexandrian delegates and drew his conclusion from this.[92] In Philo's account Isidorus is the lead spokesperson for the Alexandria delegation and accused the Jews of not offering sacrifices to Gaius. Josephus replaced him with Apion, perhaps a deliberate replacement reflecting his own view of Apion whom Philo never named.[93] Josephus then said that as Philo—the head of the Jewish delegation—began to speak, Gaius cut him off.[94] Philo never described himself as the head of the delegation, although he did indicate that he was the oldest and best educated among the delegates. He also presented himself as addressing the Jewish delegation following the first meeting when he felt compelled to check what he considered to be the naïveté of the Jewish delegation.[95] It may be that Josephus had independent knowledge of Philo's status, guessed at it, or that he made Philo's role after the first meeting with Gaius official when he collapsed the two meetings into one. Josephus concluded his account with Philo's statement to the delegates that Gaius had made God his enemy. There is no indication of this in Philo's account. However, immediately after Philo's report of the second meeting, the Alexandrian ended the *Embassy* with a promise to write a palinode.[96] The work has unfortunately been lost. However, if the *Embassy* is part of the five volume work that Eusebius mentioned,[97] it is likely that all of the volumes dealt with the divine overthrow of governing authorities that oppressed the Jews: Pilate, Sejanus, Flaccus, and Gaius.[98] The palinode

---

[90] Philo, *Legat.* 181–183, 349–367.

[91] Philo, *Legat.* 370; Josephus, *AJ* 18.257. On the embassies see François Kayser, "Ambassades Alexandrines à Rome (Iᵉʳ-IIᵉ siècle)," *REA* 105 (2003): 435–68.

[92] He knew the names of Isidorus, Lampo, and Apion. See Pieter J. Sijpesteijn, "The Legationes ad Gaium," *JJS* 15 (1964): 87–96.

[93] Philo, *Legat.* 355; Josephus, *AJ* 18.257–259.

[94] Josephus, *AJ* 18.259.

[95] Philo, *Legat.* 182–183.

[96] Philo, *Legat.* 373.

[97] Eusebius, *Hist. eccl.* 2.5.1. Cf. also 2.5.6; 2.6.3; 2.18.8.

[98] If we follow Eusebius' lead and the internal cross references in Philo we can reconstruct the five works as follows: book one, Pilate (Eusebius, *Hist. eccl.* 2.5.7); book 2, Sejanus (Philo, *Flacc.* 1, 191; Eusebius, *Chron.*; cf. *Hist. eccl.* 2.5.6–7); book 3, *In Flaccum*; book 4, *Legatio*; book 5, palinode (Philo, *Legat.* 373). For details see Pieter van der Horst, *Philo's Flaccus: The First Pogram. Introduction, Translation and Commentary* (PACS 2; Leiden: Brill, 2003), 4–6.

would have provided the story of Gaius's assassination. The two treatises would have been companions in much the way that *Against Flaccus* has two parts that revolve around the reversal of Flaccus's status.[99] Josephus may have simply made the deduction based on his own theology and knowledge of Gaius's history or could have made the statement as a summary of Philo's palinode. We can only guess.

This short exercise indicates the challenges that one faces when asking whether Josephus used Philo's works for historical events and figures. In virtually every case, they differ and it is clear that Josephus had access to information beyond Philo and that both authors adjusted the narrative to meet the needs of their own agenda. We can say that it is possible that he read *Against Flaccus* and the *Embassy*, but it is difficult to say more.

Conclusions

Did Josephus know and read the works of Philo. It appears to me very likely that Josephus had not only read but drew from *On the creation of the cosmos* and *The Life of Moses* He may have read some of the other treatises in the Exposition of the Law, especially *On the virtues*. It is also possible that he read some of the *Questions and Answers on Genesis and Exodus*, but there is little to suggest that he had read and been influenced by the Allegorical Commentary. He may also have known *Against Flaccus* and the *Embassy*, but he clearly knew more about some of the same events they address.

The textual evidence that we have considered correlates with the historical evidence that we have. Josephus had the opportunity to read Philo's works. We know that Josephus visited Alexandria[100] and lived in Rome.[101] Philo's works were certainly extant in Alexandria when Josephus visited and some of them may well have been in Rome when the historian lived in Vespasian's former house. The evidence for the preservation of Philo's works in Rome is indirect, but worth noting. In addition to Josephus, there is some evidence that Pseudo-Longinus knew *On drunkenness*[102] and even enough evidence that Plotinus knew Philo's works to generate a debate.[103] The works could have been preserved in several ways. Philo may

---

[99] Philo, *Flac.* 1–96 vs. 97–191. For details see van der Horst, *Philo's Flaccus*, 6–9.

[100] Josephus, *V* 415–16. Cf. *BJ* 4.656–662, where Josephus described the journey of Vespasian and Titus, but did not indicate that he had accompanied them.

[101] Josephus, *V* 422–23.

[102] Compare Philo, *Ebr.* 198 and Pseudo-Longinus, *Subl.* 44.1–5. For details see Sterling, "Recherché or Representative," 24–26

[103] For a summary with bibliography see Sterling, "Recherché or Representative," 29.

have brought some with him to Rome when he took up residence in the capital as a member of the Jewish embassy.[104] Allen Kerkeslager has argued that the Herodian family may have helped to preserve Philo's works in Rome.[105] It is also worth noting that Tiberius Julius Alexander lived in Rome following the revolt.[106] While he may not have had any personal interest in his uncle's works, he might have helped to see that copies were made, especially since he was the literary interlocutor in two of the dialogues.[107] There are thus several possible ways that Philo's works might have come to Rome.

When Josephus introduced Philo as the head of the Jewish delegation, he said three things about him: he was "a man of the highest repute, the brother of Alexander the alabarch, and not inexperienced in philosophy."[108] He never mentioned his writings, but this was high praise. It was as high as Josephus would offer to a compatriot whose works easily eclipsed his own in exegetical and philosophical sophistication.

Yale Divinity School

---

[104] Maren Niehoff, *Jewish Exegesis and Homeric Scholarship in Alexandria* (Cambridge: Cambridge University Press, 2011), 170–77, has suggested that Philo wrote the Exposition of the Law while in Rome (39–41 c.e.). I think that it more likely that he wrote the commentary while in Alexandria, perhaps even after he returned from Rome.

[105] Allen Kerkeslager, "Agrippa I and the Judeans of Alexandria in the Wake of the Violence in 38 c.e.," *REJ* 168 (2009): 1–49, esp. 35–45.

[106] See Juvenal, *Sat.* 1.127–31; *CPJ* 418b.

[107] Philo, *Prov.* and *Anim.*

[108] Josephus, *AJ* 18.259.

The Studia Philonica Annual 25 (2013) 115–138

PHILO, JUDAEUS? A RE-EVALUATION OF WHY CLEMENT CALLS PHILO "THE PYTHAGOREAN"*

JENNIFER OTTO

Introduction

In a well-known article, David T. Runia asks, "Why Does Clement Call Philo 'the Pythagorean'?"[1] Runia finds the epithet curious, expecting that

* This article is an expanded version of my paper of the same title presented at the 2012 SBL in Chicago, USA. I would like to express my gratitude to Ellen Birnbaum and Sarah Pearce for organizing the panel. I would also like to thank the members of the Philo group for their helpful comments and suggestions, as well as Ellen B. Aitken for reading earlier drafts of this paper. My research was supported by a Vanier Fellowship awarded by the Social Sciences and Humanities Research Council of Canada. Translations of Clement's texts are based on the Greek text of the *Sources Chrétiennes* series and are my own, with consultation of the French translations of *Sources Chrétiennes* and the English translations of Alexander Roberts and James Donaldson, *The Fathers of the Second Century* (*ANF* 2; Edinburgh: T&T Clark, 1867; reprint Grand Rapids: Eerdmans, 1979) and John Ferguson, *Clement of Alexandria: Stromateis Books one to three* (The Fathers of the Church 85; Washington: The Catholic University of America Press, 1991) unless otherwise noted.

[1] David T. Runia, "Why Does Clement Call Philo "the Pythagorean"?" *VC* 49.1 (1995): 1–22. Runia's study has been cited frequently over the past decade, with scholars generally concurring with his findings while occasionally proposing alternative possibilities. Mark J. Edwards suggests "perhaps his sobriquet for Philo means no more than that the Pythagoreans would have recognised him as an exponent of their own hermeneutical methods" in *Origen against Plato* (Burlington: Ashgate, 2002), 131. Eric F. Osborn declares that Runia's article has "elucidated" the issue but subsequently states that "Alexandrian tradition had already assimilated Philo in a stream of religious Platonism." Osborn also re-proposes Conybeare's claim that Clement is hiding Philo's Jewishness, contending, "Clement would have good reasons for not advertising his Jewish source. He is fighting on many fronts: against Marcionites who reject the OT and against Judaisers who think the Old facilitates an improvement on the New" in *Clement of Alexandria* (Cambridge: Cambridge University Press, 2008), 85. James Carleton Paget suggests the possibility that Clement's community had forgotten Philo's connection to Judaism in "Clement of Alexandria and the Jews" in *Jews, Christians and Jewish-Christians in Antiquity* (Tübingen: Mohr Siebeck, 2010), 94. Ilaria L.E. Ramelli cites Runia favourably in "The Birth of the Rome-Alexandria Connection: The Early Sources on Mark and Philo, and the Petrine Tradition" *SPhA* 23 (2011): 69–95, 79. Eugene Afonasin also avers his support of Runia in "The Pythagorean Way of Life in Clement of Alexandria and Iamblichus" in *Iamblichus and the Foundations of Late Platonism*

Clement would instead refer to Philo as a Jew or, more likely, a Hebrew, as his Christian successors did.[2] Runia begins his investigation by noting that in one of the two passages in which Clement identifies Philo as a Pythagorean, he also employs another curious epithet in reference to a Jewish source, calling Aristobulus "the Peripatetic."[3] Runia argues that since neither Philo nor Aristobulus can be shown to belong officially to either school, the epithets signal not school affiliation but "affinity of thought" with the respective traditions (p.16). Runia allows that a number of factors may have prompted Clement's description of Philo as a Pythagorean, as he would have been attuned to the Pythagorean elements of Philo's writings, especially his "penchant for arithmologizing exegesis" (p.10). Ultimately, Runia concludes that Clement's association of Philo with Pythagoreanism was intended primarily to indicate his affinity with Platonic philosophy, which by the second century C.E. was understood by many to be a continuation of a more ancient Pythagorean tradition (pp.10–12).[4]

Runia then considers the contexts in which Philo is called a Pythagorean, noting that Clement first uses the epithet while defending the

---

(ed. Eugene Afonasin, John Dillon and John F. Finamore; Leiden: Brill, 2012), 13–36. Piotr Ashwin- Siejkowski cites Runia favourably, but continues, "in my view, as the epithet 'Philo the Pythagorean' appears only once in four references to Philo, it was used spontaneously rather than deliberately as a sign of Philo's philosophical association. I believe that Clement was working simultaneously on various parts of his oeuvre, including the first Book, while reading Philo's commentaries to a specific biblical passage or reflecting on Philo's theory of achieving perfection, which included the classical Pythagorean quadrivium ..." *Clement of Alexandria: A Project of Christian Perfection* (London: T&T Clark, 2008), 50 n. 53. Ashwin-Siejkowski's argument is undercut by a factual error: Clement calls Philo "the Pythagorean" *twice*, not once, suggesting that the association is not spontaneous.

[2] "Now in my view the epithet 'Pythagorean' which Clement attaches to Philo is unexpected. It is surely surprising that he does not describe him as 'Philo the Jew' or, as might be more likely, 'Philo the Hebrew'... We would expect that Philo's role as a predecessor in the Jewish-Christian tradition, i.e., the tradition that ascribes authority to the Hebrew scriptures, was more important for Clement than an attachment to a philosophical school of thought" (Runia, "Philo the Pythagorean," 3). Neither Clement nor Origen ever refer to Philo as a Hebrew or as a Jew; Philo is first referred to as "the Hebrew" by Eusebius (*Hist. eccl.* 2.4.2; *Praep. ev.* 7.12–13), writing more than a century after Clement.

[3] *Strom.* 5.14.97.7 clarifies Aristobulus's relationship to Peripatetic philosophy, contending "he left many books, in which he demonstrated that Peripatetic philosophy is dependent on the Law of Moses and the other prophets."

[4] See also Henry Chadwick, *Early Christian Thought and the Classical Tradition: Studies in Justin, Clement, and Origen* (New York: Oxford University Press, 1966), 14: "The contemporary Neopythagoreans, for instance, had had considerable success in representing Plato as the great popularizer of Pythagorean doctrines, finding their theology especially in the *Timaeus* and the *Parmenides* and producing pseudepigraphic texts in which very early Pythagoreans expounded on Platonism."

antiquity of the Jewish people. Citing Annewies van den Hoek's analysis of Clement's Philonic borrowings in the *Stromateis*[5] and her conclusion that Philo functions for Clement primarily as an expert in the interpretation of the Pentateuch, Runia asserts that despite Clement's failure to identify Philo explicitly as a Jew, it is in "the Judaeo-Christian tradition where, also for Clement (in the light of his borrowings), [Philo] primarily belongs."[6] Clement does not bother to identify Philo as a Jew because "it is obvious enough, and does not need to be underlined" (p.13). Runia concludes that although Clement is neither embarrassed by Philo's Judaism nor attempting to hide his Jewish identity,[7] it nevertheless serves his apologetic interests to play down Philo's connection to Judaism.[8]

Runia is surely correct to conclude that Clement's description of Philo as a Pythagorean indicates Clement's recognition of his affinity with Pythagorean philosophy rather than his membership in a Pythagorean school.[9] In this article, however, I shall challenge his claim that Clement locates Philo in a "Judaeo-Christian tradition," as well as his suggestion that Clement neglects to mention Philo's Judaism because it was so obvious as to quite

---

[5] Annewies van den Hoek, *Clement of Alexandria and His Use of Philo in the Stromateis: An Early Christian Reshaping of a Jewish Model* (VCSup 3; Leiden: Brill, 1988).

[6] Runia, "Philo the Pythagorean," 16.

[7] As suggested by Frederick C. Conybeare, *Philo About the Contemplative Life* (Oxford: Clarendon, 1895, repr., New York: Garland, 1987), 328–29. Cited by Runia, "Philo the Pythagorean," 13 n. 73.

[8] "There is nothing remarkable about a Jew claiming the antiquity of his own race. Clement does not bother to tell his reader that Philo is Jewish" (Runia, "Philo the Pythagorean," 6). In the same context, as Runia admits, Clement *does* openly call Josephus a Jew. Challenging Runia's assertion, Eusebius argues in *Praep. ev.* 7.8 that the historian must consult a people's own traditions and writings if he wishes to know their history.

[9] The existence of "Pythagorean Schools" or communities in which one could be a member remains a matter of controversy. According to Dillon and Hershbell, "Tempting as it is to connect the Pythagoras legend with Pythagorean communities, there is no indisputable evidence for such communities in antiquity... But whether the Pythagorean communities portrayed by Iamblichus or his sources even existed, remains a subject for further examination. Certainly there were individuals such as Heraclides, Aristoxenus, or Iamblichus who kept Pythagoras's memory alive, but they themselves were not members of Pythagorean communities... the existence of Pythagorean communities may never be proved to everyone's satisfaction, and yet the vividness and detail with which Iamblichus or his sources portray the Pythagorean life suggests that it once flourished among a chosen few" (John Dillon and Jackson Hershbell, introduction to *On the Pythagorean Way of Life*, by Iamblichus [trans. John Dillon and Jackson Hershbell; Atlanta: Scholars Press, 1991], 16). See also Helmut Koester, *An Introduction to the New Testament Vol. I: History, Culture and Religion of the Hellenistic Age* (Philadelphia: Fortress Press, 1982), 374–76; John Dillon, *The Middle Platonists* (Ithaca: Cornell University Press, 1977), 379; Graham Anderson, *Sage, Saint, and Sophist: Holy Men and their Associates in the Early Roman Empire* (London/New York: Routledge, 1994), 12.

literally go without saying. Recent research illuminating the contested content of Christian and Jewish identities in the second and third centuries has complicated the definition of "Jew" and "Christian" in this period. A growing number of scholars argue that the criteria distinguishing Christian from Jew were not fixed until a relatively late date, with some, led by Daniel Boyarin, arguing that boundaries between Christians and Jews remained fluid into the fourth century c.e.[10] To say that Clement knew Philo to be a Jew, then, requires us to ask further, what, in Clement's mind, did it mean to be a Jew? Runia's definition of the "Judaeo-Christian tradition" as "the tradition that ascribes authority to the Hebrew scriptures" is similarly problematic, as it could potentially apply to an extremely broad variety of interpreters, including various streams of Gnostics, Neopythagoreans like Numenius, and even, as Clement contends, eminent Greeks including Plato and Pythagoras.[11] His assertion of a singular "Judaeo-Christian tradition" suggests a unity that is challenged by the diversity of hermeneutical positions and religious practices of groups who nevertheless claimed the Hebrew scriptures as authoritative.

It is therefore worthwhile once again to ask the question, why did Clement call Philo "the Pythagorean"? My investigation proceeds along two lines. I begin by illuminating Clement's conception of Pythagoreanism via an analysis of the eighty-five explicit references to Pythagoras and Pythagoreans in his corpus. I then compare my results with Clement's Philonic borrowings as evaluated by Annewies van den Hoek, mapping the overlap between Philonic material and Pythagorean references in an attempt to determine what was characteristically "Pythagorean" about Philo in Clement's mind. Secondly, I provide an overview of Clement's usage of the terms "Jew," "Hebrew," and "Israel" in order to clarify Clement's conception of what a Jew is and whether he implicitly locates Philo within

---

[10] Influential works in this field include Judith Lieu, *Image and Reality: The Jews in the World of the Christians in the Second Century* (Edinburgh: T&T Clark, 1996); Daniel Boyarin, *Border Lines: The Partition of Judaeo-Christianity* (Philadelphia: University of Pennsylvania Press, 2004); Adam H. Becker and Annette Yoshiko Reed, *The Ways that Never Parted: Jews and Christians in Late Antiquity and the Early Middle Ages* (TSAJ 95; Tübingen: Mohr Siebeck, 2003); James Carleton Paget, *Jews, Christians and Jewish Christians in Antiquity* (WUNT 251; Tübingen: Mohr Siebeck, 2010). Boyarin summarizes his argument thus: "In short, without the power of the Orthodox Church and the Rabbis to declare people heretics and outside the system—'neither Jews nor Christians,' in Jerome's words, in his famous letter to Augustine, it remains impossible to declare phenomenologically who is a Jew and who is a Christian" (Daniel Boyarin, "Martyrdom and the Making of Christianity and Judaism" *JECS* 6.4 [1998]: 577–627, 584).

[11] Runia, "Philo the Pythagorean," 3. Clement discusses foreign philosophers' reverence for the writings of Moses at *Str.* 1.22.

that category, and himself within a larger "Judaeo-Christian tradition." As a result of my analysis, I caution against the over-hasty acceptance of a theory of transmission that would have Philo's treatises passing directly from his own school or synagogue community to the so-called "Catechetical School" of Alexandria and its Christian teachers.

Clement on Pythagoras and the Pythagoreans

Clement is characteristically well-read on the subject of Pythagoras, his disciples, and his later interpreters.[12] A *TLG* search indicates that Clement mentions Pythagoras or Pythagoreans eighty-five times in his corpus, with a distribution among the individual works as indicated in the table below:

Table 1

Work	# of explicit references
Protrepticus	1
Paedogogus 1	1
Paedogogus 2	1
Paedogogus 3	0
Stromateis 1	31
Stromateis 2	7
Stromateis 3	4
Stromateis 4	9
Stromateis 5	24
Stromateis 6	4
Stromateis	2
Stromateis	0
Eclogae ex scripturis propheticus	1

[12] Eugene Afonasin has recently surveyed Clement's Pythagorean references, attempting to recreate a Clementine classroom lecture on Pythagorean philosophy: "Imagine now that we are students at the Alexandrian school allegedly founded by Clement's teacher Pantaenus, and listen to his lectures. What shall we learn about Pythagoras?" (17). Afonasin contends that traditional Pythagorean teachings "mean for [Clement] something more than just accidental references. Although sometimes he almost automatically copies from anthologies, in the majority of cases, the Pythagoreans (second only to Plato) supply him with necessary means to state his own position in a more conventional way" (21). See Eugene Afonasin, "The Pythagorean Way of Life in Clement of Alexandria and Iamblichus," *Iamblichus and the Foundations of Late Platonism*, 13–36.

The majority of the Pythagorean references are clustered in two locations, Book 1 and Book 5 of the *Stromateis*. As I shall demonstrate presently, these clusters correspond to two major rhetorical functions of Pythagoreanism in the *Stromateis*: in Book I, Pythagoras and Pythagoreans are invoked to support Clement's claim that the Greeks did not invent philosophy but derive their true doctrines from the "barbarian philosophy" communicated in the scriptures of the Jews; in Book 5, Pythagorean exegetical practices are put to use in defence of Clement's assertion that all true wisdom must be protected and promulgated via enigmas and other symbolic sayings or writings.

Pythagoras in Strom. 1

In *Stromateis* 1, Pythagoras figures prominently as an intermediary between Greek and Barbarian wisdom. Although esteemed as one of the original Greek philosophers, he is shown to have been born outside of Greece—exactly where is a matter of debate—and to have studied with many exotic teachers before introducing philosophy to Italy.[13] Although ancient, he is demonstrated to have lived centuries after Moses, the original barbarian philosopher. Clement argues that, among Pythagoras's many barbarian contacts, the ancient Hebrews had an outsized influence on his teachings. After rehearsing a tedious chronology of Greek and Hebrew history establishing the anteriority of Jewish philosophy, Clement charges the Greeks with stealing the wisdom of the Jews, citing Aristobulus's claim in *Strom.* 1.22.150 that "Pythagoras transferred many of our doctrines into his own."[14] The dependence of Plato and Pythagoras on the Jewish scriptures is also recognised by the Pythagorean Numenius, to whom Clement attributes the famous *bon mot*, "What is Plato but Moses speaking Attic Greek?"[15]

[13] On the life of Pythagoras, see *Strom.* 1.14.62–63; 1.15.66–70. Clement cites Aristarchus, Neanthes, Hippobotus, Aristoxenus, and Theopompus, none of whose works survive in full. These authors are also cited by Porphyry among the thirty-one sources for his Life of Pythagoras. Aristoxenus, floruit third-century B.C.E., wrote volumes on the Life of Pythagoras, the Pythagorean Sayings, and the Pythagorean Way of Life. Neanthes was likely a third century B.C.E. historian from Cyzicus. Theopompus, born c. 380 B.C.E. in Chios, was a historian whose works Clement criticises earlier in *Strom.* 1.1. Hippobotus, born c. 200 B.C.E., is frequently mentioned by Diogenes Laertius as a historian of philosophical schools. See Dillon and Hershbell, introduction to *Iamblichus, On the Pythagorean Way of Life*, 6–14.
[14] Πυθαγόρας πολλὰ τῶν παρ'ἡμῖν μετενέγκας εἰς τὴν ἑαυτοῦ δογματοποιίαν (*Strom.* 1.22.150.3). Here Aristobulus is quite unambiguously identified as belonging to the Jewish people.
[15] Τί γάρ ἐστι Πλάτων ἢ Μωυσῆς ἀττικίζων (*Strom.* 1.22.150.4).

Pythagorean Symbola in Strom. 5

In Book 5, Clement repeatedly invokes the Pythagorean *symbola* as examples of the enigmatic transmission of philosophical truths.[16] *Str.* 5.5 cites the agreement of the *ekklesia's* sacred texts with the highly-regarded Pythagorean *symbola* as proof that the church also teaches hidden doctrine through enigmatic expressions.[17] Clement argues that, like the Pythagoreans, the Law, the prophets, and Jesus also conceal their true teaching from outsiders, so that their hidden meaning may be understood only by initiates.[18] The hermeneutic of the Pythagoreans is thus recommended as

[16] Andrew Dinan, "Αἴνιγμα and Αἰνίττομαι in the Works of Clement of Alexandria." *Papers Presented at the Fifteenth International Conference on Patristic Studies Held in Oxford 2007* (ed. Jane Baun, Averil Cameron, Mark Edwards and M. Vinzent; Leuven: Peeters, 2010), 175–80 has demonstrated the pervasiveness of the language of enigma and esotericism throughout Clement's writings. He notes, "*Ainittomai, ainigma,* and related forms appear more than one hundred and forty times in Clement's extant works, often in connection with other words denoting oblique or allusive communication (*symbola, metaphora, parabole, allegoria, huponoia*)." These terms are most often used to describe the obscure utterances of scripture; however, "the second most common use of *ainittomai* and *ainigma* is to characterize the sayings of barbarian and Greek sages, philosophers, and poets, who foreshadow, often in astonishing ways, Christian teachings" (177). Among the barbarians and Greeks cited for their use of enigmas, Dinan affirms that "Clement, like Plutarch and others, especially finds riddles in the Pythagorean *symbola* and among Pythagoras' teachers, the Egyptians" (177).

[17] *Strom.* 5.5.27–31. Iamblichus describes the Pythagorean practice of teaching enigmatically via symbols in *On the Pythagorean Way of Life* 103–10: "Most indispensable for [Pythagoras] was his manner of teaching by means of *symbola.* For this style of teaching was treated with respect by nearly all Hellenes inasmuch as it was of ancient origin, and especially employed by the Egyptians in very subtle ways. Likewise, Pythagoras considered it of great importance if someone carefully and clearly elucidated the meanings and secret conceptions of the Pythagorean symbols (and discerned) how much rightness and truth they contained when revealed and freed from the their enigmatic form, and when adapted with simple and unadorned teaching for the lofty geniuses of these philosophers, deified beyond human thought…

But in accord with the "silence" legislated for them by Pythagoras, they engaged in divine mysteries and methods of instruction forbidden to the uninitiated, and through symbols, they protected their talks with one another and their treatises. And if someone, after singling out the actual symbols, does not explicate and comprehend them with an interpretation free from mockery, the things said will appear laughable and trivial to ordinary persons, full of nonsense and rambling. When, however, these utterances are explicated in accord with the manner of these symbols, they become splendid and sacred instead of obscure to the many, rather analogous to the prophecies and oracles of the Pythian god" (trans. Dillon and Hershbell).

[18] Clement, *Strom.* 5.4.20.1: ἐντεῦθεν αἱ προφητεῖαι οἵ τε χρησμοὶ λέγονται δι' αἰνιγμάτον καὶ αἱ τελεταὶ τοῖς ἐντυγχάνουσιν ἀνέδην οὐ δείκνυνται, ἀλλὰ μετά τινων καθαρμῶν καῖ προρρήσεων. "Thence the prophecies and the oracles are spoken in enigmas,

the correct method for interpreting the church's scriptures (*Strom.* 5.5.29.3). By maintaining that the Pythagorean teachings are derivative of those of Moses, however, Clement defends the stature and the priority of the church's holy writings as the highest source of profound hidden doctrines.

Pythagoreans in Clement's Corpus

In Clement's presentation, Pythagoreans and Christians have a lot in common. As one of the oldest philosophies, Pythagorean teachings are presented as closely mimicking the true teachings of the divine Logos revealed in the writings of Moses and the Prophets and properly interpreted by Jesus Christ.[19] Clement frequently notes agreements between Pythagorean doctrines and the Law, the Prophets, the Gospels, or Paul.[20] Pythagoreans and Christians alike are monotheists,[21] believe in providence,[22] the immortality of the soul and judgement after death.[23] Both refuse to worship images[24] or sacrifice animals,[25] face persecution with courage,[26] include virtuous women among their numbers,[27] are encouraged to pursue celibacy after having children,[28] and consider the words of their teacher to be trustworthy and a legitimate foundation for knowledge.[29] Perhaps surprisingly,

---

and the mysteries are not exhibited straightforwardly to those who happen upon them, but after certain purifications and previous instructions."

[19] Clement compares Moses and Jesus at *Strom.* 2.5.21.1–5: "Moses was a man of wisdom, a king, a legislator. But our Savior surpasses all human nature, being beautiful to the point of being the sole object of our love in our yearning for true beauty, 'for he was the true light.'... He is our lawgiver, presenting us with the Law through the mouth of the prophets, and instructing us in all that has to be done, not least when it is not clear." trans. Ferguson.

[20] *Strom.*1.1.10; 1.10.48; 1.15.70; 2.18.79; 4.3.9; 4.23.151; 4.26.171; 5.5.27; 5.5.28; 5.5.29; 5.5.30; 5.5.31.

[21] *Prot.* 6.72

[22] *Prot.* 6.72; 5.13.88

[23] *Strom.* 4.7.44; 4.22.144

[24] *Strom.* 5.1.8; 5.5.28

[25] *Strom.* 7.6.32

[26] *Strom.* 4.8.56

[27] *Strom.* 4.19.121 (x2)

[28] *Strom.* 3.3.12; 3.3.24

[29] *Strom.* 2.5.24. On Clement's defence of faith (*pistis*) in the words of the divine teacher as a legitimate foundation for knowledge (*gnosis*), see Salvatore Lilla, *Clement of Alexandria: A Study of Christian Platonism and Gnosticism* (Oxford: Oxford University Press, 1971), 118–197. Clement's contention that Pythagoreans accept doctrine on faith in the *ipse dixit* of the teacher is echoed by John Dillon, *The Middle Platonists*, 119: "All this Pythagorean activity, however, seems to have occurred on the non-philosophical, or at least sub-philosophical, level. The treatises are bald and didactic, stating their doctrine without

Clement only twice associates Pythagoreans with number symbolism or "arithmologizing exegesis."[30] The only Pythagorean doctrine that Clement openly rejects is the transmigration of the soul and vegetarianism practiced on that account.[31]

The similarity between Pythagorean teachings and those of Clement's *ekklesia* is not always presented by Clement as a good thing. Especially in Books 5 and 6 of the *Stromateis*, Clement increasingly criticizes Pythagoras and his followers for their unacknowledged and prideful plagiarism.[32] In the end, the so-called "Great Pythagoras" and "Chief among the Greeks" is criticized for offering only a distorted refraction of the true saving knowledge imparted by the Logos incarnate as Jesus.[33]

Philo the Pythagorean?

In her analysis of Clement's Philonic borrowings in the *Stromateis*, Anne-wies van den Hoek notes that 74% of the borrowings include biblical references. Thus she concludes that "the interpretation of Scripture has been Clement's most important focus of attention in the writings of Philo."[34] Runia cites this conclusion as evidence that Clement located Philo in a "Jewish-Christian tradition."[35] Runia emphasizes that Clement employs Philo to help him interpret the writings that are held sacred by both Jews and Christians. Consequently, he reasons that "If [Philo] was not a Christian, then he had to be a Jew."[36] If we look beyond the mere presence of biblical content in the Philonic borrowings, however, we find that Philo's writings—including those with biblical content—are often invoked in the same contexts for the same purposes as Pythagoreanism: to prove the barbarian origin of Greek philosophy and the necessity of propagating

---

attempt at proof, and aimed at an audience which, it would seem, was prepared to substitute faith for reason."

[30] *Strom.* 5.14.93; 6.16.139.

[31] *Strom.* 7.6.32. Vegetarianism adopted as a method of developing one's *enkrateia*, or self-control, however, is praised in *Paed.* 2.1.11.

[32] *Strom.* 5.14.89; 5.14.99; 6.2.17; 6.2.27.

[33] *Strom.* 1.21.133; 5.11.67.

[34] Van den Hoek, *Clement's use of Philo*, 223. Among the 205 borrowings identified by Stählin in his critical edition of the *Stromateis*, van den Hoek finds four lengthy blocks of Philonic material, four short sequences of borrowings, and 119 isolated references, which she evaluates as being definitely (A), probably (B), possibly (C), and unlikely (D) dependent on Philo.

[35] Van den Hoek, *Clement's Use of Philo*, 223; Runia, "Philo the Pythagorean," 3.

[36] Runia, "Philo the Pythagorean," 14.

knowledge in mysteries and enigmas. Compare the occurrence of Philonic borrowings (Table 2) with the Pythagorean references (Table 1, above):

Table 2

Book	Putative Philonic borrowings in Stählin's Critical Edition, as evaluated by van den Hoek
1	36 (2 major sequences)
2	63 (1 major sequence, 2 short sequences
3	9 (no sequences or "A" references)
4	17 (no sequences or "A" references
5	40 (1 major sequence, 2 short sequences)
6	32 (no sequences; 3 "A" references)
7	15 (no sequences or "A" references)
8	1 (no sequences or "A" references)

The clusters of Pythagorean references in Books 1 and 5 occur in the books with the second and third most numerous, and most securely identifiable, Philonic references. Likewise, Books 3, 4, and 7, which contain only a few vague indications of Philonic influence, include relatively few explicit Pythagorean references. The outlier is Book 2, which contains the most Philonic borrowings at sixty-three but only seven explicit appeals to Pythagoras or Pythagoreans. However, a closer look at the Philonic borrowings in this book also reveals significant overlap between the Philonic material and Pythagorean elements. I shall now briefly review the four major sequences identified by van den Hoek as the most extensive and surely identifiable Philonic borrowings, illuminating their Pythagorean elements and rhetorical function within Clement's broader argument.[37]

The first major sequence is found in Book 1 chapter 5. Here Clement borrows the allegorical interpretation of Hagar and Sarah as the encyclical and advanced studies, respectively, from Philo's treatise *De congressu eruditionis gratia*. Significantly, Philo is cited here as part of a larger defence of the value of *Greek* philosophy as a propaideutic path to Christian faith and knowledge. The study of foreign philosophy is valid, Clement argues, because its true doctrines ultimately derive from one single source of truth,

[37] The four major sequences contain a combined total of 69 Philonic borrowings, including 59 of the 125 borrowings van den Hoek identifies as definitely (A) or probably (B) dependent on a Philonic source.

the divine Logos.[38] The division of preliminary studies from philosophy proper parallels the separation of philosophy from the introductory *Quadrivium* of Arithmetic, Music, Geometry and Astronomy, a common feature of Greek philosophical education especially associated with the Pythagorean school.[39] Philo is explicitly named in this context, neither as a Pythagorean nor a Jew, but as someone who interprets the esoteric meanings hidden in barbarian scripture.[40]

The second major sequence follows in chapter 23, shortly after a citation from the Pythagorean Numenius deeming Plato "Moses speaking Attic Greek" and asserting that Pythagoras copied much from Moses.[41] Numenius is presented as a Pythagorean who nevertheless acknowledges his tradition's debt to Moses and, by extension, the Jews. But in spite of his interest in the exotic wisdom of the Hebrews and the Christians, Numenius is uniformly remembered by his successors as neither a Jew nor a Christian but as a Pythagorean.[42] The question of whether Numenius knew the works of Philo remains an open one; John Dillon remarks that, in any event, "he

---

[38] *Strom.* 1.5.29.

[39] Compare the testimony of Justin Martyr in the *Dialogue with Trypho*, 2 : "I came to a Pythagorean, very celebrated—a man who thought much of his own wisdom. And then, when I had an interview with him, willing to become his hearer and disciple, he said, 'What then? Are you acquainted with music, astronomy, and geometry? Do you expect to perceive any of those things which conduce to a happy life, if you have not been first informed on those points which wean the soul from sensible objects, and render it fitted for objects which appertain to the mind, so that it can contemplate that which is honourable in its essence and that which is good in its essence?' Having commended many of these branches of learning, and telling me that they were necessary, he dismissed me when I confessed to him my ignorance." Proclus describes a Pythagorean propaideutic *Quadrivium* of Arithmetic, Music, Geometry and Astronomy in his *Commentary on the First Book of Euclid's Elements*, xii.

[40] *Strom.* 1.5.31: ἑρμηνεύει δὲ ὁ Φίλων τὴν μὲν Ἄγαρ παροίκησιν ἐνταῦθα γὰρ εἴρηται· "Μὴ πολὺς ἴσθι πρὸς ἀλλοτρίαν," τὴν Σάραν δὲ ἀρχήν μου. "Philo interprets Hagar as 'sojourner,' for it is said in connection to this, 'do not be long with a strange woman'; and Sarah he interprets as 'my ruler.'" Note that Clement interprets πολὺς in a temporal sense.

[41] *Strom.* 1.22.150; cf. Numenius, fr. 1a in *Numénius: Fragments* (trans. Édouard des Places; Paris: Les Belles Lettres, 1973); Eusebius, *Prep. ev.* 9.7.1.

[42] Origen also identifies Numenius as a Pythagorean at *Cels.* 4.51. Norman Bentwich, "From Philo to Plotinus," *JQR* 1.4 (1913): 1–21, considered Numenius "certainly a Jew." This speculation of the early twentieth century has fallen out of favour and is refuted by Dillon, *The Middle Platonists*, 379: "Efforts to prove Numenius a Jew are surely also misguided. One did not have to be a Jew in the Syria of the second century c.e. to be acquainted with either Jewish or Christian writings. Numenius certainly accords to the God of the Jews high honour, declaring him to be 'without communion with others, and Father of all the gods, who will not have it that anyone should share in his honour' ... but this is a position that could be adopted by a friendly gentile philosopher with esoteric and syncretistic tendencies..."

was certainly acquainted with the results of allegorical exegesis of the Pentateuch."[43] The writings of Numenius prove that some Pythagoreans, in addition to Christians and Jews, were interested in the enigmatic teachings conveyed in the writings of Moses.

Clement then proceeds with a biographical sketch of Moses, citing Philo's *De vita Moysis* as his source.[44] Asserting the continuity between the Mosaic and Pythagorean traditions, he claims that Pythagoras copied much from Moses, whom he presents, borrowing a phrase from Philo, as an "interpreter of sacred laws."[45] Clement then excerpts Philo's depiction of Moses' education in barbarian wisdom, which bears a striking resemblance to traditions surrounding Pythagoras.[46] Pythagoras is said to have studied with Magi (including Zoroaster), Brahmans, Gauls and Assyrians, while Moses learned Chaldean astronomy and Assyrian letters. For both sages, preliminary study in the sacred traditions of the Egyptians is emphasised. Moses is taught their philosophy through symbols expressed in sacred writings, while Pythagoras is reported to have undergone circumcision in order to study mystical philosophy in their sacred sanctuaries.[47] Clement's second extended Philonic citation thus emphasizes the similarities between Moses and Pythagoras while maintaining the Lawgiver's chronological priority.

The third major sequence of borrowings, taken from Philo's *De vir-tutibus*, is twice interrupted by claims of the Law's agreement with Pythagorean teaching. *Stromateis* 2.18.81–83 reproduces abbreviated elements of the subtreatise on the subject of courage, while Philo's treatments of repentance (2.18.96) and nobility (2.19.98) are also given brief mention. The bulk

---

[43] Dillon, *The Middle Platonists*, 378.

[44] *Strom.* 1.23.153: Ἐν δὲ ἡλικίᾳ γενόμενος ἀριθμητικήν τε καὶ γεωμετρίαν ῥυθμικήν τε καὶ ἁρμονικὴν ἔτι τε μετρικὴν ἅμα καὶ μουσικὴν παρὰ τοῖς διαπρέπουσιν Αἰγυπρίων ἐδιδάσκετο καὶ προσέτι τὴν διὰ συμβόλων φιλοσοφίαν, ἣν ἐν τοῖς ἱερογλυφικοῖς γράμμασιν ἐπιδείκνυνται. τὴν δὲ ἄλλην ἐγκύκλιον παιδείαν Ἕλληνες ἐδίδασκον ἐν Αἰγύπτῳ, ὡς ἂν βασιλικὸν παιδίον, ᾗ φησι Φίλων ἐν τῷ Μωυσέως βίῳ, προσεμάνθανε δὲ τὰ Ἀσσυρίων γράμματα καὶ τὴν τῶν οὐρανίων ἐπιστήμην παρά τε Χαλδαίων παρά τε Αἰγυπτίων, ὅθεν ἐν ταῖς Πράξεσι πᾶσαν σοφίαν Αἰγυπτίων πεπαιδεῦσθαι φέρεται. "When he was old enough, he was taught arithmetic and geometry, rhythm and harmonics as well as metrics and also music by distinguished Egyptians, and further philosophy through symbols, which they display in holy inscriptions (hieroglyphics). The remaining encyclical curriculum Greeks taught him in Egypt, as though he were a royal child, as Philo says in *The Life of Moses*; he was taught the Assyrian letters and the knowledge of the heavens from Chaldeans and Egyptians; on that account he is said in the Acts [of the Apostles] 'to have been taught all the wisdom of the Egyptians.'"

[45] *Strom.* 1.22.150.

[46] cf. *Iamblichus, On the Pythagorean Way of Life*, 28.151.

[47] *Strom.* 1.15.66.2.

of the borrowing (*Strom.* 2.18.84.4–95.3) depends substantially on Philo's demonstration of *philanthropia* in the Law of Moses (*Virt.* 51–174). Although explicit Pythagorean references are rare in *Strom.* 2, its presentation of the Law as a means of inculcating virtue through enigmatic practices and prohibitions is reminiscent of Iamblichus's defence of Pythagorean practices in *On the Pythagorean Life* 106–109.[48] Immediately following the first Philonic borrowing of the sequence, asserting the Law's effective inculcation of justice and wisdom, Clement interjects a reference to Prov. 11:1, "Deceitful balances are an abomination before God; but a just balance is acceptable to Him," and he equates this proverb with the Pythagorean *symbolon*, "do not step over the balance" (*Strom.* 2.18.79.2). Both texts are interpreted as general exhortations to justice. Later, following Philo's notice of the Law's concern for the welfare of animals, Clement comments that Pythagoras must have derived his own similar teaching from Moses (2.18.92). Although not explicitly cited as the source of this material, Philo "the Pythagorean" is invoked a second time very shortly after the completion of this sequence as an expositor who demonstrates the similarity (and possible dependence) between Plato and the Law of Moses.[49] In the third borrowing, Philo's *De virtutibus* functions to demonstrate that the Law, like the Pythagorean *symbola*, inculcates virtue via enigmatic ordinances.

The fourth major sequence of borrowings, in which the Temple and vestments of the High Priest are given an allegorical interpretation, follows on the heels of a favourable description of the Pythagorean *symbola*. In Book 5, chapter four, Clement argues that the mysteries, the Egyptian hiero-

---

[48] The chapter concludes, "Pythagoras prescribed other rules like these, and thus, beginning with food, he led human beings to virtue" (trans. Dillon and Hershbell, modified). A demonstration of the Pythagorean inculcation of piety, wisdom, justice, self-control, courage, and friendship also occupies the last section of Iamblichus's work (134–240).

[49] *Strom.* 2.19.100: Πλάτων δὲ ὁ φιλόσοφος, εὐδαιμονίαν τέλος τιθέμενος, "ὁμοίωσιν θεῷ" φησιν αὐτὴν εἶναι "κατὰ τὸ δυνατόν", εἴτε καὶ συνδραμών πως τῷ δόγματι τοῦ νόμου αἱ γὰρ μεγάλαι φύσεις καὶ γυμναὶ παθῶν εὐστοχοῦσί πως περὶ τὴν ἀλήθειαν, ὥς φησιν ὁ Πυθαγόρειος Φίλων τὰ Μωυσέως ἐξηγούμενος, εἴτε καὶ παρά τινων τότε λογίων ἀναδιδαχθεὶς ἅτε μαθήσεως ἀεὶ διψῶν. φησὶ γὰρ ὁ νόμος· ὀπίσω κυρίου τοῦ θεοῦ ὑμῶν πορεύεσθε καὶ τὰς ἐντολάς μου φυλάξετε. τὴν μὲν γὰρ ἐξομοίωσιν ὁ νόμος ἀκολουθίαν ὀνομάζει· ἡ δὲ τοιαύτη ἀκολουθία κατὰ δύναμιν ἐξομοιοῖ. "And Plato the philosopher, regarding happiness to be the goal, says that it is 'to resemble God as far as possible.' Perhaps here he is discerning the teaching of the Law, 'for those with great natures and naked of passions somehow hit on the truth,' as Philo the Pythagorean said in his exegesis of the writings of Moses; perhaps, on the other hand, he was taught by certain wise men, since he was always thirsting after learning. For the Law says, 'walk in the ways of the Lord your God and guard my commandments.' For the Law calls assimilation 'following after'; and this following after renders one like God as far as possible."

glyphs and Socratic apothegms all convey truth esoterically in the same manner as the scriptures. Pythagoras, however, is the esoteric teacher *par excellence*. Clement begins with the affirmation, "the Pythagorean symbols surely were dependent upon the Barbarian philosophy in a most cryptic manner."[50] He then adduces scriptural parallels to eight Pythagorean *symbola*,[51] concluding that Pythagoras must have been acquainted with the writings of Moses.[52] Clement's borrowing of Philo's elucidation of the cosmological mysteries hidden in the Temple and the High Priest's clothing follows directly after this favourable evaluation of Pythagorean esotericism. Although Clement's exegesis combines a variety of Stoic, Platonic, Gnostic, and apocalyptic elements, the framing of the chapter emphasizes the association between correct biblical interpretation and Pythagorean exegesis. Clement thus associates Philo's allegorical interpretation of the temple with the correct interpretation of hidden wisdom practiced by Pythagoreans.

In the four major sequences of borrowings, Clement employs Philo as an especially skilled interpreter of the philosophical truths expressed enigmatically in the books of Moses which, when properly understood, inculcate virtue. Through his selection of Philonic borrowings, Clement connects the proper exegesis of the Mosaic writings with Pythagorean pedagogical and exegetical methods. Although Philo is employed by Clement as an expert in the Jewish scriptures, his expertise has a decidedly Pythagorean character.

Clement's Construction of "the Jews"

Having demonstrated Philo's conformity to Clement's idea of a Pythagorean exegete, I shall next consider how well Philo matches up to his conception of a Jew and whether he locates himself with Philo in a common "Judaeo-Christian tradition." My investigation will be attentive to the multiple shades of meaning that the terms "Jew," "Israel," and "Hebrew"

---

[50] *Strom.* 5.5.27: Αὐτίκα τῆς βαρβάρου φιλοσοφίας πάνυ σφόδρα ἐπικεκρυμμένως ἤρτηται τὰ Πυθαγόρεια σύμβολα.

[51] The principal source for the allegorical interpretation of the Pythagorean Symbols is Androcydes, whose *Peri Pythagorikon Symbolon* interprets the *symbola* as *ainigmata*. In his commentary on *Stromateis* 5, Alain Le Boulluec, *Stromate V* (SC 278; Paris: Cerf, 1981), 114–15 notes similarities between Clement's choice of *symbola* and Plutarch's *Table Talks* 8 (727c–728c), suggesting common use of the same source material.

[52] *Strom.* 5.5.27–30.

express.[53] In Clement's writings, all three terms may be used to designate the descendants of Abraham, Isaac, and Jacob, both in the ancient past and in the present. They are sometimes used interchangeably, as in *Strom.* 6.6, where the righteous dead liberated from Hades by Jesus are first referred to as Israel, then Jews, then Hebrews, and then Jews again, all in reference to the same people in the same context.

In a survey of broader usage, however, variations of meaning between the terms become apparent. When Clement refers to Old Testament teachings and exhortations to "Israel," he generally follows the supercessionist practice of interpreting the text as applicable to his own community.[54] Clement's substitution of the church as the true "Israel" is characteristic of "proto-orthodox" second-century writings, beginning with Justin Martyr.[55] Clement's usage, however, includes some peculiarities. The term "Israel" is especially applied to those Christians who voluntarily pursue the higher knowledge (*gnosis*) of God through advanced study and ascetic discipline. Clement calls these gnostics "true Israelites" at *Str.* 6.13.108. Clement's adoption of the term "Israel" for his fellow Christ-believers is more consistent than is typical of *Contra Iudaeos* literature in general; verses such as Isa 1:3, "The ox knows his owner, and the ass his master's crib; but Israel has not known me" are not used as ammunition against Jews but are interpreted as a complaint against all unbelievers.[56]

"Hebrew" and its cognates frequently occur in references to the historical people of the Hebrew scriptures. Clement does not use this term to

---

[53] Graham Harvey contends that the terms Jew, Hebrew, and Israel had varying semantic ranges in Jewish writings from the Second Temple period which were adopted by Christians, though he does not include Clement in his analysis. See Harvey, *The True Israel: The Use of the Terms Jew, Hebrew, and Israel in Ancient Jewish and Early Christian Texts* (AGJU 35; Leiden: Brill, 1996); Ellen Birnbaum argues that Philo uses the term *Ioudaioi* to refer to the physical race of the Jews while reserving the word *Israel* to refer to philosophically advanced individuals who "see God" with the eyes of the mind. See Birnbaum, *The Place of Judaism in Philo's Thought: Israel, Jews, and Proselytes* (BJS 290/SPhM 2; Atlanta: Scholars Press, 1996).

[54] See for example *Paed.* 1.10.91.3, quoting Baruch 4.4, "Blessed are we, Israel; for what is pleasing to God is known by us."

[55] *Dial.* 123.9: "As therefore your whole race, from that one Jacob, who was surnamed Israel, were called Jacob and Israel, so we, from Christ who begat us for God, are called and are Jacob and Israel and Judah and Joseph and David, and true children of God." The secondary literature on this topic is extensive; I provide here only a very partial list: Marcel Simon, *Verus Israel: Étude sur les Relations entre Chrétiens et Juifs dans l'Empire Romain 135–425* (Paris: E. de Boccard, 1964); Jeffrey S. Siker, *Disinheriting the Jews: Abraham in Early Christian Controversy* (Louisville: John Knox Press, 1991); Judith Lieu, *Image and Reality: The Jews in the World of the Christians in the Second Century* (Edinburgh: T&T Clark, 1996).

[56] *Protr.* 10.92.1; *Paed.* 1.9.77.4

describe himself or the members of his church; while Clement subsumes himself within the category of Israel, he does not count himself among the Hebrews.[57] Sometimes the term is used solely in reference to the Hebrew language (*Strom.* 6.129, 6.130.1) or as a citation of the Letter to the Hebrews, taken by Clement to have been written by Paul (*Strom.* 5.6, 5.10). In *Stromateis* 3, Clement explicitly cites a *Gospel of the Hebrews* as the source of an authoritative tradition. In *Strom.* 1.1.11.2, Clement mentions a "Hebrew of Palestine" among a list of "blessed and truly remarkable men" whose discourses he treasures. Here "Hebrew" is employed parallel to the epithets "Ionian" and "Sicilian" that Clement uses for his other teachers. Thus "Hebrew" typically carries the connotation of an innate characteristic for Clement, designating ethnicity or the ancestral race into which one is born.[58] A Hebrew may be a Christ-believer; Clement notes that Paul was "a Hebrew by birth" and the "Hebrew of Palestine" whom he so admired imparted teachings in the apostolic tradition.

"Hebrew" can have a positive connotation; the "philosophy of the Hebrews" is praised as the source of Plato's philosophy (*Paed.* 2.1.18). In *Strom.* 1.5, Clement famously compares the Law of the Hebrews to the philosophy of the Greeks; both find their value in their roles as school-masters leading their respective peoples to Christ.[59] On the other hand, "Hebrew" can also be used as a criticism of the other: the "Hebrew people" are also held guilty of crucifying Christ (*Paed.* 2.8.63.2). In *Paed.* 1.9.87.1, Clement describes the relationship of the "Hebrews" to God through the Law as one of involuntary piety, hatred, and fear, equivalent to the relationship between a slave and a harsh master.

The term "Jew" also has particular resonances for Clement.[60] In the first book of the *Stromateis*, it occurs most frequently in citations of works

[57] *Strom.* 1.21; 2.10.47; 2.18; 5.5; 5.11.68.3; *Paed.* 1.10.90.2; 1.6.41.2; 2.2.19.1; 2.4.43.3; 2.8.61.3; 2.12.126.3; *Prot.* 1.8.1; 8.80.1; 9.85.2.

[58] The fluidity of race and ethnicity in early Christian texts, including those of Clement, is illuminated by Denise Kimber Buell, *Why this New Race? Ethnic Reasoning in Early Christianity* (New York: Columbia University Press, 2005). While recognizing that race and ethnicity are discursively constructed traits, I wish only to suggest that Clement presents "Hebrew" identity as a fixed, hereditary trait, in contrast to "Jewishness" or membership in Israel, which he describes as traits that one may adopt or shed.

[59] *Strom.* 1.5.28.3: Τάχα δὲ καὶ προηγουμένως τοῖς Ἕλλησιν ἐδόθη τότε πρὶν ἢ τὸν κύριον καλέσαι καὶ τοὺς Ἕλληνας· ἐπαιδαγώγει γὰρ καὶ αὐτὴ τὸ Ἑλληνικὸν ὡς ὁ νόμος τοὺς Ἑβραίους, εἰς Χριστόν. "Perhaps [philosophy] was given beforehand to the Greeks at that time, before the Lord called them as well; for it was a pedagogue to the Greeks, just as the Law was to the Hebrews, leading them to Christ."

[60] On the evolution of the usage and meaning of the term "Jew" in the Hellenistic period, see A. T. Kraabel, "The Roman Diaspora: Six Questionable Assumptions," *JJS* 33 (1982): 445–64; Ross Kraemer, "The Meaning of the Term 'Jew' in Greco-Roman Inscrip-

compiled by the likes of Megasthenes, Apion, Ptolemy, Josephus, and Philo himself, that attempt to locate the Jewish people in universal history (*Strom.* 1.15.72; 1.21.1). References to "the Jews" quoted from authors such as Josephus (whom Clement calls a Jew explicitly) reflect their own choice of terminology rather than Clement's. When referring to the people of the Hebrew Bible, Clement usually employs terms native to the texts themselves, most often "Israel," "Hebrews," or "the people" rather than "Jews." However, he uses the term "Jew" to refer to the people of the Old Testament three times in the *Paedagogus*. Twice the connotation is clearly negative, criticising "the Jews" who "transgressed by asking for a King" and arguing that the Jews required the ascetic Law of Moses to break down their propensity for indulgence; once it is used to foreshadow Christ's title as King of the Jews.[61]

At *Strom.* 5.14.98, Clement evaluates the Jews as a people of middling rank, equating them with the "race of silver" described by Plato in *Rep.* 3, 415a 2–7. *Stromateis* 5.14, a lengthy chapter that takes up approximately the final third of the fifth *Stromateus*, contends that all Greek philosophy, even the false teachings of the Stoics and the Epicureans, is derived from the philosophers' insufficient understanding of the Hebrew Scriptures that they have plagiarized.[62] In this context, Plato's division of the human race into three classes is introduced as a prophecy of the Christians, who possess the "gold" of the Holy Spirit. Plato's race of silver corresponds to the Jews, while the Greeks make up the race of bronze. Clement's interpretation of the *Republic* reveals his perception of the Jews as occupying an intermediate place between Christians and Greeks. The Jews surpass the Greeks in their perception of the Logos who speaks through their scriptures. Their ethical behaviour, especially their monotheistic worship and conformity to the Law of Moses, is also presented as praiseworthy.[63] The Jews are inferior,

---

tions," in *Diaspora Jews and Judaism* (ed. J. Andrew Overman and Robert S. MacLennan; Atlanta: Scholars Press, 1992), 311–330; Steve Mason, "Jews, Judaeans, Judaizing, Judaism: Problems of Categorization in Ancient History," *Journal for the Study of Judaism* 38 (2007): 457–512. Shaye Cohen, *The Beginnings of Jewishness: Boundaries, Uncertainties, Varieties* (Berkeley: University of California Press, 1999), 69–106, argues that the term *Ioudaios* shifted from a geographic/ethnic to a political or cultural/religious referent during the Hasmonean period.

[61] *Paed.* 2.1.17.1; 2.8.63.4; 3.4.27.2.

[62] *Strom.* 5.14.89.2; 5.14.90.2.

[63] Clement repeatedly praises the Mosaic Law as good in its function as a pedagogue to lead the Jews to faith in Christ. He contends that those who have faith in Christ do not reject the Law but fulfill it according to its intent, which is sometimes literal and sometimes figurative, as Jesus himself demonstrated by his healing on the Sabbath. See *Strom.* 1.26–28; 2.18; 4.7.49.

however, to the Christians, who alone are characterized by the gold that results from their possession of the Holy Spirit.

Most often when Clement uses the word "Jew" to describe his contemporaries, the term applies to those who follow the Hebrew Scriptures but do not accept the Clementine claim that those scriptures enigmatically prophesy Jesus. Clement's soteriology insists that the ancestral wisdom of both the Jews and the Greeks serves as preparatory instruction for the revelation of the Logos in Christ.[64] Clement alludes to formulations similar to Gal 3:28; Eph 4:24; and Col 3:9-11, in each of his major works, taking them together as abolishing the distinction between Jew and Greek in the new creation of the Christian. Hence Paul is described by Clement in *Paedagogus* 1 as "formerly a Jew."[65] Jews by definition do not have faith (*pistis*) or the saving knowledge (*gnosis*) of Christ, as we see in his assertion at the outset of book 2 that, although the Jews are not his intended audience, he will make reference to the scriptures, so that "the Jew also, listening in, may be able to turn quietly from those things which he believed toward him in whom he has not believed."[66]

The negative uses of the term "Jew" in Clement's writings derive frequently from his quotations of early Christian texts, in which the term refers to those who belong to Jesus's ancestral people but have rejected him. He notes that Paul "became a Jew to reach the Jews"; he asks with Paul in Rom 3:29 if God is the God of Jews only (*Strom.* 5.3.18.13); and echoes what he takes to be Paul's criticism of Jews who think themselves wise by rejecting Christ in 1 Cor 3 (*Strom.* 5.4.20). Quoting the *Kerygma Petrou*, Clement urges Christians not to "worship as the Jews do, who thinking they alone know God, do not really know him, worshipping angels and archangels, the month and the moon."[67]

Reading early Christian texts, including the canonical Gospels, the letters of Paul, and the *Kerygma Petrou* as accurate representations of Jews and Judaism, the Jews are repeatedly invoked as the people who characteristically reject Christ due to their misunderstanding of the Law and the

[64] *Strom.* 1.1.1; 6.5.41–2; 6.6.48; 6.13.106.
[65] Interpreting 1 Cor. 13, Clement asserts, "'When I was a child' may be expounded in this manner: when I was a Jew (for he was a Hebrew by ancestry) I thought as a child, when I followed the law; but after becoming a man, I no longer entertain the sentiments of a child, that is, of the law, but of a man, that is, of Christ" (*Strom.* 1.6.34.2).
[66] *Strom.* 2.1.2.1: εἴ πως ἠρέμα καὶ ὁ Ἰουδαῖος ἐπαΐων ἐπιστρέψαι δυνηθείη ἐξ ὧν ἐπίστευσεν εἰς ὃν οὐκ ἐπίστευσεν.
[67] *Strom.* 6.5.41.2: μηδὲ κατὰ Ἰουδαίους σέβασθε· καὶ γὰρ ἐκεῖνοι μόνοι οἰόμενοι τὸν θεὸν γινώσκειν οὐκ ἐπίστανται, λατρεύοντες ἀγγέλοις καὶ ἀρχαγγέλοις, μηνὶ καὶ σελήνῃ.

Prophets.[68] Basing his concept of "the Jews" on their characterisation in these texts, Clement uses the term to denote a hermeneutical position he abjures rather than a tradition with which he identifies. This is well-demonstrated in *Strom.* 7.18.109.3, where Clement provides his most explicit commentary on "Jewish" scriptural exegesis. He argues, "Now those that ruminate, but do not part the hoof, are the crowd of the Jews, who have the oracles of God in their mouths, but not resting on the truth, do not have the faith and the progress from the Son to the Father that accompany them."[69] Without the "parted hoof" of the Father and the Son, Jewish exegesis lacks balance, and is prone to falling down. "Jews" become a functional equivalent in Clement's writings with those who have not recognised that the incarnation, life, crucifixion and resurrection of the Logos in the person of Jesus is foreshadowed in their ancestral scriptures.

It has been noted that Clement's writings lack the polemical zeal against Judaism found in other works by second-century Christians such as Justin Martyr, Tertullian, and Melito of Sardis.[70] Yet my analysis challenges

---

[68] I offer five examples:

Strom. 1.27.174–5: "the apostle showed the beneficent function of the Law in the passage relating to the Jews, writing [quotes Rom. 2:17–20]… For it is admitted that such is the power of the Law, although those whose conduct is not according to the Law, make a false pretence, as if they lived in the Law … In the same way as Paul, prophecy upbraids the people with not understanding the Law."

Strom. 2.5.21.2: "But our Saviour surpasses all human nature. He is so beautiful, as to be the sole object of our love, whose hearts are set on the true beauty, for 'He was the true light.' He is shown to be a king, as such hailed by unsophisticated children and by Jews without faith or knowledge of him, and heralded by the prophets."

Strom. 6.5.41.2, quoting the *Kerygma Petrou* (frag. 4): "Neither worship as the Jews; for they, thinking that they only know God, do not know Him, adoring as they do angels and archangels, the month and the moon."

Strom. 6.6.44.3–4, quoting an *agraphon* of Jesus of unknown origin: "If the prisoners are the Jews, to whom the Lord said, 'go out from the prison, those who are willing,' he designates by it those who consented to be enchained and are charged with carrying heavy burdens of human origin, and continues, 'those who are righteous according to the Law lack faith.'"

Quis div. 28: "And on His interlocutor inquiring, 'Who is my neighbour?,' he did not, in the same way with the Jews, specify the blood-relation, or the fellow-citizen, or the proselyte, or him that has been similarly circumcised, or the man who uses one and the same law."

[69] Αὐτίκα τὰ ἀνάγοντα μηρυκισμόν, μὴ διχηλοῦντα δέ, τοὺς Ἰουδαίους αἰνίσσεται τοὺς πολλούς, οἳ τὰ μὲν λόγια τοῦ θεοῦ ἀνὰ στόμα ἔχουσιν, τὴν δὲ πίστιν καὶ τὴν βάσιν δι᾽ υἱοῦ πρὸς τὸν πατέρα παραπέμπουσαν οὐκ ἔχουσιν ἐπερειδομένην τῇ ἀληθείᾳ.

[70] Responding to Miriam Taylor, *Christian Anti-Judaism: A Critique of the Scholarly Consensus* (Leiden: Brill, 1995), who argues that anti-Judaism is inherent in Christianity, James Carleton-Paget cites Clement as an example of an early Christian who was not fiercely anti-Jewish. Carleton-Paget attributes Clement's relative leniency to a lack of

Runia's claim that Clement had "on the whole a relatively neutral, or even sometimes a selectively favourable attitude to contemporary Judaism."[71] Clement loads the term "Jew" with negative connotations, charging contemporary Jews with misunderstanding the Law and preferring slavery to freedom.

The Transmission of Philo's Treatises to Clement

In a number of recent studies, Clement's use of Philo has been cited as *prima facie* evidence for a genetic relationship between the Alexandrian Church and the city's Jewish community. To give just two examples, Ronald E. Heine asserts that "One of the more obvious traces of the continuing imprint of its early Jewish-Christian origins is the acceptance and use of the works of Philo in a segment, at least, of the Alexandrian Christian community."[72] Similarly, Ilaria L. E. Ramelli claims, "The link between Philo and the early Christian community in Alexandria, although historically unfounded, reflects however the probable Jewish roots of Alexandrian Christianity, before the transformation that occurred at the beginning of the second century (115–117) when Alexandrian Judaism appears to have been swept away."[73]

In his article, "The School of Sacred Laws: The Social Setting of Philo's Treatises," Gregory E. Sterling has proposed a direct line of transmission between Clement's school and an earlier circle of disciples centred around Philo. He suggests that Philo's texts entered Christian hands when Philo's own personal teaching library was incorporated into a Christian library

---

strong local competition from Jews in Alexandria. See Carleton-Paget, "Clement of Alexandria and the Jews," in *Jews, Christians and Jewish Christians in Antiquity* (Tübingen: Mohr Siebeck, 2010), 100. For a similar argument, see also Eric F. Osborn, *Clement of Alexandria*, 23.

[71] Runia, "Philo the Pythagorean," 13. Runia cites nothing from Clement's corpus itself in support of this claim, citing instead Nicholas de Lange's *Origen and the Jews* (Cambridge: Cambridge University Press, 1976), which refers only to Origen. De Lange's study remains influential and highly valuable but is widely recognized to paint too rosy a picture of the intellectual exchange between Jews and Christians in Origen's writings. See Ruth A. Clements, "Origen's Hexapla and Christian-Jewish Encounter in the Second and Third Centuries," in *Religious Rivalries and the Struggle for Success in Caesarea Maritima* (ed. Terence L. Donaldson; Waterloo, Canada: Wilfrid Laurier Press, 2000), 311.

[72] Ronald E. Heine, *Origen: Scholarship in Service of the Church* (New York: Oxford University Press, 2010), 31.

[73] Ilaria L. E. Ramelli, "The Birth of the Rome-Alexandria Connection," 78–79.

following the conversion of a disciple, or the entire school, to Christianity.[74] Philo's library and his hermeneutic were then passed down through a succession of teachers and students, eventually including Clement. Thus, Sterling situates Clement and Philo in an uninterrupted Jewish-Christian exegetical tradition.[75]

Sterling, Heine, and Ramelli all subscribe to the plausible but by no means verifiable theory that Philo's Christian readers encountered his texts through their direct transfer from Jews to Christians, allowing for the possibility of an intermediary "Jewish-Christian" link in the chain of transmission. This reconstruction is based, in part, on the assumption that Philo's treatises, including those with apologetic features, reached only a limited audience of patrons, friends and students who were primarily, if not exclusively, Jews.[76] The extent of Philo's readership is re-evaluated in this volume by Sterling himself and I am inclined to agree with his suggestion that, within decades of his death, Philo's treatises may have been read by Josephus in Rome. I would suggest further that the circle of Philo's readers extended beyond the Roman Jewish community. Once Philo's treatises began to circulate outside of his own control, it becomes impossible to exclude the possibility of non-Jewish readers making use of his works. Although ancient books were costly and time-consuming to reproduce, philosophical texts were frequently copied and given as gifts

[74] Gregory E. Sterling, "The School of Sacred Laws: The Social Setting of Philo's Treatises" *VC* 53 (1999)· 148–164, posits a private educational setting in which Philo's treatises were kept, dubbing it "The School of Sacred Laws" and suggests—while admitting that this suggestion is highly speculative—that "a student in the school was either a Christian or became one and made arrangement for the Christian community to obtain copies of the manuscripts"; or, "a later disciple who became the head of his own school converted to Christianity and brought the library with him. While we will probably never know what actually took place, the theory that his library was preserved by a school of disciples appears the most reasonable explanation of the evidence. Either a student or a head of a subsequent school converted to Christianity and brought the library" (163).

[75] Sterling clarifies, "I am not suggesting a continuous institutional history, but the passing of the hermeneutic and its accompanying library from one private school to another. I think that it is in this sense that we may speak of Philo's 'school of sacred laws' as the forerunner of a later Christian *didaskaleion* at Alexandria" ("School of Sacred Laws," 164).

[76] This argument is made by Victor Tcherikover, "Jewish Apologetic Literature Reconsidered" *Eos* 43 (1956): 169–93. It is accepted by Naomi G. Cohen, *Philo of Alexandria: His Universe of Discourse* (Frankfurt am Main: Peter Lang, 1995), 20, who asserts: "It is immediately obvious that most of Philo's works would have been unintelligible to people unfamiliar with the Pentateuch and with the literary form of his writings. Philo's audience must therefore have been not unlike Philo himself, not only regarding their Greek *paideia* ... but also respecting their command of at least the text of the Pentateuch, together with the midrashic method and the better known midrashic *topoi*."

among the educated elite.[77] It is entirely plausible that readers interested in barbarian wisdom who shared Philo's enthusiasm for Pythagorean thought, such as Numenius of Apamea, could have acquired his treatises.

I have demonstrated that Clement's use of Philo both implicitly and explicitly associates him with Pythagorean exegesis while distancing him from "the Jews" who reject Christ. Consequently, I suggest the possibility that Clement's portrayal of Philo may not be innovative or idiosyncratic. Philo's treatises may have reached Clement as Pythagorean writings, rather than via a chain of exclusively Jewish/Christian readers. Given Philo's prominence and the fame attributed to him by Josephus,[78] it is possible that his texts circulated among a variety of philosophically-inclined readers, particularly those with an interest in Pythagorean-Platonic thought, eventually reaching the hands of one of Clement's beloved teachers in any of the major centres of the Empire. Clement's possession of Philo's writings does not compel us to conclude that the two belonged to a specifically Judaeo-Christian transmission tradition, nor should it be taken uncritically as evidence of a genetic connection between Philo's synagogue and Clement's church.

Conclusion

My analysis of the Philonic borrowings in the *Stromateis* indicates that Clement not only calls Philo a Pythagorean explicitly, but also implicitly connects him with practices he considers Pythagorean rather than Jewish, most notably the interpretation of symbols or enigmas in esoteric texts. Both in content and context, Clement associates Philo with the Pythagorean Numenius who, though not a Jew, also acknowledges the dependence of Plato and Pythagoras on the writings of Moses. Clement's Philonic borrowings dislodge the life and teachings of Moses from the sphere of Jewish life and practice, emphasising their continuity with other revelations of the Logos, both Greek and Barbarian. Clement locates Philo, together with Moses and Pythagoras, not in a "Judaeo-Christian tradition," but among a fraternity of eminent minds who understand something of the true philosophy taught by the Logos.

---

[77] Anthony Grafton and Megan Hale Williams, *Christianity and the Transformation of the Book: Origen, Eusebius and the Library of Caesarea* (Cambridge: Harvard University Press, 2006), 13–14.

[78] The testimony of Josephus in *AJ* 18.257–60, published perhaps a half-century after his death, demonstrates that Philo's actions on behalf of his community and his philosophical abilities were known outside of Alexandria.

By calling Philo a Pythagorean, Clement associates him with a tradition that comes haltingly close to grasping the teaching of the Logos. Clement does not fault Pythagorean ethics or exegesis; in his evaluation, Pythagorean teaching errs only in its doctrine of metempsychosis. Still, the Pythagoreans, like all Greeks, are *apistoi,* unbelievers who condemn themselves by their "unwillingness to believe the truth which declares that the Law was divinely given through Moses, while they honour Moses in their own writers" (*Strom.* 1.26.170.2). By associating Philo with the Pythagoreans, perhaps Clement subtly criticises him for his excessive praise of Moses and insufficient grasp of the Logos by whom he spoke.

Does Clement's description of Philo as Pythagorean disqualify him from being a Jew? If by Jew we mean a member of the people who trace their biological ancestry to the ancestors Abraham, Isaac, and Jacob—a concept for which Clement prefers to use the term "Hebrew"—then it is certainly possible that Clement knows that Philo is a Jew in spite of the fact that he never calls him one. That he does not call Philo a "Hebrew" parallel to his Palestinian teacher requires us to speculate as to whether Clement did indeed know Philo's ethnic origin. It is notable that Van den Hoek's analysis of Clement's borrowings of Philo in the *Stromateis* identify no certain borrowings from the *Hypothetica, Legatio ad Gaium* or *In Flaccum,* the treatises in which Philo's Jewishness is most clearly displayed; perhaps they were unknown to him.[79]

I have argued that Clement made a subtle rhetorical distinction between Israel, Hebrews, and Jews, reserving the latter term to indicate the people who fail to recognize the Logos incarnate as Jesus due to their misunderstanding of the Law and the Prophets. Using this definition of Jew, the term does not fit Philo very comfortably. Certainly Clement knows that Philo did not recognise Christ in the Old Testament; when he borrows Philo's allegorical exegeses, Clement frequently adds a Christological dimension to the interpretation that is not found in the source text.[80] But the fact that Clement employs Philo's allegories suggests that Clement thinks he is on the right exegetical track. In Clement's usage, "Jews" misunderstand the Law and the Prophets:

> The Law and the gospel are the work of one Lord who is 'the power and wisdom of God' (1 Cor. 1:24) ... In the same way as Paul, prophecy reproaches

[79] Van den Hoek, *Clement's use of Philo,* 210.

[80] See, for example, *Strom.* 1.5.31.3, where Clement inserts the identification of Isaac as a "type of Christ" into Philo's interpretation of Sarah and Hagar in *Congr.* This tendency is also noted by van den Hoek, *Clement's Use of Philo,* 228–229 and Eric Osborn, "Philo and Clement: Quiet Conversion and Noetic Exegesis" *SPhA* 10 (1998): 111.

the people for not understanding the Law: 'Destruction and trouble are on their roads, and they have not known the road of peace' (Isa. 59:7–8). 'There is no fear of God before their eyes' (Ps. 36:1). 'Claiming to be wise, they became fools' (Rom. 1:22).[81]

Philo, in contrast, is employed as an aid to decipher the hidden meaning of the Mosaic scriptures. Although Clement lacks the ferocity of his contemporaries, his construction of the concept "the Jews" has a pejorative edge. In Clement's estimation, Philo is a wise man among the *apistoi* who nevertheless remains outside of the *ekklesia*. Taking into account the semantic values he assigns to the term "Jew," we should not be surprised that Clement calls Philo "the Pythagorean."

McGill University

---

[81] Strom. 1.27.174.3–175.2: ἑνὸς γὰρ κυρίου ἐνέργεια, ὅς ἐστι "δύναμις καὶ σοφία τοῦ θεοῦ," ὅ τε νόμος τό τε εὐαγγέλιον … ὁμοίως δὲ τῷ Παύλῳ ἡ προφητεία ὀνειδίζει τὸν λαὸν ὡς μὴ συνιέντα τὸν νόμον. "σύντριμμα καὶ ταλαιπωρία ἐν ταῖς ὁδοῖς αὐτῶν, καὶ ὁδὸν εἰρήνης οὐκ ἔγνωσαν," "οὐκ ἔστι φόβος θεοῦ ἀπέναντι τῶν ὀφθαλμῶν αὐτῶν." "φάσκοντες εἶναι σοφοὶ ἐμωράνθησαν."

The Studia Philonica Annual 25 (2013) 139–167

INSTRUMENTA

A PRELIMINARY INDEX TO PHILO'S NON–BIBLICAL CITATIONS AND ALLUSIONS

DAVID LINCICUM

Introduction

The purpose of this index is to provide some indication of the non–biblical sources that Philo quotes or alludes to in his works. Those references that are explicit quotations of the source are marked by an asterisk (*), while the majority are more subtle allusions or echoes. The index is reasonably complete as a record of quotations, though its reckoning of allusions could doubtless be significantly expanded. The difference between a quotation, an allusion, and an echo is, of course, a matter of ongoing debate in current discussion. I have operated on the basis of a generous conception of echo and allusion, although I have mostly attempted to avoid listing references that merely supply a parallel idea, philosophical commonplace or similar lexical usage. It has not always proven easy to discern when an echo or allusion might be an indication of a significant reference to a predecessor text, but on the whole I have taken the view that a more capacious inclusion of references can then allow users to decide against certain allusions or echoes here presented without undue inconvenience. Customarily a distinction in authorial intention or 'assertorial weight' is seen to distinguish an allusion from an echo, though I have not pressed such distinctions in the presentation of the evidence here.

While Philo sometimes makes allusions to works as a whole,[1] this index is concerned with more or less identifiable allusions to and citations of

---

[1] Including, inter alia, Xenophon's *Symposium* (*Contempl.* 58), Plato's *Symposium* (*Contempl.* 59), *Laws* (*Mos.* 2.49), *Timaeus* (*Aet.* 13, 25, 141) and *Republic* (*Mos.* 2.49), Homer's *Iliad* (*QE* 2.103), Zeno's *Republic* (*Mos.* 2.49) and (Ps.-)Ocellus' *On the Nature of the Universe* (*Aet.* 12).

specific portions of text in known literary works. Questions remain as to whether and how one should include, e.g., Pythagorean number symbolism, Stoic parallels, mythological allusions, similarities with Josephus, or allusions to stories only otherwise preserved in, e.g., Cicero or Diogenes Laertius. In certain instances, references are made to authors who post-date Philo (e.g., Iamblichus, Lucian Stobaeus, etc.) when they may preserve earlier texts or opinions on which Philo may be relying. It has not always proven easy to determine whether to include as allusions certain doxographical (e.g., the discussion about Anaxagoras and Democritus in *Contempl.* 14–16; cf. Plut., *Per.* 16, or occasional statements about Epicurus) or mythological (e.g., the Argonauts in *Prob.* 128 or the stories in *Legat.* 78–113) accounts.[2] For the most part, these references are most readily available via the index of names (PLCL 10: 269–433) and the index to translators' notes (PLCL 10: 434–86) prepared by J. W. Earp, the Index Nominum prepared by J. Leisegang (*Indices ad Philonis Alexandrini opera* [vol. 7 of Cohn-Wendland's *Philonis Alexandrini quae supersunt*; Berlin: G. Reimer, 1926–1930], 3–26), and judicious use of the *TLG*. In this light, I have tried to include those allusions that appear as references to particular texts or, in some cases, to parallel accounts that may reflect a common source, though there has undoubtedly been some inconsistency in the application of this rule. More problematic have been Philo's numerous allusions to the concepts of philosophical schools; these are occasionally noted by means of important parallels or (where clear) sources in the index that follows. Doubtless the index could be further improved in this area specifically (especially for *Prob.*, *Aet.*, and *Prov.*, though also more broadly). An imperfect index should at least serve to stimulate further research.

The index proceeds in three sections. Part I includes quotations and allusions drawn from known literature (or, in a handful of cases, clearly marked citations of unknown literary texts), presented first in the order in which they appear in Philo, then in the order of the sources.[3] Part II considers some special cases not included in Part I, including a) unidentifiable short citations marked in Philo's text; b) the Delphic axiom; c) Protagoras's saying that 'the human is the measure of all things'; and d) proverbial sayings. Part III provides a list of Philo's texts that appear in Johannes von

---

[2] Doxographical material is also found in, e.g., *Opif.* 7–8, 170–171, 54; *Abr.* 162–163; *Ebr.* 170–202; *Mut.* 10, 67; *Somn.* 1.14–16, 21–24, 25, 30–34, 52–56, 145, 184; *Her.* 246; *Aet.* 7–19; *Prov.* 2.89, etc.; on this, see the authoritative discussion in David T. Runia, "Philo and Hellenistic Doxography," in *Philo of Alexandria and Post-Aristotelian Philosophy* (ed. F. Alesse; Studies in Philo of Alexandria 5; Leiden and Boston: Brill, 2008), 13–54.

[3] The Philonic evidence is presented in the order of PLCL, with the addition of fragments afterward.

Arnim's collection, *Stoicorum Veterum Fragmenta*, and in Long & Sedley's *The Hellenistic Philosophers*, in both Philonic order and the order of *SVF* and LS. Because von Arnim refers to a variety of sources before the Cohn–Wendland edition had been completed, this index standardizes the references to bring them in line with more recent editions of Philo. Von Arnim's views on Philo as a witness to Stoic thought have not gone unchallenged,[4] but his classic presentation is still influential today.

It goes without saying that this modest index owes an enormous debt to the considerable erudition of Philo's translators. The following works by Philo have been included in the index, and the majority of the references have been culled from editorial footnotes: F. H. Colson, G. H. Whitaker and R. Marcus, eds., *Philo, I–X, Supplements I–II*, (LCL; Cambridge, Mass.: Harvard University Press, 1929–1962); M. Hadas-Lebel, *De Providentia I et II: Introduction, traduction et notes* (Les œuvres de Philon d'Alexandrie 35; Paris: Cerf, 1973); Abraham Terian, ed., *Philonis Alexandrini, De animalibus: The Armenian Text with an Introduction, Translation, and Commentary* (Studies in Hellenistic Judaism 1; Chico, Calif.: Scholars Press, 1981); idem, "A Philonian Fragment on the Decad," in *Nourished with Peace: Studies in Hellenistic Judaism in Memory of Samuel Sandmel* (ed. F. E. Greenspahn, E. Hilgert and B. L. Mack; Scholars Press Homage Series 9; Chico, Calif.: Scholars Press, 1984), 173–82; F. Siegert, "The Philonian Fragment *De Deo*: First English Translation," *SPhilo* 10 (1998): 1–33. Though compiled independently, this index was afterwards checked for completeness against W. Theiler's index to Cohn-Wendland, "Sachweiser zu Philo," in PCH 7.388–92, and against the French series, *Les œuvres de Philon d'Alexandrie* (36 vols.; Paris: Cerf, 1961–1992).

Abbreviations for classical literature follow *LSJ*.[5] Note further the following:

Bowra   C. M. Bowra, ed., *Pindari Carmina cum fragmentis* (2nd ed.; Oxford: Clarendon, 1947)

Caizzi   F. D. Caizzi, *Antisthenis fragmenta* (Milan: Istituto editorial Cisalpino, 1966)

---

[4] See, for instance, A. A. Long, "Philo on Stoic Physics," in *Philo of Alexandria and Post-Aristotelian Philosophy* (ed. F. Alesse; Studies in Philo of Alexandria 5; Leiden: Brill, 2008), 121–40. I am indebted to Gregory Sterling for this reference.

[5] With the following exceptions: Aesch. for Aeschylus, Eur. for Euripides, Soph. for Sophocles; Zeno for Zeno Citieus; Hippocr. for Hippocrates; Chrysipp. for Chrysippys the Stoic; Pind. for Pindar; Dem. for Demosthenes.

DK   Hermann Diels and Walther Kranz, eds., *Die Fragmente der Vorsokratiker: griechisch und deutsch* (3 vols.; 6th ed.; Berlin: Weidmann, 1972–1973)

Düring   I. Düring, *Aristotle's Protrepticus* (Göteborg: Acta Universitatis Gothoburgensis, 1961)

HL   M. Hadas-Lebel, *De Providentia I et II: Introduction, Traduction et Notes* (Les œuvres de Philon d'Alexandrie 35; Paris: Cerf, 1973)

Kock   Theodor Kock, ed., *Comicorum Atticorum fragmenta* (3 vols.; Leipzig: Teubner, 1880–1888)

KT   A. Körte and A. Thierfelder, *Menandri quae supersunt* (2 vols.; 2nd ed.; Leipzig: Teubner, 1957–1959)

LS   A. A. Long and D. N. Sedley, *The Hellenistic Philosophers* (2 vols.; Cambridge: Cambridge University Press, 1987)

Marc.   M. Marcovich, *Heraclitus: Greek Text with a Short Commentary* (2nd ed.; Sankt Augustin: Academia, 2001)

PCG   R. Kassel and C. Austin, eds., *Poetae Comici Graeci* (8 vols.; Berlin: de Gruyter, 1983–)

Pfeiffer R. Pfeiffer, *Callimachus* (2 vols.; Oxford: Clarendon, 1965)

PMG   D. L. Page, *Poetae Melici Graeci* (Oxford: Clarendon, 1962)

Powell   J. U. Powell, *Collectanea Alexandrina. Reliquiae minores Poetarum Graecorum Aetatis Ptolemaicae 323–146 A.C.* (Oxford: Clarendon, 1925)

Rose   V. Rose, *Aristotelis qui ferebantur librorum fragmenta* (Leipzig: Teubner, 1886; repr., Stuttgart: Teubner, 1967)

SM   B. Snell and H. Maehler, *Pindari Carmina cum fragmentis* (2 vols.; Leipzig: Teubner, 1989)

SH   H. Lloyd–Jones and P. Parsons, *Supplementum Hellenisticum* (Berlin: de Gruyter, 1983)

SVF   Johannes von Arnim, ed., *Stoicorum veterum fragmenta* (4 vols.; Leipzig: Teubner, 1903–1924)

Th   W. Theiler, ed., *Poseidonios. Die Fragmente* (2 vols.; Berlin: de Gruyter, 1982)

TrGF 1   B. Snell and R. Kannicht, eds., *Tragicorum Graecorum Fragmenta Vol. 1. Didascaliae Tragicae, Catalogi Tragicorum et Tragediarum, Testimonia et Fragmenta Tragicorum Minorum* (Göttingen: Vandenhoeck & Ruprecht, 1986)

TrGF 2   R. Kannicht and B. Snell, eds., *Tragicorum Graecorum Fragmenta Vol. 2: Fragmenta Adespota* (Göttingen: Vandenhoeck & Ruprecht, 1981)

TrGF 3   S. Radt, ed., *Tragicorum Graecorum Fragmenta Vol. 3: Aeschylus* (Göttingen: Vandenhoeck & Ruprecht, 1985)

TrGF 4   S. Radt, ed., *Tragicorum Graecorum Fragmenta Vol. 4: Sophocles* (2nd
             ed.; (Göttingen: Vandenhoeck & Ruprecht, 1999)

TrGF 5   R. Kannicht, ed., *Tragicorum Graecorum Fragmenta Vol. 5: Euripides*
             (2 vols.; Göttingen: Vandenhoeck & Ruprecht, 2004)

Wehrli   F. Wehrli, *Hieronymos von Rhodos; Kritolaos und seine Schüler*
             (Schule des Aristoteles 10; Basel: Schwabe, 1959)

West   M. L. West, *Iambi et elegi Graeci ante Alexandrum cantati* (2 vols.;
             2nd ed.; Oxford: Clarendon, 1989–1992)

In addition to the online version of the *TLG* (which has proven indispensable), the following works have been helpful in preparing the index:
W. W. Fortenbaugh, P. M. Huby, R. W. Sharples and D. Gutas, *Theophrastus
of Eresus: Sources for his Life, Writings, Thought, and Influence* (2 vols.;
Philosophia Antiqua 54; Leiden: Brill, 1992); Anargyros Anastassiou and
Dieter Irmer, eds., *Testimonien zum Corpus Hippocraticum. Teil I: Nachleben
der hippokratischen Schriften bis zum 3. Jahrhundert n. Chr.* (Göttingen: Vandenhoeck & Ruprecht, 2006); E. Koskenniemi, "Philo and Classical Drama,"
in *Ancient Israel, Judaism, and Christianity in Contemporary Perspective: Essays
in Memory of Karl-Johan Illman* (ed. J. Neusner, et al.; Lanham: University
Press of America, 2006), 137–51; idem, "Philo and Greek Poets," *JSJ* 41
(2010): 301–22; Gregory E. Sterling, '"The Jewish Philosophy": Reading
Moses via Hellenistic Philosophy according to Philo' (forthcoming).

Contents

Part I: *Quotations and Allusions Drawn from Known Literature*

A. Philonic Order

Opif.

3	D.L. 6.63; 7.87; *SVF* 1.262
8	*SVF* 2.300; 2.312
12	Pl., *Ti.* 28a
13	Pl., *R.* 7.546b
21	Pl., *Ti.* 28c
21–22	Pl., *Ti.* 29e
26	*SVF* 2.509–510
38	Posidon., fr. 308b Th*; Pl., *Ti.* 37c–38c
39	Pl., *Ti.* 52e–53a
48	Pl., *Ti.* 35a–b
54	Pl., *Ti.* 47a–b
58	Pl., *Ti.* 39b–c
58–62	Pl., *Ti.* 47
66	Pl., *Ti.* 39e–40a
67	Arist., *GA* 736a
69	Pl., *Lg.* 963a
70	Pl., *Phdr.* 249c; *Tht.* 173e
72–75	Pl., *Ti.* 41–42
73	Zeno in *SVF* 1.110
79	Pl., *Ti.* 69d
97	Pl., *Ti.* 53c
100	Philol.? B20 DK*
104	Sol., fr. 27 West*
105	Hippocr., *Hebd.* 9.1–10.35 R
119	Pl., *Ti.* 75d*
124	Hippocr., *Hebd.* 1.8–13 R
131	Posidon., fr. 308c Th*
132	Pl., *Ti.* 60b; Aesch., *Pr.* 90; Ar., *Ra.* 382; Ar., *Av.* 971
133	Pl., *Mx.* 238a*
142	D.L. 6.63; *SVF* 1.262
144	Aesch., *TrGF* 3: 162 (via Pl., *R.* 3.391e?)
148	Pl., *Lg.* 776b; *R.* 328a
160	D.L. 10.128
171	Pl., *Ti.* 32c, 55d

Leg.

1.4	Arist., *EN* 3.1.6
1.5	Eur., *TrGF* 5: 839.12–14*
1.35	Arist., *EN* 1135a–b
1.61	Pl., *Phdr.* 247a
1.68	*SVF* 1.262–264

1.70	Pl., *Phdr.* 246–254; *R.* 439d; *Ti.* 69c, 69e, 90a
1.70–73	*Ti.* 69e–f
1.73	Pl., *Phdr.* 253d
1.87	*SVF* 3.262
1.91	*SVF* 2.774
1.103	Pl., *Phd.* 65a
1.105	Pl., *Phd.* 64c
1.107–108	Heraclit., fr. 47 Marc.*
1.108	Pl., *Cra.* 400b; *Grg.* 493a
2.6	D.L. 7.111
2.15	Pl., *Cra.* 390d, 401b
2.22	*SVF* 2.457–460
2.30	Pl., *Phd.* 65e–66a
2.32–33	Pl., *Phdr.* 243d
2.72	Pl., *Smp.* 191d
2.99	*SVF* 3.381–388
2.249	Pl., *Phdr.* 247a
3.2	*SVF* 3.169–177
3.7	Heraclit., fr. 54 Marc.; fr. 26 Marc.*; fr. 55 Marc.*; Pl., *Phdr.* 247a
3.97	*SVF* 2.1009
3.105	Hom., *Il.* 24.527–528; Pl., *R.* 379d
3.115	Pl., *Ti.* 69e–f
3.129	*SVF* 3.443–455
3.160	D.L. 10.136
3.175	*SVF* 2.329, 2.333
3.202	Eur., *TrGF* 5: 687*
3.210	*SVF* 3.516–517

Cher.

14–17	*SVF* 3.516–517
21–24	Pl., *Ti.* 35–36
22–23	Pl., *Ti.* 36c–d
26	Eur., *TrGF* 5: 911
69	*SVF* 2.54, 2.64
79	D.L. 7.64
109–112	Epict., *Diss.* 1.12.16
125	Arist., *Metaph.* 1013a, etc.; Pl., *Ti.* 29e

Sacr.

11	Arist., *Rh.* 1.1.1
21–33	X., *Mem.* 2.1
34	Heraclit., fr. 6 Marc.

35	Ps.–Epich., fr. 271 PCG
36	Pl., *R.* 507d–508
49	Pl., *Phdr.* 246
82	Pl., *Ti.* 30a
86	X., *Mem.* 1.6.7
93	Aesch.? TrGF 3: 394
104	Pl., *Phdr.* 229a
116	X., *Mem.* 1.6.8

Det.

7	Arist., *EN* 1098b; *SVF* 3.136
16	*SVF* 3.613
34	Pl., *Phd.* 64a, 67e
64	Hes., *Op.* 40
84–85	Pl., *Ti.* 90
85	Pl., *Ti.* 90a, 90d, 91e
119	D.L. 7.110–111
139	Antisth., fr. 44b Caizzi
141	Arist., *Rh.* 3.3; Pl., *Grg.* 484b; *Smp.* 196c
154	Pl., *Ti.* 32c
157	D.L. 10.6
160	Pl., *Ti.* 69d
168	D.L. 7.110; 7.157
178	Hom., *Od.* 12.118

Post.

5	Pl., *Ti.* 42e
36	Pl., *Cra.* 385e; *Tht.* 152a
113	Pl., *Cra.* 211c; *Smp.* 211c
138	*SVF* 3.589–603
151	Hom., *Il.* 20.361
163	Heraclit., fr. 40 Marc.
214	Epich.? fr. 214 PCG

Gig.

7	Arist., *GA* 762a
8	Pl., *Ti.* 34a; *Lg.* 897–898
13	Pl., *Phdr.* 248c; *Ti.* 43a
14	Pl., *Phd.* 64a, 67e
16	Pl., *Smp.* 202e
31	Pl., *Phdr.* 247a
33	D.L. 6.41
38	D.L. 7.104–105
56	Pl., *Phd.* 60b; Soph., TrGF 4: 910

Deus

14	Pl., *Tht.* 156a
18	*SVF* 3.21
22	*SVF* 3.548

24	Pl., *Lg.* 653b; *R.* 554f
31–32	Pl., *Ti.* 37–38b
32	Pl., *Ti.* 37d, 38b
34	*SVF* 2.847
35–48	*SVF* 2.457–460
43	Pl., *Tht.* 191c
44	D.L. 7.88
46	Arist., *Rh.* 3.10.7; Heraclit., fr. 68 Marc.
57	Arist., *Ph.* 2.3
62	*SVF* 1.164
65–69	Pl., *R.* 389b; *SVF* 3.554–555
79	Pl., *Ti.* 45b–c
84	Pl., *Ti.* 80b; *SVF* 2.836, 2.872
90	Theoc., *Id.* 14.48
111	Dem., *F.Leg.* 133
129	Pl., *R.* 488b–489c
146–147	Cic., *Tusc.* 5.91; D.L. 2.25
162–165	Arist., *EN* 2.6–7

Agr.

24	Hom., *Il.* 5.487
40	Pl., *Grg.* 505a, etc.
41	Hom., *Il.* 1.263, etc.; *SVF* 3.617–624
110	Dem. via Stob., *Flor.* 19.4
128–129	Pl., *R.* 379b–c; *Ti.* 29–30, 40–41
140–141	D.L. 7.64–76
144	Heraclit., fr. 36 Marc.*
160	*SVF* 3.510
161	*SVF* 3.539–540

Plant.

6	Pl., *Ti.* 32c
17	Pl., *Ti.* 90a; 91
21	Pl., *Ti.* 91e
40	Heraclit., fr. 68 Marc.
65	Cic., *Tusc.* 5.91; D.L. 2.25
80	Pl., *Ap.* 21a–23b
106	*SVF* 3.432*
118	Pl., *Ti.* 47a
129	Hes., *Th.* 50–61
131	Pl., *Ti.* 29a*
163	Arist. apud Ath., *Epit.* 2.40c
171	Pl., *Erx.* 397e
172	Pl., *Phd.* 105
173	Arist., *Rh.* 1.15

Ebr.

8	Pl., *Phd.* 60b; Soph., TrGF 4: 910
56	Pl., *Sph.* 263f
61	Pl., *Ti.* 51a
70	*SVF* 2.135
88	*SVF* 3.560
103	Hom., *Il.* 2.489
126	Aesch., *Eu.* 107
142	*SVF* 3.613
146	Pl., *Phdr.* 249d
150	Hes., *Op.* 289–292*
158	*SVF* 3.548
170–202	D.L. 9.79–88; S.E., *P.* 1.36–37, 1.40–163

Sobr.

12	Pl., *Smp.* 218e
18	D.L. 7.88
34	*SVF* 3.11
56	*SVF* 3.589–603
57	*SVF* 3.617–624

Conf.

4	Hom., *Od.* 11.315, 318*
5	Arist., *Cael.* 293a
6	Call., fr. 193 Pfeiffer
57	Heraclit., fr. 6 Marc.*
81	Pl., *Phdr.* 247d–e
90	D.L. 7.93
141	Dem., *C.Eub.* 1300; Heraclit., fr. 6 Marc.*
164	Pl., *R.* 9.576b
167	Pl., *Phd.* 15e
170	Hom., *Il.* 2.204–205*
175	Pl., *Ti.* 41–42
179	Pl., *Lg.* 860e
184–187	*SVF* 2.471
187	*SVF* 2.473

Migr.

14	D.L. 7.40
37	Pl., *Ti.* 29d–e; *Phdr.* 247a
40	Pl., *R.* 508e
105	Pl., *Phdr.* 274a
126	Pind., *P.* 4.286–287
147	Arist., *EN* 1100b
156	Hom., *Il.* 6.484*
180	*SVF* 2.1013
181	Pl., *Ti.* 41a
183	Pl., *Phdr.* 253a; *Ti.* 29e
188	Pl., *Phd.* 109b

194	Pl., *Ti.* 90c–d
195	Hom., *Od.* 4.392*
218	Arist., *Protr.* fr. 5 Düring
220	Pl., *Sph.* 226a*

Her.

5	Men., fr. 312 KT*
14	D.L. 7.158
38	Pl., *Phdr.* 245a
76	Pl., *Phdr.* 248a
83	Pl., *Ti.* 47b–e
86	Pl., *Ti.* 41d
88	Pl., *Ti.* 47
116	Hes., *Op.* 40
132	D.L. 7.46
136	*SVF* 1.120
156	*SVF* 3.92, 3.525
158	Th. 2.40
165	Pl., *Ti.* 37d
181	Pl., *Tht.* 191c*
185	Pl., *Ti.* 47b
189	Hom., *Il.* 9.97*
190	D.L. 8.25
233	Pl., *Ti.* 36d
246	Pl., *Tht.* 152; *Ti.* 32c; 41b
247	Pl., *Tht.* 151c
249	Pl., *Phdr.* 244e, 245a
265–266	Pl., *Ion* 534
282	Pl., *Ti.* 42e
283	Arist., *Cael.* 1.2–3
301	Pl., *Phdr.* 246e
304	Pl., *Lg.* 854c
307	Pl., *Lg.* 770a

Congr.

18	Arist., *Rhet.* 1.1.1
21	Pl., *Ti.* 44a
54	*SVF* 1.205
71	Pl., *Phdr.* 247a
79	*SVF* 2.36
114	Pl., *Lg.* 855c
141	*SVF* 1.68, 1.73, 2.93–94
143	Pl., *Tht.* 184b–d

Fug.

8	Pl., *Phd.* 96–98
10	Anaxag. A1 DK
12	Pl., *Ti.* 28a
11–13	*SVF* 2.395
31	Hom., *Od.* 21.294
55	Heraclit., fr. 47 Marc.

61	Heraclit., fr. 76 Marc.*; Hom., *Od.* 12.118*
62	Pl., *Phdr.* 247a
63	Pl., *Tht.* 176a–b*
72	Pl., *Ti.* 41d
74	Pl., *Phdr.* 247a
75	*SVF* 2.504–505
82	Pl., *Tht.* 176c*
134	*SVF* 2.787–789
179	Heraclit., fr. 8 Marc.*

Mut.

32	D.L. 7.117; *SVF* 3.637–639
34	*SVF* 3.32
46	Pl., *Ti.* 29d–e
60	Heraclit., fr. 8 Marc.*
77	*SVF* 2.166
114	*SVF* 3.613–614
135	*SVF* 2.915–921
144	Pl., *Tht.* 149d
146	Pl., *Phlb.* 14c, 15b–c
152	Eur., TrGF 5: 484.1; *SVF* 3.617
153	*SVF* 3.262
160	*SVF* 3.169
179	Hom., *Od.* 7.36*
212	Pl., *Tht.* 191c
243	D.L. 9.37; Ps.–Plu., *Lib.Ed.* 14
267	Pl., *Ti.* 37d

Somn.

1.1–2	Posid. via Cic., *Div.* 1.64
1.6	Heraclit., fr. 8 Marc.*
1.10	Hippocr., *Aph.* 4.458.3*; Thphr. via D.L. 5.40–41
1.21	Stob., *Ecl.* 1.23–26
1.21–23	Aët., *Plac.* 2.11, 13, 15, 28
1.22	Anaxagoras via D.L. 2.3
1.23	Stob., *Ecl.* 1.26
1.30	Iamb. via Stob., *Ecl.* 1.41; Pl., *Phlb.* 16, 23; Zeno via Cic., *Scip.* 1.14.19
1.30–32	Aët., *Plac.* 4.2–7
1.31	Pl., *Cra.* 399e; Stob., *Ecl.* 1.40; *SVF* 2.804–808
1.32	Pl., *Ti.* 70a
1.53	Anaximand. via Stob., *Ecl.* 1.25; Heraclit., fr. 57 Marc.
1.57	Hom., *Od.* 4.392*

1.138	Pl., *R.* 10.617; *Phdr.* 248e–249c
1.140	X., *Cyr.* 8.2.10
1.141	Pl., *Smp.* 202e
1.145	Aët., *Plac.* 2.25, 30
1.147	Pl., *Ti.* 43a
1.150	Hom., *Od.* 11.303
1.153–156	Heraclit., fr. 33 Marc.*
1.154	Eur., TrGF 5: 420*
1.172	Eur., TrGF 5: 484
1.233	Hom., *Od.* 17.485[6]
1.245	Dem., *Cor.* 21, 87
2.1–2	Posidon., fr. 373b Th*
2.14	Pl., *R.* 588c
2.50	Hom., *Il.* 9.211–214
2.52	Hom., *Od.* 15.529
2.70	Hom., *Od.* 12.219
2.109	Heraclit., fr. 40 Marc.
2.144	Hom., *Od.* 4.535
2.148	Hom., *Il.* 22.60, etc.
2.209	Cic., *Tusc.* 5.34.95; D.L. 10.136
2.244	*SVF* 3.617
2.260	Hom., *Il.* 2.212
2.275	Hom., *Il.* 2.246
2.294	Pl., *Phdr.* 246e

Abr.

20	Pl., *R.* 492b
32	Antisth., fr. 44b Caizzi
99	*SVF* 2.42, 2.44
134	Men., fr. 786 KT*
150	Heraclit., fr. 6 Marc.*
156	Pl., *R.* 508–509
158–159	Pl., *Ti.* 47
164	Pl., *Ti.* 47a
261	*SVF* 3.617

Jos.

2	Hom., *Il.* 1.263, etc.
20	Pl., *Grg.* 469c, 508b, 509c
24	Th. 2.43
25	Arist., *Rh.* 1.13
28	*SVF* 1.262, 3.322
32	Pl., *R.* 557c

[6] Contrast Pl., *R.* 2.380d–381d; see H. Jacobson, "A Philonic Rejection of Plato," *Mnemosyne* 57 (2004): 488.

38	Arist., *Pol.* 3.10.2; Pl., *Plt.* 259c
48	Eur., *Hipp.*?; Soph., *Hipp.*?
62	Pl., *Grg.* 464d–465b, 500b, 501a
78	Eur., *Ph.* 521*; Eur., TrGF 5: 687*
79	Arist., *Pol.* 5.9
88	Pl., *Lg.* 908a
126–128	Heraclit., fr. 40 Marc.
265	Hom., *Il.* 3.277; *Od.* 11.109; 12.323

Mos.

1.22	Luc., *Pisc.* 9; Pl., *Tht.* 183d
1.23	Hdt. 4.87; Pl., *Lg.* 656d, 799a, 819a
1.30	Hom., *Il.* 18.104, etc.
1.31	Heraclit., fr. 93 Marc.; fr. 33 Marc.*; Eur., TrGF 5: 420*
1.135	Eur., *IA* 122
1.274	Heraclit., fr. 6 Marc.
1.279	Aesch., TrGF 3: 162 (via Pl., *R.* 3.391e?); Heraclit., fr. 108 Marc.

2.2	Pl., *R.* 5.473d
2.4	Muson. via Stob., *Flor.* 47.67; Pl., *Smp.* 196c
2.13	Men., fr. 786 KT
2.51	Pl., *Lg.* 723a
2.213	Heraclit., fr. 6 Marc.

Decal.

12	Pl., *Sph.* 230
30	Arist., *Cat.* 4; *Top.* 1.9
54	D.L. 7.147; Pl., *Cra.* 404c
56	Hom., *Od.* 11.303; S.E., *M.* 9.37
58	Pl., *Ti.* 41a
69	Hes., *Op.* 218 (apud Pl., *Smp.* 222b?); Hom., *Il.* 17.32
77	Hdt. 2.65–74
103	Pl., *Ti.* 36c–d
104	Pl., *Lg.* 821c–d
133	Pl., *Lg.* 869b
142–146	D.L. 7.112; *SVF* 3.389, 3.404

Spec.

1.2	Hdt. 2.36
1.6	*SVF* 2.96, 2.838
1.10	Heraclit., fr. 114 Marc.*
1.25	Pl., *Lg.* 631c
1.27	Arist., *Ph.* 8.3 253b; Pl., *Cra.* 402a; *Tht.* 160d
1.32–35	*SVF* 2.1009
1.33–34	*SVF* 2.1009–1020
1.65	Pl., *Ion* 534
1.74	Hom., *Il.* 18.104; *Od.* 20.379; Pl., *Tht.* 1.176d; Soph., TrGF 4: 945
1.90–92	Pl., *Ti.* 47
1.103	Pl., *Grg.* 524e
1.146	Pl., *Ti.* 69e
1.148	Pl., *Ti.* 70e; Heraclit., fr. 36 Marc.*
1.208	D.L. 9.8; Heraclit., fr. 25 Marc.*; fr. 55 Marc.*
1.210	Pl., *Ti.* 32c
1.219	Pl., *Ti.* 71
1.318	*SVF* 3.88; 3.208
1.321	Pl., *Phdr.* 243a; 243d; 247a
1.337	Arist., *de An.* 435b
1.339	Pl., *Ti.* 47a

2.2	Pl., *Phdr.* 236d
2.4	Pl., *Grg.* 466e
2.6	Hom., *Il.* 6.266
2.46	Cic., *Tusc.* 3.24–34; 3.52–53; *SVF* 3.482
2.56	Arist., *Metaph.* 1.5 985b
2.62	Pl., *Phdr.* 243d
2.73	D.L. 7.101
2.91	Pl., *Phdr.* 239c
2.133	Eur., *IA* 122
2.185	*SVF* 3.431–432
2.188	*SVF* 3.267
2.232	Pl., *Lg.* 866e
2.249	Pl., *Phdr.* 247a*

3.16	D.S. 4.66
3.43	D.S. 4.77
3.50	Hom., *Il.* 18.104; *Od.* 20.379; Pl., *Tht.* 1.176d; Soph., TrGF 4: 945
3.117	*SVF* 2.806
3.120	Pl., *Lg.* 866d–867c
3.185	Pl., *Ti.* 47a

4.14	Aesch., TrGF 3: 162 (via Pl., *R.* 3.391e?)
4.20	Unknown text*
4.34	Dem., *Mid.* 119.9, etc.
4.40	Arist., *Rh.* 1.15.2
4.47	Eur., TrGF 5: 200.3–4*
4.49	Pl., *Ion* 534
4.51	Heraclit., fr. 8 Marc.*
4.54	*SVF* 2.121
4.60	Heraclit., fr. 6 Marc.; Hdt. 1.8*
4.63	Pl., *R.* 352c
4.63–66	Pl., *Lg.* 955c–d
4.64	Arist., *Rh.* 1.15.24
4.73	Ael., *VH* 12.59
4.92	Pl., *Ti.* 69e–f
4.94	Pl., *Ti.* 70e
4.116	*Let.Arist.* 145–147
4.137	Heraclit., fr. 6 Marc.
4.145	*SVF* 1.262–264
4.149–150	Arist., *Rh.* 1.14.7
4.188	Pl., *Cra.* 400b, etc.; *Grg.* 493a, etc.; *Tht.* 176a–b
4.235	Pl., *Cra.* 410d
4.236	Aesch., TrGF 3: 162 (via Pl., *R.* 3.391e?)

Virt.

5	Pl., *Lg.* 631c
13	Pl., *Phdr.* 253d
14	Pl., *Cra.* 411e
23	Pl., *R.* 468a
28	*SVF* 1.216; 3.567
80	Aesch., TrGF 3: 162 (via Pl., *R.* 3.391e?)
152	Arist., *Rh.* 2.13.4; 2.21.13; D.L. 1.5.87
172	Pind., fr. 292 Bowra[7]*

Praem.

---

[7] Otherwise unknown, though either reminiscent of Pindar, *Ol.* 2.2 (as SM 2.161 suggest), or reflecting a lost text; so Enrica Salvaneschi, "Between Philo and Pindar: the Delos Quotation (*Aet.* 120–122)," in *Italian Studies on Philo of Alexandria* (ed. Francesca Calabi; Studies in Philo of Alexandria and Mediterranean Antiquity 1; Boston and Leiden: Brill, 2003), 75–89, here 86.

9	Pl., *Men.* 81
46	D.L. 8.25
55	Cic., *Leg.* 1.6.18
111	Call., *Epigr.* 25; Iamb., *VP* 208; Theoc. 14.48

Prob.

2	D.L. 8.17
5	Pl., *R.* 7.514–517; 533d
8	Pl., *Phdr.* 259c
13	Pl., *Phdr.* 243d; 247a
14	Zeno A18 DK
19	Soph., TrGF 4: 755*
22	Eur., TrGF 5: 958*
25	Eur., TrGF 5: 687*
28	Antisth., fr. 91 Caizzi
31	Hom., *Il.* 1.263, etc.
42	Soph., *OC* 1293
48	Chrysipp.(?), *SVF* 3.361*
53	Zeno, *SVF* 1.228*
97	Zeno, *SVF* 1.218*
98–104	Eur., TrGF 5: 687–691*
109	Anaxarch. (via D.L. 9.59)*
112	Hom., *Il.* 6.407*
116	Eur., *Hec.* 548–551*
121	D.L. 6.29
122	Hom., *Il.* 24.602–604*
123	D.L. 6.29
125	Hom., *Il.* 1.180–181*
127	D.L. 2.98–102
134	Ion? TrGF 1: 53*
141	Eur., TrGF 5: 275.3–4*
143	Aesch., TrGF 3: 20(*)*
145	TrGF 2: 318; Eur., TrGF 5: 893.1*
152	TrGF 2: 327*
155	Thgn., *El.* 5.535–536*

Contempl.

9	Hom., *Il.* 2.216–219
10	Pl., *R.* 533d
16	Hippocr., *Aph.* 4.458.3*
17	Hom., *Il.* 13.5–6*
35	Pl., *Phdr.* 259c
36	Pl., *Mx.* 238a
40	Hom., *Od.* 9.373
43	Comic Poet (PCG 8: 475)
57	X., *Smp.* 2–3; Pl., *Smp.* 173a
58	X., *Smp.* 2.1–23
62	Pl., *Lg.* 838e
74	Pl., *Ti.* 70e

78	Pl., *Men.* 81

Aet.

1	Pl., *Ti.* 27c
4	*SVF* 2.509–510
5	Emped. B12 DK*; Eur., TrGF 5: 839.12–14*
8	Hom., *Il.* 5.4
10	Arist., fr. 18 Rose
13	Pl., *Ti.* 41a*
14	Arist., *Cael.* 1.10 (279b 34)
15	Pl., *Ti.* 30b; 31a; 49a; 50c; 50d
16	Arist., *Cael.* 280a
17	Hes., *Th.* 116–117*
18	Zeno, *SVF* 1.103; Arist., *Ph.* 4.1 (208b 29)
19	Pl., *Ti.* 51a
21	Pl., *Ti.* 32c
25–26	Pl., *Ti.* 32c*
27	TrGF 2: 327a*
29	Pl., *Ti.* 42e
30	Eur., TrGF 5: 839.8–14*
37	Hom., *Od.* 6.107–108*
38	Pl., *Ti.* 33c*
41	Unknown poet[8]*
42	Heraclit., fr. 93 Marc.; Hom., *Il.* 15.362–364
47	Anaxagoras via D.L. 2.3
48	D.L. 7.138
48–51	Chrysipp., *SVF* 2.397
49	Aesch., TrGF 3: 139*
52	Pl., *Ti.* 39c
52–53	Pl., *Ti.* 37e
55	Critol., fr. 13 Wehrli
57	Eur., TrGF 5: 839
69	Pl., *Smp.* 206c
70	Critol., fr. 12 Wehrli
74	Pl., *Phlb.* 35a; *Ti.* 73a
79	Posidon., fr. 272 Th*
90	Cleanthes, *SVF* 1.511; Chrysipp., *SVF* 2.611
94	Chrysipp., *SVF* 2.618
109–110	Heraclit., fr. 33 Marc.*

[8] Xenophanes of Colophon? So Andrei Lebedev, "Xenophanes on the Immutability of God: A Neglected Fragment in Philo Alexandrinus," *Herm* 128 (2000): 385–91.

109–111	Heraclit., fr. 66 Marc.*
110	Heraclit., fr. 53 Marc.*
117–149	Thphr., fr. 184*
117–150	Posidon., fr. 310 Th*
121	Pind., fr. 33c SM*
127	Hom., *Il.* 18.397
132	Hom., *Il.* 6.147–148*
139	Aesch.? TrGF 3: 402
140	SH 1134a*
141	Pl., *Ti.* 24e*; 25c–d*
144	Eur., TrGF 5: 839.12–14*
146	Pl., *Phd.* 96a
146–149	Pl., *Lg.* 3.676–77; *Ti.* 22a–f

Flacc.

85	Hdt. 1.109; 3.119; 5.72

Prov.

1.7 HL	Pl., *Ti.* 30a
1.9 HL	D.L. 7.141
1.16 HL	Pl., *Ti.* 28b
1.19 HL	Pl., *Ti.* 32c
1.20 HL	Pl., *Ti.* 38b*
1.21 HL	D.L. 7.138; *SVF* 2.527; 2.529; Pl., *Ti.* 28b*; 29b*
1.22 HL	Pl., *Ti.* 30b
1.29 HL	D.L. 7.138
1.34 HL	*SVF* 2.169
1.61 HL	Pl., *Ap.* 17b
2.8 HL	Aesch., TrGF 3: 344*
2.13 HL	Democr. A14 DK
2.13 LCL	Hom., *Il.* 13.599, etc.
2.15 HL	Hom., *Il.* 1.544
2.16 HL	Pl., *Tht.* 144a; *Ti.* 90a; Hom., *Il.* 20.234–235*
2.17 HL	Pl., *R.* 7.519b, etc.
2.19 HL	Hom., *Od.* 1.443
2.22 HL	Pl., *Phlb.* 39e
2.23 HL	D.L. 7.115; Pl., *Phlb.* 64c
2.24 LCL	Emped. B121 DK*
2.27 HL	X., *Mem.* 2.1.22–26
2.28 HL	Paus. 10.2.2; 10.35.2–3
2.35 HL	Hes., *Th.* 154–210; 459–506
2.36 HL	Hes., *Th.* 23*
2.37 HL	Hom., *Il.* 1.591–592; 5.330; 15.18–19*
2.39 HL	Xenoph. A26 DK
2.42 HL	Xenoph. A26 DK; Pl., *Phdr.* 245a*
2.44 HL	Pl., *Prt.* 335e–336a

2.50 HL	Pl., *Ti.* 53b	4.203	Epich., fr. 260 PCG (46
2.52 HL	Pl., *Cri.* 46b; *Phd.* 91c		DK)*; Eur., TrGF 5: 954*
2.53 HL	*SVF* 2.505	4.211	Eur., *Hipp.* 331
2.56 HL	Pl., *Ti.* 33b	4.238	Hom., *Il.* 13.206; 14.191
2.60 HL	Emped. A49 DK	4.265	Heraclit., fr. 8 Marc.*
2.61 HL	Emped. A66 DK		
2.66 HL	Emped. B55 DK	*QE*	
2.70 HL	Emped. B43 DK*	2.6	Aesch., TrGF 3: 162 (via
2.80 HL	Pind., *Pae.* 9.1–10*		Pl., *R.* 3.391e?)*
2.89 HL	Anaxag. A42 DK; A1 DK;	2.118	Pl., *Ti.* 75d–e
	Eratosth., fr. 14 Powell*		
		Anim.	
2.90 HL	Th. 2.49; Aesch., TrGF 3:	1	Pl., *Phdr.* 228b
	345*	2	Pl., *Phdr.* 235a; 238d
2.95 HL	Hom., *Od.* 9.106–111	3	Pl., *Phdr.* 227b; 227c; 228c;
2.100 HL	Pind., *Pae.* 9.1–10		228e; 236a
2.107 HL	D.S. 2.4.2–6	4	Pl., *Phdr.* 228a
2.109 HL	Pl., *Ti.* 90a; Heraclit., fr.	5	Pl., *Phdr.* 236c
	68 Marc.*	6	Pl., *Phdr.* 230e; 236a
2.113 HL	Ps–Pind., fr. 281 SM =	7	Pl., *Phdr.* 235c–d
	Simon., PMG 582*	8	Pl., *Phdr.* 228a
		9	Pl., *Phdr.* 228b
Legat.		11	*SVF* 2.1012; 2.1131
80	Hom., *Od.* 4.454–459	12	Arist., *APo.* 76b24; Pl.,
84	Pind., *N.* 10.73–90		*Sph.* 263e; *Tht.* 189e; *SVF*
149	Hom., *Il.* 2.204*		2.135; 2.223
211	Pl., *R.* 526e	17	Pl., *Ti.* 33b; *SVF* 3.83
		23	Ael., *NA* 5.26
QG		27	Ael., *NA* 2.11; Plin., *HN*
1.6.	Pl., *Ti.* 29e; 92c		8.4
1.7	Hom., *Il.* 12.239; *Od.*	28	Ael., *NA* 2.11; Plin., *HN*
	20.242		8.6; Unknown ode*
1.76	Hom., *Od.* 12.118*	30–65	Pl., *R.* 419–445e
		37	Ael., *NA* 2.42; Plin., *HN*
2.5	Heraclit., fr. 108 Marc.*		10.23
2.12	Heraclit., fr. B 118(*)	46	S.E., *P.* 1.69
2.27	Hom., *Il.* 4.299*	47	Aesch., TrGF 3: 159*;
			Aesch., TrGF 3: 162 (via
3.3	Hom., *Od.* 12.39–45; Pl.,		Pl., *R.* 3.391e?)*
	Phdr. 246e	54	Hom., *Il.* 20.170–171*
3.5	Heraclit., fr. 27 Marc.*	58	Plin., *HN* 8.160–161
3.16	Hom., *Od.*, 14.258*	59	Hom., *Od.* 11.541–562;
			Plin., *HN* 8.11–12
4.1	Heraclit., B123.10 DK	61	Pl., *Ti.* 31a–b; 32c–33a;
4.2	Hom., *Od.* 17.485–488*		Hes., *Th.* 599*
4.8	Hom., *Il.* 15.189*	69	Hom., *Il.* 22.310, etc.
4.20	Hom., *Od.* 15.74*	72	Pl., *Phdr.* 234c
4.120	Men., fr. 581 Kock*	73	Pl., *Phdr.* 228d; 234d;
4.152	Heraclit., fr. 47 Marc.*		234d; 235c
4.159	Pl., *Phd.* 60b; Soph., TrGF	74	Pl., *Phdr.* 235b
	4: 910	75	Pl., *Phdr.* 227b; 235a
4.183	Hom., *Il.* 3.179*	76	Pl., *Phdr.* 227b

Decad. (Terian)
11   Pl., *Ti.* 35b*
38   Pl., *Ti.* 55c
40   Pl., *Ti.* 55e; 56a

Deo (Siegert)
4   Pl., *Ep.* 7 341c; *Prm.* 142a;
            Ti. 28c
6   Heraclit. 22B 30 DK; Pl.,
            Ti. 30a; 92c; *SVF* 1.504;
            2.527
8   Pl., *Ti.* 32c
9   Pl., *Ti.* 34b
12   Pl., *Phdr.* 247a; *Ti.* 29e

                B. Order of the Sources

Aelian
NA 2.11   *Anim.* 27, 28
NA 2.42   *Anim.* 37
NA 5.26   *Anim.* 23
VH 12.59   *Spec.* 4.73

Aeschylus
Eu. 107   *Ebr.* 126
Pr. 90   *Opif.* 132
TrGF 3: 20*   *Prob.* 143*
TrGF 3: 139   *Aet.* 49*
TrGF 3: 159   *Anim.* 47*
TrGF 3: 162 (via Pl., *R.* 3.391e?) *Opif.*
                144; *Mos.* 1.279; *Spec.*
                4.14; 4.236; *Virt.* 80;
                Anim. 47*
TrGF 3: 344   *Prov.* 2.8 HL*
TrGF 3: 345   *Prov.* 2.90 HL*
TrGF 3: 394   *Sacr.* 93
TrGF 3: 402   *Aet.* 139

Aëtius
Plac. 2.11   *Somn.* 1.21–23
Plac. 2.13   *Somn.* 1.21–23
Plac. 2.15   *Somn.* 1.21–23
Plac. 2.25   *Somn.* 1.145
Plac. 2.28   *Somn.* 1.21–23
Plac. 2.30   *Somn.* 1.145
Plac. 4.2–7   *Somn.* 1.30–32

Anaxagoras
via D.L. 2.3 *Aet.* 47; *Somn.* 1.22
A1 DK   *Fug.* 10; *Prov.* 2.89 HL
A42 DK   *Prov.* 2.89 HL

Anaxarchus
via D.L. 9.59   *Prob.* 109*

Anaximander
via Stob., *Ecl.* 1.25   *Somn.* 1.53

Antisthenes
fr. 44b Caizzi   *Det.* 139; *Abr.* 32
fr. 91 Caizzi   *Prob.* 28

Aristophanes
Av. 971   *Opif.* 132
Ra. 382   *Opif.* 132

Aristotle
apud Ath., *Epit.* 2.40c   *Plant.* 163

APo.
76b24   *Anim.* 12

Cael.
269b–270b *Her.* 283
279b 34   *Aet.* 14
280a   *Aet.* 16
293a   *Conf.* 5

Cat.
4   *Decal.* 30

de An.
435b   *Spec.* 1.337

EN
1098b   *Det.* 7
1100b   *Migr.* 147
1106b–1108ab   *Deus* 162–165
1110a   *Leg.*1.4
1135a–b   *Leg.* 1.35

fr. 18 Rose   *Aet.* 10

GA
736a   *Opif.* 67
762a   *Gig.* 7

Metaph.
985b   *Spec.* 2.56
1013a, etc.   *Cher.* 125

Ph.
194b–195a *Deus* 57
208b29   *Aet.* 18

253b   *Spec.* 1.27

Pol.
3.10.2   *Jos.* 38
5.9   *Jos.* 79

Protr.
fr. 5 Düring   *Migr.* 218

Rh.
1.1.1   *Sacr.* 11; *Congr.* 18
1.13   *Jos.* 25
1.14.7   *Spec.* 4.149–150
1.15   *Plant.* 173
1.15.2   *Spec.* 4.40
1.15.24   *Spec.* 4.64
2.13.4   *Virt.* 152
2.21.13   *Virt.* 152
3.10.7   *Deus* 46
3.3   *Det.* 141

Top.
1.9   *Decal.* 30

Athenaeus
Epit. 2.40c *Plant.* 163

Callimachus
Epigr. 25   *Praem.* 111
fr. 193 Pfeiffer   *Conf.* 6

Chrysippus
SVF 2.397   *Aet.* 48–51
SVF 2.611   *Aet.* 90
SVF 2.618   *Aet.* 94
SVF 3.361   *Prob.* 48*

Cicero
Leg.
1.6.18   *Praem.* 55

Tusc.
3.24–34   *Spec.* 2.46
3.52–53   *Spec.* 2.46
5.34.95   *Somn.* 2.209
5.91   *Deus* 146–147; *Plant.* 65

Cleanthes
SVF 1.511   *Aet.* 90

Critolaus
fr. 12 Wehrli   *Aet.* 70
fr. 13 Wehrli   *Aet.* 55

Democritus
A14 DK   *Prov.* 2.13 HL

Demosthenes
via Stob., *Flor.* 19.4   *Agr.* 110

C.Eub.
1300   *Conf.* 141

Cor.
21   *Somn.* 1.245
87   *Somn.* 1.245

F.Leg.
133   *Deus* 111

Mid.
119.9, etc.   *Spec.* 4.34

Diogenes Laertius
1.87   *Virt.* 152
2.25   *Deus* 146–147; *Plant.* 65
2.98–102   *Prob.* 127
6.29   *Prob.* 121; 123
6.41   *Gig.* 33
6.63   *Opif.* 3; 142
7.40   *Migr.* 14
7.46   *Her.* 132
7.64   *Cher.* 79
7.64–76   *Agr.* 140–141
7.87   *Opif.* 3
7.88   *Deus* 44; *Sobr.* 18
7.93   *Conf.* 90
7.101   *Spec.* 2.73
7.104–105   *Gig.* 38
7.110   *Det.* 168
7.110–111   *Det.* 119
7.111   *Leg.* 2.6
7.112   *Decal.* 142–146
7.115   *Prov.* 2.23 HL
7.117   *Mut.* 32
7.138   *Aet.* 48; *Prov.* 1.21 HL;
              1.29 HL
7.141   *Prov.* 1.9 HL
7.147   *Decal.* 54
7.157   *Det.* 168
7.158   *Her.* 14
8.17   *Prob.* 2

8.25	*Her.* 190; *Praem.* 46
9.8	*Spec.* 1.208
9.37	*Mut.* 243
9.79–88	*Ebr.* 170–202
10.6	*Det.* 157
10.128	*Opif.* 160
10.136	*Leg.* 3.160; *Somn.* 2.209

Diodorus Siculus

2.4.2–6	*Prov.* 2.107 HL
4.66	*Spec.* 3.16
4.77	*Spec.* 3.43

Empedocles

A49 DK	*Prov.* 2.60 HL
A66 DK	*Prov.* 2.61 HL
B12 DK	*Aet.* 5*
B43 DK	*Prov.* 2.70 HL*
B55 DK	*Prov.* 2.66 HL
B121 DK	*Prov.* 2.24 LCL*

Epicharmus

| fr. 260 PCG (46 DK) | *QG* 4.203* |
| fr. 214 PCG | *Post.* 214 |

(Ps.–)Epicharmus

| fr. 271 PCG | *Sacr.* 35 |

Epictetus

| *Diss.* 1.12.16 | *Cher.* 109–112 |

Eratosthenes

| fr. 14 Powell | *Prov.* 2.89 HL* |

Euripides

Hec.

| 548–51 | *Prob.* 116* |

Hipp.

| *Hipp.?* | *Ios.* 48 |
| 331 | *QG* 4.211 |

IA

| 122 | *Mos.* 1.135; *Spec.* 2.133 |

Ph.

| 521 | *Ios.* 78* |

TrGF 5: 200.3–4	*Spec.* 4.47*
TrGF 5: 275.3–4	*Prob.* 141*
TrGF 5: 420	*Somn.* 1.154*; *Mos.* 1.31*

TrGF 5: 484	*Somn.* 1.172
TrGF 5: 484.1	*Mut.* 152
TrGF 5: 687	*Leg.* 3.202*; *Ios.* 78*; *Prob.* 25*
TrGF 5: 687–91	*Prob.* 98–104*
TrGF 5: 839.8–14	*Aet.* 30*
TrGF 5: 839.12–14	*Leg.* 1.5*; *Aet.* 5*; 57; 144*
TrGF 5: 893.1	*Prob.* 145*
TrGF 5: 911	*Cher.* 26
TrGF 5: 954	*QG* 4.203*
TrGF 5: 958	*Prob.* 22*

Heraclitus

fr. 6 Marc.	*Sacr.* 34; *Conf.* 57; 141*; *Abr.* 150*; *Mos.* 1.274, 2.213; *Spec.* 4.60; 4.137
fr. 8 Marc.	*Fug.* 179*; *Mut.* 60*; *Somn.* 1.6*; *Spec.* 4.51*; *QG* 4.265*
fr. 25 Marc.	*Spec.* 1.208*
fr. 26 Marc.	*Leg.* 3.7*
fr. 27 Marc.	*QG* 3.5*
fr. 33 Marc.	*Somn.* 1.153–156*; *Mos.* 1.31*; *Aet.* 109–110*
fr. 36 Marc.	*Agr.* 144*; *Spec.* 1.148*
fr. 40 Marc.	*Post.* 163; *Somn.* 2.109; *Ios.* 126–128
fr. 47 Marc.	*Leg.* 1.107–108*; *Fug.* 55; *QG* 4.152*
fr. 53 Marc.	*Aet.* 110*
fr. 54 Marc.	*Leg.* 3.7
fr. 55 Marc.	*Leg.* 3.7*; *Spec.* 1.208*
fr. 57 Marc.	*Somn.* 1.53
fr. 66 Marc.	*Aet.* 109–111*
fr. 68 Marc.	*Deus* 46; *Plant.* 40; *Prov.* 2.109 HL*
fr. 76 Marc.	*Fug.* 61*
fr. 93 Marc.	*Mos.* 1.31; *Aet.* 42
fr. 108 Marc.	*Mos.* 1.279; *QG* 2.5*
fr. 114 Marc.	*Spec.* 1.10*
22 B30 DK	*Deo* 6 (Siegert)
B118* DK	*QG* 2.12
B123.10 DK	*QG* 4.1

Herodotus

1.8	*Spec.* 4.60*
1.109	*Flacc.* 85
2.36	*Spec.* 1.2
2.65–74	*Decal.* 77
3.119	*Flacc.* 85
4.87	*Mos.* 1.23

5.72   *Flacc.* 85

Hesiod
Op.
40   *Det.* 64; *Her.* 116
218 (apud Pl., *Smp.* 222b?) *Decal.* 69
287   *Ebr.* 150*
289–92   *Ebr.* 150*

Th.
23   *Prov.* 2.36 HL*
50–61   *Plant.* 129
116–117   *Aet.* 17*
154–210   *Prov.* 2.35 HL
459–506   *Prov.* 2.35 HL
599   *Anim.* 61*

Hippocrates
Aph.
1.1 (4.458.3)   *Somn.* 1.10*; *Contempl.*
                16*

Hebd.
1.8–13 R   *Opif.* 124
9.1–10.35 R   *Opif.* 105

Homer
Il.
1.180–181   *Prob.* 125*
1.263, etc.   *Agr.* 41; *Jos.* 2; *Prob.* 31
1.544   *Prov.* 2.15 HL
1.591–592   *Prov.* 2.37 HL
2.204   *Legat.* 149*
2.204–205   *Conf.* 170*
2.212   *Somn.* 2.260
2.216–219   *Contempl.* 9
2.246   *Somn.* 2.275
2.489   *Ebr.* 103
3.179   *QG* 4.183*
3.277   *Jos.* 265
4.299   *QG* 2.27*
5.4   *Aet.* 8
5.330   *Prov.* 2.37 HL
5.487   *Agr.* 24
6.147–148   *Aet.* 132*
6.266   *Spec.* 2.6
6.407   *Prob.* 112*
6.484   *Migr.* 156*
9.97   *Her.* 189*
9.211–214   *Somn.* 2.50
12.239   *QG* 1.7
13.5–6   *Contempl.* 17*

13.206   *QG* 4.238
13.599, etc.   *Prov.* 2.13 LCL
14.191   *QG* 4.238
15.18–19   *Prov.* 2.37 HL*
15.189   *QG* 4.8*
15.362–364   *Aet.* 42
17.32   *Decal.* 69
18.104   *Mos.* 1.30; *Spec.* 1.74; 3.50
18.397   *Aet.* 127
20.170–171   *Anim.* 54*
20.234–235   *Prov.* 2.16 HL*
20.361   *Post.* 151
22.60, etc.   *Somn.* 2.148
22.310, etc.   *Anim.* 69
24.527–528   *Leg.* 3.105
24.602–604   *Prob.* 122*

Od.
1.443   *Prov.* 2.19 HL
4.392   *Migr.* 195*; *Somn.* 1.57*
4.454–459   *Legat.* 80
4.535   *Somn.* 2.144
6.107–108   *Aet.* 37*
7.36   *Mut.* 179*
9.106–111   *Prov.* 2.95 HL
9.373   *Contempl.* 40
11.109   *Jos.* 265
11.303   *Somn.* 1.150; *Decal.* 56
11.315, 318   *Conf.* 4*
11.541–562   *Anim.* 59
12.39–45   *QG* 3.3
12.118   *Det.* 178; *Fug.* 61*; *QG*
                1.76*
12.219   *Somn.* 2.70
12.323   *Jos.* 265
14.258   *QG* 3.16*
15.74   *QG* 4.20*
15.529   *Somn.* 2.52
17.485[9]   *Somn.* 1.233
17.485–488   *QG* 4.2*
20.242   *QG* 1.7
20.379   *Spec.* 1.74; 3.50
21.294   *Fug.* 31

Iamblichus
via Stob., *Ecl.* 1.41   *Somn.* 1.30

---

[9] See Jacobson, "Philonic Rejection,"
(n. 6).

VP
208   *Praem.* 111

Ion?
TrGF 1: 53   *Prob.* 134*

Letter of Aristeas
145–147   *Spec.* 4.116

Lucian
Pisc. 9   *Mos.* 1.22

Menander
fr. 312 KT   *Her.* 5*
fr. 581 Kock   *QG* 4.120*
fr. 786 KT   *Abr.* 134*; *Mos.* 2.13

Musonius
via Stob., *Flor.* 47.67 *Mos.* 2.4

Pausanias
10.2.2   *Prov.* 2.28 HL
10.35.2–3   *Prov.* 2.28 HL

Philolaus?
B20 DK   *Opif.* 100*

Pindar
fr. 33c S-M *Aet.* 121*
fr. 292 Bowra[10] *Virt.* 172*

N.
10.73–90   *Legat.* 84

P.
4.286–287   *Migr.* 126

Pae.
9.1–10   *Prov.* 2.80 HL*; 2.100 HL

Plato
Ap.
17b   *Prov.* 1.61 HL
21a–23b   *Plant.* 80

Cra.
211c   *Post.* 113
385e   *Post.* 36

[10] See n. 7 above.

390d   *Leg.* 2.15
399e   *Somn.* 1.31
400b   *Leg.* 1.108
400b, etc.   *Spec.* 4.188
401b   *Leg.* 2.15
402a   *Spec.* 1.27
404c   *Decal.* 54
410d   *Spec.* 4.235
411e   *Virt.* 14

Cri.
46b   *Prov.* 2.52 HL

Ep.
7, 341c   *Deo* 4 (Siegert)

Erx.
397e   *Plant.* 171

Grg.
464d–465b *Ios.* 62
466e   *Spec.* 2.4
469c   *Ios.* 20
484b   *Det.* 141
493a   *Leg.* 1.108
493a, etc. *Spec.* 4.188
500b   *Ios.* 62
501a   *Ios.* 62
505a   *Agr.* 40
508b   *Ios.* 20
509c   *Ios.* 20
524e   *Spec.* 1.103

Ion
534   *Her.* 265–266; *Spec.* 1.65;
          4.49

Lg.
631c   *Spec.* 1.25; *Virt.* 5
653b   *Deus* 24
656d   *Mos.* 1.23
676–677   *Aet.* 146–149
723a   *Mos.* 2.51
770a   *Her.* 307
776b   *Opif.* 148
799a   *Mos.* 1.23
819a   *Mos.* 1.23
821c–d   *Decal.* 104
838e   *Contempl.* 62
854c   *Her.* 304
855c   *Congr.* 114
860e   *Conf.* 179

866d–867c *Spec.* 3.120
866e *Spec.* 2.232
869b *Decal.* 133
897–898 *Gig.* 8
908a *Jos.* 79
955c–d *Spec.* 4.63–66
963a *Opif.* 69

Men.
81 *Praem.* 9; *Contempl.* 78

Mx.
238a *Opif.* 133*; *Contempl.* 36

Phd.
15e *Conf.* 167
60b *Gig.* 56; *Ebr.* 8; *QG* 4.159
64a *Gig.* 14; *Det.* 34
64c *Leg.* 1.105
65a *Leg.* 1.103
65e–66a *Leg.* 2.30
67e *Gig.* 14; *Det.* 34
91c *Prov.* 2.52 HL
96a *Aet.* 146
96–98 *Fug.* 8
105 *Plant.* 172
109b *Migr.* 188

Phdr.
227b *Anim.* 3; 75; 76
227c *Anim.* 3
228a *Anim.* 4; 8
228b *Anim.* 1; 9
228c *Anim.* 3
228d *Anim.* 73
228e *Anim.* 3
229a *Sacr.* 104
230e *Anim.* 6
234c *Anim.* 72
234d *Anim.* 73
235a *Anim.* 2; 75
235b *Anim.* 74
235c *Anim.* 73
235c–d *Anim.* 7
236a *Anim.* 3; 6
236c *Anim.* 5
238d *Anim.* 2
239c *Spec.* 2.91
243a *Spec.* 1.321
243d *Leg.* 2.32–33; *Spec.* 1.321; 2.62; *Prob.* 13
244e *Her.* 249

245a *Her.* 38; 249; *Prov.* 2.42 HL*
246–254 *Leg.* 1.70
246 *Sacr.* 49
246e *Her.* 301; *Somn.* 2.294; *QG* 3.3
247a *Leg.* 1.61; 2.249; 3.7; *Gig.* 31; *Migr.* 37; *Congr.* 71; *Fug.* 62; 74; *Spec.* 1.321; 2.249*; *Prob.* 13; *Deo* 12 (Siegert)
247d–e *Conf.* 81
248a *Her.* 76
248c *Gig.* 13
248e–249c *Somn.* 1.138
249c *Opif.* 70
249d *Ebr.* 146
253a *Migr.* 183
253d *Leg.* 1.73; *Virt.* 13
259c *Prob.* 8; *Contempl.* 35
274a *Migr.* 105

Phlb.
14c *Mut.* 146
15b–c *Mut.* 146
16 *Somn.* 1.30
23 *Somn.* 1.30
35a *Aet.* 74
39e *Prov.* 2.22 HL
64c *Prov.* 2.23 HL

Plt.
259c *Jos.* 38

Prm.
142a *Deo* 4 (Siegert)

Prt.
335e–336a *Prov.* 2.44 HL

R.
328a *Opif.* 148
352c *Spec.* 4.63
379b–c *Agr.* 128–129
379d *Leg.* 3.105
389b *Deus* 65–69
419–445e *Anim.* 30–65
439d *Leg.* 1.70
468a *Virt.* 23
473d *Mos.* 2.2
488b–489c *Deus* 129

492c	*Abr.* 20	25c–d	*Aet.* 141*
507d–508	*Sacr.* 36	27c	*Aet.* 1
508–509	*Abr.* 156	28a	*Opif.* 12; *Fug.* 12
508e	*Migr.* 40	28b	*Prov.* 1.16 HL; 1.21 HL*
514–517	*Prob.* 5	28c	*Opif.* 21; *Deo* 4 (Siegert)
519b, etc.	*Prov.* 2.17 HL	29–30	*Agr.* 128–129
526e	*Legat.* 211	29a	*Plant.* 131*
533d	*Prob.* 5; *Contempl.* 10	29b	*Prov.* 1.21 HL*
546b	*Opif.* 13	29d–e	*Mut.* 46
554f	*Deus* 24	29e	*Opif.* 21–22; *Cher.* 125;
557c	*Jos.* 32		*Migr.* 183; *QG* 1.6; *Deo* 12
576b	*Conf.*164		(Siegert)
588c	*Somn.* 2.14	29d–e	*Migr.* 37
617	*Somn.* 1.138	30a	*Sacr.* 82; *Prov.* 1.7 HL; *Deo*
			6 (Siegert)
Smp.		30b	*Aet.* 15; *Prov.* 1.22 HL
General	*Contempl.* 59–63	31a	*Aet.* 15
173a	*Contempl.* 57	31a–b	*Anim.* 61
191d	*Leg.* 2.72	32c	*Opif.* 171; *Det.* 154; *Plant.*
196c	*Det.* 141; *Mos.* 2.4		6; *Her.* 246; *Spec.* 1.210;
202e	*Gig.* 16; *Somn.* 1.141		*Aet.* 21; 25–26*; *Prov.* 1.19
206c	*Aet.* 69		HL; *Deo* 8 (Siegert)
211c	*Post.* 113	32c–33a	*Anim.* 61
218e	*Sobr.*12	33b	*Prov.* 2.56 HL; *Anim.* 17
		33c	*Aet.* 38*
Sph.		34a	*Gig.* 8
226a	*Migr.* 220*	34b	*Deo* 9 (Siegert)
230	*Decal.* 12	35a–b	*Opif.* 48
263e	*Anim.* 12	35b	*Decad.* 11 (Terian)*
263f	*Ebr.* 56	35–36	*Cher.* 21–24
		36c–d	*Cher.* 22–23; *Decal.* 103
Tht.		36d	*Her.* 233
144a	*Prov.* 2.16 HL	37–38b	*Deus* 31–32
149d	*Mut.* 144	37c–38c	*Opif.* 38
151c	*Her.* 247	37d	*Deus* 32; *Mut.* 267; *Her.*
152	*Her.* 246		165
152a	*Post.* 36	37e	*Aet.* 52–53
156a	*Deus* 14	38b	*Deus* 32; *Prov.* 1.20 HL*
160d	*Spec.* 1.27	39b–c	*Opif.* 58
173e	*Opif.* 70	39c	*Aet.* 52
176a–b	*Fug.* 63*; *Spec.* 4.188	39e–40a	*Opif.* 66
176c	*Fug.* 82*	40–41	*Agr.* 128–129
176d	*Spec.* 1.74; 3.50	41–42	*Opif.* 72–75; *Conf.* 175
183d	*Mos.* 1.22	41a	*Migr.* 181; *Decal.* 58; *Aet.*
184b–d	*Congr.* 143		13*
189e	*Anim.* 12	41b	*Her.* 246
191c	*Deus* 43; *Mut.* 212; *Her.*	41d	*Her.* 86; *Fug.* 72
	181*	42e	*Post.* 5; *Her.* 282; *Aet.* 29
		43a	*Gig.* 13; *Somn.* 1.147
Ti.		44a	*Congr.* 21
22a–f	*Aet.* 146–149	45b–c	*Deus* 79
24e	*Aet.* 141*		

2.135	*Ebr.* 70; *Anim.* 12
2.166	*Mut.* 77
2.169	*Prov.* 1.34 HL
2.223	*Anim.* 12
2.300	*Opif.* 8
2.312	*Opif.* 8
2.329	*Leg.* 3.175
2.333	*Leg.* 3.175
2.395	*Fug.* 11–13
2.457–460	*Leg.* 2.22; *Deus* 35–48
2.471	*Conf.* 184–187
2.473	*Conf.* 187
2.504–505	*Fug.* 75
2.505	*Prov.* 2.53 HL
2.509–510	*Opif.* 26; *Aet.* 4
2.527	*Prov.* 1.21 HL; *Deo* 6 (Siegert)
2.529	*Prov.* 1.21 HL
2.774	*Leg.* 1.91
2.787–789	*Fug.* 134
2.804–808	*Somn.* 1.31
2.806	*Spec.* 3.117
2.836	*Deus* 84
2.838	*Spec.* 1.6
2.847	*Deus* 34
2.872	*Deus* 84
2.915–921	*Mut.* 135
2.1009	*Leg.* 3.97; *Spec.* 1.32–35
2.1009–1020	*Spec.* 1.33–34
2.1012	*Anim.* 11
2.1013	*Migr.* 180
2.1131	*Anim.* 11
3.11	*Sobr.* 34
3.21	*Deus* 18
3.32	*Mut.* 34
3.83	*Anim.* 17
3.88	*Spec.* 1.318
3.92	*Her.* 156
3.136	*Det.* 7
3.169	*Mut.* 160
3.169–177	*Leg.* 3.2
3.208	*Spec.* 1.318
3.262	*Leg.* 1.87; *Mut.* 153
3.267	*Spec.* 2.188
3.322	*Jos.* 28
3.381–388	*Leg.* 2.99
3.389	*Decal.* 142–146
3.404	*Decal.* 142–146
3.431–432	*Spec.* 2.185
3.432	*Plant.* 106*
3.443–455	*Leg.* 3.129

3.482	*Spec.* 2.46
3.510	*Agr.* 160
3.516–517	*Leg.* 3.210; *Cher.* 14–17
3.525	*Her.* 156
3.539–540	*Agr.* 161
3.548	*Deus* 22; *Ebr.* 158
3.554–555	*Deus* 65–69
3.560	*Ebr.* 88
3.567	*Virt.* 28
3.589–603	*Post.* 138; *Sobr.* 56
3.613	*Det.* 16; *Ebr.* 142
3.613–614	*Mut.* 114
3.617	*Mut.* 152; *Somn.* 2.244; *Abr.* 261
3.617–24	*Agr.* 41; *Sobr.* 57
3.637–39	*Mut.* 32

Thucydides
2.40	*Her.* 158
2.43	*Jos.* 24
2.49	*Prov.* 2.90 HL

Theocritus
14.48	*Deus* 90; *Praem.* 111

Theognis
El. 5.535–536	*Prob.* 155*

Theophrastus
via D.L. 5.40–41	*Somn.* 1.10
fr. 184	*Aet.* 117–149*

Unidentified texts
Comic Poet (PCG 8: 475) *Contempl.* 43
TrGF 2: 318 *Prob.* 145
TrGF 2: 327 *Prob.* 152*
TrGF 2: 327a *Aet.* 27*
Unknown ode *Anim.* 28*
Unknown poet[11] *Aet.* 41*
Unknown text *Spec.* 4.20*
SH 1134a *Aet.* 140*

Xenophon
Cyr.
8.2.10	*Somn.* 1.140

[11] See n. 8 above.

Mem.
1.6.7   *Sacr.* 86
1.6.8   *Sacr.* 116
2.1   *Sacr.* 21–33; *Prov.* 2.27 HL

Smp.
2.1–23   *Contempl.* 58
2–3   *Contempl.* 57

Xenophanes
A26 DK   *Prov.* 2.39 HL; 2.42 HL

Zeno
via Cic., *Scip.* 1.14.19   *Somn.* 1.30
A18 DK   *Prob.* 14
SVF 1.103   *Aet.* 18
SVF 1.110   *Opif.* 73
SVF 1.218   *Prob.* 97*
SVF 1.228   *Prob.* 53*

Part II: *Special Cases Not Included in Part I*

1. Unidentifiable short citations marked in Philo's text: *Ebr.* 116; *Somn.* 1.22; *Abr.* 194 (cf. Lib., *Or.* 64.48.6); *Spec.* 2.77; *Spec.* 3.69; *Aet.* 66 (cf. *Mos.* 2.84; *Spec.* 3.33, 109; *Legat.* 56); *Anim.* 33 (cf. Arist., *HA* 611a26)

2. Delphic axiom (γνῶθι σαυτὸν): *Fug.* 46; *Somn.* 1.57–58; *Spec.* 1.44; *Legat.* 69; *Deo* 2 (Siegert)

3. Protagoras, 'The human is the measure of all things' (cf. Pl., *Tht.* 152a; *Cra.* 385e): *Post.* 35; *Her.* 246; *Somn.* 2.193

4. Proverbial phrases, often marked by "as they say" (ὥς φασι), or as κατὰ τὴν παροιμίαν, etc.: a second best voyage (*Somn.* 1.44, 180; *Abr.* 123; *Decal.* 84; cf. Pl., *Pol.* 297e, etc.); friends have all things in common (*Abr.* 235; *Mos.* 1.156; cf. Pl., *Phdr.* 279c); like the horse to the meadow (*Mos.* 1.22; cf. Pl., *Tht.* 183d; Luc., *Pisc.* 9); adding fire to fire (*Legat.* 125); beginning with the sacred line (*Somn.* 2.119); like washing brick or carrying water in a net (*QG* 2.54); blind wealth (*Fug.* 19; *Abr.* 25; *Jos.* 258; *Mos.* 1.153; *Spec.* 1.25; 2.23; *Virt.* 5, 85; *Praem.* 54; *Prov.* 2.13; note Pl., *Lg.* 1.631c); not too much of anything (*Spec.* 2.83; *QE* 1.6); to reslay the slain (*Spec.* 4.202; cf. D.L. 2.135.10); excels by the whole and all (*Virt.* 11); lives from day to day (*Virt.* 88); satiety begets insolence (*Post.* 145; *Agr.* 32; *Abr.* 228; *Spec.* 3.43; *Virt.* 162; *Flacc.* 91; cf. Sol., fr. 6 West; Thgn., *Eleg.* 1.153); beginning is half the whole (*Det.* 64; *Agr.* 125; *Her.* 116; cf. Pl., *Lg.* 6.753e; Hes., *Op.* 40)

Part III: *Philo in Stoicorum Veterum Fragmenta and Long & Sedley*[12]

A. Philonic Order

		68	2.453	
		78	3.739	
Opif.		82–83	3.304	
3	3.336	84	3.304	
8–9	2.302	111	3.609	
26	2.511	115	3.505	
36	2.358	121	3.636	
43	2.713	123	3.636	
66	2.722	136–138	2.842	
67	2.745			
73	3.372	*Det.*		
117	2.833	7–9	3.33	
142–144	3.337	72	3.209	
166	2.57	168	2.833	
Leg.		*Post.*		
1.11	2.833	75	3.670	
1.30	2.844; LS 53P	126	2.862	
1.56–58	3.202	133	3.31	
1.59	2.843	138	3.364	
1.61	2.843			
1.63–68	3.263	*Gig.*		
1.79	3.263	67	3.680	
1.87	3.263			
1.93–94	3.519	*Deus*		
2.22–23	2.458; LS 47P	22	3.566	
3.113	3.679	31	2.512	
3.175	2.334	35–36	LS 47Q	
3.177	3.116	35–37	2.458	
3.201–202	3.676	41–46	2.458	
3.210	3.512	100	3.518	
3.246	3.406			
3.247	3.671	*Agr.*		
		14, 16	2.39	
Cher.		30	2.833	
14–15	3.513; LS 59H	139–142	2.182	
		160–161	3.541	
Sacr.				
43	3.522			
46	3.375			

[12] In this part of the index, references to Long & Sedley are marked "LS", while all other references are to *SVF*.

Plant.	
49	3.7
69	3.596
142–144	3.712
149–150	3.712
154–156	3.712
176	1.229

Ebr.	
88–92	3.301

Sobr.	
34–41	3.244
56–57	3.603

Conf.	
5	2.560
156–157	2.664
184–187	2.472

Migr.	
128	3.8
156–157	3.436
178–180	2.532
197	3.621

Her.	
232	2.833
299	3.222

Congr.	
141–142	2.95
146–150	2.99

Fug.	
13	2.760
112	2.719
182	2.861

Mut.	
152	3.620

Somn.	
1.145	2.674

Jos.	
28–39	3.323

Mos.	
2.7	3.303
2.139–140	3.392
2.151	3.10

2.181	3.227

Decal.	
56?[13]	2.1009

Spec.	
1.32–35	2.1010
1.208	2.616
1.210	2.695
1.246	3.559
2.47	3.610
2.49	3.610
2.69	3.352
2.73	3.330
2.122	3.352
4.79	3.446
4.145	3.286

Virt.	
6	3.707
138	2.759

Praem.	
33–34	2.1171
71	3.388
112–13	3.558

Prob.	
32–34	3.357
36	3.357
37–38	3.358
42	3.359
45–47	3.360
48–52	3.361
53	1.228
59	3.362
60–61	3.363
97	1.218; LS 67N
160	1.179

Aet.	
4	2.621
8–9	2.620
18	2.437

[13] Von Arnim simply has: "Cf. Philo *Leg. Alleg.* III p. 107 M. Sextus adv. math. IX 26.27." This page number in Mangey does not correspond to *Leg.*, but *Decal.* 56 is paralleled in the passage of Sextus Empiricus to which von Arnim refers.

47	2.613		2.4	2.802; LS 47R
47–51	LS 28P		2.85	2.562
48–49	2.397		3.48	2.740
52–54	2.509; LS 52A		4.5	2.566
72	2.636		4.11	3.207
75	2.459		4.73	3.571
75	2.913		4.74	3.634
76–77	LS 46P		4.76	3.681
76–84	3.Boeth.7		4.92	3.583
77	3.Diog.27		4.99	3.592
81	2.611		4.117	2.145
86	2.612		4.136	3.271
90	1.511; 2.611; LS 46M		4.165	3.624
94	2.618		4.165	3.678
97	2.874		4.188	2.635
101–103	2.619		4.215	2.643
117–131	1.106			
117–131	1.106a		*QE*	
			1.1	2.584
Prov.			2.81	2.561
1.9 HL	2.577		2.88	2.561
1.10 HL	2.578		2.90	2.548
1.13 HL	2.591		2.112	3.277
1.15 HL	2.592		2.120	2.803
1.18–19 HL	2.592			
1.22 HL	1.85		*Anim.*	
1.25 HL	2.1111		45–46	2.726
1.29 HL	2.1112		60–61	2.728
1.32 HL	2.1113		77	2.731
1.40 HL	2.1114		78–80	2.732
2.41 HL	2.1079		80	2.732
2.48–49 HL	1.509		84–85	2.726
2.55 HL	2.1141		91–92	2.733
2.56 HL	2.1143		93–95	2.730
2.57 HL	2.1142		96	2.834
2.58 HL	2.86		98	2.734
2.62 HL	2.1144		*Deo* (Siegert)	
2.62 HL	2.568		6	2.422
2.64 HL	2.1145			
2.67 HL	2.1146			
2.73 HL	2.1147		B. *SVF* Order	
2.74 HL	1.548			
2.74 HL	2.1150		1.85	*Prov.* 1.22 HL
2.74 HL	2.688		1.106	*Aet.* 117–131
2.76 HL	2.1148		1.106a	*Aet.* 117–131
2.77 HL	2.680		1.179	*Prob.* 160
2.78 HL	2.694		1.218	*Prob.* 97
2.84 HL	2.1149		1.228	*Prob.* 53
			1.229	*Plant.* 176
QG			1.509	*Prov.* 2.48–49 HL
1.64	2.567		1.511	*Aet.* 90
1.75	2.832		1.548	*Prov.* 2.74 HL

2.39	*Agr.* 14, 16		2.688	*Prov.* 2.74 HL
2.57	*Opif.* 166		2.694	*Prov.* 2.78 HL
2.86	*Prov.* 2.58 HL		2.695	*Spec.* 1.210
2.95	*Congr.* 141–142		2.713	*Opif.* 43
2.99	*Congr.* 146–150		2.719	*Fug.* 112
2.145	*QG* 4.117		2.722	*Opif.* 66
2.182	*Agr.* 139–142		2.726	*Anim.* 45–46
2.302	*Opif.* 8–9		2.726	*Anim.* 84–85
2.334	*Leg.* 3.175		2.728	*Anim.* 60–61
2.358	*Opif.* 36		2.730	*Anim.* 93–95
2.397	*Aet.* 48–49		2.731	*Anim.* 77
2.422	*Deo* 6 (Siegert)		2.732	*Anim.* 78–80
2.437	*Aet.* 18		2.732	*Anim.* 80
2.453	*Sacr.* 68		2.733	*Anim.* 91–92
2.458	*Leg.* 2.22–23		2.734	*Anim.* 98
2.458	*Deus* 35–37		2.740	*QG* 3.48
2.458	*Deus* 41–46		2.745	*Opif.* 67
2.459	*Aet.* 75		2.759	*Virt.* 138
2.472	*Conf.* 184–187		2.760	*Fug.* 13
2.509	*Aet.* 52–54		2.802	*QG* 2.4
2.511	*Opif.* 26		2.803	*QE* 2.120
2.512	*Deus* 31		2.832	*QG* 1.75
2.532	*Migr.* 178–180		2.833	*Leg.* 1.11
2.548	*QE* 2.90		2.833	*Opif.* 117
2.560	*Conf.* 5		2.833	*Agr.* 30
2.561	*QE* 2.81		2.833	*Her.* 232
2.561	*QE* 2.88		2.833	*Det.* 168
2.562	*QG* 2.85		2.834	*Anim.* 96
2.566	*QG* 4.5		2.842	*Sacr.* 136–138
2.567	*QG* 1.64		2.843	*Leg.* 1.59
2.568	*Prov.* 2.62 HL		2.843	*Leg.* 1.61
2.577	*Prov.* 1.9 HL		2.844	*Leg.* 1.30
2.578	*Prov.* 1.10 HL		2.861	*Fug.* 182
2.584	*QE* 1.1		2.862	*Post.* 126
2.591	*Prov.* 1.13 HL		2.874	*Aet.* 97
2.592	*Prov.* 1.15 HL		2.913	*Aet.* 75
2.592	*Prov.* 1.18–19 HL		2.1009	*Decal.* 56?[14]
2.611	*Aet.* 90		2.1010	*Spec.* 1.32–35
2.611	*Aet.* 81		2.1079	*Prov.* 2.41 HL
2.612	*Aet.* 86		2.1111	*Prov.* 1.25 HL
2.613	*Aet.* 47		2.1112	*Prov.* 1.29 HL
2.616	*Spec.* 1.208		2.1113	*Prov.* 1.32 HL
2.618	*Aet.* 94		2.1114	*Prov.* 1.40 HL
2.619	*Aet.* 101–103		2.1141	*Prov.* 2.55 HL
2.620	*Aet.* 8–9		2.1142	*Prov.* 2.57 HL
2.621	*Aet.* 4		2.1143	*Prov.* 2.56 HL
2.635	*QG* 4.188		2.1144	*Prov.* 2.62 HL
2.636	*Aet.* 72		2.1145	*Prov.* 2.64 HL
2.643	*QG* 4.215			
2.664	*Conf.* 156–157			
2.674	*Somn.* 1.145		[14] See n. 13 above.	
2.680	*Prov.* 2.77 HL			

2.1146	*Prov.* 2.67 HL		3.512	*Leg.* 3.210
2.1147	*Prov.* 2.73 HL		3.513	*Cher.* 14–15
2.1148	*Prov.* 2.76 HL		3.518	*Deus* 100
2.1149	*Prov.* 2.84 HL		3.519	*Leg.* 1.93–94
2.1150	*Prov.* 2.74 HL		3.522	*Sacr.* 43
2.1171	*Praem.* 33–34		3.541	*Agr.* 160–161
			3.558	*Praem.* 112–113
3.7	*Plant.* 49		3.559	*Spec.* 1.246
3.8	*Migr.* 128		3.566	*Deus* 22
3.10	*Mos.* 2.151		3.571	*QG* 4.73
3.31	*Post.* 133		3.583	*QG* 4.92
3.33	*Det.* 7–9		3.592	*QG* 4.99
3.116	*Leg.* 3.177		3.596	*Plant.* 69
3.202	*Leg.* 1.56–58		3.603	*Sobr.* 56–57
3.207	*QG* 4.11		3.609	*Sacr.* 111
3.209	*Det.* 72		3.610	*Spec.* 2.47
3.222	*Her.* 299		3.610	*Spec.* 2.49
3.227	*Mos.* 2.181		3.620	*Mut.* 152
3.244	*Sobr.* 34–41		3.621	*Migr.* 197
3.263	*Leg.* 1.63–68		3.624	*QG* 4.165
3.263	*Leg.* 1.87		3.634	*QG* 4.74
3.263	*Leg.* 1.79		3.636	*Sacr.* 121
3.271	*QG* 4.136		3.636	*Sacr.* 123
3.277	*QE* 2.112		3.670	*Post.* 75
3.286	*Spec.* 4.145		3.671	*Leg.* 3.247
3.301	*Ebr.* 88–92		3.676	*Leg.* 3.201–202
3.303	*Mos.* 2.7		3.678	*QG* 4.165
3.304	*Sacr.* 82–83		3.679	*Leg.* 3.113
3.304	*Sacr.* 84		3.680	*Gig.* 67
3.323	*Jos.* 28–39		3.681	*QG* 4.76
3.330	*Spec.* 2.73		3.707	*Virt.* 6
3.336	*Opif.* 3		3.712	*Plant.* 142–144
3.337	*Opif.* 142–144		3.712	*Plant.* 149–150
3.352	*Spec.* 2.69		3.712	*Plant.* 154–156
3.352	*Spec.* 2.122		3.739	*Sacr.* 78
3.357	*Prob.* 32–34		3.Diog.27	*Aet.* 77
3.357	*Prob.* 36		3.Boeth.7	*Aet.* 76–84
3.358	*Prob.* 37–38			
3.359	*Prob.* 42			
3.360	*Prob.* 45–47			
3.361	*Prob.* 48–52			
3.362	*Prob.* 59			
3.363	*Prob.* 60–61			
3.364	*Post.* 138			
3.372	*Opif.* 73			
3.375	*Sacr.* 46			
3.388	*Praem.* 71			
3.392	*Mos.* 2.139–140			
3.406	*Leg.* 3.246			
3.436	*Migr.* 156–157			
3.446	*Spec.* 4.79			
3.505	*Sacr.* 115			

C. Long & Sedley Order

LS 28P	*Aet.* 47–51
LS 46M	*Aet.* 90
LS 46P	*Aet.* 76–77
LS 47P	*Leg.* 2.22–23

LS 47Q	*Deus* 35–36
LS 47R	*QG* 2.4
LS 52A	*Aet.* 52–54
LS 53P	*Leg.*1.30
LS 59H	*Cher.* 14–15
LS 67N	*Prob.* 97

Mansfield College, Oxford[15]

[15] Thanks are due to Professors David Runia and Greg Sterling for generous comments that measurably improved this index.

The Studia Philonica Annual 25 (2013) 169–209

BIBLIOGRAPHY SECTION

PHILO OF ALEXANDRIA
AN ANNOTATED BIBLIOGRAPHY 2010

D. T. Runia, K. Berthelot, E. Birnbaum, A. C. Geljon, H. M. Keizer,
J. Leonhardt-Balzer, J. P. Martín, M. R. Niehoff, S. J. K. Pearce,
T. Seland

2010[1]

S. Al-Suadi, 'Wechsel der Identitäten: Philos Therapeuten im Wandel der Wissenschaftsgeschichte,' *Judaica* 66 (2010) 209–228.

The author describes the reception history of Philo's account of the Therapeutae in *Contempl.* as an expression of the *Zeitgeist* of each period. In the 19th century the debate focused on the identity of the Therapeutae: Jewish context with an ascetic and mystical interest, Bellermann (1821); Christian orders, Gförer (1831); mixture of pagan and Jewish elements, Neopythagorean ideas, Ritschl (1855); theosophic-mystical Hellenism, Baur (1876). Lucius (1879), and also Schürer and Harnack, regard the author of *Contempl.* as a Christian of the 3rd-4th century, reflecting on Christian monasticism. Against this, Massebieau (1888), Conybeare (1895) and Wendland (1895), argue for Philo's authorship and the Therapeutae's historicity, a position generally accepted ever since (Wagner 1960). Scholarship in the 20th century focuses on the Therapeutae's name (Schönfeld 1960, Vermes 1961)and their relationship with Qumran (Klinghardt 1996). At the turn to the 21st century the emphasis shifts to the cultural diversity within Judaism and a variety of hermeneutical approaches are used: social historical (Taylor 1998, Davies 2003), cultural–anthropological (McGowan 1999), rhetorical (Engberg-Pedersen 1999), allegorical (Sterling 2004) or political (Niehoff 2010). (JLB).

---

[1] This bibliography has been prepared by the members of the International Philo Bibliography Project, under the leadership of D. T. Runia (Melbourne). The principles on which the annotated bibliography is based have been outlined in *SPhA* 2 (1990) 141–142, and are largely based on those used to compile the 'mother works,' R-R, RRS and RRS2 (on the inclusion of works in languages outside the scholarly mainstream see esp. RRS2 xii). The division of the work this year is as follows: material in English (and Dutch) by D. T. Runia (DTR), E. Birnbaum (EB), A. C. Geljon (ACG) and S. J. K. Pearce (SJKP); in French by K. Berthelot (KB); in Italian by H. M. Keizer (HMK); in German by Jutta Leonhardt-Balzer (JLB); in Spanish and Portuguese by J. P. Martín (JPM); in Scandinavian languages (and by Scandinavian scholars) by T. Seland (TS), and in Hebrew and by Israeli scholars by M. R. Niehoff (MRN). Once again this year much benefit has been derived from the related bibliographical labours of L. Perrone (Bologna) and his team in the journal *Adamantius* (studies on the Alexandrian tradition). Other scholars who have given assistance this year

T. ALEKNIENÉ, 'L'«extase mystique» dans la tradition platonicienne: Philon d'Alexandrie et Plotin,' *The Studia Philonica Annual* 22 (2010) 53–82.

At the end of the ninth treatise of Plotinus' *Enneads*, the neoplatonic philosopher uses the word ἔκστασις in connection with a kind of mystical experience, which he describes as a state of complete rest, as well as an exit out of the self which is simultaneously an intensification of the self. This description has been compared to Philo's discourse about ἔκστασις in connection with the migration of the soul. At the end of the 19th century and the beginning of the 20th, in particular, the issue of a possible influence of Philo upon Plotinus has been hotly debated. In Philo's work, the main text concerning the notion of ἔκστασις is the passage in *Her.* (249ff.) about Genesis 15 and Abraham's *tardemah* (ἔκστασις in the Septuagint). In *Her.* 257, however, Philo also uses the term to speak about the sleep of Adam when God creates the woman; there it designates the inactivity of the intellect, which corresponds to the awakening of sensation. Plotinus' remark in *Tr.* 49 (V,3) would appear to be a polemical response to Philo's use of ἔκστασις in that sense. In his distinction between four types of ἔκστασις Philo is influenced by the four kinds of divine madness (μανία) discussed in Plato's *Phaedrus*. The deepest meaning of ἔκστασις for Philo consists in the 'sleep' of the intellect that leaves space to divine possession. For both Plato and Philo only the mind of the wise can experience ἔκστασις. However, in contrast to Philo, Plato does not state that the mind has to go beyond its intellectual capacities to reach the ultimate experience of the divine, and never connects ἔκστασις with the fact of leaving one's self behind. Moreover, in Philo's system, prophetic ecstasy actually takes the place of Plato's philosophical μανία. Philo thus attributes a new meaning to the term ἔκστασις: it designates an experience of intimacy with the divine, beyond the intellect, by a soul which has already reached ethical perfection. When Plotinus describes ἔκστασις as an exit out of the self, it is therefore probable that this notion goes back to Philo, whose work Plotinus may well have discovered during his stay in Alexandria. (KB)

M. ALESSO, 'Qué es Israel en los textos de Filón,' *Circe de clásicos y modernos* 14 (2010) 12–29.

After a brief description of how in the Torah Israel is named the people of God, the author discusses Philo's reading of Gen 32:29–31, finding an innovative exegesis by which the Alexandrian establishes the particularity of Israel as 'one who sees' or 'one who can see.' She shows that the Greek theme of the superiority of vision over hearing enables

---

are Giovanni Benedetto, Francesca Calabi, Maurizio Olivieri, Jean Riaud, Sami Yli-Karjanmaa. My research assistant in Melbourne, Kyle Conrau-Lewis, helped me with various tasks. This year once again I owe much to my former Leiden colleague M. R. J. Hofstede, who laid a secure foundation for the bibliography through his extremely thorough electronic searches. However, the bibliography remains inevitably incomplete, because much work on Philo is tucked away in monographs and articles, the titles of which do not mention his name. Scholars are encouraged to get in touch with members of the team if they spot omissions (addresses below in 'Notes on Contributors'). In order to preserve continuity with previous years, the bibliography retains its own customary stylistic conventions and has not changed to those of the Society of Biblical Literature used in the remainder of the Annual. Investigations are still in progress in relation to the possibility of making an online version of the Bibliography which will cover the entire history of Philonic scholarship, including the material included in G-G.

Philo to describe the contemplative character of the Jewish people in relation to its universal priestly role. According to Philo, any human who reaches the ability to see and love God, whether native Jew or proselyte, belongs to the people of vision. The concept of Israel thus becomes a philosophical category, including not only who belongs to the nation (ἔθνος) but also to a class (γένος). (JPM)

L. Alexidze, 'Imago et similitudo Dei (Platon–Philon von Alexandrien– Kirchenväter–Ioanne Petrizi),' *Phasis: Greek and Roman Studies (Ivane Javakhishvili Tbilisi State University)* 12 (2010) 48–72.

The article studies the concept of the concept *imago dei* in the commentary of Iane Petrizi on Proclus' *Elementatio theologica* in the context of the (Neo-)Platonic and Patristic tradition. The issue of the human being as image of God is already discussed in Platonism, but is particularly prominent in the interpretation of Gen 1:26. The article focuses on New Testament and Patristic approaches. The Alexandrian theologians Philo, Clement, Origen and Athanasius, along with the Gnostics and various church fathers propose that the divine Logos is the image of God. For Philo God is the paradigm, the Logos is the image of God, therefore subordinated, and the pneumatic (never the bodily, material) human being, the highest part of the human soul, is created after God's image, image of the image. (JLB)

P. Ashwin-Siejkowski, *Clement of Alexandria on Trial: the Evidence of 'Heresy' from Photius' Bibliotheca*, Supplements to Vigiliae Christianae 101 (Leiden 2010), passim.

This interesting and original study examines the eight accusations of 'heretical' doc- trines that the ninth cent. Byzantine patriarch Photius makes against the early Christian thinker Clement of Alexandria. For four of these the Philonic background is separately studied. (1) For the accusation of the existence of eternal matter and the eternity of the ideas there is a section entitled 'Philo of Alexandria as an important precursor of Clement' (pp. 27–31). (2) For the accusation regarding the teachings of the two Logoi of the Father there is a section entitled 'Philo of Alexandria and the nature of the Logos' (pp. 58–65). (3) For the accusation of the assumption that the Son of God is a creature there is a section entitled 'The origin of the Logos in Philo of Alexandria's philosophy' (pp. 77–80). (4) For the accusation regarding the creation of Eve from Adam in a blasphemous and shameful way there is a section entitled 'Eve as a metaphor in Philo's philosophy' (pp. 134–136). Philo is also relevant for two other accusations regarding the transmigration of souls (p. 125) and the sexual encounters of angels with human women (p. 151). In his conclusion the author emphasises that Clement was a 'very original, creative theologian' (p. 162). Philo was his closest ally in theological creativity, but Clement goes even further than he, not only in his assimilation of Platonism, Stoicism and Neopythagoreanism, but also in his more open approach to the Bible. (DTR)

M. Baretta, *Una biografia guidaico-ellenistica: il De vita Mosis die Filone Alessandrino* (diss. Pisa 2010).

The work starts with the analysis of passages of Philo's *Mos.* (1.5–84; 94–146; 163–180; 191–209; 220–238; 263–304; 2.159–186; 246–292) in the quest for its sources, whether biblical, Jewish, or Greek, and especialy for Philo's originality in re-writing his material on Moses. It emerges that Philo follows the biblical narrative without significant changes, but at the same time he slightly modifies it in order to idealise the character of Moses and to create an attractive Greek narrative. Particular attention is paid to central themes such as God, prophecy, the portrait of Moses, Philo's style and the hypothetical public of the biography. Throughout his work Philo is able to mix Jewish and Greek culture as far as politics, religion and philosophy are concerned. The style is classical, lively, never boring. The didactic aim, however, remains quite apparent. There can be no doubt that Philo is addressing his work to a non-Jewish public. The dissertation offers as its main conclusion an original thesis about the real target of his work: Philo has in mind the Romans who controlled Egypt and needed to judge the ethnic and religious clashes of the time. (HMK; based on the author's summary)

C. T. BEGG, 'Moses' First Moves (Exod 2:11–22) as Retold by Josephus and Philo,' *Polish Journal of Biblical Research* 9 (2010) 67–93.

Exod 2 speaks of various actions done by Moses, namely his killing of an Egyptian, his exchange with two Hebrews, his flight to Midian, his encounter with the daughters of the Midian priest, and his marriage with one of the priest's daughters. In this article the author examines the rewriting of these events by Josephus (*AJ* 2.254–263) and by Philo (*Mos.* 1.44–59). Josephus narrates the events very freely, making substitutions for and additions to or modifications of the biblical data. Furthermore, Moses' image is strikingly ameliorated. Philo's rewriting also deviates from the biblical account in many ways. He does not mention, for instance, Moses' encounter with the fighting Hebrews. He takes care to answers questions raised by the biblical text, and he retouches the various biblical characters. Philo also accentuates the positive image of Moses, having Moses live a philosophical life in Midian. In this way Philo makes the story a vehicle for his philosophical, psychological and ethical lessons. Finally, the author compares Philo and Josephus, pointing out similarities and differences. (ACG)

C. T. BEGG, 'Joseph's two dreams according to Josephus and Philo,' *Antonianum* 85 (2010) 355–375.

The author examines two rewritings of the story of Joseph as told in Gen 37:1–11, namely Josephus' *AJ* 2.7–17 and Philo's *Ios.* 1–9. Josephus leaves aside certain data (e.g. Joseph's shepherding with his brothers) and elaborates others (Joseph's telling of his first dream). Philo's rewriting is characterized by elaboration of the biblical data, for instance the digression on Joseph as shepherd. Other amplifications are Jacob's predilection for Joseph, the brothers' negative reaction to this fact, their response to Joseph's telling of his first dream, and Jacob's reaction to the second dream. In this way Philo's retelling of the story obtains a didactic character. But at the same time he retains virtually all of the biblical narrative. Just as in the Genesis account Philo does not explicitly mention God's role in the events. The author ends by comparing Philo and Josephus mentioning similarities (e.g. attributing positive characteristics to the brothers, giving the story a didactic turn) and differences (Philo, for instance, does not refer to God, as Josephus does; Philo's elaboration of Joseph's shepherding is absent in Josephus). (ACG)

M. BELTRAN, and J. L. LLINAS, 'El dios incomprehensible de Filón y su huella en el neoplatonismo,' *Anales del Seminario de Historia de la Filosofía* 27 (2010) 49–61.

The authors of this short article return to the thesis of Henri Guyot (1906), arguing that there was a Philonic influence on Plotinus on the topic of the unknowability of God.

Noting that Wolfson in his celebrated study does not quote Guyot, they state that the issue should be revisited. The authors argue that God, according to Philo, is without qualities (ἄποιος) and that nothing can be predicated of Him except properties (ἰδιότητες). This latter statement is not supported by texts of Philo, which, in general, are cited with inaccuracies, and are not compared exactly with Plotinan texts. (JPM)

B. A. Berkowitz, 'Allegory and Ambiguity: Jewish Identity in Philo's *De Congressu,' Journal of Jewish Studies* 61 (2010) 1–17.

Addressing the broad question of what was Jewish identity in the period of the Roman Empire, the author argues that Philo's exegetical practice should be considered as 'a critical means by which he crafts Jewish identity.' The focus of the article is on Philo's exegesis of Lev 18:1–5 (*Congr.* 85–88), a text which strongly insists on the separateness of the people of Israel from other peoples. It proposes that Philo's allegorical interpretation of this text creates a 'strategic ambiguity regarding Jewish exclusivism.' A similar ambiguity is also related to Philo's exegesis of Hagar in Gen 16:2–3. Viewing Philo's work in the context of stereotypes of Jewish misanthropy in Graeco-Roman Egypt, the author concludes that Philo appears to conceal 'a potentially dangerous particularist reading of the Pentateuch within his universalising philosophical discourse.' (SJKP)

M. F. Bird, Crossing Over Sea and Land. Jewish Missionary Activity in the Second Temple Period (Peabody, Mass. 2010), esp. 103–109.

This study of the extent and nature of Jewish proselytizing activity among non-Jews in the first centuries b.c.e./c.e. includes a brief overview of relevant aspects of Philo's thought (pp. 103–109): his conception of the purpose of the Greek Torah translation, his emphasis on Jewish openness to outsiders, and his positive appraisal of proselytes. (SJKP)

E. Birnbaum, 'Exegetical Building Blocks in Philo's Interpretation of the Patriarchs,' in P. Walters (ed.), *From Judaism to Christianity: Tradition and Transition. A Festschrift for Thomas H. Tobin, S.J. on the Occasion of His Sixty-fifth Birthday* (Leiden 2010) 69–92.

Underlying some of Philo's most elaborate and ingenious interpretations is the notion that Abraham, Isaac, and Jacob exemplify the acquisition of virtue through learning, nature, and practice, respectively. Although Philo himself does not explain the basis of this motif, it appears to be constructed from several smaller units of interpretation, or 'exegetical building blocks.' At the foundation is an ancient debate about whether and how virtue can be taught. Several Greek and Roman sources identify nature, learning, and practice as essential to acquiring not only virtue but also other qualities and skills. Based on intricate interpretations—some, perhaps, traditional—of specific biblical verses or episodes, Philo links each patriarch with a different path to virtue: He connects Abraham with learning on the basis of complex interpretations of Abraham's mating with Hagar, his journey from Chaldea, and, secondarily, the change of his name from Abram to Abraham. Isaac becomes associated with one who is naturally gifted on the basis of an interpretation of one or possibly two verses from Gen 21. An involved exegesis of Jacob's wrestling with an adversary in Gen 32 leads this patriarch to be understood as one who acquires virtue through practice. Finally, Philo also hints that an allegorization of the Graces, figures in

Greek mythology, may have served as a model, which was adopted and adapted in Jewish exegesis of the biblical patriarchs. An understanding of how this trope about the patriarchs was formed thus provides a fascinating window on the learned and sophisticated world of Alexandrian Jewish exegesis. (EB)

M. D. Boeri, 'Platonismo y estoicismo en el *De aeternitate mundi* de Filón de Alejandría,' in J.-F. Pradeau (ed.), *Études Platoniciennes VII: Philon d'Alexandrie* (Paris 2010) 65–94.

Focusing on *Aet.*, though also taking into account the entire corpus Philonicum, the author revisits again the issue of Philo's Platonism in relation to his Stoicism. Generally the author argues that Philo does not embrace any philosophical school as his own, but he is an unusual eclectic, choosing aspects of almost all philosophical trends to produce a thinking oriented towards the understanding of biblical text. Having stated this, the author accepts that Philo is favorable to Platonism and a critic of Stoicism. However, Philo's Platonism appears innovative, with developments that go beyond the Platonic text. As for the criticism of Stoicism, Philo does not hesitate to take over many of its themes. Among the most important points mentioned by the author are: the figure of the Logos as power, as cohesive principle, and the identification with *pneuma*; the psychology of action; the rejection of the Stoic theory of ἐκπύρωσις, though accepting the concept of διακόσμησις. (JPM)

D. Boesenberg, 'Philo's Descriptions of Jewish Sabbath Practice,' *The Studia Philonica Annual* 22 (2010) 143–163.

Philo's *Hypoth.* and *Contempl.* have often been categorized as 'apologetic' works. This article explores the aptness of such a classification through a comparative analysis of the treatment of Sabbath observance in these works and in the rest of the Philonic corpus (*Mos.* II; *Spec.* II; *Decal.*; *Prob.*; *Legat.*). Boesenberg concludes that Philo's description of Sabbath practice in the *Hypoth.* is clearly consistent with an apologetic agenda (as in *Legat.*, responding directly to pagan criticism of Sabbath observance), while the treatment of the Sabbath in *Contempl.* is less easily classed as apologetic in function (together with *Mos.*, *Spec.*, *Decal.* and *Prob.*, it is an implicit response to pagan accusations). Philo's regular mode of describing the Sabbath is set out in a comparative chart at the end of the article. (SJKP)

A. P. Bos, 'De uitleiding uit Egypte in de Openbaring van Johannes, bij Philo van Alexandrië en in de Hymne van de Parel [Dutch: The exodus from Egypt in the Revelation of John, in Philo of Alexandria, and in the Hymn of the Pearl],' in K. van der Ziel and H. Holwerda (eds.), *Het stralend teken. 60 jaar exegetische vergezichten van dr. D. Holwerda,'* (Franeker 2010) 18–27.

In his allegorical interpretations Philo regards the human being as a composite of a material, mortal body and an immaterial, immortal soul. In this line of thought Egypt is seen as the land of body and of corporeality, from which the human soul has to been liberated. It is probable that Philo's anthropological view has influenced the Christian Gnostics. They also think that the human soul, which is the divine element in the human being, has to be freed from the material body. The hymn of the pearl shows also a Gnostic world-view, in which Egypt represents the land of the body, which the divine soul should leave in order to return to its celestial homeland. (ACG)

A. P. Bos, 'Hagar and the 'Enkyklios Paideia' in Philo of Alexandria,' in M. Goodman, G. H. van Kooten and J. van Ruiten (eds.), *Abraham, the Nations, and the Hagarites: Jewish, Christian, and Islamic Perspectives on Kinship with Abraham*, Themes in Biblical Narrative (Leiden 2010) 163–175.

The author begins by giving a short overview of Philo's presentation of Hagar, the female slave of Sarah. Generally, Philo interprets the name Hagar as 'foreigner' or 'asylum-seeker.' The story of Hagar and Sarah as told in Gen 16:1–6 is extensively dealt with in *Congr*. Sarah, Abraham's wife, does not bear children for him, because he has not yet attained perfection or spiritual adulthood. Abraham, symbol of the soul who yearns for knowledge, first has to study the preparatory studies, the so-called *enkyklios paideia*. The figure of Hagar is related to the theme of the migration of Abraham from the land of the Chaldeans, which is seen as the transition from worship of cosmic gods to worship of transcendent nature. Philo's interpretation of Hagar has been derived from Greek thought. The Stoics, for instance, interpret Penelope and her bondmaids as wisdom and the branches of science. Finally, the author argues that Philo's distinction between the disciplines that are related to sense-perceptible reality (of which Hagar is a symbol) and the highest knowledge, Wisdom (represented by Sarah) has its origin in the works of Aristotle. It would seem that Aristotle is the first author who distinguished study of reality that surrounds us (*enkyklios*) and knowledge of transcendent reality. (ACG)

A. Bosch-Veciana, *Judaisme alexandrí i filosofia* (Barcelona 2010).

The author includes in this volume two articles previously published in *Revista Catalana de Teología* 34 (2009) 167–188 and 503–521, and summarized in *SPhA vol.* 24 pp. 187–188. (JPM)

M.-O. Boulnois, 'Les péricopes de Sara 'sœur-épouse' (Gn 12, 10–20 et Gn 20, 1–18) chez les Pères grecs,' in M. Arnold, G. Dahan and A. Noblesse-Rocher (eds.), *La sœur-épouse (Genèse 12, 10–20),'* (Paris 2010) 27–66.

The Church Fathers addressed the problematic issue of Abraham's lie about Sarah, when he presents her as his sister instead of presenting her as his wife (Gen 12:10-20; 20), in basically two ways. These two ways correspond to a historical (or literal) and an allegorical reading that can be traced back respectively to Flavius Josephus on the one hand and to Philo on the other. The literal reading consists in arguing that Sarah was not Abraham's sister *stricto sensu*, but rather his niece. This interpretation, testifying to the difficulty of making sense of the word 'sister,' which according to Leviticus implies an incest between Abraham and Sarah, can be found in Josephus, Eusebius of Emesus, Theodoret of Cyrus, Diodorus of Tarsus, Didymus the Blind and John Chrysostomus, who all put the emphasis on the fact that Pharaoh and Abimelech did not touch Sarah and sent her back to her husband as pure as she originally was. The allegorical reading, in contrast to the literal one, is precisely based on the word 'sister,' which is viewed positively. Philo is the first author who proposes to identify Sarah with virtue and Abraham with the intellect, and who suggests that the sage does not keep virtue for himself as a spouse, but rather calls her 'sister' in order to share it with others, so that others will become virtuous too. Origen follows Philo's interpretation and adds another biblical proof-text supporting this reading, namely Prov 7.4. However, whereas Philo considers that the persons who are making progress towards virtue and wisdom have virtue as a sister so that only the perfect ones can call virtue their wife, Origen inverts the order and presents the perfect ones as those who share virtue with others, thus having virtue as a sister. Origen also dwells at length on the reasons why Pharaoh and Abimelech could not possess Sarah. He re-interprets Sarah as divine virtue and grace, of the kind that only Christ could offer to the Gentiles (whereas in the time of Abraham it was not yet possible). Origen therefore switches from an allegorical and moral reading to a typological and historical one (insofar as the history of salvation is concerned). Finally, Didymus' allegorical interpretation is compared to those of Philo and Origen. (KB)

G. BUCH-HANSEN, *'It is the Spirit that Gives Life': a Stoic Understanding of Pneuma in John's Gospel*, Beihefte zur Zeitschrift für die neutestamentliche Wissenschaft und die Kunde der älteren Kirche 173 (Berlin–New York 2010), esp. 105–158.

In this magnum opus (502 pages) the Danish scholar, now professor at the University of Copenhagen, presents her analysis of the role that the phenomenon of *pneuma* plays in the Fourth Gospel. She suggests that the Gospel should be examined in light of the idea of the *pneuma* as found in ancient philosophy, pre-eminently in Stoic physics. In fact it is Philo's allegorical exposition of biblical texts in terms of Stoic philosophy that seems to be the tradition within which the Fourth Gospel is to be situated. In order to go beyond Stoic theory, Philo develops and expands several core Stoic ideas. First, of special importance is Philo's development of the Stoic's ontological hierarchy into an ordering of successive generations brought about by the addition of pneumatic bodies. In Philo's reformulated hierarchy, man's generation culminates in his divinely executed 'second generation.' Second, and also important, is Philo's application of the Stoics' understanding of cosmic conflagration to individual human beings, who may in extraordinary cases be transformed from bodily beings into pneumatic mind stuff. The book consists of eight chapters, which develop, step by step, her understanding of John's pneumatic narrative. Chapter one introduces the project; chapters two and three analyse the contextual material that serves as a foundation for the exegetical section. The second of these, chapter three (pp. 105–158), accounts for Philo's development of and critical stance towards Greek philosophy in general and Stoic philosophy specifically. Special attention is given to Philo's anthropology and his thesis of different type of men and their different manners of generation. Philo is dealt with in several subsections in the following chapters too. Chapters Four to Eight constitute the exegetical section dealing with the Johannine texts. (TS; based on the author's abstract)

G. BUCH-HANSEN, 'The Emotional Jesus: Anti-Stoicism in the Fourth Gospel?,' in T. RASIMUS, T. ENGBERG-PEDERSEN and I. DUNDERBERG (eds.), *Stoicism in Early Christianity,'* (Grand Rapids 2010) 93–114, esp. 106–111.

The article focuses on the presentation of the emotional Jesus in the second half of John's Gospel. In Origen's interpretation of the Gospel, Jesus' emotional upheavals were justified by their Stoic character. In giving the background to this interpretation Philo's evidence and use of the Stoic doctrine of the εὐπάθειαι is examined, drawing on the work of Dillon and Terian (R-R 7713) and Graver (RRS2 9931, cf. *SPhA* vol. 22, p. 225). Philo's presentation of the virtuous lament of the sage seems more consistently Stoic than that of Hellenistic doxographers and modern interpreters. So, although impossible to prove, a Stoic background for the presentation of Jesus' emotions in John cannot be a priori ruled out. (DTR)

D. K. Burge, *First Century Guides to Life and Death in the Roman East: a Comparative Study of Epictetus, Philo and Peter* (diss. Macquarie University, Sydney 2010).

The thesis is a comparative study of three prominent ethical guides in the Roman East during the Julio-Claudian and Flavian period. Epictetus the Stoic, Philo the Alexandrian Jew, and Peter, the Christian Apostle drew from their differing philosophical or ideological perspectives to teach about God, life, and death. The aim is to examine the resonance and dissonance between the three guides and to discuss reasons for their differences. Part I analyses Epictetus' *Discourses* and *Encheiridion* under four subheadings: (i) Epictetus in his first-century Setting; (ii) Epictetus' Guide to θεός; (iii) Epictetus' Guide to Life; and (iv) Epictetus' Guide to Death. Parts II and III examine a selection of Philo's treatises and 2 Peter 1 respectively, using in each the same four-fold structure as used with Epictetus. Part IV compares the three Guides, again using the same structure (the setting; the Guides to θεός; life; and death) to highlight points of resonance and dissonance. It is concluded that although there were numerous points of contact between the three Guides in a general sense, significant differences exist between them on these same points when examined in detail. It also unexpectedly emerged in the course of this dissertation that the three Guides faced an enemy with common features: a movement that was spreading rapidly through-out the Roman Empire known as the Second Sophistic. It rejected sound reason and truth in favor of more immediate fame and influence and pleasure. The close proximity of deceitful teachers to the Guides is reflected in the vehement polemical style with which they set forth their superior path of life. Since each Guide was motivated by, and responded in unique ways to, the threat posed by this common enemy, it was possible to compare their responses. (DTR; based on the author's abstract)

F. Calabi, *Storia del pensiero guidaico ellenistico* (Brescia 2010), esp. 39–94.

In a monograph of 280 pages (including indices) on the history of Jewish Hellenistic thought, the third (and longest) of the ten chapters is dedicated to Philo. After a brief sketch of his context and a categorized list of his works, a brief description (10–25 lines) is given for each treatise. A section entitled 'the Philonic analysis' then deals with the follow-ing fourteen key issues: 'In six days God created the world'; rules and modes of exegesis; Platonist comments and Biblical exegesis; unity and coherence of the text; references to the *Timaeus*; the *Logos* and the powers; powers, causes, *middot*; transcendence, unknowability and unnameability of God; revelation; allegorical meaning of Biblical personages; literality and observance; the Therapeutae; Philo and the Church Fathers; Philo in the Hebrew tradition. The treatment is profound but very accessible (there are no notes). An extensive bibliography concludes the chapter. (HMK)

F. Calabi, 'Giuseppe e i sogni della folla in Filone di Alessandria,' in J.-F. Pradeau (ed.), *Études Platoniciennes VII: Philon d'Alexandrie* (Paris 2010) 145–164.

This study about 'Joseph and the dreams of the crowd' argues that in Philo we can distinguish three rather than two types of the 'political man': the good and inspired kind who aims at unity, the good but not inspired kind who keeps to plurality, and the bad kind who is the prey of the crowd (*ochlos*), of passions and of disunity. Philo's views on the patriarch Joseph are varied, reflecting these three types. The task of the political man is to interpret the dreams of the crowd, which are characterized in essence not just by the desire of riches and honour, but by plurality and discord. The good politician will not only not be slave of the crowd's desires, but will create order and stability out of the disordered confusion characterizing the dreams of the crowd. True stability and order can be seen in the heavens, and is truly found only in God; to strive after assimilation to God belongs to the good governor's task. (HMK)

J. J. Collins and D. C. Harlow (eds.), *The Eerdmans Dictionary of Early Judaism* (Grand Rapids 2010), esp. 1063–1080.

Philo is a constant presence in this large-scale (1360 pages) encyclopedia of Second Temple Judaism. Specifically dedicated to him is a multi-authored entry under the title 'Philo' (pp. 1063–1080), which focuses primarily on his life and writings. It consists of an initial overview by Gregory E. Sterling, which includes a useful two page listing of all his treatises (with shortened English titles), their biblical base (when applicable) and their textual base. There follow separate sections on the Allegorical Commentary by Maren Niehoff, the Apologetic treatises by Sterling, the Exposition of the Law by Niehoff, the Philosophical writings by Annewies van den Hoek, and the Questions and Answers on Genesis and Exodus by David T. Runia. Each section of the article concludes with a selective bibliography. In addition sections on Philo are included as parts of articles on many other subjects, e.g. Allegory, Ascent to Heaven, Creation, Ethics, Greek philosophy, Sabbath etc. We note also articles devoted to topics based on or relevant to Philo, such as on the Therapeutae, Tiberius Julius Alexander, and the scholars Erwin Ramsdell Goodenough and Harry Austryn Wolfson. There is an overview of entries on pp. xix–xxix (alphabetically and by topic), but no general index. (DTR)

M. Cover, 'Reconceptualizing Conquest: Colonial Narratives and Philo's Roman Accuser in the *Hypothetica*,' *The Studia Philonica Annual* 22 (2010) 183–207.

Eusebius' prefatory comments, introducing the first fragment of Philo's *Hypoth.*, raise a number of significant questions about the character of this work, Philo's self-presentation as a Jew, and the identity and influence of those 'accusers' against whom, according to Eusebius, Philo wrote this 'defense on behalf of the Jews.' Cover approaches such questions with a treatment of the *Hypoth.* as the product of an imperial Roman context, arguing for the position that Philo wrote this work in anticipation of his role in the embassy to Gaius, following the mass violence against Alexandrian Jews under the prefect Flaccus. This article begins with a critical survey of the sort of Roman accusations that Philo might have anticipated in the *Hypoth.*, focusing on comments about the conquest of Canaan as constructed in Alexandrian and Roman historiography (Manetho, Lysimachus, traditions preserved in Tacitus). Cover argues that Philo's presentation of the conquest narratives in

Hypoth. both responds to such charges and reflects contemporary Roman accounts of the colonization of Rome (Livy, *Ab urbe condita* 1) in order to represent the foundation of Jerusalem in terms that would elicit sympathy and understanding in a Roman context. In the final part of this article, Cover tries to reconstruct the details of the Roman imperial court which Philo might have anticipated when writing the *Hypoth.*, focusing on the evidence of *Legat., Flacc.* and the *Acta Alexandrinorum.* (SJKP)

M. DELCOGLIANO, *Basil of Caesarea's Anti-Eunomian Theory of Names: Christian Theology and Late-Antique Philosophy in the Fourth Century Trinitarian Controversy,* Supplements to Vigiliae Christianae 103 (Leiden 2010), esp. 79–87.

In this study of Basil of Caesarea's attack on the theory of names in the trinitarian theology of Eunomius the author argues that 'if Platonist speculations on names had an influence on the Heteroousians, it was mediated through Philo of Alexandria and Eusebius of Caesarea,' but 'even in these cases there are only scattered points of contact, and these not without considerable modification' (p. 51). In order to substantiate this claim there is a section on Philo and the exegesis of Hebrew names, in which it is argued that Philo's influence on Eunomius is best seen in the latter's theory of the origin of names (pp. 80–86). It is surprising, the author concludes (p. 93), that Philo has not been proposed as a source for the Heteroousians. (DTR)

J. DILLON, 'Philo of Alexandria and Platonist Psychology,' in J.-F. PRADEAU (ed.), *Études Platoniciennes VII: Philon d'Alexandrie* (Paris 2010) 165–172.

A brief discussion on the essential philosophical aspects of Philo's doctrine of the soul. The main philosophical influence on Philo is the type of Platonism initiated by Antiochus of Ascalon which absorbs Stoic formulations (and also some Peripatetic ideas) into a basically Platonic framework, overlaid with a Pythagoreanizing, transcendentalist turn associated with the figure of Eudorus of Alexandria. Topics discussed as the nature and structure of the soul, a doctrine of two souls?, and the immortality of the soul. Philo appears to elide the awkward issue of reincarnation, while seeming to adhere to some kind of pre-existence of the human soul. The most troublesome biblical doctrine for Philo is the statement that 'the soul is the blood' (Lev 17:11 etc.), which Philo solves with a reference to pneuma, possibly anticipating later Platonist ideas of a 'pneumatic vehicle' for the soul. (DTR)

A. DINAN, 'Another Citation of Philo in Clement of Alexandria's Protrepticus,' *Vigiliae Christianae* 64 (2010) 435–444.

In *Protr.* 10.93.1–2 Clement is partly dependent on a passage found in Philo *Virt.* 181. This dependence has not been noticed earlier. Similarities between the Philonic and the Clementine passages are the description of conversion through the language of politics and the image of looking at the light. Furthermore, their respective lists of virtues and vices are largely identical. Clement has been attracted by Philo's description of conversion as a 'desertion to freedom' in *Virt.* 181. At the same time, Clement changes Philo's text in several ways, particularly by introducing the term κίνδυνος. In this way he makes explicit a citation that is partially found in Plato *Phaed.* 114d (καλὸς γὰρ ὁ κίνδυνος) and more fully in

Horace *Carm.* 3.25. Clement thus makes clear that deserting to God is a 'good risk or an 'advantageous venture.' (ACG)

P. DRUILLE, 'Los Querubines, la espada flamígera y la Causa en Filón de Alejandría,' *Nova Tellus. Anuario del Centro de Estudios Clásicos* 28 (2010) 73–95.

The author studies the treatise *Cher.* as a reading of the biblical text that incorporates philosophical elements in order to present Jewish monotheism. She examines especially *Cher.* 21–30 and 124–127. The first passage illustrates the figure of the Logos as a mediator between cosmic dualism and divine oneness. The second passage discusses the theory of the four causes, the introduction of the concept of instrumental cause assigned to the Logos, and finally, the Philonic preference for the term αἴτιον to designate the only true cause, the creator of the world. (JPM)

L. DUPRÉE SANDGREN, *Vines Intertwined: A History of Jews and Christians from the Babylonian Exile to the Advent of Islam* (Peabody, Mass. 2010), esp. 217–224, 565–568.

True to its subtitle, this history covers an impressive amount of material spanning 1280 years. Philo appears primarily in Part Three, which covers 14–138 C.E., in which he is treated as a historical source for events in Alexandria. One can also find several references to Philo's legacy in later sections, however, particularly in Part Five (312–455 C.E.), which devotes several pages to Philo's importance to and reputation among later Christians and includes a discussion entitled 'Philo Christianus.' Scattered throughout are references to selected opinions of Philo on such topics as anthropology, laws, and people of God. Often embedded in larger contexts, these various references help to illustrate Philo's similarities to and differences from other thinkers across different times, places, and cultures. (EB)

D. M. FRIEDENBERG, *Tiberius Julius Alexander: a Historical Novel* (Amherst NY 2010).

Philo is one of the main characters in this racy novel based on the eventful life of his nephew, who, speaking throughout in the first person, frequently refers to him as 'Uncle Philo.' Allusions are made on many occasions to Philo's writings and to the religious and philosophical discussions that occurred between the two men. On p. 154 an imaginitive depiction is given of Philo's death: 'I was glad that Philo at the age of sixty-five ... had been struck down and killed by a horse and carriage on the Canopus Way in Alexandria while absentmindedly walking to the Great Library.' (DTR)

A. C. GELJON, 'Philo's Interpretation of Noah,' in M. E. STONE, A. AMIHAY and V. HILLEL (eds.), *Noah and his Book(s)*, Early Judaism and its Literature 28 (Atlanta 2010) 183–191.

Noah belongs to the first triad, together with Enos and Enoch. Basing himself on Gen 6:9 Philo characterizes Noah as righteous and perfect, but he is also good, holy, wise and a lover of virtue. Noah is, however, not absolutely good but only in comparison with the men of his time. The patriarchs of the second triad—Abraham, Isaac and Jacob—are superior in virtue. The name Noah means 'rest' and this indicates that Noah has rest in his mind because he has expelled the passions. Because Noah is perfect he survives the flood and becomes the founder of a new race. The flood is a symbol of the stream of passions and vices that attack the mind. In *Agr.* Philo deals with Noah as a cultivator (Gen 9:20) and explains that a good cultivator has to cut down and destroy the trees of passions and vices. Noah, as a cultivator of the soul, is contrasted with Cain, who is a worker of the earth, i.e. he is a lover of earthly passions. Presenting Noah as virtuous and controlling the passions, Philo depicts Noah with the terminology of a Stoic sage. The author concludes that Philo offers first and foremost an ethical reading of Noah along the lines of Stoic ethics. By presenting Noah as a Stoic sage, Philo sought to make the biblical figure acceptable for non-Jewish readers. (ACG)

M. Gonzalez Fernandez, "Sacerdos, propheta et rex': filosofía, religión y políitica en Filón de Alejandría,' in P. Roche Arnas (ed.), *El pensamiento político en la Edad Media* (Madrid 2010) 451–462.

The article quotes passages of *Legat.*, *Jos.* and *Mos.* at length in order to show some aspects of Philo's political ideal. This ideal implies the Platonic-Aristotelian preference for the monarchical form of the wise king, who in the monotheistic theological context becomes priest and prophet. Philo accepts the political value of the Roman Empire but, as a Jew, awaits a future for his people corresponding to the memory of a brilliant past. (JPM).

H.-G. Gradl, 'Kaisertum und Kaiserkult: ein Vergleich zwischen Philos Legatio ad Gaium und der Offenbarung des Johannes,' *New Testament Studies* 56 (2010) 116–138.

A comparison is made between the way in which Philo in *Legat.* and the author of Revelation both address the impact of the imperial cult in the first century c.e. on their monotheistic belief. Both position their respective communities differently with regard to the Roman state. While Philo aims at 'critical integration and social cohabitation' (p. 116), the seer advocates self-isolation. Philo regards Gaius' claim to divinity as a threat to the peaceful integration of the Jewish minority within the Roman empire. In the face of an acute threat to the community, he does not emphasize covenantal privilege to advocate separation from the world, but promotes a synthesis of biblical and Greek thought and uses pagan concepts of the gods to criticize Gaius' hubris. Faced with the emperor's attack on the Temple Philo attempts a peaceful dialogue. For him, the Jews are integral part of the general society and loyal to the emperor, but this must not to interfere with God's exclusivity. Philo suggests resistance and martyrdom against such a threat, albeit more as a literary device with effect on the reader than as an actual option. His argument is historical, not apocalyptic, he blames individuals for the conflict and believes in God's providence. (JLB).

C. van Heijne, *The Messenger of the Lord in Early Jewish Interpretations of Genesis*, Beihefte zur Zeitschrift für die alttestamentliche Wissenschaft 412 (Berlin 2010), esp. 192–234.

Based on a PhD dissertation supervised by Tord Fornberg, this study explores the identity of 'the angel of the Lord' in early Jewish Bible interpretation and theology, focusing on relevant texts in Genesis (including 16:7–14, 18; 21:17–20, 22:1–19; 24:7, 40;

28:10–22, 32). How did early Jewish interpreters resolve the question of the apparently ambiguous relationship between God and 'the angel of the Lord' in these texts? The main part of the study includes a substantial discussion of Philo's view of 'the angel of the Lord' and the angel's relationship to God (pp. 192–234), covering the narratives of Hagar, the Aqedah, the wooing of Rebekah, and Jacob's encounters with the angel. In general, Philo identifies 'the angel of the Lord' with the divine Logos, though in some contexts (the interpretation of Gen. 28 and 31), the Logos is more closely identified with God than in others where it is clarified that the Logos/angel is not to be identified with God (interpreting Gen 16). (SJKP)

G. HERTZ, 'L'exégèse philonienne entre sacré et profane : Philon, un nouvel Aaron?,' in M. ADDA (ed.), *Textes sacrés et culture profane: de la révélation à la création* (Bern 2010) 53–88.

The author first deals with the sacred nature of the biblical text in Philo's eyes, both in Hebrew and in Greek, and recalls that Philo's version of the story of the translation into Greek differs from that of the *Letter of Aristeas* because it insists on the miraculous character of the translation, therefore showing that Philo considered the Greek text truly inspired. Since the very letter of the Greek text is sacred, the contradictions, the grammatical problems or the apparently mythological language used in some passages all serve to indicate the necessity to look for the allegorical, deeper meaning of the text. In the passages which document the way Philo thought about his own exegetical activity, it appears that for him, the work of the exegete is connected with the prophetic experience, both of which depend on divine grace and inspiration. The commentator is similar to Aaron, who served Moses as 'the prophetic word.' Just as Aaron was called 'the prophet of Moses' (Exod 7.1), so Philo wants to be the prophet of the biblical *logos*, that is, to make its hidden meaning explicit for others. Finally, it seems that Philo was seeking not only to *hear* the divine word, but also to *contemplate* it, therefore achieving the same kind of experience of the divine which Moses experienced. (KB)

P. W. VAN DER HORST, 'Philo and the Problem of God's Emotions,' in J.-F. PRADEAU (ed.), *Études Platoniciennes VII: Philon d'Alexandrie* (Paris 2010) 173–180.

The two traditions in which Philo stands, the Bible and Greek philosophy, have very different approaches to the question of God's passions and it is no wonder that Philo, being the Platonist that he is, found the biblical presentation of God having strong emotions such as anger and repentance difficult. The article first usefully sketches in the biblical (and also Jewish) and the Greek philosophical background, noting that in the latter the group of philosophers who object to the notion of divine emotions is certainly not restricted to Platonists only. Philo's starting point, taken over from Plato, is the notion of the *theoprepes* or the *dignum deo*, i.e. that one should only attribute to the deity what is worthy of him. In some texts he does mention God's anger etc., but these are just concessions to biblical usage. His deep conviction is that these emotions are not suitable for the deity and he explains their presence in the Bible as needed for purposes of education, i.e. so that Moses could direct his message to different levels of understanding on the part of his readers. This solution was highly influential in the Alexandrian tradition (Clement, Origen), but contrasts strongly with the view of Lactantius in his treatise on God's anger. For earlier versions of this article see *SPhA* vol. 8, pp. 130–131 and vol. 21, p. 85. (DTR)

F. JOURDAN, *Orphée et les Chrétiens: La réception du mythe d'Orphée dans la littérature chrétienne grecque des cinq premiers siècles. Tome I Orphée, du repoussoir au préfigurateur du Christ* (Paris 2010), esp. 284–286.

A brief systematic overview is given of Philo's doctrine of the Logos as part of the background on Clement of Alexandria's comparison of Orpheus and Christ and the motif of the 'new song' in the *Protrepticus*. (DTR)

J. S. KLOPPENBORG, 'James 1:2–15 and Hellenistic Psychagogy,' *Novum Testamentum* 52 (2010) 37–71.

In James' elaboration of the Jesus tradition we can see philosophical ideas on the soul that were also current in Hellenistic Judaism. Within this context the author refers, among others, to Philo, 4 Maccabees and *The Testaments of the Twelve Patriarchs* and points to similarities concerning the passions, especially desire and pleasure as threats to the soul. The author concludes that James can be located 'within those circles of educated or semi-educated Judaeans, probably urban, who understood the Torah to be consistent with the best of Greek philosophy' (p. 71). (ACG)

N. KOLTUN-FROMM, *Hermeneutics of Holiness: Ancient Jewish and Christian Notions of Sexuality and Religious Community* (New York 2010), esp. 177–179, 184–186.

From the Bible onward, the concept of holiness became entwined with ideas about sexual practice. The mid-fourth century Syriac Christian Aphrahat associates holiness with celibacy and reflects tension with the rabbinic value of procreation. Currents of asceticism, however, run through both Jewish and Christian sources and can be traced through biblical interpretive traditions. Although Philo is discussed only briefly, he is an important witness to the notion that Moses became celibate in order to fulfill his priestly and prophetic role (*Mos.* 2.68–69). This tradition may have begun earlier than Philo, but he is the first writer in whom this claim of Moses's celibacy is found. Unlike *Sifre* and Aphrahat, other sources that make a similar claim, Philo was influenced primarily by Greek and Roman ideals of self-control. By contrast *Sifre* saw celibacy as an ideal limited to Moses alone in connection with his prophetic role and Aphrahat viewed Moses' celibacy as a model of holiness that can be achieved. (EB)

D. KONSTAN, 'Of Two Minds: Philo On Cultivation,' *The Studia Philonica Annual* 22 (2010) 131–138.

In the first part of *Agr.* interpreting Gen 9:20 Philo contrasts Noah, who is a true cultivator, with Cain, who is a mere worker of the earth. Explained in an allegorical way, a cultivator cares for the soul, cutting off all vices and passions, whereas a worker of the earth looks only after the body and its pleasures. In the Pentateuch Philo discovers two other comparable distinctions, viz. between herdsman and tender of sheep, and between horseman and rider. Konstan argues that Philo in his treatment of these distinctions constructs something like a double nature of the mind, one good, the other bad. The good one strives for virtue and has to be preserved, but the bad has to be killed. Philo regards making distinctions as useful but at the same time he sees an excessive passion for logical distinctions as dangerous. In the second part of *Agr.* Philo discusses the fact that Noah only begins to be a cultivator, that is he starts but does not fully achieve excellence. Philo sets out the dangers that beset a novice in the sciences, especially in making distinctions, which is the core theme of *Agr.* (ACG)

G. H. VAN KOOTEN, 'The Anthropological Trichotomy of Spirit, Soul and Body in Philo of Alexandria and Paul of Tarsus,' in M. LABAHN and O. LEHIPUU (eds.), *Anthropology in the New Testament and Its Ancient Context; Papers from the EABS-Meeting in Piliscaba/Budapest* (Leuven 2010) 87–119.

The article aims to show how a tripartite anthropology, already present in Plato, was adopted by Philo of Alexandria and Paul of Tarsus, and how they reworked it on the basis of the Jewish Scriptures. The author also argues that Philo and Paul do not differ in their understanding of the heavenly and earthly human being, but both adopt the same tripartite anthropology which distinguishes between body, *psyche* and *pneuma*. Both thinkers develop a soteriological tripartite anthropology which aims at humankind's re-spiritualization. The author carries out his investigation by first looking in detail at Philo's view on the relation between the heavenly and earthly human being at creation, as expressed in Philo's exegesis of the creation narrative of Gen 1–2. Then he focuses on Philo's views on the degeneration of humankind, to be followed by his views on the restoration of human beings. Finally he compares Philo's view of the two types of human beings with that of Paul. This article is also integrated in his dissertation, published in 2008 (pp. 269–312). See *SPhA* vol. 23 p. 114 and also the review of that work in vol. 22, pp. 294–298. (TS)

G. H. VAN KOOTEN, 'Ancestral, Oracular and Prophetic Authority: 'Scriptural Authority' according to Paul and Philo.,' in M. POPOVIC (ed.), *Authoritative Scriptures in Ancient Judaism,* Journal of the Study of Judaism Supplements 141 (Leiden 2010) 267–308.

This study is primarily a study of Paul's views on the authoritative Jewish writings, but it is presented partly in comparison to Philo's views on the same writings. His thesis is that to Paul these writings are authoritative for a variety of reasons, and he finds a comparable variety in the works of Philo. Philo has, however, reflected more theoretically on what in Paul are his more implicit views on the issue. In the first two main sections the author deals with the various characterizations and labels Paul uses for the Scriptures. In the section on Philo (pp. 283–297), he finds that Philo too uses a varied and rich vocabulary when referring to the Jewish writings. He draws here especially on *Mos.* 2.188 and 192–245; but also on *Migr.* 14; *Cher.* 49 and *Mut.* 139 and others. In Paul there seems, according to the author, a clear difference between ancestral, oracular and prophetic authority. In essence he finds the same distinction in Philo; in his differentiation between three types of oracles. (TS)

E. KOSKENNIEMI, 'Philo and Greek Poets,' *Journal for the Study of Judaism* 41 (2010) 301–322.

The article deals with how Philo uses and refers to the Greek poets, not only Homer (pp. 305–311), but also Hesiod (pp. 312–315), Solon (pp. 315–316), Theognis (p. 317), Pindar (pp. 317–319) and others. He knows the poets as well any Greek writer. In most cases, the author argues, Philo quotes the verses exactly as we have them from other sources, preserving all the dialectic peculiarities. However, he may correct the quotation theologically, make a mistake or drop a line, and sometimes he might have learned a text that differed from ours. He often gives the words a new sense and makes them speak for his own view, or he changes the context, following the manner of the Stoics. Philo's works allow us a glimpse of the learned circles of the Alexandrian Jews. The author suggests that Philo had memorized poets when studying in the gymnasium, and that he did not lose contact with them after his early years, having a library in his own home, so that he could enjoy its treasures with his friends during his lifetime. Homer, Hesiod and others were not dangerous: if interpreted properly, they supported the Jewish religion. (TS)

A. B. Kovelman, 'Hellenistic Judaism on the Perfection of the Human Body,' *Journal of Jewish Studies* 61 (2010) 207–219.

The article addresses issues of body and soul raised by Daniel Boyarin's influential argument about 'carnal Israel' (see RRS 9312a), which is contrasted to Hellenistic-Jewish and Christian 'spirituality.' While Boyarin saw the rabbis in opposition to Hellenistic-Christian notions, Kovelman argues for a distinct similarity between them, stressing that Hellenistic Jews also experienced every day physical experience as a miracle to be appreciated. Kovelman presents passages from the *Letter of Aristeas* and Philo which resonate with the Psalms as evidence for a conscious appreciation of the bodily dimension of human existence. The following Philonic passages receive special attention: *Ebr.* 145–1466, *Cher.* 71–73, *Somn.* 1.14. (MRN)

W. Kullmann, *Naturgesetz in der Vorstellung der Antike, besonders der Stoa: eine Begriffsuntersuchung*, Philosophie der Antike 30 (Stuttgart 2010), esp. 59–69.

The book studies ancient, particularly Stoic, ideas of the law of nature. For Philo the concept of the divine law serves to link the Torah with Stoic philosophy. The law of nature and that of Moses are identical. He uses the Stoic concept of the king as living law, and refers to the patriarchs as embodied Torah. The person who lives according to the Torah lives according to the law of nature; he is a cosmopolitan citizen and a good Stoic (*Opif.*). Of all legislators it is only Moses who combines admonition and commandments. The Stoic treatise *Prob.* emphasizes that living according to the laws of nature makes one free, even in slavery or imprisonment. But Philo also uses law of nature in a non-Stoic way for natural laws, the parents' love for their children, prohibition of pederasty etc. In the Stoic sense the natural law derives its prescriptive character from its relationship with God. In the less philosophical, more common, sense the link to God is not implied. The Logos, which in the Stoa is closely linked with the concept of the law of nature, in Philo can have quite different roles, e.g. the architect or the place of the ideas, image or firstborn son of God, archangel, even a second god. (JLB).

J. Lagouanère, 'Les songes et les signes : l'interprétation dans le «De Iosepho» de Philon d'Alexandrie,' *Mélanges de sciences religieuses* 67 (2010) 3–19.

Dream interpretation was highly developed in Antiquity, as Artemidorus' work *The Interpretation of Dreams* (2nd cent. c.e.) shows. His distinction between different categories of dreams (such as τὰ ἐνύπνια and οἱ ὄνειροι) was probably known to Philo. Philo's classification, however, was mostly influenced by that of Posidonius, who considered that in some cases, the gods communicate with human beings through dreams. The beginning of each book of *Somn.* (I and II) reproduces Posidonius' tripartition of dreams, which are characterized by a decreasing degree of clarity: in the first category of dreams God directly communicates with man; in the second the soul communicates with the divine through the Soul of the Universe or the angels; in the third the soul foresees the future thanks to its own power. Joseph's dreams in Genesis belong mainly to the third category. Philo's description of the analysis of the dreams recalls Artemidorus' analytical tools, but he also develops an ethics of interpretation, stating that the interpreter can reveal the meaning of the dream only if this is God's will. The onirocritical art is both hermeneutical and prophetic. Moreover, since Joseph is inspired by God he can also offer a solution to the problem foretold in the dream. In *Ios.* 140–142, Philo indulges in a surprisingly sceptic argument. The idea that life is a dream does not, however, deprive it of a meaning, based on an interpretation that has to be divinely inspired. Therefore the wise can attain true knowledge only with the help of God, and all knowledge is in a way the result of a hermeneutical activity. Finally, the author argues that in *Ios.* both the literal and the allegorical reading aim at emphasizing the relationships that unite all the elements of Joseph's story, and that the two readings should not be opposed to each other. (KB)

J. Leemans, 'After Philo and Paul: Hagar in the Writings of the Church Fathers,' in M. Goodman, G. H. van Kooten and J. van Ruiten (eds.), *Abraham, the Nations, and the Hagarites: Jewish, Christian, and Islamic Perspectives on Kinship with Abraham,* Themes in Biblical Narrative 13 (Leiden 2010) 435–447.

First the author discusses the Philonic interpretation of Hagar and Sarah in Clement of Alexandria and Didymus the Blind. In *Str.* 1.28–32 Clement interprets Hagar as *paideia*, Sarah as philosophy or virtue, and Abraham as the man of faith, seeing *paideia* as a preparatory stage for attaining true wisdom. The same Philonic exegesis of Hagar and Sarah is also found in Didymus, who refers to Philo by name in his treatment in *In Gen.* Thereafter Leemans shows how Paul's allegorical interpretation of Hagar and Sarah in Gal 4:24 has been used by Tertullian, Origen and Gregory of Nyssa in defending allegorical exegesis. Finally, the author demonstrates how the duality between Hagar and Sarah gave rise to very diverse interpretations of oppositional types: for instance, Christianity versus non-Christian religions, or old covenant versus new covenant. (ACG)

J. Leonhardt-Balzer, 'Philo und die Septuaginta,' in M. Karrer and W. Kraus (eds.), *Die Septuaginta — Texte, Theologien, Einflüsse: Internationale Fachtagung veranstaltet von Septuaginta Deutsch (LXX.D), Wuppertal 20.-23. Juli 2006,* Wissenschaftliche Untersuchungen zum Neuen Testament 252 (Tübingen 2010) 623–637.

Philo's works are relevant for research on the LXX because of his account of the production of the translation, which emphasizes the traits of divine inspiration, and because of his extensive use of the work. The article engages in a critical dialogue with N. Cohen, *Philo's Scriptures: Citations from the Prophets and Writings: Evidence for a Haftarah Cycle in Second Temple Judaism* (Leiden 2007). Philo calls Scripture by various terms indicating their inspiration, e.g. 'holy writings,' 'divine word,' 'oracle,' but he also knows the names of the different biblical books. Quotations from the non-Pentateuchal texts never occur for their own sake but only serve the interpretation of the Torah, frequently where there is no Pentateuch text to make the same point. The prophets are introduced by terms relating them to Moses, e.g. the prophet as 'disciple' or 'friend' of Moses, similarly the rare references to the writings. Psalm quotations sometimes link the psalmist to Moses or refer to the psalm as hymn, prayer or as prophecy. Thus the non-Pentateuchal texts are treated as valid, prophetic interpretation of the Torah. In the same way the LXX translation of the Pentateuch is characterized as an inspired, valid rendition of the Torah of Moses. (JLB).

C. LÉVY, 'À propos d'un rêve de puissance de Joseph (Philon, *Somn.* II, 17–109),' in J.-F. PRADEAU (ed.), *Études Platoniciennes VII: Philon d'Alexandrie* (Paris 2010) 133–144.

At the beginning of each book of *Somn.* Philo explains that there are different kinds of dreams: (1) those in which God communicates directly and clearly with the dreamer; (2) those in which the Soul of the World communicates with the soul of the person asleep, and which require some interpretation; (3) those in which the soul moves by itself, which require onirocritical deciphering. Beyond the similarities with Posidonius' classification of dreams, some differences are to be noted: in the third case, whereas Posidonius attributes to the soul an intrinsic power of divination, Philo does not go so far, because for him God's role is more pervasive. Concerning the second category, Posidonius probably refers to the role of *daimones* in the inspiration of dreams, whereas Philo uses the term ἄγγελοι, which has a different meaning insofar as angels convey messages and commands from God. The author then deals at length with Philo's allegorical interpretation of Joseph's dreams in *Somn.* 2.17–109 (on Gen 37:7, 9). The image of the 'wise architect' in §8 recalls the way it is used by Plutarch in his *Life of Alexander* (26), in connection with Homer. But Philo applies the expression to the allegorical interpretation of the text. Joseph represents the Aristotelian type of ethics, which integrates the soul, the body and exterior objects. However, in Philo's interpretation of the second dream (Gen 37.9), it is the Stoic notion of one common world for gods and human beings which is criticized through the condemnation of Joseph, whose identification with the 12th star is interpreted as meaning that the universe was created for humanity. The reason that Philo considers Joseph's dreams difficult to interpret, in contrast with their apparently obvious signification, lies in the fact that, in Philo's eyes, Joseph's dreams of power cannot represent a legitimization of the political life. Only the allegorical reading can therefore reveal the true meaning of the dreams. (KB)

D. LINCICUM, *Paul and the Early Jewish Encounter with Deuteronomy*, Wissenschaftliche Untersuchungen zum Neuen Testament 2.284 (Tübingen 2010), esp. 100–116.

The study offers a reading of Paul as a Jewish interpreter of Deuteronomy among others Jewish interpreters of this biblical book. It examines approaches in Jewish literature from the third century B.C.E. to the first century C.E. (Qumran, the Apocrypha and Pseudepigrapha, Josephus, *Sifre* and Targums), including Philo's writings. First, the way in which Philo refers to Deuteronomy is examined. He often refers to the book's hortatory character. He sees it as a separate book of the Pentateuch but also recognizes subunits, such as the Song of Moses (ch. 33). Next, Philo's use of Deut in the Exposition (including *Mos.*) and in the Allegorical Commentary is discussed. In *Mos.* Deut appears as the source for the retelling of Moses' death. Philo discusses the law extensively in *Decal.* and *Spec.* Remarkable in his treatment of the particular laws is the principle used to order them. The Decalogue serves as a series of headings under which the particular laws can be classed. Philo often gives these laws in updated form to preserve the immediacy of Deuteronomy's appeal. Obedience to the laws in their literal sense is crucial for Philo, and is a precondition for personal blessing. In the Allegorical Commentary Philo makes use of Deut in different ways. Sometimes the quotation from Deut is starting point for a long digression, at other times Philo adduces to Deut to provide authoritative maxims. The author concludes: 'For Philo, Deuteronomy is above all a *useful* book of exhortation, of law, of theological reflection, and he employs it accordingly to all these ends.' (p. 116). (ACG)

F. L. Lisi, 'Filón de Alejandría, ¿un judío platónico o un platónico judío?,' in J.-F. Pradeau (ed.), *Etudes platoniciennes VII: Philon d'Alexandrie* (Paris 2010) 5–10.

Although the general editor of the series is the French scholar Jean-François Pradeau, this particular volume was put together by the Spanish scholar Francisco Lisi, who has also written the introductory section. In addition to summarising each of the articles, he also briefly sets out a general framework for the interpretation of Philo's writings, which should not be conceived in the categories of modern Judaism, but rather as the work of a thinker who wants to read Moses as a Homer in an environment in which the Platonic philosophy is dominant. Finally he notes that while this volume was in preparation the first volumes of the translation of Philo's complete works appeared in Spanish; see *SPhA* vol. 24 (2012) 208–209. (JPM)

N. E. Livesey, *Circumcision as a Malleable Symbol*, Wissenschaftliche Untersuchungen zum Neuen Testament 2.295 (Tübingen 2010).

In this revised version of a 2007 PhD dissertation supervised by Jouette Bassler (on which see *SPhA* vol. 22 p. 232), Livesey aims to demonstrate the variety and richness in the understanding of circumcision among early Jewish sources (1, 2, 4 Maccabees; Josephus; Philo; Paul). For such interpreters, the meaning of circumcision is 'malleable' and tied to context; later interpreters (reviewed in the final main chapter) would distort the perspective of earlier sources by reading early Jewish statements about circumcision out of context. A substantial part of the monograph is dedicated to Philo's discussions of circumcision (pp. 41–76), focusing on passages in *Spec.* 1 ('The mark of circumcision as the promotion of health, life and well-being'); *QG* 3 ('The mark of circumcision draws the mind closer to God'); and *Migr.* ('The mark of circumcision benefits the mind and gains the respect of fellow Jews'). In all three passages, the significance of circumcision is shaped by the rhetorical context of Philo's work as interpreter of specific scriptural texts. (SJKP)

N. E. Livesey, 'Paul the Philonic Jew: (Philippians 3,5–21),' *Annali di Storia dell'Esegesi* 27 (2010) 35–44.

In this article Livesey argues that Paul's words in Phil 3 should be read, not as a departure from Judaism, but as a description of his own sense of undertaking a journey towards immortality, represented by the immortal Christ. In describing this journey, Paul draws on Greco-Roman discourse to express ideas about departure from self in terms of the ideal of self-mastery. His use of this motif echoes the writings of Philo on this subject (cf. *Migr.*). Both Paul and Philo follow a 'three-step model' of self-mastery: departure from self; use of reason; the idea of the journey forward. Philo's conception of Abraham as exemplar of one who successfully undertakes such a journey may have influenced Paul's thinking in Philippians. Neither Paul nor Philo speaks of exchanging one form of religious identity for another; instead, both 'share the common final goal of immortality and communion with the divine' (p. 44). (SJKP)

P. MAKIELLO, 'Abraham and the Nations in the Works of Philo of Alexandria,' in M. GOODMAN, G. H. VAN KOOTEN and J. VAN RUITEN (eds.), *Abraham, the Nations, and the Hagarites: Jewish, Christian, and Islamic Perspectives on Kinship with Abraham*, Themes in Biblical Narrative (Leiden 2010) 139–161.

This article deals with Philo's interpretation of Gen 12:3 in *Migr.* 109–127. Generally, Philo associates blessing or 'eulogy' with reason and speech. He interprets Gen 12:3a ('I will bless those who bless you, and I will curse those who curse you') as referring to one of the gifts given for the wise man's sake. Philo attaches more importance to the intention of one who blesses than the words he speaks. In his exegesis of Gen 12:3b ('in you all the nations of the earth shall be blessed') Philo focuses upon the role of the just man as a mediator between God and the rest of humanity. God's providential care extends to the unworthy as well as the virtuous and well intentioned. Being a suppliant the virtuous man reflects the working of the divine Logos, who is also presented as curing wounds. It is likely that Philo constructs the wise and virtuous man as Jewish. Philo also regards Abraham as a symbol of the righteous mind, who can bestow many benefits upon the irrational part of the soul, especially in the area of sense-perception. (ACG)

J. P. MARTÍN, 'Inmortalidad del alma y destino del cuerpo en la escatología de Filón,' in J.-F. PRADEAU (ed.), *Études Platoniciennes VII: Philon d'Alexandrie* (Paris 2010) 181–202.

In the first part of the article the author describes the studies on Jewish eschatology during the early part of the twentieth century, noting that Philo is generally considered a Platonist philosopher with little sense of community or history. In the second part the author analyses the change of perspective introduced by researchers such as Wolfson, and especially P. Borgen, who draws attention to *Praem.* In the third part, the author argues that *Praem.* must be seen as an essential text for a comprehensive interpretation of Philo, the primary weight of which is not orientated towards an eschatology of the postmortem salvation of the soul, but to sustain a hope in a providential view of history, which, within the context of the Greek œcumene and the pax Romana, will allow the rise of Israel as a priesthood of humanity. (JPM)

J. P. MARTÍN (ed.), *Filón de Alejandría Obras Completas Volumen II* (Madrid 2010).

The second volume of the Philo's complete works in Spanish translation is the third in order of publication. It contains ten treatises of the Allegorical Commentary, the translation of which began in the first volume and will end in the third. The order of publication follows the conventional orderalready established by Cohn and Wendland. After a presentation by the general editor, José Pablo Martín, Paola Druille, Professor of Greek at the Universidad Nacional de La Pampa, is responsible for the introduction, translation and notes of *Cher.* followed by *Sacr.* translated by Raquel Martín Hernández, Researcher of the Universidad Complutense of Madrid. Marcela Coria, Professor of Greek at the Universidad Nacional de Rosario, takes care of two works, *Det.* and *Plant.* The general editor has taken care of *Post.* and *Deus*, while Pura Nieto, Professor at Brown University, has translated *Gig.* Juan Pablo Lewis, Researcher in classical philology at the University of Edinburgh, is the translator of *Agr.* and Lena Balzaretti, Professor of Greek at the Universidad

Nacional de Rosario, is responsible for *Ebr.* and *Sobr.* The volume is brought to a close with indices of biblical and Philonic passages, of ancient and modern authors, of Greek language and of subjects. (JPM)

M. W. Martin, *Judas and the Rhetoric of Comparison in the Fourth Gospel*, New Testament Monographs 25 (Sheffield 2010), esp. 61–63.

Philo's account of Moses is studied as an example of *synkrisis*. The praise of Moses as legislator better than any other can be found at the beginning of the interpretation of the Mosaic laws in *Opif.* 1–2. Syncrisis also shapes the whole narrative of *Mos.*: Moses is praised as the greatest of all legislators. In each of his offices Moses surpasses all Greeks and barbarians: as king (1.152), legislator (2.12) and priest (2.66) and prophet (2.187, 192). He surpasses others with regard to his parents (1.7), his training (1.21), his mind (1.27), his deeds (1.63,152; 2.12, 67, 187) and his burial (2.291). (JLB)

E. Matusova, 'Allegorical Interpretation of the Pentateuch in Alexandria: Inscribing Aristobulus and Philo in a Wider Literary Context,' *The Studia Philonica Annual* 22 (2010) 1–51.

Recent studies have attempted to situate Philo's allegorical commentary within the wider context of an allegorical tradition among Alexandrian Jews, based in local synagogues, including Aristobulus and the unnamed exegetes to whom Philo himself refers. In this article, Matusova challenges some aspects of this approach to Philo and suggests an alternative way to a better understanding of the context of the exegetical tradition that connects Aristobulus and Philo. Part One of the study compares Philo's exegetical method with non-Alexandrian exemplars of the 'indirect' interpretation of Jewish Scripture (Qumran pesharim; CD; Pauline exegesis), observing that Philo's approach differs significantly in terms of subject matter, technique and goal. Part Two explores the thesis of 'alleged Stoic influence' on the allegorical interpretation of Philo and his predecessors, against which Matusova raises a number of objections, related to content, form and method, and historical considerations. Thus far, Matusova's analysis aims to cast doubt on the value of locating the origins of Philo's allegorical commentary within a synagogue context, associated with a tradition of Stoic allegorical interpretation. In the final part of the discussion, she outlines a 'new' way of explaining Philo and other Alexandrian Jews as allegorists, focusing on evidence for close connections with Pythagorean traditions, and with the interpretation of *hieroi logoi* (sacred discourse) in the Derveni papyrus and Graeco-Egyptian modes of interpreting traditional Pharaonic religion. (SJKP)

A. M. Mazzanti, 'Fra superstizione ed empietà. La definizione intermedia di εὐσέβεια in Filone di Alessandria,' *Adamantius* 16 (2010) 193–205.

Starting from Philo's qualification of εὐσέβεια as 'intermediate' (μέση) with regard to both δεισιδαιμονία and ἀσέβεια (*Deus* 163–164), the article reviews Philo's interpretation and evaluation of the latter two concepts throughout his œuvre, with reference also to Philo's philosophical context. δεισιδαιμονία refers to ritual and ethical conformism with neither existential participation nor an intellectual basis (or based on erroneous notions), ἀσέβεια amounts to an intellectual and ethical κακόν. The fundamental virtue of εὐσέβεια represents the stable balance of intellectual and existential adhesion to the one and only God. (HMK)

L. MAZZINGHI, 'Law of Nature and Light of the Law in the Book of Wisdom (Wis 18:4c),' in G. G. XERAVITS and J. ZSENGELLÉR (eds.), *Studies in the Book of Wisdom* (Leiden 2010) 185–218.

What kind of relationship exists between the author of the Book of Wisdom and philosophy contemporary with the composition of this work? Taking his starting point from Wis 18:4, which treats the Law of Moses under the metaphor of light, Mazzinghi explores the possibilities of a relationship between this passage and the concept of the law of nature in Stoicism. A significant part of the discussion is devoted to Philo's 'restatement of 'the law of nature',' focusing on some characteristics and basic conceptions which may help to illuminate the way in which the author of Wisdom refers to the Law. Among the notions considered, Mazzinghi includes: the concept of Mosaic Law as the direct revelation of God; the cosmic law of nature as the law of God; the incorruptible character of the Law and its identification with right reason; unwritten and embodied law; and the superiority of Mosaic Law, a true copy of the law of nature, over all human-made bodies of law. (SJKP)

E. MENA SALAS, 'Publio Petronio, una aproximación a su imagen literaria e histórica,' *Estudios Bíblicos* 68 (2010) 185–218, esp. 189-195.

The article studies the figure of Publius Petronius, an important Roman personage during the crisis before the Jewish war. The research has two well-documented parts: (a) analysis of the testimonies of Philo and Josephus, (b) comparison with historiographical data from other sources. Philo's report in *Legat.* and *Flacc.* presents Petronius as an example of Roman virtue, with goodwill towards foreigners and respectful of the Jewish traditions, the complete opposite to the madness of Caligula. The study of Josephus and other historiographical evidence show that Philo, in addition to using the story for his apologetic strategy, reflected real aspects of Petronius' character. (JPM)

K. METZLER, *Origenes Die Kommentierung des Buches Genesis*, Origenes Werke mit deutscher Übersetzung 1.1 (Berlin 2010).

Frequent references are given to Philo in this landmark new collection of the surviving fragments of Origen's commentaries on Genesis presented in Greek and Latin and in German translation on facing pages. It includes material from both the *Commentary on Genesis* (which covered only the creation account up to Gen 5:1) and from the *Scholia* on the same book covering Gen 5:2 to 49:9. Philo is cited in Testimonium C II 1 (Calcidius) and is frequently referred to in the annotations to the fragments. See the listing in the index on p. 339. (DTR)

M. MIRA, 'Philo of Alexandria,' in L. F. MATEO-SECO and G. MASPERO (eds.), *The Brill Dictionary of Gregorius of Nyssa*, Supplements to Vigiliae Christianae 99 (Leiden–Boston 2010), 601–603 and passim.

English translation of the article devoted to Philo in this comprehensive encyclopedia on the writings and thought of Gregory of Nyssa first published in Italian in 2007. See the summary at *SPhA* vol. 22, p. 234–235. The many other references to the Alexandrian throughout the work are indexed on p. 800. (DTR)

F. Morelli, 'Philo Vindobonensis restitutus. Non c'è due senza tre: P. Vindob. G 30531 + 60584 + 21649,' *Zeitschrift für Papyrologie und Epigraphik* 173 (2010) 167–174.

A small fragment from the Viennese collection of papyri, G21649, can be added to the two recently identified by Ursula and Dieter Hagedorn as presenting the text of Virt. 62–71; see *SPhA* vol. 24, p. 196. The new identification allows some more conclusions to be drawn about the distribution of the text among the fragments and some features of the original from which they derive. (DTR)

H. Najman, 'Text and Figure in Ancient Jewish *paideia*,' in M. Popovic (ed.), *Authoritative Scriptures in Ancient Judaism*, Journal of the Study of Judaism Supplements 141 (Leiden 2010) 253–265.

Najman's study explores the interconnections between figures, scriptures and *paideia* in Philo's Jewish-Greek context within the early Roman imperial world, in which, Najman argues, he 'had to authorize Judaism itself to both Jews and non-Jews' (p. 254). Philo aims to achieve this goal by 'inscribing' Mosaic tradition into the school of Plato, treating Mosaic laws 'in light of the Greek concept of *paideia*.' Najman emphasizes the importance, in this context, of Philo's notion of the human goal of becoming mind alone, an ostensibly Platonic concept of perfection attained through *paideia*. Philo reads this conception into his Jewish sources (Torah), thereby demonstrating that the goal of perfection through *paideia* is attainable through a life lived according to Mosaic Torah. Philo's strategy involves the identification of three figures of different modes of instruction within the Torah: the self-taught who follow their 'internal' teacher (the first Adam; Abraham; Isaac; Moses); the self-taught sage who is a model for others to follow, 'an internal teacher *at a second remove*' (Abraham; Moses); and textual instruction (Mosaic Torah as the most perfect copy of the laws of nature). (SJKP)

H. Najman, *Past Renewals: Interpretative Authority, Renewed Revelation and the Quest for Perfection in Jewish Antiquity*, Supplements to the Journal for the Study of Judaism 53 (Leiden 2010).

This volume brings together a collection of fourteen of the author's previously published essays, reprinted as originally published, with minor corrections and updating of references where relevant. In her Introduction (xvii–xxii) to the volume, Najman explains the structure of the collection, the three parts of which correspond to three key questions which have underpinned her work of the last decade: (1) how did ancient Jewish authors claim authority for their interpretation of Scripture? (2) how, after the 'end of prophecy,' could Jewish authors claiming prophetic authority for their interpretation expect to find people to listen to them? (3) what sort of person might have been considered as meriting authority as an interpreter? Najman's studies on Philo figure prominently in each section. Under the first heading, 'Interpretive Authority,' she includes her essays on 'The Law of Nature and the Authority of Mosaic Law,' (RRS 9960), and 'A Written Copy of the Law of Nature: an Unthinkable Paradox?,' (RRS 20389). In the second section, 'Renewed Revelation,' Najman includes 'Philosophical Contemplation and Revelatory Inspiration in Ancient Judean Traditions,' (summary in *SPhA* vo. 22, p. 235). The final part of the volume, 'Soul Formation and the Quest for Perfection,' includes three essays touching on different aspects of Philo's thinking about allegorical interpretation, *paideia* and perfection: 'Cain and Abel as Character Traits: A Study in the Allegorical Typology of Philo of Alexandria,'

(RRS 20387); 'The Quest for Perfection in Ancient Judaism,' originally published in French as 'La Recherche de la Perfection dans le Judaïsme ancien,' (summary in *SPhA* vol. 23, p. 122); and 'Text and Figure in Ancient Jewish *Paideia*' (summary above). (SJKP)

M. R. Niehoff, 'The Symposium of Philo's Therapeutae: Displaying Jewish Identity in an Increasingly Roman World,' *Greek, Roman, and Byzantine Studies* 50 (2010) 95–117.

The article argues that for Philo the symposium has become an arena where national identity is displayed and ancestral values are transmitted. In the case of the Therapeutae it exemplifies the stern demands of Jewish ethics, which are diametrically opposed to the hedonistic and reckless ways of the Greek Other. This antagonistic construction of Jewish identity emerged in the more mature stages of Philo's career and differs significantly from his earlier positions. This change of perspective can be explained by reference to Philo's increasing integration into distinctly Roman forms of discourse, which rendered him close to intellectuals such as Seneca. The Therapeutic symposium, as seen by Philo, moreover provides a crucial background for understanding subsequent Christian writers, such as Clement, who shared his familiarity with Greek literature as well as his ascetic tendency and Roman affinities. (MRN)

M. R. Niehoff, 'Philo's Scholarly Inquiries into the Story of Paradise,' in M. Bockmuehl and G. G. Stroumsa (eds.), *Paradise in Antiquity: Jewish and Christian Views* (Cambridge 2010) 28–42.

The article argues that Philo's approach to the story of Paradise was exceptionally scholarly. He combined for the first time stringent scholarship in the style of the Jewish exegete Demetrius and Homeric scholars with systematic allegorical readings. Philo thus hoped to show that his allegorical interpretations of Paradise were not whimsical, but had instead been intended by Moses himself. In this way Philo rendered the biblical story relevant to his critical readers in first century Alexandria, showing that problems of consistency and verisimilitude can be solved in the same way as they had been solved with regard to the Homeric epics. (MRN)

M. R. Niehoff, 'Philo's Role as a Platonist in Alexandria,' in J.-F. Pradeau (ed.), *Études Platoniciennes VII: Philon d'Alexandrie* (Paris 2010) 37–64.

The article argues for Philo's active and creative engagement with Plato's thought, distinguishing between different phases and orientations of his writings. The starting point of Philo's thought on Plato was distinctly Alexandrian. Like his predecessors Eudorus and the anonymous commentator on the *Theaetetus*, he assumed that Plato advocated dogma. For him, too, epistemology and man's assimilation to God were central concerns, which were discussed in the context of the *Theaetetus*. Philo's Jewish background thus contributed to his exegesis of Plato's works. His firm belief in the truth of Scripture led him to take a pioneering role in the interpretation of the *Timaeus*. He drew attention to this dialogue in Alexandria, fervently opposing Stoic notions and advocating a scholastic, literal approach to the text. Philo's contribution to Platonism in the later part of his career is similarly significant, because he offers an innovate synthesis of Platonic transcendentalism and Stoic immanentism. His treatise *Opif.* exemplifies the importance of Rome, whose political role had crucial implications for the philosophical discourse of the time. As a Jew, who had experienced ethnic violence in Alexandria and was awaiting Claudius' verdict, he was especially sensitive to current discourses in Rome. (MRN)

M. R. NIEHOFF, '[Hebrew: The story of Joseph: from narrative to character] סיפור יוסף: מטקסט לדמות,' *Bet Mikra* 55 (2010) 107–122.

The article addresses the famous crux of Philo's different interpretations of the Joseph story in his Allegorical Commentary and in *Ios*. It is argued that these differences of perspective are best interpreted in light of Philo's different series of writings and his different audiences. In the Allegorical Commentary he offers a systematic interpretation of consecutive verses, enriching his textual work by Platonic assumptions, which lead to a highly critical view of Joseph. In *Ios.*, by contrast, Philo has embraced the biographical style and presents Joseph's overall traits, which are no longer discussed in light of a stringent contrast between body and soul. (MRN)

E. PARKER, 'Philo of Alexandria's *Logos* and *Life of Moses*,' *Dionysius* 28 (2010) 27–44.

To determine Moses's ontological status in the *Mos.*, the author reviews several scholarly positions and discerns that Philo's understanding of the triple role of the Logos in creation is key to this question. The relationship between Philo's creation theology and Moses's ontology is reflected in the Exposition treatise on Moses, which stands 'at the culmination of Philo's divine history as the fulfillment and perfection of creation' (p. 34). Like the Logos, Moses functions as a mediating figure between creation and the divine. His stages of development, from his early education to his exile in Arabia to his experience at the burning bush, as well as the different roles that he plays as philosopher-king, lawgiver, priest, and prophet correspond to the three functions of the Logos in creation, which Roberto Radice terms as 'the Logos in the world,' 'the Logos in itself,' and 'the Logos in God.' The implications of these observations for Moses's ontology are that Moses is human, divine, and a mixture of the two: 'As philosopher undertaking the contemplative ascent, Moses is fully human. As consubstantial with God as an aspect of his self-knowledge, Moses is fully God. As inspired prophet and miracle worker, Moses is fully both God and man.' (p. 43) (EB)

J.-F. PRADEAU (ed.), *Études platoniciennes VII: Philon d'Alexandrie* (Paris 2010).

This volume in the series devoted to the study of Plato and Platonism is largely devoted to the thought and writings of Philo and contains eleven articles written by specialists in the field of Philonic and related studies. In addition a twelfth article by F. Trabbatoni includes a section on Philo as part of its investigation into the presence of an onto-theology in pre-Plotinian platonism. All twelve articles are summarised elsewhere in this bibliography. (DTR)

V. RABENS, 'Geistes-Geschichte. Die Rede vom Geist im Horizont der griechisch-römischen und jüdisch-hellenistischen Literatur,' *Zeitschrift für Neues Testament* 25 (2010) 46–55.

The author locates different concepts of *pneuma* in Philo, that of air, of the rational aspect of the human soul and of divine inspiration. Against the assumption of a Stoic influence on Philo's idea of *pneuma* there are no indications of its material character. The divine spirit is immaterial. The effect of the spirit on human beings cannot be described as 'infusion transformation.' There is no ontological transformation but a dynamic, religious-ethical change. When Philo seeks to describe the experience of the divine presence he uses visual, mystic terminology, in the context of which the spirit plays an important part in shaping the relationship with God. The religious-ethical effect of the spirit is relational. The spirit pulls up the human soul, and thus enables virtuous behaviour. Because of the indwelling of the divine spirit humankind can live lives that are pleasing to God, as demonstrated in specific examples, e.g. Abraham and Moses. (JLB).

R. RADICE, 'L'allegoria di Filone di Alessandria,' in J.-F. PRADEAU (ed.), *Études Platoniciennes VII: Philon d'Alexandrie* (Paris 2010) 95–114.

This study starts with an outline of the historical development and context of Alexandrian Jewish allegory as found in the work of Aristobulus and Philo. There follows a systematic analysis of Philo's allegorical procedures, culminating in a definition of the nature and origin of the *Quaestiones et solutiones* and in the identification of four possible relationships between the *Questions* and the *Allegorical Commentary*, as well as four rules or allegorical methods applied by Philo. A comparison between *Leg.* 1 and the corresponding *Quaestiones* illustrates the possible relationships: (i) *QG* instigates *Leg.*; (ii) *QG* and *Leg.* are in perfect correspondence; (iii) *QG* and *Leg.* do not show any relationship; (iv) *QG* functions as archive or database from which *Leg.* makes a selection. Philo in writing the Allegorical Commentary seems to have applied the following methods: (1) agglomeration, with ensuing variation and amplification, of *quaestiones* (due to the necessary exegetical continuity of a running commentary as opposed to the fragmentary *Quaestiones*); (2) lemmatic ladders (my rendering of the author's *procedimento scalare*: a first biblical lemma poses a *quaestio* that leads to another lemma etc.); (3) etymology—for which the author refers to D. T. Runia in *SPhA* 16 (2004) 101–121 (= RRS2 204108); (4) digressions of a scholarly, philosophical, or exegetical nature which move away from a direct relationship to the biblical text under discussion. (HMK)

M. J. REDDOCH, *Dream Narratives and their Philosophical Orientation in Philo of Alexandria*, OhioLINK Electronic Theses and Dissertations Center (diss. University of Cincinnati 2010).

In *Somn.* I–II, Philo provides an exegesis of various dreams in the book of Genesis. He organizes the dreams into a classification system based on how the dreams were conveyed and to what extent they are enigmatic. The purpose of this dissertation is to explain the relationship between Philo's tripartite classification system and his actual exegesis of the dreams. The approach taken is based on the idea that Philo's goals in these treatises are best understood within the Greek philosophical tradition. The condition of one's soul remains central to philosophical approaches to dreams from Plato through the Neoplatonists. Philo's tripartite dream classification, which is most similar to the one attributed by Cicero (*Div.* 1.64) to the Stoic Posidonius, also stresses the role and condition of the soul in prophetic dreaming. Stoic ideas about the moral and spiritual progress of the soul are central to Philo's philosophical and exegetical project throughout his corpus, and his treatment of dreams is no exception. Each class of dreams corresponds to a different level of progress for the dreamer. The one whose dreams are obscure is the one whose moral and spiritual progress is not sufficient to enable clarity of mental vision. Philo's interpretation of the biblical text does not isolate the dreams themselves but takes into consideration the larger narrative contexts in which the descriptions of the dreams are embedded. Moreover, Philo's exegesis of these biblical dream narratives operates simultaneously on both literal and allegorical levels. A literal reading of the text provides evidence to Philo that certain dreamers lacked mental clarity and required assistance in interpreting their dreams. For example, Joseph expresses uncertainty when describing his first dream, and Philo says this is indicative of his lack of mental clarity and thus moral and spiritual progress. On the level of the allegorical exegesis, Philo no longer treats the dreams as prophetic mediums, and they become allegories themselves. For example, Philo interprets Jacob's dream of the ladder as the life of the practitioner who is subject to constant ups and downs as he strives for moral and spiritual improvement. This dissertation is divided into three parts. The first part deals exclusively with the philosophical background. The second part explains how Philo approaches the biblical dreams within their narrative contexts (ch. 3) and also explains the philosophical background to Philo's figurative use of sleep and dreaming (ch. 4). The last two chapters examine the two treatises individually and in linear fashion in order to show how Philo's ideas about the condition of the soul and its moral and spiritual progress are developed within each class of dreams. In the conclusion, the study returns to the question of the subject of Philo's first class of dreams, which was discussed in a no longer extant treatise. Having shown how Philo situates his ideas about the moral and spiritual progress of the soul within the context of his dream classification, the author argues that Isaac must have been central to the first class. (DTR; based on the author's abstract)

E. Regev, 'From *Enoch* to John the Essene: an Analysis of Sect Development – 1 *Enoch, Jubilees* and the Essenes,' in E. G. Chazon, B. Halperin-Amaru and R. Clements (eds.), *New Perspectives on Old Texts: Proceedings of the Tenth International Symposium of the Orion Center for the Study of the Dead Sea Scrolls and Associated Literature, 9–11 January, 2005* (Leiden 2010) 67–93.

The article deals with the origin of the community at Qumran and asks to what extent it was a sect or when it assumed sectarian features. While the main parts of the article focus on *Enoch* and the *Book of Jubilees,* pointing to similarities with writings from Qumran, the last section discusses Philo and Josephus as witnesses to the Essenes, asking whether they can be identified with the group at Qumran. In this section Philo plays a secondary role next to Josephus, who is used as an important source in the argument for essential differences between Qumran and the Essenes. (MRN)

J. R. Royse, 'Some Observations on the Biblical Text in Philo's *De Agricultura,*' *The Studia Philonica Annual* 22 (2010) 111–129.

In this article Royse discusses some quotations from the LXX in *Agr.*, paying special attention to the question how they differ from the LXX text as it has been transmitted and from other citations in Philo. Having examined six quotations (*Agr.* 1: Gen 9:20–21; §12: Deut 20:20; §94: Gen 49:17–18; §127: Gen 4:7; §148: Deut 20:5b–7; §172: Deut 8:18), he concludes as follows: 'Philo basically uses the LXX, but omits words that seem superfluous or irrelevant to his discussion, adds words for clarificaton of grammar, rewrites constructions, and shifts to preferred grammatical forms.' (p. 129). (ACG)

D. T. Runia, 'The Structure of Philo's Allegorical Treatise *De Agricultura,'* *The Studia Philonica Annual* 22 (2010) 87–109.

The author returns to the subject of the structure of Philo's allegorical treatises, which he had dealt with extensively in two earlier articles published in the eighties (R–R 8447, RRS 8781) and applies to the case of *Agr.*, on which he and A. C. Geljon are preparing a commentary in the Philo of Alexandria Commentary Series. It is plain the Allegorical Commentary is a running commentary on the text of Genesis, but *Agr.* plainly deviates from earlier and later treatises in treating only a single verse of scripture, Gen 9:20. In the absence of any comments on the part of Philo or others on how the biblical commentaries are structured, we have no alternative to adopt an empirical approach to the evidence before us. The method of analysing the treatise in terms of the biblical texts cited—not just the primary biblical text, but also those cited at a secondary or even tertiary level—works very well and will be utilised in the commentary. In addition Philo uses other techniques that are part of his 'prose rhetoric,' e.g. the use of transitional and structuring phraseology, various rhetorical tropes, attacks on opponents reminiscent of the diatribe, and exhortatory passages that bring home the relevance of the exegesis for the moral and spiritual life of the reader. In the final part of the paper a detailed analysis of the treatise's structure is set out and briefly commented upon. This structure fits in well with the method that the Director of the series, Prof. Gregory E. Sterling, outlined when he established the series in 1995 (see *SPhA* vol. 7, p. 165). The commentary itself was published in 2013; see the provisional bibliography for that year below. (DTR)

D. T. Runia, '*Dogma* and *doxa* in the Allegorical Writings of Philo of Alexandria,' in J.-F. Pradeau (ed.), *Études Platoniciennes VII: Philon d'Alexandrie* (Paris 2010) 115–132.

The article follows on from an earlier study of Philo's use of Greek philosophical doxography (see *SPhA* vol. 23, p. 128). Philo frequently uses the terms δόγμα and δόξα to refer both to specifically doxographical material and also to philosophical and religious positions in general. The article examines this usage, particularly in relation to Philo's use of the allegorical method of exegesis. After some initial comments on the etymology and general Greek usage of the terms, it is noted that they are both used very frequently by Philo and that the exact meaning is generally determined by the context. In many cases the meaning seems to be virtually identical, denoting 'opinion,' 'belief' or 'line of thinking.' But there are sometimes subtle differences. In general *dogma* has a more positive resonance, whereas *doxa* is quite often negatively marked (a striking case is his use of the Epicurean phrase κενὴ δόξα, often translated 'vainglory'). Against this background the article then examines how Philo links the two terms to biblical characters who thereby come to be represent directions of thought in his allegories. Seven characters or groups are discussed, including Cain, the Chaldeans, Laban, Pharaoh, Joseph and groups excluded from the holy congregation. This list shows how Philo makes his own idiosyncratic adapations of Greek philosophical material, with most of the characters having a negative bias that is contrasted with the pious and virtuous attitudes of positive characters such as Abel, Abraham and Moses. When compared with Greek practice, e.g. allegories of Homeric stories, Philo shows himself to be quite innovative, identifying doctrines more closely with characters and emphasising the narrative element more strongly. In addition his allegorical exegesis presumes a much more complex and more deeply spiritual system. In the final part of the paper brief remarks are made on Patristic trajectories, noting how Philo's practice finds a famous later sequel in Augustine's *City of God*. Although the notion of orthodoxy is wholly foreign to Philo's thought, his emphasis on normative thinking as seen in his use of *dogma* and *doxa* contributed to the development of such religious and theological thought patterns. (DTR)

D. T. RUNIA, 'Early Alexandrian Theology and Plato's *Parmenides*,' in J. D. TURNER and K. CORRIGAN (eds.), *Plato's Parmenides and its Heritage, Writings from the Greco-Roman World Supplements* 2–3 (Atlanta 2010) 2.177–187.

The two volumes record the results of a six-year project entitled 'Rethinking Plato's Parmenides and its Platonic, Gnostic and Patristic Reception' that was carried out at the Annual meetings of the Society of Biblical Literature from 2001 to 2006. A chapter is devoted to Philo and Clement of Alexandria as representatives of the Judaeo-Christian thought that developed in Alexandria in the first two centuries of the common era. Philo never refers to Plato's dialogue and only mentions Parmenides three times in *Prov.* However, three themes in his thought and writings are relevant to the Nachleben of Plato's dialogues and these are briefly discussed in turn: (1) the knowability of the ideas; (2) negative theology; and (3) dialectical categories of thought. As for Clement, he too makes no explicit references to the dialogue. But there are two passages in the *Stromateis* in which we can definitely see the theological interpretation of the Parmenides lurking in the background, 5.81.4–6 and 4.156. These two passages are briefly analysed. The article concludes with the observation that in the century and a half separating the two Alexandrians philosophy did not stand still. Just as there was a shift from a strong focus on Plato's *Timaeus* to a broader reading of the dialogues including the *Parmenides,* so Clement moves beyond Philo's strong emphasis on the relation between God and the cosmos to a broader and more developed theological doctrine. (DTR)

D. T. RUNIA, and G. E. STERLING (eds.), *The Studia Philonica Annual*, Vol. 22 (Atlanta 2010).

The twenty-second volume of the Journal dedicated to Philonic studies contains two general articles, two special sections on Philo's *De agricultura* and Hypothetica respectively, the usual bibliography section (see summary below), and thirteen book reviews. These are followed by the customary News and Notes section, Notes on contributors and Instructions for contributors. The various articles are summarised elsewhere in this bibliography. (DTR)

D. T. RUNIA, K. BERTHELOT, E. BIRNBAUM, A. C. GELJON, H. M. KEIZER, J. LEONHARDT BALZER, J. P. MARTÍN, M. R. NIEHOFF, and T. SELAND, 'Philo of Alexandria: an Annotated Bibliography 2007,' *The Studia Philonica Annual* 22 (2010) 209–256.

The yearly annotated bibliography of Philonic studies prepared by the members of the International Philo Bibliography Project covers the year 2007 (114 items), with addenda for the years 1998–2006 (20 items, including 5 studies by the Armenian scholar O. G. Vardazarjan), and provisional lists for the years 2008–10. (DTR)

G. Schöllgen (ed.), *Reallexikon für Antike und Christentum Band 23* (Stuttgart 2010).

W. Löhr, art. Logos, 327–435, esp. 345–354 (Logos); A. Hoffmann, art. Los, 471–510, esp. 495–496 (lot); M. Frenchkowski, art. Magie, 857–957, esp. 908–909 (magic); B. Eckhardt, art. Mahl V (Kultmahl), 1012–1105, esp. 1060–1061 (cultic meal, focusing on the Therapeutae). (DTR)

I. W. Scott, 'Revelation and Human Artefact: The Inspiration of the Pentateuch in the Book of Aristeas,' *Journal for the Study of Judaism* 41 (2010) 1–28.

In the *Book of Aristeas* (as the author calls this work) the Pentateuch is presented as a purely human composition. Moses was endowed by God with a sharp intellect so that he could write a superior law. This view stands in sharp contrast with other Hellenized Jews, among whom should be counted Philo, who depicts Moses as a divinely inspired prophet. Sometimes Moses is possessed by God's spirit and carried away out of himself. The same underscoring of Moses' inspiration is also found in other Alexandrian Jewish literature, for instance in the Wisdom of Solomon and Aristobulus. This implies that the author of the *Book of Aristeas* deliberately rejects the prophetic model for Moses' work, i.e. the Greek translation is also seen as a purely human intellectual endeavour, in contrast to Philo's view. It should be noted, however, that the writer of the *Book of Aristeas* does claim that the Torah has its origin in God. (ACG)

T. Seland, "'Colony' and 'Metropolis' in Philo. Examples of Mimicry and Hybridity in Philo's writing back from the Empire?,' in J.-F. Pradeau (ed.), *Études Platoniciennes VII: Philon d'Alexandrie* (Paris 2010) 13–36.

Philo is often read as one who finds his position in general quite well situated in the Diaspora, and as one who exhibits a very positive attitude towards the Roman Empire. At the same time, we also know that the Jewish Diaspora communities of Alexandria of his time underwent severe social troubles, and for some time in the late thirties c.e. even suffered from an anti-Jewish pogrom in the city. The present study attempts an anti-imperial and postcolonial reading, focusing especially on Philo's use of the terms for colony (ἀποικία) and mother-city (μητρόπολις). The first section deals with Philo in the world of imperialism, colonialism, mimicry and hybridity (pp. 12–18), focusing on central aspects of Philo's social world, and discussing the heuristic values of postcolonial perspectives, especially as represented by the last two categories. The second deals with Philo 'writing back from the Empire' (pp. 18–29), discussing *apoikia* and *metropolis* in recent Philonic research (pp. 20–23), in the LXX and in Philo's works, except *Flacc.* and *Legat.* (pp. 24–25), and then focusing on the terms in those two treatises as cases of mimicry and hybridity (pp. 25–29). In conclusion the author suggests that there is a kind of double message from Philo to the readers. The warnings are there, and the underlying self understanding of Philo is associated with his view of the Jewish settlements as being a kind of colonies sent out from Jerusalem up through the decades and centuries. In this there is mimicry of both Greek and Roman colonization. The Romans might smile at the hybridity involved in Philo's characterizations. But to Philo they were real issues. In writing in these ways, he tried to support and defend his Jewish people and their presence in the Roman Empire, while also presenting his negative attitudes to the Roman authorities. (TS)

G. Sfameni Gasparro, *Dio unico, pluralità e monarchia divina. Esperienze religiose e teologie nel mondo tardo-antico*, Scienze e storia delle religioni 12 (Brescia 2010).

This collection of studies argues that the confrontation between polytheism and monotheism was a debate that was fundamental for the development of western culture. It includes as its first chapter (pp. 35–77) the study on Philo published previously in 2009, on which see *SPhA* vol. 24 p. 219. (HMK)

R. W. Sharples, *Peripatetic Philosophy 200 BC to AD 200: an Introduction and Collection of Sources in Translation*, Cambridge Source Books in Post-Hellenistic Philosophy (Cambridge 2010).

Following the method of vol. 1 of Long and Sedley's The Hellenistic Philosophers (see RRS 3016), this valuable collection of sources on Peripatetic philosophy in the first two centuries B.C.E. and C.E. includes translations of eleven texts from Philo: *Leg.* 1.3–4; *Det.* 7; *Ebr.* 111; *Migr.* 147; *Decal.* 30–31; *Aet.* 55–57, 70, 71–73, 74, 75; *QG* 3.16 (DTR)

M. G. Steinhilber, *Die Fürbitte für die Herrschenden im Alten Testament, Frühjudentum und Urchristentum : eine traditionsgeschichtliche Studie*, Wissenschaftliche Monographien zum Alten und Neuen Testament 128 (Neukirchen-Vluyn 2010), esp. 195–206.

The chapter entitled 'Die Fürbitte für die Herrschenden bei Philo von Alexandrien' (The prayers for the rulers in Philo of Alexandria) focuses on Philo's *Flacc.* and *Legat.*, both of which have an apologetic outlook. According to *Flacc.* 48–49 the destruction of the Alexandrian *proseuchai* prevented the Jewish community from honoring the emperor, probably not a reference to actual prayer for the ruling house, but rather a reference to the practice of putting up inscriptions and other honors for benefactors, similar to what occurred in pagan associations. *Legat.* 157 and 317 describe the daily sacrifices and prayers are offered in the Jewish Temple on behalf of the emperor as having been instituted and paid for by Augustus. Philo interprets this as an *aparche*, i.e. offering or Temple tax on the part of the emperor. After Augustus the daily sacrifices retained the purpose of prayer for the emperors (*Legat.* 232), which for Philo was an expression of the particular loyalty of the Jews, especially to Gaius (*Legat.* 279–280 and 356–357). The latter text is the only evidence of a Roman emperor not being satisfied with this form of honoring the emperor. (JLB).

G. E. Sterling, 'Philo's *De Agricultura*: Introduction,' *The Studia Philonica Annual* 22 (2010) 83–85.

Brief remarks on Philo's aims and exegetical methods in the Allegorical Commentary that serve as an introduction to a Special section of the Journal devoted to the treatise *De agricultura*, on which A. C. Geljon and D. T. Runia are preparing a commentary for the Philo of Alexandria Commentary Series. See also the articles by J. R. Royse and D. T. Runia summarised above. (DTR)

G. E. Sterling, '*The Hypothetica*: Introduction,' *The Studia Philonica Annual* 22 (2010) 139–142.

Brief remarks on Philo's treatise *Hypothetica*, of which fragments have been preserved by Eusebius in his *Praeparatio Evangelica*. They serve as an introduction to a Special section of the Journal devoted to this treatise. See further the articles by D. Boesenberg, M. Cover and H. Vela summarised elsewhere in this bibliography. (DTR).

G. E. Sterling, M. R. Niehoff, A. van den Hoek, and D. T. Runia, 'Philo,' in J. J. Collins and D. C. Harlow (eds.), *The Eerdmans Dictionary of Early Judaism* (Grand Rapids 2010) 1063–1080.

See the notice above under the names of the editors, J. Collins and D. C. Harlow.

H. Svebakken, 'Exegetical Traditions in Alexandria: Philo's Reworking of the Letter of Aristeas 145–149 as a Case Study,' in P. Walters (ed.), *From Judaism to Christianity: Tradition and Transition. A Festschrift for Thomas H. Tobin, S.J., on the Occasion of His Sixty-fifth Birthday* (Leiden 2010) 93–112.

To test the conclusions of his teacher, Thomas H. Tobin S.J., about Philo's interpretive practices, the author examines Philo's interpretation in *Spec.* 4.100–118 of Lev 11:13–19, a passage about birds that Israelites are forbidden to eat, in light of interpretation of this biblical passage in the *Letter of Aristeas* 145-149. Agreements between the two interpretations suggest that Philo knew and reworked the earlier tradition. These agreements include a listing, not found in Leviticus, of permitted birds; similar characterizations of the birds, some of which Philo applies to land animals instead of birds; and Philo's reference to carnivores, a category found in the *Letter,* in his discussion of land animals. But whereas the *Letter* disregards literal observance of the prohibition and focuses on its symbolic role of promoting justice, Philo believes that literal observance leads to self-control and the management of passions and desire. The study confirms Tobin's conclusions that Philo knew, honored, and employed earlier interpretive traditions as well as contemporary philosophical currents of thought. Instead, however, of introducing the allegory of the soul which Tobin found in the Philonic interpretations of the creation of man, Philo shows concern for the inner life by emphasizing the moral psychology of the prohibitions. This difference is attributable to the different kinds of treatments necessitated by biblical narrative and legal texts. (EB)

J. E. Taylor, 'The Classical Sources on the Essenes and the Scrolls Communities,' in T. H. Lim and J. J. Collins (eds.), *The Oxford Handbook of the Dead Sea Scrolls* (Oxford 2010) 173–199.

This expert overview of the classical sources on the Essenes and their relationship to the scrolls communities begins with a brief discussion of the Philonic evidence (pp. 174–177), in which the author analyzes Philo's treatment of the Essenes as exemplars of the excellence of Jewish religious life (in *Prob.* and in Eusebius' *Apology for the Jews*), and as the subject of a now lost treatise on the active life of philosophy (*Contempl.*). Taylor's conclusions challenge several common assumptions about the Essenes, notably her emphasis on the idea that the Essenes did not reject animal sacrifices but rather prioritized obedience to the divine law, and her insistence that Philo's evidence does not permit the conclusion that the Essenes were pacifists—they in her view reject the business of both war and peace. (SJKP)

F. TRABATTONI, 'Y a-t-il une onto-théologie dans le platonisme antérieur à Plotin ?,' in J.-F. PRADEAU (ed.), *Études Platoniciennes VII: Philon d'Alexandrie* (Paris 2010) 203–215.

The articles argues for the view that one should not attribute any kind of onto-theology to Plato or Middle Platonist authors, but that this interpretation is the result of Aristotelian and Christian influence on modern interpreters. A brief discussion is devoted to Philo, who is the first author to make an explicit identication of God with being based on the biblical text Exod 3:14. Basing his view on the texts *Mut.* 7, *Mos.* 1.75, *Det.* 160 and esp. *Opif.* 12, the author argues that Philo speaks of God as being in order to make clear the distinction between God and his creatures, and that this should not be called 'onto-theology.' The same result is reached when the writings of Plutarch and Numenius are examined. True 'onto-theology' does not occur until the advent of Neoplatonism. (DTR)

L. TROIANI, 'La colère de Dieu : «blke» et le démiurge des gnostiques,' *Mythos* 4 (2010) 113–127.

The source of the Gnostic exegesis which attributes, as we read in the Nag Hammadi treatises, the characteristic of anger to the demiurge and the archons, if not to the great archon himself in the account of the universal flood of Gen 6:6–7, can be traced back to the *Timaeus* of Plato and the *Enneads* of Plotinus. A further parallel is also encountered in the exegesis of Philo of Alexandria. (DTR; based on the author's abstract)

H. VELA, 'Philo and the Logic of History,' *The Studia Philonica Annual* 22 (2010) 165–182.

Starting-point of the article is the recently expressed view of Barclay that Philo is not author of the fragmentary work *Hypothetica* attributed to Philo (see *SPhA* vol. 22 pp. 211–212). A key argument is that Philo would not have treated biblical history in the manner found in this treatise. The author returns to the approach of Sterling (cf. RRS 9068) that Philo's reasoning makes use of the methods of Stoic logic and that this is the reason for the work's puzzling title. First a brief survey of the relevant arguments on history in *Hypoth.* 8.6.1–9 is given. Then two kinds of hypothetical Stoic argument are analysed. The first of these is the disjunction, which has two forms, the exclusive and the inclusive type. Sterling had argued that *Hypoth.* 8.6.4 was an inclusive disjunction. The author argues against this view and proposes that it uses the method of the logical and rhetorical device of the dilemma. Finally he returns to the text of *Hypoth.* and analyses its arguments in terms of dilemmatic argumentation. Philo's strategy is use this form of argument to counter conflicting reports about the Jews and thereby 'trap' his readers into a positive understanding of Judean history and culture. 'Whatever his audience might have heard about the exodus, settlement, and Jewish law, they could not help but admit that the Jews were favoured by God's providence.' (p. 182) Therefore this particular text need not worry Philonic interpreters any more. Its approach to biblical history is both Philonic and intelligible in light of ancient modes of argumentation. (DTR)

P. WALTERS (ed.), *From Judaism to Christianity: Tradition and Transition. A Festschrift for Thomas H. Tobin, S.J., on the Occasion of His Sixty-fifth Birthday*, Supplements to Novum Testamentum 136 (Leiden 2010).

Dedicated as a 'tribute to a scholar of the highest caliber,' this volume of contributions from students, colleagues, and friends of Thomas H. Tobin S.J. is divided into two parts— 'Tradition and Transition: Jewish Responses to a Hellenistic World,' consisting of five papers, and 'Foundations Amid Flux: Christian Responses to a Transitory World,' consisting of eight papers—together with an introductory paper in a section entitled, 'A Paradigm for Biblical Interpretation.' Two papers by E. Birnbaum and H. Svebakken (both summarized elsewhere in the bibliography) will be of particular interest to Philonists, as will also be P. Walters' introductory essay about the honorand and a bibliography of his works. (EB)

D. WINSTON, 'Philo of Alexandria,' in L. GERSON (ed.), *The Cambridge History of Philosophy in Late Antiquity* (Cambridge 2010) 2.235–257.

The second part of this splendid history of philosophy in antiquity is entitled The first encounter of Judaism and Christianity with ancient Greek philosophy commences with a chapter on Philo. David Winston gives a judicious and mature survey of his views on key questions in the study of Philo's thought. The view that Philo is an exegete *tout court* is quite misleading. He is thoroughly Hellenized Jew who has clearly been intellectually seduced by Platonic philosophy but nevertheless remained loyal to his Jewish faith and so felt compelled to do whatever he could to reconcile the two opposing passions that energized his existence. For his interpretation of scripture the key technique was allegory, the principles of which he derived from the Greek allegorical tradition but which he may have developed further than his Greek models. For an interpretation of Philo's philosophical thought two themes are central, his theory of creation and his doctrine of noetic prophecy. Further sections follow on the themes of freedom and determinism and the soul and its passions. Philo's mysticism is placed in perspective by a comparison with the great Sufi theosophist Ibn 'Arabi. The vision of God is more than a vision of God's incorporeal or intelligible light. It must be seen as a self-evident intellectual grasp of God's existence which takes place at the level of the Logos. The chapter ends with some comments on the Philonic heritage in the Church fathers. (DTR)

O. WISCHMEYER, 'Cosmo e cosmologia in Paolo,' *Protestantesimo* 64 (2010) 163–179.

The article offers a reflection on Paul's cosmology, which it compares to Plato's cosmology in the *Timaeus* and to Philo's reading of the latter in *Opif* . The cosmology of Plato and Philo are not only reflections on the structure of the cosmos, but also on its origin and evolution as well as on humanity and history. The author notes Engberg-Pedersen's emphasis on the interrelatedness of Paul's cosmological and apocalyptic views: Paul's cosmology does not only refer to the creation of the universe, but also includes an apocalyptic vision of its end. According to the author Paul's understanding differs from Philo's and Plato's because he believes that perfection comes only at the end of the universe, not at its beginning. Paul's vision of the universe is thus subordinate to his Christology and eschatology, and entails a new anthropology which is no longer focussed on the 'first man'—as in Philo—but on the new creation in Christ. (HMK, based on the author's summary)

M. Zugmann, 'Philo Iudaeo-Hellenisticus: Judentum und Hellenismus in der Sicht des alexandrinischen Gelehrten,' *Studien zum Neuen Testament und seiner Umwelt* 35 (2010) 189–229.

Philo exemplifies the openness towards Hellenistic culture and education combined with a commitment to Jewish traditions, but he is not an isolated phenomenon. Philo's family are Hellenized Jews, his writings are a synthesis of biblical revelation and Greek thought, Greek is his language, he is educated to the highest standards of Greek education, and participates in the full range of Greek culture in Alexandria. On the other hand he is also deeply immersed in Jewish customs and traditions, oral and written, a prominent member of the Jewish community of Alexandria as well as faithful to the Temple in Jerusalem, even expecting an eschatological gathering of the gentiles there. Nevertheless, following the Stoic cosmopolitan ideal, he praises the Hellenization, the spread of Greek culture, under Augustus, which turns barbarians into civilized people. Greeks and Jews are never placed in opposition to each other (in the pogrom the opponents are not called *Hellenes*). Yet ultimately Moses is the best lawgiver for Philo, attracting barbarians as well as Greeks, but in the Greek translation. Thus Philo is *the* 'Hellenist' *par excellence*. (JLB).

Extra items from before 2010

P. CAZIER, 'Du serpent et de l'arbre de la connaissance: lectures patristiques (Philon, Grégoire de Nysse, Jean Chrysostome, Augustin),' *Graphè* 4 (1995) 73-103.

After pointing out the exegetical difficulties contained in the biblical text, the author examines Philo's interpretation of the 2nd and 3rd chapters of Genesis, and then those of Origen, Gregory of Nyssa, John Chrysostom and Augustine. Philo struggles to show that the biblical story is not a myth despite the fact that an allegorical reading is required to discover the true meaning of the text. Man's choice is between the tree of life, understood as perfect piety, and the tree of knowledge of good and evil, which stands for 'intermediate *phronèsis*,' which is an incomplete choice for the Good. Philo does not locate the origin of evil in the snake which deceives Adam and Eve, but in the desire for pleasure; the snake is then interpreted as a symbol of pleasure. However, P. Cazier argues, it is not pleasure itself which Philo condemns, but rather the fact that the intellect does not master pleasure. The interpretations of the texts by Origen and Gregory show clear similarities with that of Philo. However, both Christian writers differ from Philo in connecting the snake with the devil, thus understanding evil and the Fall as due partly to an external factor. Moreover, Gregory's monastic background prompts him to conceive human beings as originally similar to angels. In contrast, John Chrysostom and Augustine focus on a literal reading of the texts. In all cases the author shows how the author's exegetical choices are connected with his theological, cultural and personal background. (KB)

M. HARL, 'Socrate – Silène. Les emplois métaphoriques d'ἄγαλμα et le verbe ἀγαλματοφορέω: de Platon à Philon d'Alexandrie et aux Pères grecs,' *Semitica et Classica* 2 (2009) 51–71.

This article explores the metaphorical use of the terms ἄγαλμα (the cultic statue of a god) and ἀγαλματοφορέω, a composite verb first attested in Philo. It starts with general considerations about the term ἄγαλμα and with an analysis of Plato's use of the term, and ends with the Church Fathers' use of Philo's neologism. The verb ἀγαλματοφορέω has a different meaning according to the way ἄγαλμα is used, either in the plural or in the singular. Plato describes Socrates as a Silenus who has statues of the gods within himself, that is, who conceals treasures of wisdom behind deceptive social behaviour or apparently ridiculous discourses, which actually are 'statues of virtue.' Later on, humanists such as Erasmus or Pico della Mirandola applied the image of the Silenus to Scriptures, which also contain hidden treasures. Philo already wrote that when one studies Scripture in depth, one may find in the words of the text *agalmata* of virtues, located in the human soul which is the temple of God. The assimilation of the virtues with the *agalmata* derives from Plato's *Symposium*, and is found later on in Origen as well. Plato, however, also uses the term *agalma* in the singular, to designate the human intellect, which is a divine image of the deity (*Tim.* 37b); moreover, the world too is an *agalma* of the eternal gods (*Tim.* 29b). The religious literature of late Antiquity often uses the metaphor of the *agalma* to describe the divine part within the human being, together with other terms such as *eikôn*. Before Philo, this association can already be found in Cicero. As for Philo, he describes the intellect as the *eikôn* of the divine Intellect and as an *agalma* within the human being, therefore combining a biblical term and a Platonic notion (*Opif.* 69). Human beings carry within themselves a rational soul like a divine statue. This Philonic usage of the term(s) is found appropriated by several Church Fathers influenced by Platonism and by Philo's work, such as Clement of Alexandria, Origen, Eusebius, Methodius of Olympus and Didymus of Alexandria. Considering that for Christian theologians the image of God was first and foremost Christ himself, the association of the image of God with the Greek religious notion of *agalma* was not self-evident. It shows that the term *agalma* retains only its metaphorical, abstract meaning (that of 'image'). With Eusebius, however, one encounters another meaning of *agalma*, referring to the exterior, material body which God took upon himself through the incarnation. (KB)

G. HINGE and J. KRASILNIKOFF, *Alexandria: a Cultural and Religious Meltingpot* (Aarhus 2009).

This volume contains some of the papers presented at the Centre for the Study of Mediterranean Antiquity, the University of Aarhus, Denmark, at an international confe-rence on Alexandria in 2004. Some papers have also been added to the volume, making up a total of eight contributions, prefaced by an Introduction by the editors. The volume is divided into two parts. The first entitled Alexandria from Greece and Egypt, deals with the relationship between Ptolemaic Alexandria and its Greek past. The second deals with various aspects of contact and development between Rome, Judaism and Christianity. Two articles by P. Bilde and A. Klostergaard Petersen discuss Philo. The former was summa-rized in *SPhA* vol 22 p. 214. For the latter see below. (TS)

A. KLOSTERGAARD PETERSEN, 'Alexandrian Judaism: Rethinking of a Problematic Category,' in G. HINGE and J. KRASILNIKOFF (eds.), *Alexandria: a Cultural and Religious Meltingpot* (Aarhus 2009) 115–143.

The essay focuses on the theoretical aspects of how to reconstruct past cultural entities more than on the Alexandrian Jewry or Philo as such, though using Alexandrian Jewry as a kind of sample test case. Hence the author pays especial attention to reconstruction on the basis of limited sources, and secondly, to the problems of how to conceive past cultural entities. In his 'Listing of Problems' (pp. 120–128), and in his section on 'Alexandrian Jewry; Historical reality or Scholarly Phantom' (pp. 128–135), and 'Different Stages in the History of Alexandrian Judaism' (pp. 134–139) he deals extensively with Philo as one of the relevant sources. He emphasizes that Philo did not embody Alexandrian Judaism in its cultural and social breadth, nor should he be thought of as a homogenous thinker who always subscribed to the same understanding of reality: 'Philo's writings should be interpreted as the creations of a composite being who under particular circumstances and with particular aims and situations in mind attempts to conquer the cultural battlefield of his time' (p. 139). (TS)

A. MCGOWAN, *Ascetic Eucharists. Food and Drink in Early Christian Ritual Meals*. (Oxford 1999), esp. 56–57, 79–80.

A study on food and drink in early Christian ritual meals that wishes to take into account both the Jewish and the pagan background can hardly fail to make reference to Philo's account of the Therapeutae. The author judiciously weighs up the value of Philo's testimony, concluding that his philosophical bent may lessen our confidence in the historicity of the description, but that the meal of the Therapeutae that Philo describes does not step very far outside the bounds of expectation, given what we know about other Jewish meals and the Greco-Roman tradition. (DTR)

M. Olivieri, *Il secondo libro del De Providentia di Filone di Alessandria: i frammenti greci e la tradizione armena* (diss. Bologna 2000).

The dissertation submitted to the University of Bologna in 2000 consists of five chapters. In the first the author reviews both the Greek (via Eusebius *Praep. Evang.*) and the Armenian witnesses of *Prov.*, using the one tradition to judge the other. Even though it is a case of an 'open' *recensio*, applying the method of Martin West, he defines a *stemma codicum* and identifies the witnesses which are useful for the *constitutio textus*. The second chapter deals with the problem of the ancient Armenian translations of Philo, relating them to the lexicographical Greek texts, which often seem to be used in Armenian translations (this section has also been published elsewhere, see RRS2 20053). The third chapter is a true critical edition of the text of the four large fragments handed down in Greek by Eusebius. The text is presented synoptically in Armenian, Greek and Italian side-by-side. The text of Armenian and Greek are given with a critical *apparatus* and followed by a continuous commentary, which mainly focuses on those aspects of the *constitutio textus* presented in the *apparatus*. A new text division and numbering is proposed, based on the work of Philo (and not, as hitherto, on that of his indirect witnesses). Comparative tables between the numberings of previous editors are provided. Conjectures and proposals for additions to both the Greek and Armenian text are put forward, with both traditions used to judge and correct the other. The fourth chapter discusses recognizable quotations from other authors (e.g. Plato, Homer, Hesiod) for which it is possible to make a further comparison with the Greek, and also contains a list of fragments from Greek authors, of which the Greek text in Philo is not preserved (e.g. Aeschylus and Simonides). The fifth and final chapter is a Greek-Armenian and Armenian-Greek, dictionary, based on correspondences found in the text of *Prov.* and in translations of other works by the so-called 'Hellenizing School.' *Prov.* is quoted according to the new proposed text division and numbering. The dictionary also collects the contents of several similar works (e.g. Marcus, Terian, Adontz, Calzolari). With about 4000 entries, it is one of the most extensive lists of Greek-Armenian correspondences compiled so far. The author uses it as a tool to attempt some retroversions from Armenian to Greek. (DTR; based on the author's abstract)

C. Rodriguez, 'P. Mich. inv. 4800: un témoignage du conflit judéo-alexandrin de 38-41 de n.è.?,' *Journal of Juristic Papyrology* 39 (2009) 161–197.

The papyrus Mich inv. 4800, which is dated to the second half of the 2nd cent. c.e. and includes 17 fragments, has been incorporated in H. Musurillo's 1961 edition of the *Acta Alexandrinorum*. The author provides a new edition of the papyrus, with some comments and a translation, and suggests that it may represent a document related to the riots against the Jews in 38 c.e., based on a Jewish account. Some elements, such as the prominent role of a mother, recall Jewish stories of martyrdom such as those of 2 Maccabees, and the reference to an ingathering in the theater is reminiscent of both 3 Maccabees and Philo's *Flacc.* The motif of prisoners in the chains also looks like a *topos* of Jewish martyrdom literature. The author of the text seems to have known Philo's *Flacc.* A first possibility would be to consider the text a passage from a longer version of *Flacc.*, *Legat.* or a lost treatise on the persecutions of the Alexandrian Jews mentioned by Eusebius and called the Περι ἀρετῶν. Another possibility would be to identify the text as a paraphrase of Philo's works written by an anonymous Jew. Finally, one cannot exclude the possibility that the papyrus was related to the revolt of 115–117 c.e., which was brutally repressed. It may have been a kind of legal drama similar to 3 Maccabees and characterized by the same *poikilia*. In any case, the author concludes that the papyrus shows that Philo's works were read during the 2nd century c.e. Finally, the issue of the provenance of the papyrus is discussed. It was found in the house of Socrates, son of Sarapion, an Egyptian tax collector in Karanis, a place where the Jewish community had disappeared in the 2nd cent. c.e. Socrates, however, was a learned man who may have been interested in a Jewish work, particularly if he was connected in some way with the Sambathions, a group of Egyptians who observed the sabbat and had a presence in Karanis. Although the fragmentary state of the papyrus precludes reaching definitive conclusions, it does represent the first testimony of the reception of Philo's works in Egypt. (KB)

F. L. Schuddeboom, *Greek Religious Terminology—Telete & Orgia. A Revised and Expanded English Edition of the Studies by Zijderveld and Van der Burg*, Religions in the Graeco-Roman World 169 (Leiden 2009).

Part One of this book is a revised edition of C. Zijderveld, Τελετή: *Bijdrage tot de kennis der religieuze terminologie in het Grieksch* [Dutch: Teletê: Contribution to the understanding of religious terminology in Greek] (diss. Utrecht, Purmerend 1934). Part Two contains a revised edition of N. M. H. van der Burg, Ἀπόρρητα – δρώμενα - ὄργια : *Bijdrage tot de kennis der religieuze terminologie in het Grieksch* [Dutch: Aporrhêta-Drômena-Orgia: Contribution to the understanding of religious terminology in Greek] (diss. Utrecht, Amsterdam 1939). Among the Jewish and Christian authors Philo is also examined. The term τελετή has several meanings in Philo: A. Pagan ritual acts (as in the LXX), of which he disapproves; B. Greek mysteries; C. Jewish ritual acts; D. Hidden meaning of Scripture; E. Generally τελετή (and μυστήριον) often also means supreme revelation of the deity, divine truth. The term ὄργια (and ὀργιάζειν) is used in various ways. It can refer to Greek religious rites, but also to the divine rites of Jewish religion. (ACG)

M. Scopello, 'L'âme en fuite : le traité gnostique de l'«Allogène» (NH XI, 3) et la mystique juive,' in J.-M. Narbonne and P.-H. Poirier (eds.), *Gnose et philosophie : études en hommage à Pierre Hadot* (Quebec 2009) 123–145.

The Gnostic treatise known as the *Allogenes* or 'Stranger,' originally composed in Greek in the 3rd cent. c.e. and later translated into Coptic, contains revelations made by an angel (Youel) to an initiated person called Allogenes, who then teaches them to his disciple Messos. The author focuses on a passage that describes a mystical experience in which Allogenes is driven both outside of himself and deep within himself, and declares that he has become (a part of) God. After having examined some similarities between the *Allogenes* and the Book of Daniel, as well as with the 3 Enoch, he analyses the motif of the flight of the soul, which also appears in the *Apocalypse of Abraham* and in Philo. According to Philo the flight of the soul beyond the confines of the intellect leads to the experience of ἔκστασις, but also to the experience of penetrating into the most inner part of the self. The story of Abraham is the story of the soul, called to leave its own self behind in order to be filled by God. Allogenes, the foreigner, is similar to Abraham as interpreted by Philo, and Philo's discourse about the escape of the soul sheds much light on the Gnostic treatise. (KB)

B. G. WOLD, *Women, Men and Angels: The Qumran Wisdom Document Musar leMevin and its Allusions to Genesis Creation Traditions*, Wissenschaftliche Untersuchungen zum Neuen Testament 2.201 (Tübingen 2005), esp. 102, 133–135, 141–147.

The author argues against J. J. Collins' explanation of the dualism of two distinct kinds of humanity in 4Q417 1 i with reference to Philo's account of the creation of two kinds of human beings, i.e. the heavenly man and the earthly man. But he observes that on four occasions in his exegesis of Gen 1:26 Philo refers to the role of the angels. He argues that a comparison of these texts with the Qumran text will aid in placing the sapiential texts in a broader exegetical context. The Philonic texts discussed as *Opif.* 72–76, *Conf.* 171–180, *Fug.* 65–70 and *Mut.* 27–34. Emphasis is placed on the correlation between angels and humans based on the role of angels in the first creation. (DTR)

S. YLI-KARJANMAA, 'The *Timaeus*, Philo Judaeus and Reincarnation,' in G. af HÄLLSTRÖM (ed.), *Människan i universum. Platons Timaios och dess tolkningshistoria i Åbo 2007. Texter från Platonsällskapets symposium [Swedish: The Human Being in the Universe. Plato's Timaeus and Its History of Interpretation. Proceedings of the Symposium of the Nordic Plato Society in Turku, Finland, 2007]* (Åbo 2009) 217–243

The Finnish scholar examines whether Philo's interpretation of Plato's *Timaeus* left room for a reincarnationist view of the soul. The balance of evidence does not suggest a direct, explicitly reincarnationist Timaean influence in Philo's works. Nevertheless, the way in which he utilizes this dialogue, in the anthropology of which *metempsychosis* plays a clear role, can be seen to indicate rather a positive than a neutral or negative attitude towards the doctrine. Philo does not express reservations in anticipation of possible suspicions about his accepting the tenet. (DTR; based on the author's abstract)

SUPPLEMENT

A Provisional Bibliography 2011–2013

The user of this supplemental Bibliography of the most recent articles on Philo is reminded that it will doubtless contain inaccuracies and red herrings because it is not in all cases based on autopsy. It is merely meant as a service to the reader. Scholars who are disappointed by omissions or are keen to have their own work on Philo listed are strongly encouraged to contact the Bibliography's compilers (addresses in the section 'Notes on Contributors').

2011

F. Alesse, '*Prohairesis* in Philo of Alexandria,' in B. Decharneux and S. Inowlocki (eds.), *Philon d'Alexandrie. Un penseur à l'intersection des cultures gréco-romaine, orientale, juive et chrétienne*, Monothéismes et philosophie (Turnhout 2011) 185–204.

F. Alesse, 'La 'radice alla mente' in Phil. Alex. *Quod deter.* 84–85. Breve analisi di una metafora astrologica,' *MHNH* 11 (2011) 218–228.

M. Alesso, 'Qué son las potencias del alma en los textos de Filón,' *Circe de clásicos y modernos* 15 (2011) 15–26.

M. Alesso, 'Problemas sobre traducción e interpretación de términos que refieren a la eucaristía (siglos I a IV),' in S. Filippi (ed.), *Controversías Filosóficas, Científicas y Teológicas en el Pensaimento Tardo-Antiquo y Medieval* (Rosario, Argentina 2011) 49–58.

M. Alexandre Jr. (ed.), *Fílon de Alexandria nas origens da cultura ocidental*, Centro de Estudos Clássicos (Lisbon 2011).

M. Alexandre Jr., 'Fílon de Alexandria na Interpretação das Escrituras,' in idem (ed.) *Fílon de Alexandria nas origens da cultura ocidental*, Centro de Estudos Clássicos (Lisbon 2011) 9–22.

M. Alexandre Jr., 'Fílon entre os sofistas de Alexandria. A Sofística Alexandrina sob o olhar crítico de Fílon de Aenxandria,' in idem (ed.) *Fílon de Alexandria nas origens da cultura ocidental*, Centro de Estudos Clássicos (Lisbon 2011) 121–136.

M. Alexandre, 'Monarchie divine et dieux des nations chez Philon d'Alexandrie,' in B. Decharneux and S. Inowlocki (eds.), *Philon d'Alexandrie. Un penseur à l'intersection des cultures gréco-romaine, orientale, juive et chrétienne*, Monothéismes et philosophie (Turnhout 2011) 117–147.

C. A. Anderson, *Philo of Alexandria's Views of the Physical World*, Wissenschaftliche Untersuchungen zum Neuen Testament 2.309 (Tübingen 2011).

S. Badilita, 'Caïn, figure du mal chez Philon d'Alexandrie,' in Y.-M. Blanchard, B. Pouderon and M. Scopello (eds.), *Les forces du bien et du mal aux premiers siècles de l'Église: Actes du Colloque de Tours, septembre 2008,* Théologie historique 118 (Paris 2011).

T. Bénatouïl, E. Maffi and F. Trabattoni, *Plato, Aristotle, or Both? Dialogues between Platonism and Aristotelianism in Antiquity,* Europaea memoria. Reihe 1, Studien, Bd 85, Diatribai 4 (Hildesheim 2011).

K. Berthelot, 'Grecs, Barbares et Juifs dans l'œuvre de Philon,' in B. Decharneux and S. Inowlocki (eds.), *Philon d'Alexandrie. Un penseur à l'intersection des cultures gréco-romaine, orientale, juive et chrétienne,* Monothéismes et philosophie (Turnhout 2011) 47–61.

K. Berthelot, 'Philo's Perception of the Roman Empire,' *Journal for the Study of Judaism* 42 (2011) 166–187.

K. Berthelot, 'The Canaanites who 'Trusted in God': an Original Interpretation of the Fate of the Canaanites in Rabbinic Literature,' *Journal for the Jewish Studies* 62 (2011) 233–261.

K. Berthelot, 'Philon d'Alexandrie, lecteur d'Homère: quelques éléments de réflexion,' in A. Balansard, G. Dorival and M. Loubet (eds.), *Prolongements et renouvellements de la tradition classique: en homage à Didier Pralon,* Textes et documents de la Méditerraneée antique et médiévale (Aix-en-Provence 2011) 145–157.

K. Berthelot, M. R. Niehoff, and M. Simonetti, 'Discussione su The Cambridge Companion to Philo a cura di A. Kamesar,' *Annali di Storia dell'Esegesi* 28 (2011) 367–390.

E. Birnbaum, 'Who Celebrated on Pharos with the Jews? Conflicting Philonic Currents and Their Implications,' in B. Decharneux and S. Inowlocki (eds.), *Philon d'Alexandrie. Un penseur à l'intersection des cultures gréco-romaine, orientale, juive et chrétienne,* Monothéismes et philosophie (Turnhout 2011) 63–82.

R. Bloch, *Moses und der Mythos: Die Auseinandersetzung mit der griechischen Mythologie bei jüdisch-hellenistischen Autoren,* Journal for the Study of Judaism Supplements 145 (Leiden 2011).

G. Bolognesi, 'Marginal Notes on the Armenian Translation of the *Quaestiones et Solutiones in Genesim* by Philo,' in S. Mancini Lombardi and P. Pontani (eds.), *Studies on the Ancient Armenian Version of Philo's Works,* Studies in Philo of Alexandria 6 (Leiden 2011) 45–50.

A. Botica, *The Concept of Intention in the Bible, Philo of Alexandria, and the early Rabbinic Literature: a Study in Human Intentionality in the Area of Criminal, Cultic and Religious and Ethical Law,* Perspectives on Hebrew Scriptures and its Contexts 9 (Piscataway N.J. 2011).

M. Broze, 'L'Égypte de Philon d'Alexandrie: approches d'un discours ambigu,' in B. Decharneux and S. Inowlocki (eds.), *Philon d'Alexandrie. Un penseur à l'intersection des cultures gréco-romaine, orientale, juive et chrétienne,* Monothéismes et philosophie (Turnhout 2011) 105–113.

F. Calabi, 'Le repos de Dieu chez Philon d'Alexandrie,' in B. Decharneux and S. Inowlocki (eds.), *Philon d'Alexandrie. Un penseur à l'intersection des cultures gréco-romaine, orientale, juive et chrétienne,* Monothéismes et philosophie (Turnhout 2011) 185–204.

F. Calabi, 'Metafore del *logos* in Filone di Alessandria,' in R. Radice and M. Sordi (eds.), *Dal Logos dei Greci e dei Romani al Logos di Dio* (Milano 2011) 65–84.

M. Ceglarek, *Die Rede von der Gegenwart Gottes, Christi und des Geistes: eine Untersuchung zu den Briefen des Apostels Paulus* (Frankfurt am Main 2011).

N. G. Cohen, 'Philo's Place in the Chain of Jewish Tradition,' *Tradition* 44 (2011) 9–17.

M.-H. Congourdeau, 'De l'exil à la migration. À propos de *La migration d'Abraham* de Philon,' *Christus* 230 (2011) 169–175.

J. T. Conroy Jr., 'Philo's "Death of the Soul": Is This Only a Metaphor?' *The Studia Philonica Annual* 23 (2011) 23–40.

R. R. Cox, 'Travelling the Royal Road: the Soteriology of Philo of Alexandria,' in D. M. Gurtner (ed.), *This World and the World to Come: Soteriology in Early Judaism* (London 2011) 167–180.

B. Decharneux, 'Le Logos philonien comme fondation paradoxale de l'Évangile de Jean,' in B. Decharneux and S. Inowlocki (eds.), *Philon d'Alexandrie. Un penseur à l'intersection des cultures gréco-romaine, orientale, juive et chrétienne,* Monothéismes et philosophie (Turnhout 2011) 317–333.

B. Decharneux and S. Inowlocki (eds.), *Philon d'Alexandrie. Un penseur à l'intersection des cultures gréco-romaine, orientale, juive et chrétienne,* Monothéismes et philosophie 12 (Turnhout 2011).

M. Duarte, 'Λόγος ἐνδιάθετος e προφορικός na Formação da Cristologia Patrística,' in M. Alexandre Jr. (ed.) *Fílon de Alexandria nas origens da cultura ocidental,* Centro de Estudos Clássicos (Lisbon 2011) 47–79.

T. Faia, 'Embaixada de Calígula, Agustina Bessa-Luís e uma Memória de Fílon de Alexandria,' in M. Alexandre Jr. (ed.) *Fílon de Alexandria nas origens da cultura ocidental,* Centro de Estudos Clássicos (Lisbon 2011) 37–467.

M. Fernandes, 'O Profetismo no Tratado De Iosepho de Fílon de Alexandria,' in M. Alexandre Jr. (ed.) *Fílon de Alexandria nas origens da cultura ocidental,* Centro de Estudos Clássicos (Lisbon 2011) 81–90.

M. FERNANDES, 'Φύσις no Tratado de Fílon de Alexandria De Iosepho,' in M. ALEXANDRE JR. (ed.) *Fílon de Alexandria nas origens da cultura ocidental*, Centro de Estudos Clássicos (Lisbon 2011) 111–120.

A. C. GELJON, 'Philo's Influence on Didymus the Blind,' in B. DECHARNEUX and S. INOWLOCKI (eds.), *Philon d'Alexandrie. Un penseur à l'intersection des cultures gréco-romaine, orientale, juive et chrétienne*, Monothéismes et philosophie (Turnhout 2011) 357–372.

M. GOODMAN, 'Philo as a Philosopher in Rome,' in B. DECHARNEUX and S. INOWLOCKI (eds.), *Philon d'Alexandrie. Un penseur à l'intersection des cultures gréco-romaine, orientale, juive et chrétienne*, Monothéismes et philosophie (Turnhout 2011) 37–45.

E. S. GRUEN, 'Jews and Greeks as Philosophers: a Challenge to Otherness,' in D. C. HARLOW, K. MARTIN HOGAN, M. GOFF AND J. KAMINSKY (edd.), *The "Other" in Second Temple Judaism: Essays in Honor of John J. Collins* (Grand Rapids Mich. 2011) 402–422.

N. GUPTA, 'The Question of Coherence in Philo's Cultic Imagery: a Socio-literary Approach,' *Journal for the Study of the Pseudepigrapha* 20, no. 4 (2011) 277–297.

M. HARL, 'L'association du Cosmos au culte sacerdotal selon Philon d'Alexandrie,' in A. BALANSARD, G. DORIVAL and M. LOUBET (eds.), *Prolongements et renouvellements de la tradition classique: en homage à Didier Pralon*, Textes et documents de la Méditerraneée antique et médiévale (Aix-en-Provence 2011) 173–186.

J. G. HARRISSON, 'Jewish Memory and Identity in the First Century AD: Philo and Josephus on Dreams,' in M. BOMMAS (ed.), *Cultural Memory and Identity in Ancient Societies* (London 2011) 61–78.

M. HATZIMICHALI, *Potamo of Alexandria and the emergence of eclecticism in late Hellenistic Philosophy* (Cambridge 2011).

S. HONIGMAN, 'Les juifs dans la société de l'Égypte romaine au croisement des sources documentaires et littéraires,' in C. CLIVAZ and J. ZUMSTEIN (eds.), *Reading New Testament Papyri in Context*, Bibliotheca Ephemeridum Theologicarum Lovaniensium 242 (Leuven 2011).

S. INOWLOCKI-MEISTER, 'Relectures apologétiques de Philon par Eusèbe de Césarée: le cas d'Enoch et des Thérapeutes,' in B. DECHARNEUX and S. INOWLOCKI (eds.), *Philon d'Alexandrie. Un penseur à l'intersection des cultures gréco-romaine, orientale, juive et chrétienne*, Monothéismes et philosophie (Turnhout 2011).

O. KAISER, 'Aretê and Pathos bei Philo von Alexandrien,' *Deuterocanonical and Cognate Literature Yearbook* (2011) 379–429.

S. KOTTEK, 'Les Esseniens et la médecine,' *Histoire des sciences medicales* 45 (2011) 315–320.

R. S. KRAEMER, *Unreliable Witnesses: Religion, Gender, and History in the Greco-Roman Mediterranean* (Oxford 2011), esp. ch. 3.

F. LEDEGANG, *Philo van Alexandrië Over de tien woorden, De Decalogo* (Budel, Netherlands 2011).

J. LEONHARDT-BALZER, 'Priests and Priesthood in Philo: Could He Have Done without Them?,' in D. R. SCHWARTZ and Z. WEISS (eds.), *Was 70 CE a Watershed in Jewish History? On Jews and Judaism Before and After the Destruction of the Second Temple,* Ancient Judaism and Early Christianity 78 (Leiden 2011) 121–147.

C. LÉVY, 'La notion de signe chez Philon d'Alexandrie,' in B. DECHARNEUX and S. INOWLOCKI (eds.), *Philon d'Alexandrie. Un penseur à l'intersection des cultures gréco-romaine, orientale, juive et chrétienne,* Monothéismes et philosophie (Turnhout 2011) 149–161.

C. LÉVY, 'L'aristotélisme, parent pauvre de la pensée philonienne?,' in T. BÉNATOUÏL, E. MAFFI and F. TRABATTONI (eds.), *Plato, Aristotle, or Both? Dialogues between Platonism and Aristotelianism in Antiquity,* Europaea memoria. Reihe 1, Studien, Bd 85. Diatribai, 4 (Hildesheim 2011) 17–33.

Y. LI, 'A Comparative Study of Philo's Allegory and Origen's Allegory [Chinese],' *CGST Journal* (2011) 47–74.

D. LINCICUM, 'Philo on Phinehas and the Levites: Observing an Exegetical Connection,' *Bulletin for Biblical Research* 21 (2011) 43–49.

W. LOADER, *Philo, Josephus, and the Testaments on Sexuality: Attitudes towards Sexuality in the Writings of Philo and Josephus and in the Testaments of the Twelve Patriarchs* (Grand Rapids 2011).

E. Z. LYONS, *Hellenic Philosophers as Ambassadors to the Roman Empire: Performance, Parrhesia, and Power* (diss. University of Michigan 2011).

S. MANCINI LOMBARDI, and P. PONTANI (eds.), *Studies on the Ancient Armenian Version of Philo's Works,* Studies in Philo of Alexandria 6 (Leiden 2011).

A. B. McGOWAN and K. RICHARDS (eds.), *Method and Meaning: Essays on New Testament Interpretation in Honor of Harold W. Attridge* (Atlanta 2011).

E. MATUSOVA, 1 Enoch in the Context of Philo's Writings,' in A. LANGE, E. TOV, M. WEIGOLD AND B. H. REYNOLDS III (edd.), *The Dead Sea Scrolls in Context: Integrating the Dead Sea Scrolls in the Study of Ancient Texts, Languages, and Cultures,* 2 vols., Vetus Testamentum Supplements 140 (Leiden 2011) 1.385–397.

A. M. MAZZANTI, 'Il λόγος nell'antropologia di Filone d'Alessandria: Considerazione sulla creazione dell'uomo in *De opificio mundi* e in *Legum Allegoriae*,' in R. Radice and M. Sordi (eds.), *Dal Logos dei Greci e dei Romani al Logos di Dio* (Milano 2011) 85–101.

D. S. Meca, J. A. López Férez, A. Díaz Hernandez, and A. Martínez Lorca, *Pensadores judíos: de Fílon de Alejandría a Walter Benjamin*, Coleccío Juadica (Palma de Mallorca 2011).

J. Mélèze Modrzejewski, 'Philon d'Alexandrie notable juif et philosophe politique. La bible d'Alexandrie: quand le judaisme rencontre le monde grec,' *Le Monde de la Bible* (2011) 50–55.

F. Mirguet, 'Introductory Reflections on Embodiment in Hellenistic Judaism,' *Journal for the Study of the Pseudepigrapha*. 21 (2011) 5–19.

W. Moon, *Your Love is Better than Wine: a Reading of Love in the Gospel according to John* (diss. The Claremont Graduate University 2011).

J. Moreau, 'Entre Écriture sainte et *paideia*: le langage exégétique de Philon d'Alexandrie. Étude sur la pistis d'Abraham dans le *Quis rerum divinarum heres sit* 90–95,' in B. Decharneux and S. Inowlocki (eds.), *Philon d'Alexandrie. Un penseur à l'intersection des cultures gréco-romaine, orientale, juive et chrétienne*, Monothéismes et philosophie (Turnhout 2011) 241–263.

O. Munnich, 'La fugacité de la vie humane (*De Josepho* § 125–147): la place des motifs traditionnels dans l'élaboration de la pensée philonienne,' in B. Decharneux and S. Inowlocki (eds.), *Philon d'Alexandrie. Un penseur à l'intersection des cultures gréco-romaine, orientale, juive et chrétienne*, Monothéismes et philosophie (Turnhout 2011) 163–183.

O. Munnich, 'Travail sur la langue et sur le texte dans l'exégèse de Philon d'Alexandrie,' in A. Balansard, G. Dorival and M. Loubet (eds.), *Prolongements et renouvellements de la tradition classique: en homage à Didier Pralon*, Textes et documents de la Méditerranée antique et médiévale (Aix en Provence 2011).

G. Muradyan, 'The Armenian Version of Philo Alexandrinus. Translation Technique, Biblical Citations,' in S. Mancini Lombardi and P. Pontani (eds.), *Studies on the Ancient Armenian Version of Philo's Works*, Studies in Philo of Alexandria 6 (Leiden 2011) 51–85.

M. R. Niehoff, 'Recherche homérique et exégèse biblique à Alexandrie: un fragment sur la Tour de Babel préservé par Philon,' in B. Decharneux and S. Inowlocki (eds.), *Philon d'Alexandrie. Un penseur à l'intersection des cultures gréco-romaine, orientale, juive et chrétienne*, Monothéismes et philosophie (Turnhout 2011) 83–103.

M. R. Niehoff, *Jewish Exegesis and Homeric Scholarship in Alexandria* (Cambridge 2011).

M. R. Niehoff, 'Jüdische Bibelexegese im Spiegel alexandrinischer Homerforschung,' *Biblische Notizen* NF 148 (2011) 19–33.

M. R. Niehoff, 'Philo's Exposition in a Roman Context,' *The Studia Philonica Annual* 23 (2011) 1–21.

F. Nobilio, 'Le chemin de l'Esprit dans l'œuvre de Philon d'Alexandrie en dans l'évangile de Jean,' in B. Decharneux and S. Inowlocki (eds.), *Philon d'Alexandrie. Un penseur à l'intersection des cultures gréco-romaine, orientale, juive et chrétienne,* Monothéismes et philosophie (Turnhout 2011) 283–315.

S. Nordgaard Svendsen, 'Paul's Appropriation of Philo's Theory of 'Two Men' in 1 Corinthians 15:45–49,' *New Testament Studies* 57 (2011) 348–365.

P. van Nuffelen, *Rethinking the Gods: Philosophical Readings of Religion in the Post-Hellenistic Period* (Cambridge 2011).

M. Olivieri, 'Philo's *De Providentia*: a Work Between Two Traditions,' in S. Mancini Lombardi and P. Pontani (eds.), *Studies on the Ancient Armenian Version of Philo's Works,* Studies in Philo of Alexandria 6 (Leiden 2011) 87–124.

J. Otto, 'Conflicting Christian Reactions to Philo's Ark Door Exegesis,' *Theoforum* 43 (2011) 89–98.

J. Otto, 'An Education in Virtue: Philosophical Speculation and Religious Observance in the Thought of Philo of Alexandria,' *Dionysius* 29 (2011) 135–146.

D. Pastorelli, 'La lecture de Lv 5, 20–26 par Philon, *Lois spéciales* 1, 237: la conscience accusatrice, un paraclet pour le péché volontaire,' in A. Balansard, G. Dorival and M. Loubet (eds.), *Prolongements et renouvellements de la tradition classique: en homage à Didier Pralon,* Textes et documents de la Méditerraneée antique et médiévale (Aix-en-Provence 2011) 217–228.

P. A. Patterson, *Visions of Christ: The Anthropomorphite Controversy of 399 CE* (diss. Saint Louis University 2011).

F. Petit, L. van Rompay and J. J. S. Weitenberg, *Eusèbe d'Émèse. Commentaire de la Genèse. Texte arménien de l'édition de Venise (1980), fragments grecs, avec traductions,* Traditio Exegetica Graeca 15 (Louvain 2011).

P. Pontani, 'Saying (Almost) the Same Thing. On Some Relevant Differences Between Greek-Language Originals and their Armenian Translations,' in S. Mancini Lombardi and P. Pontani (eds.), *Studies on the Ancient Armenian Version of Philo's Works,* Studies in Philo of Alexandria 6 (Leiden 2011) 125–146.

R. Radice, 'Logos tra stoicismo e platonismo. Il problema di Filone,' in R. Radice and M. Sordi (eds.), *Dal Logos dei Greci e dei Romani al Logos di Dio* (Milano 2011) 131–145.

I. L. E. Ramelli, 'The Birth of the Rome–Alexandria Connection: the Early Sources on Mark and Philo, and the Petrine Tradition,' *The Studia Philonica Annual* 23 (2011) 69–95.

E. Regev, ' From Qumran to Alexandria and Rome: Qumranic Halakhah in Josephus and Philo,' in A. I. Baumgarten, H. Eshel, R. Katzoff and S. Tzoref (eds.), *Halakhah in the Light of Epigraphy*, Journal of Ancient Judaism Supplements 3 (Göttingen 2011) 43–63.

C. M. Rios, 'Exílio, Diáspora e Saudades de Jerusalém: Estudo em Jeremias 29:1–14 em Fílon de Alexandria,' in M. Alexandre jr. (ed.) *Fílon de Alexandria nas origens da cultura ocidental*, Centro de Estudos Clássicos (Lisbon 2011) 91–109.

P. Robertson, 'Toward an Understanding of Philo's and Cicero's Treatment of Sacrifice,' *The Studia Philonica Annual* 23 (2011) 41–67.

D. Roure, 'Forgiveness in Ben Sira and in Philo of Alexandria,' *Studia Monastica* 53 (2011) 7–19.

D. T. Runia, 'Why Philo of Alexandria is an Important Writer and Thinker,' in B. Decharneux and S. Inowlocki (eds.), *Philon d'Alexandrie. Un penseur à l'intersection des cultures gréco-romaine, orientale, juive et chrétienne*, Monothéismes et philosophie (Turnhout 2011) 13–33.

D. T. Runia, 'Ancient Philosophy and the New Testament: "Exemplar" as Example,' in A. B. McGowan and K. Richards (eds.), *Method and Meaning: Essays on New Testament Interpretation in Honor of Harold W. Attridge*, Society of Biblical Literature Resources for Biblical Study 67 (Atlanta 2011) 347–361.

D. T. Runia and G. E. Sterling (eds.), *The Studia Philonica Annual*, Vol. 23 (Atlanta 2011).

D. T. Runia, K. Berthelot, E. Birnbaum, A. C. Geljon, H. M. Keizer, J. Leonhardt Balzer, J. P. Martín, M. R. Niehoff, and T. Seland, 'Philo of Alexandria: an Annotated Bibliography 2008,' *The Studia Philonica Annual* 23 (2011) 97–159.

L. Saudelli, 'Les fragments d'Héraclite et leur signification dans le *corpus philonicum*: le cas du fr. 60 DK,' in B. Decharneux and S. Inowlocki (eds.), *Philon d'Alexandrie. Un penseur à l'intersection des cultures gréco-romaine, orientale, juive et chrétienne*, Monothéismes et philosophie (Turnhout 2011) 265–280.

G. Schöllgen (ed.), *Reallexikon für Antike und Christentum*, Lieferungen 188–191 (Stuttgart 2011).
C. Tornau, art. Materie, 346–410, esp. 370–373 (Matter); M. Durst, R. Amedick, E. Enss, art. Meer 505–609, esp. 549–552 (Sea). (DTR)

G. Sellin, *Allegorie – Metapher – Mythos – Schrift. Beiträge zur religiösen Sprache im Neuen Testament und in seiner Umwelt*, edited by D. Sänger, Novum Testamentum et orbis antiquus 90 (Göttingen 2011).

R. Sgarbi, 'Philo's Stylemes vs Armenian Translation Stylemes,' in S. Mancini Lombardi and P. Pontani (eds.), *Studies on the Ancient*

Armenian Version of Philo's Works, Studies in Philo of Alexandria 6 (Leiden 2011) 147–154.

M. E. SHIRINIAN, 'Philo and the *Book of Causes* by Grigor Abasean,' in S. MANCINI LOMBARDI and P. PONTANI (eds.), *Studies on the Ancient Armenian Version of Philo's Works,* Studies in Philo of Alexandria 6 (Leiden 2011) 155–189.

F. SIEGERT, 'Philon et la philologie alexandrine. Aux origines du fondamentalisme chrétien,' in B. DECHARNEUX and S. INOWLOCKI (eds.), *Philon d'Alexandrie. Un penseur à l'intersection des cultures gréco-romaine, orientale, juive et chrétienne,* Monothéismes et philosophie (Turnhout 2011) 393–402.

A. SIRINIAN, "Armenian Philo': a Survey of the Literature,' in S. MANCINI LOMBARDI and P. PONTANI (eds.), *Studies on the Ancient Armenian Version of Philo's Works,* Studies in Philo of Alexandria 6 (Leiden 2011) 7–44.

J. SMITH, *Christ the Ideal King,* Wissenschaftliche Untersuchungen zum Neuen Testament 2.313 (Tübingen 2011).

G. J. STEYN, '"On Earth as it is in Heaven …" The Heavenly Sanctuary Motif in Hebrews 8:5 and its Textual Connection with the "Shadowy Copy" [ὑποδείγματι σκίᾳ] of LXX Exodus 25:40,' *HTS Teologiese Studies/ Theological Studies* 67 (2011) 6 pages (electronic publication).

C. TASSIN, *Les juifs d'Alexandrie et leur écrits,* Les Suppléments aux Cahiers Évangile 156 (Paris 2011).

T. H. TOBIN SJ, 'Hellenistic Judaism and the New Testament,' in A. B. MCGOWAN and K. RICHARDS (eds.), *Method and Meaning: Essays on New Testament Interpretation in Honor of Harold W. Attridge,* Society of Biblical Literature Resources for Biblical Study 67 (Atlanta 2011) 363–380.

P. J. TOMSON, 'Le temple céleste: pensée platonisante et orientation apocalyptique dans l'Épître aux Hébreux,' in B. DECHARNEUX and S. INOW-LOCKI (eds.), *Philon d'Alexandrie. Un penseur à l'intersection des cultures gréco-romaine, orientale, juive et chrétienne,* Monothéismes et philosophie (Turnhout 2011) 337–356.

S. TORALLAS TOVAR, 'Orphic Hymn 86 "To Dream": On Orphic Sleep and Philo,' in M. HERRERO DE JÁUREGUI and e. al. (edd.), *Tracing Orpheus: Studies of Orphic Fragments* (Berlin 2011) 405–411.

S. TORALLAS TOVAR, 'La lengua de Filón de Alejandría en el panorama lingüistico del Egipto Romano,' in M. ALEXANDRE JR. (ed.) *Fílon de Alexandria nas origens da cultura ocidental,* Centro de Estudos Clássicos (Lisbon 2011) 23–36.

C. TOUATI, 'L'allégorisation de la guerre sainte,' *Revue de l'histoire des Religions* 227 (2011) 231–247.

O. S. VARDAZARYAN, 'The 'Armenian Philo': a Remnant of an Unknown Tradition,' in S. MANCINI LOMBARDI and P. PONTANI (eds.), *Studies on the*

Ancient Armenian Version of Philo's Works, Studies in Philo of Alexandria 6 (Leiden 2011) 191–216.

M. VERMAN, 'Earthly and Heavenly Jerusalem in Philo and Paul: a Tale of Two Cities,' in D. V. ARBEL and A. A. ORLOV (eds.), *With Letters of Light; Studies in the Dead Sea Scrolls, Early Jewish Apocalypticism, Magic and Mysticism in Honor of Rachel Elior* (Berlin 2011) 133–156.

J. B. WALLACE, *Snatched into Paradise (2 Cor 12:1–10). Paul's Heavenly Journey in the Context of Early Christian Experience*, Beihefte zur Zeitschrift für die neutestamentliche Wissenschaft 179 (Berlin 2011).

J. WEINBERG, 'La quête de Philon dans l'historiographie juive du XVIᵉ s.,' in B. DECHARNEUX and S. INOWLOCKI (eds.), *Philon d'Alexandrie. Un penseur à l'intersection des cultures gréco-romaine, orientale, juive et chrétienne*, Monothéismes et philosophie (Turnhout 2011) 403–432.

S. WEISSER, 'La figure du progressant ou la proximité de la sagesse,' in B. DECHARNEUX and S. INOWLOCKI (eds.), *Philon d'Alexandrie. Un penseur à l'intersection des cultures gréco-romaine, orientale, juive et chrétienne*, Monothéismes et philosophie (Turnhout 2011) 221–239.

S. WEISSER, 'Philo's Therapeutae and Essenes : a Precedent for the Exceptional Condemnation of Slavery in Gregory of Nyssa?,' in K. BERTHELOT and M. MORGENSTERN (eds.), *The Quest for a Common Humanity: Human Dignity and Otherness in the Religious Traditions of the Mediterranean*, Numen Book Series 134 (Leiden 2011) 289–310.

M. WIEGER, 'Εὐσέβεια et «crainte de Dieu» dans la Septante,' in J. JOOSTEN and E. BONS (eds.), *Septuagint Vocabulary: Pre-History, Usage, Reception*, SBL Septuagint and Cognate Studies 58 (Atlanta 2011) 101–156.

W. T. WILSON, *Philo of Alexandria On Virtues. Introduction, Translation, and Commentary*, Philo of Alexandria Commentary Series 3 (Leiden 2011).

J. D. WORTHINGTON, *Creation in Paul and Philo*, Wissenschaftliche Untersuchungen zum Neuen Testament 2.317 (Tübingen 2011).

B. WYSS, 'Philon und die Philologen,' *Biblische Notizen* 148 (2011) 67–83

D. ZELLER, *Studien zu Philo und Paulus*, Bonner Biblische Beiträge 165 (Göttingen 2011).

D. ZELLER, 'Leben und Tod der Seele in der allegorischen Exegese Philo's. Gebrauch und Ursprung einer Metapher,' in IDEM (ed.), *Studien zu Philo und Paulus* (Göttingen 2011) 55–99.

2012

H. W. ATTRIDGE, 'Creation and Sacred Space: the Reuse of Key Penta-teuchal Themes by Philo, the Fourth Evangelist, and the Epistle to the Hebrews,' in A. MORIYA and G. HATA (eds.), *Pentateuchal Traditions in the Late Second Temple Period: Proceedings of the International Workshop in Tokyo, August 28–31, 2007,* Supplements to the Journal for the Study of Judaism 158 (Leiden 2012) 243–255.

K. BERTHELOT, 'Philo and the Allegorical Interpretation of Homer in the Platonic tradition (with an Emphasis on Porphyry's *De Antro Nympharum*),' in M. R. NIEHOFF (ed.), *Homer and the Bible in the Eyes of Ancient Interpreters,* Jerusalem Studies in Religion and Culture 16 (Leiden 2012) 155–174.

R. BLOCH, 'Alexandria in Pharaonic Egypt: Projections in *De Vita Mosis*,' *The Studia Philonica Annual* 24 (2012) 69–84.

F. BORCHARDT, 'The LXX Myth and the Rise of Textual Fixity,' *Journal for the Study of Judaism* 43 (2012) 1–21.

F. CALABI, 'Il giardino delle delizie e la storia delle origini secondo Filone di Alessandria,' in F. Calabi and S. Gastaldi (eds.), *Immagini delle origini — la nascità della civiltà e delle culture nel pensiero antico,* Contributions to Classical Political Thought 5 (Sankt Augustin 2012) 173–194.

F. CALABI, La trasgressione di Adamo e la torre di Babele nella rilettura di Filone di Alessandria,' in E. MANICARDI AND L. MAZZINGHI (edd.), *Genesi 1–11 e le sue interpretazioni canoniche: un caso di teologia biblica. XII Settimana Biblica Nazionale (Roma, 6-10 Settembre 2010),* Ricerche Storico-Bibliche (Bologna 2012) 155–170.

F. CALABI, 'Filone di Alessandria e l'*Epinomide*,' in F. ALESSE and F. FERRARI (eds.), *Epinomide: studi sull'opera e la sua ricezione,* Elenchos 60.1 (Naples 2012) 235–261.

D. CREESE, 'Rhetorical Uses of Mathematical Harmonics in Philo and Plutarch,' *Studies in History and Philosophy of Science* 43 (2012) 258–269.

C. D'ANCONA, 'Plotin,' in R. GOULET (ed.), *Dictionnaire des philosophes antiques* (Paris 2012) 5.885–1070, esp. 966–969.

J. M. DILLON, *The Platonic Heritage. Further Studies in the History of Platonism and Early Christianity,* Variorum Collected Studies (Abingdon 2012).

C. FRAENKEL, *Philosophical Religions from Plato to Spinoza: Reason, Religion, and Autonomy* (Cambridge 2012) esp. 24–32, 100–122.

E. L. GALLAGHER, *Hebrew Scripture in Patristic Biblical Theory,* Supplements to Vigiliae Christianae 114 (Leiden 2012).

E. S. GRUEN, 'Caligula, the Imperial Cult, and Philo's *Legatio*,' *The Studia Philonica Annual* 24 (2012) 135–147.

M. HADAS-LEBEL, *Philo of Alexandria: a Thinker in the Jewish Diaspora*, Studies in Philo of Alexandria 7 (Leiden 2012).

M. HILLAR, *From Logos to Trinity: The Evolution of Religious Beliefs from Pythagoras to Tertullian* (Cambridge 2012).

S. J. JOSEPH, *Q, and the Dead Sea Scrolls: a Judaic Approach to Q (on Qumran and the Essenes)*, Wissenschaftliche Untersuchungen zum Neuen Testament 2.333 (Tübingen 2012), esp. 94–123.

J. L. KUGEL, 'Jubilees, Philo and the Problem of Genesis,' in N. Dávid, A. Lange, K. DE TROYER and S. TZOREF (eds.), *The Hebrew Bible in Light of the Dead Sea Scrolls* (Göttingen 2012) 295–311.

J. L. KUGEL, 'Jubilees, Philo and the Problem of Genesis,' in *A Walk through Jubilees: Studies in the Book of Jubilees and the World of its Creation* (Leiden 2012) 391–405.

S. D. MACKIE, 'Seeing God in Philo of Alexandria: Means, Methods, and Mysticism,' *Journal for the Study of Judaism* 43 (2012) 147–179.

P. MARTENS, *Origen and Scripture: the Contours of the Exegetical Life*, Oxford Early Christian Studies (Oxford 2012).

P. W. MARTENS, '*On the Confusion of Tongues* and Origen's Allegory of the Dispersion of Nations,' *The Studia Philonica Annual* 24 (2012) 107–127.

J. MORE, 'On Kingship in Philo and the Wisdom of Solomon,' in J. COOK AND H.-J. STIPP (edd.), *Text-Critical and Hermeneutical Studies in the Septuagint,* Vetus Testamentum Supplements 157 (Leiden 2012) 499–525.

M. R. NIEHOFF (ed.), *Homer and the Bible in the Eyes of Ancient Interpreters*, Jerusalem Studies in Religion and Culture 16 (Leiden 2012).

M. R. NIEHOFF, 'Philo and Plutarch as Biographers: Parallel Responses to Roman Stoicism,' *Greek, Roman, and Byzantine Studies* 52 (2012) 361–392.

M. R. NIEHOFF, 'Philo and Plutarch on Homer,' in M. R. NIEHOFF (ed.), *Homer and the Bible in the Eyes of Ancient Interpreters,* Jerusalem Studies in Religion and Culture 16 (Leiden 2012) 128–153.

C. S. O'BRIEN, 'The Middle Platonist Demiurge and Stoic Cosmobiology,' *Horizons: Seoul Journal of the Humanities* 3 (2012) 19–39, esp. 31–33.

S. J. K. PEARCE, 'Philo and Roman Imperial Power: Introduction,' *The Studia Philonica Annual* 24 (2012) 129–133.

S. J. K. PEARCE, 'Philo and the *Temple Scroll* on the Prohibition of Single Testimony,' in N. DÁVID, A. LANGE, K. DE TROYER AND S. TZOREF (edd.), *The Hebrew Bible in Light of the Dead Sea Scrolls*, Forschungen zur Religion und Literatur des Alten und Neuen Testaments 239 (Göttingen 2012) 321–336.

J. M. ROGERS, *Didymus the Blind and his Use of Philo of Alexandria in the Tura Commentary on Genesis* (diss. Hebrew Union College 2012).

T. A. ROGERS, 'Philo's Universalization of Sinai in *De Decalogo* 32–49,' *The Studia Philonica Annual* 24 (2012) 85–105.

J. R. ROYSE, 'Philo of Alexandria, *Quaestiones in Exodum* 2.62–68: Critical Edition,' *The Studia Philonica Annual* 24 (2012) 1–68.

D. T. RUNIA, 'Philon d'Alexandrie,' in R. GOULET (ed.), *Dictionnaire des philosophes antiques* (Paris 2012) 5.362–390.

D. T. RUNIA, 'Jewish Platonism (Ancient),' in G. A. PRESS (ed.), *The Continuum Companion to Plato* (London 2012) 267–269.

D. T. RUNIA, 'God the Creator as Demiurge in Philo of Alexandria,' *Horizons: Seoul Journal of the Humanities* 3 (2012) 41–59.

D. T. RUNIA and G. E. STERLING (eds.), *The Studia Philonica Annual*, Vol. 24 (Atlanta 2012).

D. T. RUNIA, K. BERTHELOT, A. C. GELJON, H. M. KEIZER, J. LEONHARDT BALZER, J. P. MARTÍN, M. R. NIEHOFF, S. J. K. PEARCE, and T. SELAND, 'Philo of Alexandria: an Annotated Bibliography 2009,' *The Studia Philonica Annual* 24 (2012) 183–242.

K.-G. SANDELIN, *Attraction and Danger of Alien Religion: Studies in Early Judaism and Christianity*, Wissenschaftliche Untersuchungen zum Neuen Testament 1.290 (Tübingen 2012).

L. SAUDELLI, *Eraclito ad Alessandria. Studi e ricerche intorno alla testimonianza di Filone*, Monothéismes et Philosophie 16 (Turnhout 2012).

G. SCHÖLLGEN (ed.), *Reallexikon für Antike und Christentum Band 24* (Stuttgart 2012).

G. SCHÖLLGEN (ed.), *Reallexikon für Antike und Christentum Lieferungen 194–197* (Stuttgart 2012).

D. R. SCHWARTZ, 'Philo and Josephus on the Violence in Alexandria in 38 C.E.' *The Studia Philonica Annual* 24 (2012) 149–166.

G. E. STERLING, 'The Interpreter of Moses: Philo of Alexandria and the Biblical Text,' in M. HENZE (ed.), *A Companion to Biblical Interpretation in Early Judaism* (Grand Rapids Mich. 2012) 415–435.

G. E. STERLING, 'When the Beginning is the End: the Place of Genesis in the Commentaries of Philo,' in C. A. EVANS, J. N. LOHR and D. L. PETERSEN (eds.), *The Book of Genesis: Composition, Reception, and Interpretation,* Vetus Testamentum Supplements 152 (Leiden 2012) 427–446.

G. E. STERLING, '"Prolific in Expression and Broad in Thought": Internal References to Philo's Allegorical Commentary and Exposition of the Law', *Euphrosyne* 40 (2012) 55–76.

G. E. STERLING, M. R. NIEHOFF, A. VAN DEN HOEK, and D. T. RUNIA, 'Philo,' in J. J. COLLINS and D. C. HARLOW (eds.), *Early Judaism: a Comprehensive Overview* (Grand Rapids Mich. 2012)?

G. J. Steyn, 'Can We Reconstruct an Early Text Form of the LXX from the Quotations of Philo of Alexandria and the New Testament: Torah Quotations Overlapping between Philo and Galatians as a Test Case,' in S. Kreuzer, M. Meiser and M. Sigismund (eds.), *Die Septuagina — Entstehung, Sprache, Geschichte*, Wissenschaftliche Untersuchungen zum Neuen Testament 2.309 (Tübingen 2012) 444–464.

A. Timotin, *La démonologie platonicienne. Histoire de la notion de daimôn de Platon aux derniers néoplatoniciennes*, Philosophia Antiqua 128 (Leiden 2012), esp. 100–112.

S. Weisser, 'Why Does Philo Criticize the Stoic Ideal of Apatheia in *On Abraham* 257? Philo and Consolatory Literature,' *Classical Quarterly* 62 (2012) 242–259.

M. R. Whitenton, 'Rewriting Abraham and Joseph: Stephen's speech (Acts 7:2–16) and Jewish Exegetical Traditions,' *Novum Testamentum* 54 (2012) 149–167.

B. Wyss, 'Philon und der Sophistendiskurs,' in M. Hirschberger (ed.), *Jüdisch-hellenistische Literatur in ihrem interkulturellen Kontext* (Frankfurt am Maim 2012) 89–105.

J. Yoder, 'Sympathy for the Devil? Philo on Flaccus and Rome,' *The Studia Philonica Annual* 24 (2012) 167–182.

2013

S. C. Byers, *Perception, Sensibility, and Moral Motivation in Augustine: a Stoic-Platonic Synthesis* (Cambridge 2013).

P. Frick, 'Monotheism and Philosophy: Notes on the Concept of God in Philo and Paul (Romans 1:18–21),' in S. E. Porter and A. W. Pitts (eds.), *Christian Origins and Hellenistic Judaism: Social and Literary Contexts for the New Testament,* Texts and Editions for New Testament Study 10 (Leiden 2013).

A. C. Geljon and D. T. Runia, *Philo On Cultivation: Introduction, Translation and Commentary*, Philo of Alexandria Commentary Series 4 (Leiden 2013).

S. E. Porter and A. W. Pitts (eds.), *Christian Origins and Hellenistic Judaism: Social and Literary Contexts for the New Testament*, Texts and Editions for New Testament Study 10 (Leiden 2013).

C. M. Rios, *O próprio e o comum: rastros de interculturalidade na escrita de Fílon de Alexandría* (diss. Universidade Federal de Minas Gerais 2013).

H. Svebakken, *Philo of Alexandria's Exposition on the Tenth Commandment* Studia Philonica Monographs 6 (Atlanta 2013).

BOOK REVIEW SECTION

ALBERT C. GELJON AND DAVID T. RUNIA. *Philo of Alexandria: On Cultivation: Introduction, Translation, and Commentary.* Philo of Alexandria Commentary Series 4. Leiden: Brill, 2013. xxii + 312. ISSN 1570-095X; ISBN: 978 90 04 24303 3. Price €112, $156 (hb).

Though it is the fourth in the Philo of Alexandria Commentary Series, Geljon's and Runia's *On Cultivation* represents a significant development for the series and for Philonic scholarship generally. The previous volumes gave us fresh translations and elucidations of writings in the vein of Philo's apologetic works (*Philo's Flaccus:The First Pogrom* by Pieter Van Der Horst) and his Exposition of the Laws (*On the Creation of The World according to Moses* by David Runia and *On Virtues* by Walter Wilson). But though *On Cultivation* follows the format of these others, it provides PACS' first foray into Philo's most intriguing and most demanding group of writings, the Allegorical Commentary (AC). If any of Philo's writings invite commentary, it is these treatises that provide the Alexandrian's allegorical interpretations of Gen 2:1–18:4. They are characterized by intricate interpretive machinations that arise from reading the first book of the Bible as focusing on the soul over against often uncomfortable (to Philo) literal understandings and that rely upon a network of supporting biblical texts functioning in ways obscure to readers not familiar with the Greek version of the Jewish scriptures as well as Philo's literary and intellectual milieu. Geljon and Runia rise admirably to the herculean challenge of guiding a modern reader through such a complex in their introduction, translation and commentary on Philo's treatment of Gen 9:20, *De agricultura*.

Geljon and Runia preface their work by explaining their distribution of labor even as they both share responsibility for the work as a whole. Most noteworthy is that Runia translated the treatise from Greek to English with the assistance of Geljon's literal Dutch version, that Geljon drafted most of the introduction and commentary with subsequent assistance from Runia, and that they relied in part upon an unpublished commentary on *Agr.* by Andreas Kilaniotis (they clearly designate material from Kilaniotis they use in their commentary). The volume then commences with a forty-one page introduction that is helpful for understanding both *Agr.* and Philo's allegorical enterprise more broadly. *De agricultura's* place in the AC is clearly demonstrated as well as distinctive characteristics that set it apart within that collection. Unlike prior treatises in the AC, *Agr.* and its companion *Plant.*, form a commentary on only one verse and do so in a thematic approach (*Agr.* on cultivation and *Plant.* more specifically on planting); also, *Agr.*, focusing only on one verse, has a systematic structure where earlier AC treatises find structure in progressing from verse to verse. That said, *Agr.* shares with other AC treatises the same type of exegetical approach. Focusing on two words from Gen 9:20, the treatise has two parts; the first part (§§1–123) deals with the skills of the "cultivator" (γεωργός), whom Philo identifies as the lover of virtue (Noah), and the second (§§124–181) with "beginning" (ἤρξατο), which shows that Noah has only began the path to virtue but did not finish it. The authors provide a four-plus page (pp. 11–15) outline of *Agr.* that demonstrates how secondary and tertiary biblical texts form the skeleton of Philo's exposition of these two words in the main lemma. For each secondary and tertiary lemma, the authors briefly describe Philo's argument as well as identify the exegete's "Mode of Transition" (or MOT, the way in which Philo connects verses, be it verbally, thematically or both). This outline is invaluable to understanding the treatise and to appreciating Philo's interpretations. The introduction also discusses, with much useful detail, Philo's use of the Bible, the main themes of the treatise, its intellectual setting, its Nachleben among patristic authors, its textual transmission, and the state of scholarship on *Agr.*

Next is a translation the chief aim of which is "to present a highly accurate and relatively literal rendering of the Greek text," since many expected "users of the translation will not be able to read the treatise in its original Greek" (p. 39). A literal translation also prepares for the later commentary. The translation succeeds for the most part, especially with headings and sub-headings derived from the outline in the introduction. Those unfamiliar with Philo's style would do well to keep a finger in the pages of the outline so they can flip back to find out what he is doing exegetically (especially his MOT). In keeping with earlier PACS volumes, biblical references are in bold and biblical allusions are italicized; footnotes identify these references and endnotes explain textual and translation matters. The latter will be of much interest and value to those proficient in Greek. Indeed, if there is an issue with the translation (besides matters of preference over how to render a word here and there), it is that while Runia and Geljon seek to provide an accessible translation to non-Greek readers, they provide notes and detailed commentary that skew considerably toward scholarly awareness and concerns. Obviously, this is a boon to scholars but it means that novice readers will find less assistance for understanding Philo's writing.

Geljon and Runia's commentary on *Agr.* (pages 85–266) also helpfully follows the aforementioned outline. The approach to the commentary is consistent with previous PACS volumes. First, for each outline segment there is a general analysis that is accessible and provides useful guidance for all readers in understanding the flow of Philo's thought. Segments then receive detailed commentary, replete with references to Philo's writings, Greek and Roman literary and philosophical authors, and occasional Jewish writings that help explain specific words, grammatical issues, and concepts. What is more, *On Cultivation*'s detailed commentary proves reliable for tackling the many complexities in Philo's writing, thinking and/or his literary or cultural contexts. So when expounding upon Lev 11:4's "split the hoof," Philo lists several forms of division, including musicians in §137. "Do not musicians divide their own science into rhythm, metre and melody, with melody further divided into the chromatic, the harmonic and the diatonic kind, into fourths and fifths and octaves, and into melodies of conjoined and separated elements?" Geljon and Runia provide a two page (pp 225–27) explication of this one sentence, including an explanation of Greek musical theory with three accompanying illustrations of musical notation. Third comes a discussion of parallel exegesis elsewhere in the Philonic corpus; this portion synthesizes the data from the Philonic references in the detailed commentary. Finally, for each section, there is a survey of its reception (if any) in Patristic writings. These surveys, when combined with the introduction's general discussion of the treatise's Nachleben, make for a substantive and authoritative look at how *Agr.* was later read (especially by Clement of Alexandria, Origen, Didymus the Blind, and Gregory of Nyssa).

On Cultivation also provides an exhaustive bibliography (secondary literature is well treated throughout the book, with the authors carefully describing others' researches, regardless whether they agree with their conclusions) and a set of indices that includes the sundry types of texts cited, mentions of names and subjects, and Greek terms that occur in the volume. The indices are reliable though not always comprehensive. For example, the Christian texts index is very good for the commentary but does not include all the Patristic writings cited in the introduction. This means readers who enter the book through its indices might miss out on some valuable information. This fault joins the volume's few others, which also include occasional mistakes that slipped passed the copyeditor, omissions such as *Conf.* from the list of AC treatises (2), stylistic missteps (e.g., the redundancy on p. 122, "showing in this way a kinship and relationship"), and rare moments where the commentary is insufficient. The detailed commentary on §50's calling the Logos πρωτόγονος ("first born") ably discusses Heb 1:6's use of the similar term πρωτότοκος in reference to Christ and reviews scholarship about Hebrews' relationship to Philo. However, the commentary fails to mention the use of πρωτότοκος for Christ in the Pauline corpus (especially Col 1:15, 17), which is similar to both Hebrews and Philo's writings and would have added weight to the authors' view that while Philo does not directly influence the NT, the Alexandrian's writings and the earliest Christian documents do share a common Greek-speaking Jewish background.

However, these are minor issues, especially compared to the major contribution Geljon and Runia make here to Philonic studies and to the investigation in particular of the mechanics and themes of the Allegorical Commentary. Scholars and industrious general readers will be rewarded time and time again in their use of this valuable resource. And as the first of the PACS volumes on the AC, *On Cultivation* establishes a high bar for future commentaries on related treatises.

Ronald Cox
Pepperdine University
Malibu, California, USA

HANS SVEBAKKEN. *Philo of Alexandria's Exposition of the Tenth Commandment*. Studia Philonica Monographs 6. Atlanta: Society of Biblical Literature, 2012. xx + 228 pages. ISBN 978-1589836181. Price $29.85 (pb).

This book, the revised version of a 2009 dissertation directed by Thomas Tobin at Loyola University Chicago, examines Philo's commentary on the Tenth Commandment of the Decalogue in *Spec.* 4.78b-131. As is well-known, the Alexandrian reformulates the prohibition of desire for the wife and goods of a neighbor in Exod 20:17 as a prohibition of desire itself (*ouk epithumêseis*), thereby introducing ambiguities with regard to both the commandment's object(s) and intent. Svebakken's discussion of these matters is organized into four chapters and a brief conclusion.

Chapter One introduces the study by situating the text of *Spec.* 4.78b-131 within what is conventionally referred to as Philo's "Exposition of the Law" and specifically within a section of the Exposition (i.e., *Decal.* 1 – *Spec.* 4.132) that provides an overview of the Mosaic legislation. This section is remarkably systematic in its approach, with each injunction of the Decalogue serving as a general heading under which are subsumed various specific laws. The subordinate laws understood to correspond with the Tenth Commandment pertain largely to matters of food and drink, a fact that immediately raises questions regarding the Alexandrian's principle of selection. The chapter is rounded off with a survey of previous research on the topic, especially that of Harry Wolfson and Kathy Gaca.

Chapters Two and Three are similarly introductory in nature. Chapter Two inspects some of the major terms and concepts found in *Spec.* 4.78b-131 in light of both Middle-Platonic moral psychology and their use elsewhere in the *corpus Philonicum*. In keeping with Middle-Platonic doctrine, Philo assumes a fundamental bipartition between rational and non-rational components of the soul. Among the capacities involved in the operation of the latter are instances of desire (*epithumia*), which is oriented toward the pursuit of pleasures deriving from the sense-perceptible world. Accordingly, desire can be characterized variously as an irrational "appetite" (*orexis*), a type of "impulse" (*hormê*), or as one of the emotions (*pathoi*), the last of these serving according to Philo as "helpers" (*boêthoi*) for human existence, that is, as non-rational motivators for activities (e.g., eating and drinking) necessary for the perpetuation of the species. It is from this perspective that the operation of desire within the soul can be described as both "natural" and "amoral" (pp. 64-65). A certain ambiguity arises, however, in that Philo also operates with a concept of what Svebakken refers to as "problematic malfunctions" (p. 65) of desire, which can take two forms. The first of these, labeled "passionate" desire, occurs when non-rational desire oversteps the bounds of reason, thereby becoming immoderate (*ametros*). This is distinguished from a second and more insidious form of problematic desire, which Svebakken refers to as "tyrannical" desire (*erôs*). While the former corresponds to "lack of self-control" (*akrasia*), that is, a contest of power between reason and desire, the latter corresponds to "intemperance" (*akolasia*), that is, a state in which reason has been overpowered by desire. Philo understands the two forms of problematic desire to be related inasmuch as passionate desire, if left unchecked, will ultimately give way to tyrannical desire. Svebakken argues that although for the Alexandrian the explicit object of the prohibition (*ouk epithumêseis*) is passionate desire, "Philo sees it ultimately as a *preemptive* prohibition of tyrannical desire" (p. 185, emphasis original).

In Chapter Three, self-control (*enkrateia*) is then presented as the ability of the moral agent to assert reason's control over the non-rational inclinations of the soul, including those prompted by the activity of desire. Such ability is not simply to be had, however, but must be acquired through a regimen of practice (*askêsis*). Not surprisingly, Philo contends that the agenda for this practice has been articulated most effectively by the laws of Moses. It is in this specific capacity that Svebakken proposes that we refer to the dietary laws as "ascetic precepts" (p. 103), a designation that brings to mind the *praecepta* discussed by Seneca (e.g., *Ep.* 94 and 95) and other

Stoic moralists, though possibilities for comparative analysis in this regard
are not pursued.

Chapter Four, a commentary on *Spec.* 4.78b-131, represents the heart of
the book. Philo's exposition of the Tenth Commandment is divided into
sixteen sections, a translation being provided for each section, accompanied
by one to seven pages of comments. Where applicable, detailed comparisons are drawn with material in *Decal.* 142-54, where a separate treatment
of the commandment is found, and (especially in places where the author
indulges in symbolic interpretation of the laws) the *Aristeae epistula*. As for
the organization of *Spec.* 4.78b-131 itself, an analysis of the nature and
forms of desire (§§79-94) is accompanied by a survey of Mosaic laws
thought to check desire, especially provisions that pertain to matters of
food and drink, with particular attention to provisions concerning clean
and unclean animals (§§98-125). As Svebakken explains, these provisions
are shown to promote self-control by mandating either the temporary
restraint of desire or the avoidance of especially pleasurable foods. He also
explains that together they constitute a rigorous program of *askêsis*, one
whose purpose is to remove incitements to desire, thereby obviating the
risk of desire becoming immoderate and (eventually) overpowering reason.

As Svebakken acknowledges (p. 32), what he offers in this chapter is not
a commentary in the conventional sense of the word but a focused analysis
guided by the conceptual nexus of desire, self-control, and practice. While
this lends the investigation coherence, it also leaves a number of questions
unanswered. For example, at one point the genre of *Spec.* 4.78b-131 is
identified as that of a *Seelenheilungsschrift* (p. 113), which, as such, consists
of a "diagnosis" of the problem (§§79-94) followed by a prescription for its
"treatment" (§§95-130). A more robust approach would have included
some discussion both of whether this identification applies to Philo's presentation of other commandments in *De specialibus legibus* and how it might
relate to the genre of *De specialibus legibus* as a whole. Also of interest here is
the utilization of medical terminology to characterize the purpose of the
unit's sub-sections (and, by implication, the unit as a whole), terminology
that brings to mind a passage like §83, where Philo likens desire to a "disease" that "infects" the soul. Such language, in turn, reflects the widespread
use of medical imagery in moral philosophy as studied, for example, by
Martha Nussbaum, *The Therapy of Desire: Theory and Practice in Hellenistic
Ethics* (3d ed.; Princeton: Princeton University Press, 2009), an important
resource that Svebakken mentions in passing (p. 9 n. 33) but does not utilize
in analyzing *Spec.* 4.78b-131 itself.

Similar observations can be made regarding the analysis of §96, where
Philo explains that the legislation on dietary restrictions is "paradigmatic,"

by which he means that in framing these laws Moses "builds a comprehensive program on the chastisement and training of just one desire, desire involving the belly, supposing that once the most primal and commanding desire has learned to submit to the laws of self-mastery, all other desires will likewise quit resisting the reins of reason" (translation from pp. 141-42). Here the Alexandrian makes a critical supposition, one that in fact represents a linchpin for his whole argument, namely, that it is possible to root out all forms of harmful desire by controlling desire involving the belly. According to Svebakken, Philo's idea that the desire for food and drink constitutes the originating and/or predominant form of desire "comes from Plato himself," though the passage cited in support of this claim (*Resp.* 437D, cf. *Leg.* 782E) refers to the desires known as thirst and hunger not as "the most primal and commanding" forms of desire (as Philo does) but simply as the "most palpable" (*enargestatai*) forms. In order to appreciate the full context and import of the Alexandrian's supposition, then, it seems that we are in need of a more comprehensive approach for examining how ancient moralists categorized the different forms of desire and their relation (if any) to one another. What can we surmise regarding his intentions in composing this unit that Philo not only endeavors to prove that the Mosaic law promotes self-control but that he sees the dietary laws in particular as establishing such proof? This question is especially pertinent given how such laws "often placed observant Jews at odds with the broader culture" (p. 11) and given Philo's acknowledgement that desire can have for its object not only food and drink but also such things as wealth, reputation, power, and beauty (§§86-91). In this regard, it seems that some attention to other philosophical ruminations on dietary matters is in order, for example, Porphyry, *De abstinentia* and Plutarch, *De esu carnium*. As Philo asserts in §97 (cf. §129), the Mosaic dietary laws inculcate a number of virtues besides self-control, especially piety (*eusebeia*), a point that would resonate with such sources (cf. Porphyry, *Abst.* 2.10-11, 27-28; 4.5-6, 18).

Walter T. Wilson
Emory University

JOHN J. COLLINS AND DANIEL C. HARLOW, eds. *Early Judaism. A Comprehensive Overview*. Grand Rapids, MI: Eerdmans, 2012. Pp. xxi + 467. ISBN 978-0-80286922-7. Price $35 (pb).

As explained in the preface, thirteen of the fifteen essays that comprise this edited volume are reprints from *Eerdman's Dictionary of Early Judaism* (2010) with only minor changes. The additional two essays are on Philo and

Josephus respectively and were drawn from the alphabetical entries in the *Dictionary*. The fifteen essays as a whole are intended to be an authoritative overview of Judaism from the time of Alexander the Great (late fourth century B.C.E.) to the Bar Kokhba Revolt (early second century C.E.), and thus "early Judaism" designates the latter half of the Second Temple Period and slightly beyond. The book is a welcome addition to an area of Judaism that has been historically ignored but that is receiving increased attention and is better understood, especially as a result of the Dead Sea Scrolls. The editors further explain in the preface the significance of the phrase "early Judaism," which is not only an attempt to describe a period of Judaism accurately but also an attempt to rethink the broader history of Judaism. For example, whereas the German word *Spätjudentum* (late Judaism) has derogatory overtones in suggesting that Hellenistic and early Roman Judaism was late coming and in a state of decline, "early Judaism" is more neutral and reflects a revised understanding of the overall chronology of ancient Judaism. Collins' opening chapter, "Early Judaism in Modern Scholarship," provides a more extensive history of scholarship and should be required reading for any graduate student in a related field. In what follows, I will first discuss the overall collection of essays more generally, and then I will touch on some specific features that will be of particular interest to readers of this journal.

One of the strengths of this volume is that it is designed to maximize the reader's interaction with the information. There are thirteen maps covering everything from the conquests of Alexander the Great to Qumran. There is also an extensive four-page timeline identifying key events and developments in early Judaism. Multiple indices organized by modern authors, subjects, and ancient texts also make this book particularly easy to use for quick reference. Furthermore, the appropriately sized bibliographies at the end of each essay offer helpful resources. The book also includes thirty-two pages of black and white images of architecture, inscriptions, papyri, and other archaeological evidence.

Each essay covers a topic or author relating to early Judaism: "Early Judaism in Modern Scholarship," by John J. Collins; "Jewish History from Alexander to Hadrian," by Chris Seeman and Adam Kolman Marshak; "Judaism in the Land of Israel," by James C. VanderKam; "Judaism in the Diaspora," by Erich S. Gruen; "The Jewish Scriptures: Texts, Versions, and Canons," by Eugene Ulrich; "Early Jewish Biblical Interpretation," by James L. Kugel; "Apochrypha and Pseudepigrapha," by Loren T. Stuckenbruck; "The Dead Sea Scrolls," by Eibert Tigchelaar; "Early Jewish Literature Written in Greek," by Katell Berthelot; "Philo," by Gregory E. Sterling, David T. Runia, Maren R. Niehoff, and Annewies van den Hoek; "Josephus," by

Steve Mason, James S. McLaren, and John M. G. Barclay; "Archaeology, Papyri, and Inscriptions," by Jürgen K. Zangenberg; "Jews among the Greeks and Romans," Miriam Pucci Ben Zeev; "Early Judaism and Early Christianity," by Daniel C. Harlow; and "Early Judaism and Rabbinic Judaism," by Lawrence H. Schiffman.

The picture of Judaism that emerges from these essays collectively is one marked by complexity and plurality. In the opening essay, Collins explains the scholarly debate over whether it is more accurate to refer to "Judaism" in the singular (e.g. E. P. Sanders) or "Judaisms" in the plural (e.g. J. Neusner). Regardless of one's preference, the debate illustrates the complexity of the problem. There were unifying factors in early Judaism like monotheism, Torah, and covenant; however, literary, geographical, and linguistic diversity brought about by ever changing political milieux resulted in a range of Jewish responses that are difficult to categorize. For example, as Berthelot explains, designations such as "Hellenistic" and "Hellenized" become increasingly complicated. If "Hellenistic" is simply used to describe texts chronologically, then it is vague and not very helpful in classifying early Jewish literature. The term "Hellenized" is problematic because it suggests that Judaism and Hellenism were at odds when in fact Hellenistic culture was itself the product of the multi-cultural melting pot of the Hellenistic Mediterranean (p. 229). Referring to the adoption of Greek genres by Jews such as Ezekiel the Tragedian, Berthelot says, "one might well speak of Greek literature that is Jewish instead of Jewish literature written in Greek" (p. 229). Using Pseudo-Phocylides as an example, Berthelot also illustrates how simply identifying whether a text is Jewish at all can be extremely complicated (pp. 229–30). Gruen's essay emphasizes the complexities of generalizing about the Diaspora as a shared Jewish experience. In addition to geographical and linguistic diversity, some Jews would have voluntarily remained in the Diaspora while others would have pined for return (pp. 96–97). Even the term "Diaspora" itself is complicated since there was limited uniformity in Diaspora communities and the original Greek term most often simply refers to a colony in a neutral way and not to exile (pp. 97–98).

One of the most exciting things about this collection is that it generates discussion about broader issues related to the field. For example, Ulrich discusses the transformation of Jewish law and literature into authoritative scripture. Emphasizing the Dead Sea Scrolls and the relationship between the Samaritan Pentateuch, the Old Greek and the Masoretic text, Ulrich discusses the plurality of the biblical text and the extent to which a stable and permanent canon was a much later development than previously thought.

In the course of his essay, Ulrich provides some speculative comments comparing the reception of the Bible among Jews to the reception of the *Iliad* and *Odyssey* among Greeks and Romans (pp. 124–127). Ulrich asserts that one indication the Bible was gaining traction as an authoritative and holy text is that it was translated into vernacular languages relatively early. In contrast, Ulrich says, "The *Iliad* and the *Odyssey*, despite their central cultural importance when the Romans took over the Greek culture, were apparently never translated into Latin in antiquity" (p. 127). The analogy is somewhat problematic because asking why Romans did not create an authoritative translation of a foreign text is not the same thing as asking why Jews needed authoritative translations as they themselves adopted new languages. I am also perplexed by Ulrich's analogy because as early as the third century B.C.E., Livius Andronicus translated the *Odyssey* into Latin, and we have twenty-one fragments that have been identified with certainty (*OCD*, "Livius Andronicus"). Nonetheless, while the *Iliad* and the *Odyssey* never became authoritative scripture for the masses of Greeks or Romans in the same way as scripture was for Jews and Christians, there were individuals who venerated Homer and his poems as infallible sources of wisdom (e.g. Heraclitus the Allegorist). In my own opinion, the biggest difference between the reception of the Homeric poems and the Bible has to do with daily religion. The Homeric poems had nothing to do with day-to-day worship at particular cults, but the Torah had everything to do with the Temple, the synagogue, and daily life for Jewish communities.

Although dense, all of the essays are extremely readable. They provide continuous narratives of their topics without footnotes, but there are abundant citations of primary material. Actually, one of the strengths of the essays overall is the effective use of illustrative examples and key pieces of evidence. Kugel provides a somewhat speculative discussion of the rise of biblical interpretation and reminds us that from our modern perspective it is easy to take biblical interpretation for granted but that it was necessarily an innovation in itself (152). Kugel explains that attitudes to biblical texts and laws likely underwent a major shift after the return from Babylonian exile. Kugel cites key pieces of evidence like the account in Nehemiah of Ezra reading the Torah publically (157–58) and then locates the motivation for interpretation in apparent ambiguities such as the laws in Exodus and Deuteronomy regarding how to prepare the Passover meal (159–61). In order to illustrate how interpretation worked, Kugel uses the story of the sacrifice of Isaac to show how the biblical text must have challenged its early readers with difficult questions that inevitably generated complex solutions. Although selective, this approach fosters clarity and understanding. In general, all of the essays follow this practice.

The two essays on Philo and Josephus stand out among the others since they focus on particular authors and not themes or collections of material from different sources. The essay on Philo is organized as a generic overview of what we know about his life and writings and provides a thorough and lucid account. Treatises are primarily discussed in traditional groupings such as *Questions and Answers on Genesis and Exodus*, the *Allegorical Commentary*, and the *Exposition of the Law*, and there is also some considerable discussion of individual treatises such as *De opificio mundi, De Abrahamo, De Iosepho*, etc. My only criticism is that the essay on Philo is too general since it does not address specific issues related to early Judaism that emerge throughout the overall collection (e.g. the unity vs. the diversity of Judaism, life in the Diaspora, Hellenization, the development of canon and scriptural authority, Temple, synagogue, etc.). In other words, the essay is an introduction to Philo in general but not a general introduction to Philo as a representative of early Judaism. Despite this relatively isolated picture of Philo, a more synthetic approach that relates Philo to other Jewish authors and texts can be found scattered throughout the remaining essays, and the index makes these passages easily identifiable. The essay on Josephus is similar to the one on Philo in that it also primarily provides a generic overview of his life and works; however, a central claim does emerge more clearly over the course of the essay: the need to evaluate Josephus as an author in his own right and not simply to understand his sources. Discussing the *Life of Josephus*, the *Jewish War, Jewish Antiquities*, and *Against Apion* in relation to one another, the authors of the essay emphasize Josephus' literary skill and the importance of not assuming that he is only an instrument of Roman political propaganda.

The audience for this volume is academic, but it would be useful to anyone from advanced undergraduates to senior scholars. The book is physically well published. In my reading, I did not find a single typo and this is not something I can often say. My one complaint about the format is that the individual essays are not numbered or identified by anything other than chapter title and author(s). This unnecessary omission gains nothing and only makes it more difficult to navigate one's way through the essays. Nevertheless, on the whole, this collection is a user-friendly and extremely readable resource that packs a lot of information in a relatively small space. Most will probably read individual essays in isolation, but anyone seriously interested in this topic would benefit from reading it cover-to-cover.

M. Jason Reddoch
Colorado Mesa University

Myrto Hatzimichali, *Potamo of Alexandria and the Emergence of Eclecticism in Late Hellenistic Philosophy*. Cambridge: Cambridge University Press, 2011. ix + 198 pages. Hardcover. ISBN 978-0-521-19728-1. Price £58, $99 (hb).

The scholarly epithet usually used to describe the self-styled Eclectic philosopher Potamo of Alexandria, who lived a generation before Philo, is "mysterious." The main reason is that we have so little evidence about him—just a brief notice in Diogenes Laertius, a further sentence in the *Souda*, an Ephesian inscription most likely dedicated to him, two mentions in Simplicius' commentary on Aristotle's *De caelo*, and a few more uncertain references. This might seem to be a very thin basis for writing an entire scholarly monograph. Yet this was the aim of the young Greek–English scholar Myrto Hatzimichali in her study, first presented as a Cambridge doctorate. Students of ancient philosophy, including Philonic scholars, will find it both an interesting and an instructive read.

After an introductory chapter on the notion of eclecticism in ancient and modern thought, Hatzimichali gives a lengthy and detailed background account of the history and development of philosophical activity in first century B.C.E. Alexandria. She concludes that all the principal trends of that century were represented in the eastern metropolis and that together they formed the conditions that would make it particularly favourable for Potamo to introduce his novel sect. This is by far the best account of intellectual life and philosophy in Alexandria in the century of Philo's birth that I have read and I warmly recommend it. Next is a brief chapter on what we know about Potamon's life and work, followed by a detailed examination of what we are told were the chief features of his eclectic system in the domains of epistemology, physics and ethics as set out in his work *Stoicheiôsis* (*Elementary teaching*). Based on what Diogenes tells us, Potamo took as his basis well-known teachings in other *haireseis*, added refinements of his own, and presented the result with the help of didactic techniques such as the use of prepositional phrases. So in the domain of physics he lists the principles as matter (ὕλη) and the maker (τὸ ποιοῦν) (cf. Philo *Opif.* 8), but then adds two more, quality (ποιότης) and place, summarizing them as ἐξ οὗ, ὑφ᾽ οὗ, ποίῳ and ἐν ᾧ respectively. There follow two chapters on the references to Potamo in Simplicius and in other texts, and the study ends with a quite detailed summary of the conclusions reached in the study as a whole.

Hatzimichali concludes that what chiefly characterizes Potamo as an eclectic philosopher is his method, which as Diogenes tells us involved selecting doctrines from other schools of thought and melding them into a system of his own. This method distinguishes him from other philosophers, such as sceptics (particularly of the Ciceronian variety), who also claim the freedom to choose, but express fundamental doubt that what they chose can be given the status of "infallible truths" that allow some kind of systematisation. It also separates him from syncretistic philosophers, such as perhaps Antiochus of Ascalon, who see a general agreement between differing philosophical traditions and deliberately set out to harmonize them. He also differs, we might add, from a thinker such as Philo, who sets himself the task of expounding the doctrines of Moses, and then selects those philosophical doctrines which might assist in explicating the hidden wisdom in the scriptural texts (see especially Jaap Mansfeld's fine paper on this subject, first presented to a conference on the "question of 'eclecticism'", RRS 8847). Hatzimichali does not include discussion of Philo's thought in the volume on chronological grounds, "as his main period of activity falls about a generation after Potamo's" (p. 4). This is correct. Potamo can be seen as a final product of late Hellenistic philosophy, whereas Philo clearly belongs to the emerging Imperial philosophy with its emphasis on the exposition of the thought of the great master. It remains the case, however, that he might have been used to shed light on Potamo's chief doctrines (note extra references to Philo not included in the index on pp. 53 and 59). It is very likely that Potamo was a leading figure in Alexandria at about the time that Philo received his philosophical training and much of Philo's knowledge of philosophical sources is derived from the late Hellenistic period.

I add a final comment. It is perhaps a pity that the author did not collect the very restricted textual basis for her work and present it in an "edition." This would have provided a little more information on the precise text and made it easy to refer to the testimonia on Potamo in future scholarly work. But this observation should not detract from our appreciation of a very fine piece of scholarship.

David T. Runia
Queen's College
The University of Melbourne

PETER W. MARTENS, *Origen and Scripture: the Contours of the Exegetical Life*. Oxford Early Christian Studies. Oxford: Oxford University Press, 2012. xii + 280 pages. ISBN 978-0-19-963955-7. Price £68, $125 (hb).

R. E. HEINE, *Origen: Scholarship in the Service of the Church*. Christian Theology in Context. Oxford: Oxford University Press, 2011. xii + 275 pages. ISBN 978-0-19-920907-1 (hb), 978-0-19-920908-8 (pb). Price £59, $99 (hb), £19, $29.95 (pb).

Of all the exegetes and theologians in the Alexandrian tradition Origen was the most prolific and the most controversial. Not for nothing did he receive the nickname Adamantius, man of steel. The two books under review, both by American scholars and published by Oxford University Press, approach the same subject from different but complementary angles. Both have much to offer Philonist readers.

Peter Martens' monograph is a much reworked version of a Notre Dame dissertation prepared under the supervision of Prof. Brian Daley. As he himself notes in his introduction, many studies have been devoted to Origen's methods of biblical interpretation. What is new and valuable in this study is the focus on the interpreter himself, not just in the activity of engaging in biblical study, but in the broader context of the spiritual life of the committed and dedicated Christian. The book sets out a portrait of the ideal reader and interpreter, as envisaged and outlined by Origen in his writings. But this is also the ideal that he himself strove to attain, so that there is a strong autobiographical component in the portrait, both implicitly and explicitly when he refers to his own experiences.

The first chapters set out essential requirements. Scripture is to be read in the manner of the textual scholar and this requires the techniques of Greco-Roman philology, including the crucial method of allegorical interpretation. Though mostly not part of the biblical tradition itself, the instruments of philology can legitimately be borrowed as a divine providential gift. But soon the focus turns to a broader picture of the biblical scholar whom Origen presents to his readers and hearers as living the consummate sanctified life of the advanced Christian. Scriptural interpretation is the 'epitome of rational activity' (p. 104), made possible because humanity was created in the image of God. For this activity boundaries are placed through the doctrines of the church as handed down in the apostolic succession. Both the heterodox and the Jews placed themselves outside through their literal, i.e. non-spiritual, understanding of scripture.

We now come to the most interesting and innovative part of the book. Martens portrays the interpreter as a participant in the Christian drama of salvation. Engaging in scriptural study will not succeed without a commitment to the moral life and the practice of exegesis will serve to deepen and strengthen that commitment. Origen frequently refers to necessary virtues such as love of learning and exactness, but also to the importance of trust in the transforming power of scripture and to the need and efficacy of prayer. Through the practice of scriptural interpretation the exegete himself thus embarks on the journey of the soul and makes progress towards the ultimate goal, the encounter with God and his Logos. But controversially Origen's vision is not confined to what happens to human beings in this life. In the final chapter Martens expands the horizon and argues that for Origen the study of scripture can reverse the fall of the rational minds before creation and the encounter with God in this life can prefigure the perfection of knowledge in the eschaton.

Philonist readers might at first be a little disappointed that the book plays so little attention to the background of Origen's thought in earlier Alexandrian exegetical practice. Philo receives only the briefest of mentions on pages 62 and 135. But to set the book aside for this reason would certainly be an opportunity missed. Two of the perennial problems facing the interpreter of Philo's thought is that he makes so few meta-comments on what he is doing and that he never undertakes a systematic presentation of his religious and philosophical views. Much of the textual evidence that Martens collects on Origen's conception of his role as biblical interpreter is derived from the prolegomena that he, following ancient practice, writes at the beginning of his commentaries and from his great systematic work, the Περὶ ἀρχῶν. It is of course not possible to extrapolate these views directly back to Philo. Nevertheless Marten's synoptic and systematic presentation can stimulate Philonists to think harder about how Philo would have understood his own role as scriptural interpreter. The idea that he might have regarded it as a kind of salvific process involving moral and intellectual progress and leading to an encounter with God through the divine Logos is stimulating and by no means fanciful. Origen's famous self-description of the exegete as the bride who experiences the bridegroom drawing near and then withdrawing (*Homilies on the Song of Songs* 1.7, see p. 184) brings to mind Philo's statement about his own experience at *Migr.* 34–35. In addition, Origen's understanding of himself as a teacher and a moral and intellectual guide may well have been similar to Philo's role in the context of the Alexandrian Jewish community. Another stimulating view is Marten's contention that Origen's frequent condemnation of literal exegesis of scripture is not meant as a general criticism, but relates to a limited number of specific interpretations to which he is sharply opposed (see pp. 140–41). To sum up, the similarities and differences between Philo's rare pronouncements on his exegetical activity and what Origen tells us much more copiously about his own practice is a subject worth pursuing further.

In the second book, published by Oxford in its Christian Theology in Context series, Ronald Heine distills more than thirty years of research that he has dedicated to the study of the exegetical and other writings of Origen. (Other Patristic authors treated in the series so far are Irenaeus, Athanasius and Augustine.) Not surprisingly many of the same texts that Martens cites and discusses are also highlighted in Heine's study. But the emphasis is different. Heine's approach is more diachronic and less synoptic. He follows the development of Origen's career as thinker, author and man of the church, focusing on his writings and the context in which they were written. The result is a succinctly written and highly informative guide to a field of study in which it is not always easy for the incipient scholar to find his or her way. The bibliography pp 256–72 is particularly valuable (but does show a strong bias towards English language scholarship, with relatively few references to the burgeoning French, Italian and German research, for which one should consult the journal dedicated to Origenian studies, *Adamantius*).

But there is also much that more experienced scholars can learn from this book. Heine argues persuasively that the focus of Origen's thought, as reflected in his writings, shifts during his career. In Alexandria the struggle against Gnostic thought is at the centre of his preoccupations. But the move to Caesarea in mid-career confronts him with a different context and particularly the question of the relationship between the church and the active Jewish community. In the final chapter Heine tentatively argues that the "senior scholar" in his final years might have been rethinking some of his earlier views.

This second study pays a good deal more attention to Philo and Hellenistic Judaism as an important precursor and influence on Origen's methods as a biblical commentator. Somewhat paradoxically, however, Heine sees this influence as much stronger in his earlier period in Alexandria, when he most likely had relatively little contact with Jews, than later in Caesarea, when his contacts with the Jewish community and individual learned rabbis were much more extensive. It is true that the early Alexandrian church fathers tended to see Philo as an exegetical predecessor, but they were certainly aware that he was a Jew, whose views on the law and the role of the divine Logos were not the same as theirs. Heine notes at various points Origen's debt to the man whom he appears to have met early on in Alexandria and whom he calls "the Hebrew" (pp. 56, 133, 208). The man, who was a Christian, obviously cannot be identified with Philo, but the method that is ascribed to him in a famous text (*Philocalia* 2.3), which emphasizes the obscurity of scripture and the need to search through the whole of it to find the key to the meaning hidden in specific texts, could hardly be more Philonic (even if scripture for Philo is restricted almost exclusively to the Pentateuch). On the other hand, Heine is reticent when discussing the evidence of contact with particular rabbis (p. 148), and does not mention the famous text in *Genesis Rabbah* 1.1 which strongly suggests a triangular relationship between Origen, rabbi Hoshaya and Philo. I suspect that, speaking more generally, further research on Origen's use of Philo and what it might tell us about how he sees the relationship between learned Jews in the past and in the present might lead to interesting results. Peter Martens has already made a start with his article on Origen's use of *De confusione linguarum* in his allegorical reading of the dispersion of the nations in Gen 11 in last year's volume of *The Studia Philonica Annual*.

David T. Runia
Queen's College
The University of Melbourne

RICHARD A. NORRIS JR. (trans.), *Gregory of Nyssa: Homilies on the Song of Songs*. Writings from the Greco-Roman World 13; Atlanta: Society of Biblical Literature, 2012. liv + 517 pages. ISBN 978-1-58983-105-6. Price $59.95 (pb).

After a delay of many years, the late Richard A. Norris Jr.'s (1930–2005) much-anticipated translation of Gregory of Nyssa's *Homilies on the Song of Songs* is finally in print. It is the last major project that Professor Norris completed—he passed away only weeks after submitting the final portion of the manuscript—and is, in many ways, a fitting capstone to a distinguished career devoted to the study of patristic Christology and the history of biblical interpretation. Norris's most important and enduring contributions to the field have been sourcebooks of translated texts, which include *The Christological Controversy* (1980), published in William Rusch's *Sources of Early Christian Thought* series, and *The Song of Songs: Interpreted by Early Christian and Medieval Commentators* (2003), published in Robert Wilken's *The Church's Bible* series. He was thus well-positioned to produce the authoritative English translation of Nyssen's *Homilies*, and he certainly has accomplished this. His translation is lucid and readable, and accurately captures the sense of Gregory's prose without giving an overly literal rendition of the Greek. The reader will also welcome the inclusion of Langerbeck's critical edition (minus the apparatus) on facing pages, which makes this volume all the more valuable.

Gregory's *Homilies on the Song of Songs* is an incredibly important text for understanding the history of Christian interpretation of the Song of Songs and the development of Christian mysticism more broadly. It is one of Gregory's most mature works, dating to the early 390s, and it is roughly contemporary with his other great work of mystical exegesis, the *Life of Moses*. Unlike the *Life of Moses*, however, which has long been available to a wide audience in Everett Ferguson and Abraham Mahlherbe's excellent translation in the *Classics of Western Spirituality* series (1978), the *Homilies* has had a much more restricted readership. The only previous English translation—and, as far as this reviewer knows, the only one in any modern language—was produced by Alister McCambley for the Hellenic Press and was rather inexpertly done; it has also since gone out of print. Those not fluent in patristic Greek would, therefore, have had difficulty accessing the text, and this surely explains why the *Homilies* has been so little studied in comparison with the *Life of Moses* and also Origen's *Homilies* and *Commentary on the Song of Songs*, which have been ably translated by R. P. Lawson. The present volume will, the reviewer sincerely hopes, go a long way towards redressing this lacuna, especially since Nyssen's *Homilies* is actually the earliest sequential interpretation of the Song to survive in Greek. This is often forgotten since he is chronologically so much later than the earliest Greek commentary writers Hippolytus and Origen, but their works survive in translations (Georgian and Armenian for Hippolytus, Latin for Origen), with only a few extant Greek fragments.

There are few reasons to quibble with Norris' translation, which vividly and carefully brings out the richness of Gregory's thought. Norris does, however, have a tendency to go rather beyond the Greek at times for the sake of explanation. The most striking example comes quite early on, at the bottom of p. 21, where the rather succinct phrase μετὰ δὲ ταῦτα νυμφοστολεῖν ἄρχεται τὸν νέον πρὸς τὴν τοιαύτην συνοίκησιν is fleshed out and rendered, "Then, after this, our Solomon begins to array the youth as a bridegroom, wanting to prepare him for this marriage with Wisdom." His use of a verb of desiring with a complementary infinitive of preparation seems to be placing much more weight on the *pros* with accusative clause—which here must denote purpose—than is due, although I would not say he has misconstrued the clause. One might also note that the addition of the adjective "our" near the beginning of the sentence makes it sound rather like Gregory himself included Solomon's name, rather than it being the addition of the translator for clarifying the subject of the verb. (It is worth noting that the infinitive form νυμφοστολεῖν is only found elsewhere twice, both in Philo at *Congr.* 72 and *Abr.* 250).

The translation is accompanied by an informative introduction and a number of helpful annotations. The introduction acquaints us briefly with the other two Cappadocian fathers, Basil and Gregory Nazianzen, before proceeding with a fairly detailed account of Nyssen's career and a dating of the *Homilies*. But the bulk of the introduction is concerned with technical exegetical and rhetorical matters. We are treated, in particular, to learned analyses of the terms *skopos* and *akolouthia*. Surely matters of interpretation do need to be dealt with at some length, since the prefatory letter to Olympias appended to the *Homilies* is, in effect, an apology for allegory against the criticisms of Antiochene exegetes. But it is surprising that certain major themes of the work—*philosophia* (which Gregory comes to define as mystical union with the Divine), apophaticism, ontology and nuptial theology—are treated only tangentially (esp. at pp. xxiv–xxix and xxxvii–xxxviii). And there is no attempt made to situate Gregory's *Homilies* within the broader traditions of early Christian interpretation of the Song, something Norris was uniquely positioned to do. This task is left to the notes, which do highlight parallels, but are not particularly helpful in systematically delineating relationships and influence. The reason for this may at least be in part the goals of the *Writings from the Greco-Roman World* series, which aims to make available "pagan" and Christian works that illustrate important features of Greco-Roman grammatical and rhetorical education and exegetical practice. Norris may also have been prevented from writing a more detailed introduction due to failing health.

Despite these omissions, this is a volume that will endure, and which ought to be owned by anyone interested in early Christian biblical interpretation, historical theology, and mysticism. It will also be of particular interest to scholars of Philo, even though it does not draw as explicitly on Philonic works as do the *Life of Moses* or *On the Making of Man*. The hermeneutical presupposition that governs the entirety of Gregory's exegesis of the Song—namely, that within the words of the Song divine *philosophia* is concealed—can be traced back to Philo's concern to discern the moral and cosmological significance of the Torah. Moreover, Gregory's frequent attempts to use the language of the Song, particularly in the sixth homily, to present a Christianized version of Plato's cosmology has striking overlap with Philo's *De Opificio Mundi*. The *Homilies on the Song of Songs* will provide yet more material for assessing the legacy of Philo in Late Antiquity.

Karl Shuve
University of Virginia
Charlottesville, Virginia

Bibleworks9: Software for Biblical Exegesis and Research for PC or Mac. Norfolk, Va.: Bibleworks, LLC, 2011. Price $359; upgrade from two most recent earlier editions, $159–199 (standard price includes Works of Philo in Greek)

Since the publication of *SPhA* vol. 19 pp. 210–212, where we reviewed Bibleworks 7 as a representative of available Bible software programs that include the Greek and English (Yonge's) translation of Philo of Alexandria, Bibleworks has released two significant upgrades in its software. While much of the content and many of the basic functions detailed in that earlier review have not changed, there have been some noteworthy improvements in the latest edition (Bibleworks9) that invite additional comments. As a reminder, Bibleworks includes in its standard package fully searchable editions of the Hebrew/Aramaic Tanakh (incl. BHS[4corr]), Rahlf's Septuagint, the Greek NT (now incl. NA[28]), the Latin Vulgate[5th revised], the Targumim (Aramaic), the Works of Josephus (in Greek, Latin and Whiston's English), Apostolic Fathers (in Greek, Latin and English), along with numerous Bible translations in many modern languages (from Swedish to Swahili, including several recent versions). In the case of Hebrew, Aramaic, and Greek texts, each has morphological tags and is fully lemmatized. There are also several Lexical-Grammatical references including: Hebrew and Aramaic Lexica by BDB and Holladay; Greek Lexica by Gingrich/Danker, Newman, and the Abridged LSJ; as well as several grammars focusing on biblical texts. These tools include hyperlinks to biblical references that allow one to see (by placing the mouse pointer above the link) the text of the reference in its original language and in translation. Also available, each for an additional fee, are modules containing such major resources as LSJ[9th revised], BDAG, Koehler, Baumgartner and Stamm's Hebrew/Aramaic lexicon, and the The Dead Sea Scrolls English translation (Biblical and Sectarian texts).

Noteworthy additions in content since version 7 include a fully tagged and searchable Greek text of the Old Testament Pseudepigrapha (in addition to the Charles 1913 and Evans 2008 English translations). Also available is the complete text of Schaff's *Ante-Nicene, Post-Nicene, and Nicene Fathers*. The text opens in a separate resource window and specific biblical references therein can be accessed via the analysis resources tab discussed below. Highly touted is the integration into BW9 of seven biblical manuscripts (incl. Sinaiticus, Vaticanus, and Alexandrinus), fully transcribed as well as complete digital image sets (with verse location tags imbedded), with morphological tagging and, again, fully searchable.

Though there have been some modest aesthetic alterations to the software, the most noticeable formal difference in the latest version is a fourth column. Now, from left to right, there is a search column (with a space for various kinds of searches [word, phrase, Boolean, etc.] as well as a results vertical list that provides the word(s) or phrases in context that appear in a version or some subset thereof); a browse column (that provides the full text of a treatise, either in a continuous text of one version or multiple versions viewable passage by passage); and an analysis column (that includes thirteen tabs, where one can choose to display lexical analysis, reference works, use statistics, NT manuscript images, biblical textual apparati, a mini word processor for writing notes, etc., most of which changes simply [if you wish] by passing the cursor over a passage or word in the Browse column). This last column can now be split vertically to form two columns, making it possible to have two analysis tabs (e.g., lexical analysis statistics) and so providing even more information about a word or passage.

There are also a number of new functions. One significant development is the ability to search words and phrases across either all or selected same language corpora. So, for example, one can select the word δημιουργός in *Conf.* 144 and search for either that form or all forms of the lemma not just in Philo's treatise but in every Greek text in BW9 or in specific texts one chooses. The inter-version search reveals that δημιουργός occurs, for example, seven times in the Apostolic Fathers, eight times in Josephus, twice in the Greek versions of the Old Testament Pseudepigrapha, and only once in LXX. One can then select, say, the Pseudepigrapha from the initial search results and find where and what context δημιουργός occurs there (once in Apocalypse of Ezra 7:5 and once in Testament of Job 39:12).

BW9 is fully Unicode compatible, making cutting and pasting Greek words, phrases (even whole treatises) into word processors or on-line very easy. Indeed, for teachers it is a very useful tool both in the classroom and for class preparation, generating lists, providing definitions and statistics, offering different translations (of the Bible and a few other writings, but not Philo), as well as easy exports of manuscript and map images. Technical and content support for Bibleworks is accessible and substantive. In addition to six hours of training videos and an extensive digital manual that come with the program, the software is regularly updated via the internet and new translations and editions of resources are thereby made available to users (usually without additional fee) as they come out. There is a growing Bibleworks community on the internet providing "unofficial" assistance and even (for the tech savvy) "homemade" modules, often providing valuable older materials in the public domain in digital form (for example, there is a wealth of texts, grammars and lexcia focused around Latin literature). On the occasions I have contacted Bibleworks customer support, they have been prompt to respond and very helpful and on a couple of occasions even made modest changes in the software to conform to my usage. Such changes come in the previously mentioned regular updates.

While the software is clearly oriented toward scripture scholars, the Philonist will have little difficulty using most of BW9's tools for lexical investigation as well as translation work in the Alexandrian's corpus and related literature. With all of its searchable databases, it is also a ready-to-hand digital library. As far as ease of use, one can use basic functions right away but BW9 rewards those who explore its many and various tools and texts. It is a powerful program that increases in utility the more you spend time with it.

Ronald Cox,
Pepperdine University,
Malibu, California

The Studia Philonica Annual 25 (2013) 247–250

NEWS AND NOTES*

Philo of Alexandria Group of the Society of Biblical Literature

At the 2012 Annual Meeting of the Society for Biblical Literature in Chicago, the Philo of Alexandria Group met for three sessions—one on who read and used Philo's writings in the past and two on Philo's treatises *Legum Allegoriae* 1–3, of which a translation and commentary are being prepared by Thomas H. Tobin, S.J., for the Philo of Alexandria Commentary Series. On the morning of November 18, Torrey Seland (School of Mission and Theology, Norway) presided over a panel entitled "Philo's Graeco-Roman Readers," which included the following speakers and presentations: James R. Royse (Claremont, California), "Did Philo Publish His Works?"; Gregory Sterling (Yale University), "'A Man of the Highest Repute': Did Josephus Know the Works of Philo of Alexandria?"; Frederick E. Brenk (Pontifical Institute, Rome), "Philo and Plutarch on the Nature of God"; Jennifer Otto (McGill University), "Philo, Judaeus? A Re-evaluation of Why Clement Calls Philo 'the Pythagorean'"; and Gretchen Reydams-Schils, "Calcidius, Philo, and Origen." (Torrey Seland presided in place of Sarah Pearce [University of Southampton, U.K.], who was unable to attend.)

The first session on Philo's *Legum Allegoriae* 1–3 met later the same day and was presided over by Ronald Cox (Pepperdine University), in place of Walter Wilson (Emory University), who was unable to attend. Speakers and presentations included Francesca Calabi (University of Pavia, Italy), "Adam's Solitude in Philo"; Valéry Laurand (Université Michel de Montaigne Bordeaux 3), "Giving of Names and Double Meaning in *Legum Allegoriae* (2.14–18)"; Hans Svebakken (Loyola University Chicago), "Middle-Platonic Moral Psychology as a Unifying Theme in Philo's Allegorical Interpretations of Genesis 2:21 and Deuteronomy 23:13"; and Caroline Carlier (Independent Scholar), "Pleasure and Self-Mastery in *Allegorical Interpretation* II 71–208."

The second session on Philo's *Legum Allegoriae* 1–3 met on November 20 and was presided over by Ellen Birnbaum (Cambridge, Massachusetts). In his presentation entitled, "Neuralgic Issues in the Interpretation of Philo of

---

* Items of general interest to Philo scholars to be included in this section can be sent to the editor, David Runia (contact details in Notes on Contributors below).

Alexandria's Treatises *Legum Allegoriae*," Thomas H. Tobin, S.J.—whose translation of *Leg*. 1.43–55 and paper were distributed beforehand—discussed some of the challenges involved in working with this set of treatises. Responding were Ronald Cox and Ellen Birnbaum (the latter, in place of Sarah Pearce). Following a break, Manuel Alexandre Jr. (Universidade de Lisboa) summarized his paper "Philo's Rhetorical Strategies in the Allegorical Interpretation of Genesis 2:1–3:19."

All sessions included ample time for discussion. The program concluded with a Business Meeting, at which it was announced that Ronald Cox will succeed Sarah Pearce as Co-Chair of the Philo Group after next year's meeting and that in accordance with SBL regulations, the Group will be submitting a renewal application in 2013. Attendees also welcomed news of the following Group-related publications: *The Studia Philonica Annual*, vol. 24 (2012); *Philo of Alexandria* On Cultivation: *Introduction, Translation, and Commentary*, by Albert C. Geljon and David T. Runia, Philo of Alexandria Commentary Series 4 (Leiden-Boston: Brill, 2013); and Hans Svebakken, *Philo of Alexandria's Exposition of the Tenth Commandment*, Society of Biblical Literature Studia Philonica Monographs 6 (Atlanta: Society of Biblical Literature, 2012). As a follow-up to this year's topic about who read Philo, at the 2013 meeting the Group will focus on what sources Philo himself read and used (with thanks to Greg Sterling for suggesting both topics).

In keeping with a long tradition, several members and friends of the Philo Group enjoyed dinner together, this year in a private room at the Italian Village Restaurant.

Ellen Birnbaum
Cambridge, Massachusetts

Philo in a New Prayer Book

Readers of *The Studia Philonica Annual* may be interested to know that the Reform synagogue "Kol ha-Neshama" in Jerusalem has decided to include some sentences of Philo in the new prayer book for the pilgrimage holidays. The liturgy for this Pessach opens with Philo's words on the meaning of the holiday. To the best of my knowledge this is the first time in the history of Jewish prayer that Philo's voice is heard.

Maren Niehoff
Hebrew University Jerusalem

Vale Robert Hamerton-Kelly (1938–2013)

Philonists will be deeply saddened to hear the news that Robert Hamerton-Kelly passed away in Portland, Oregon on 7 July 2013 at the age of 74 after suffering a severe stroke two weeks earlier.

Born and raised in South Africa, Bob attended the University of Cape Town and Rhodes University. He pursued his studies in theology at Cambridge University and then moved to the United States, where he completed a Th.D under W. D. Davies at the Union Theological Seminary in New York in 1965. From 1966 to 1970 he was an assistant professor in Religion at Scripps College, Claremont, and from 1970 to 1972 associate professor of New Testament at McCormick Theological College in Chicago. In 1972 he became Dean of the Chapel at Stanford University, a post that he held until 1987. He then took on the role of Senior Research Fellow at the Center for International Security and Arms Control, before returning to the ministry in 1994. He moved to Portland in 2010. While at Stanford he met the philosopher René Girard and became deeply attracted to his theory of mimetic desire, writing a number of books which interpret the New Testament from a Girardian perspective.

It was while he was teaching in Chicago that Bob took the initiative to found the Philo Institute. As Earle Hilgert recounts "he envisioned a new approach [to Philo studies] through a cooperative group of scholars working in the fields of Hellenistic Judaism and early Christianity who would focus together on an analysis of the sources behind and traditions in the Philonic corpus" (*SPhA* vol. 13 p. 13). A first meeting was held at the McCormick campus on June 23–25, 1971. Bob presented a programmatic address in which he laid out his vision for the proposed task. This remains a seminal piece of scholarship in the history of Philonic scholarship. It was agreed to form an organization called the Philo Institute, which would publish a journal called *Studia Philonica* (the predecessor of *The Studia Philonica Annual*). Bob was elected as Director of the Institute and he guided it through its first two years. But in 1973 he accepted the role of Dean at Stanford and so a parting of the ways had to take place. He retained his interest in Philonic studies, however, not only publishing further articles on Philo in 1976 and 1991, but also attending meetings of the Philo group at the Society of Biblical Literature and the Society of New Testament Scholars from time to time. But it is for his great initiative to found the Institute and its journal that he will be above all remembered by Philonic scholars.

I would also like to add some personal words to the above tribute. I first met Bob at the SNTS meeting in Trondheim in Norway in 1985, where he caused fellow scholars to raise their eyebrows by racing around in a sporty convertible. I was immediately attracted to his larger-than-life character and the breadth of his vision on religion and theology. During one of our conversations he suggested that I travel to California to attend the SBL meeting of the Philo group at Anaheim, and that afterwards we could drive to Palo Alto together and he would show me Stanford and San Francisco. I took him up on the offer and it was then that I first met Philonists, including David Winston and Greg Sterling, who would become close friends and collaborators over the next decades. I will be forever grateful to Bob for extending that invitation.

All members of the Philo community will join me in paying tribute to Bob for the great contribution that he made to our collective enterprise. We extend our heartfelt condolences to Rosemary, his life-long partner whom he first met in Cambridge, their three children with their partners, and their seven grandchildren. Vale, Bob.

David T. Runia
Queen's College
The University of Melbourne

NOTES ON CONTRIBUTORS

KATELL BERTHELOT is currently appointed at the Centre Paul-Albert Février at the University of Aix-Marseille, Aix-en-Provence. Her postal address is Maison Méditerranéenne des Sciences de l'Homme, 5 rue du château de l'horloge, BP 647, 13094 Aix-en-Provence Cedex 2, FRANCE; her electronic address is katell.b@free.fr.

ELLEN BIRNBAUM has taught at several Boston-area institutions, including Boston University, Brandeis, and Harvard. Her postal address is 78 Porter Road, Cambridge, MA 02140, USA; her electronic address is ebirnbaum78@gmail.com.

RONALD COX, the Blanche E. Seaver Professor of Religion, is Associate Professor in the religion division at Pepperdine University. His postal address is Religion Division, Pepperdine University, Malibu, CA 90263-4352, USA; his electronic address is ronald.cox@pepperdine.edu.

ALBERT C. GELJON teaches classical languages at the Christelijke Gymnasium in Utrecht. His postal address is Gazellestraat 138, 3523 SZ Utrecht, THE NETHERLANDS; his electronic address is geljon@ixs.nl.

HELEEN M. KEIZER is Dean of Academic Affairs at the Istituto Superiore di Osteopatia in Milan, Italy. Her postal address is Via Guerrazzi 3, 20900 Monza (MB), ITALY; her electronic address is h.m.keizer@virgilio.it.

JUTTA LEONHARDT-BALZER is Lecturer in New Testament at the University of Aberdeen. Her postal address is School of Divinity and Religious Studies, King's College, University of Aberdeen, Aberdeen AB24 3UB, UNITED KINGDOM; her electronic address is j.leonhardt-balzer@abdn.ac.uk.

DAVID LINCICUM is University Lecturer in New Testament Studies at the University of Oxford and Caird Fellow in Theology at Mansfield College. His postal address is Mansfield College, Oxford OX1 3TF, UNITED KINGDOM; his electronic address is david.lincicum@theology.ox.ac.uk.

José Pablo Martín is Professor Consultus at the Universidad Nacional de General Sarmiento, San Miguel, Argentina, and Senior Research fellow of the Argentinian Research Organization (CONICET). His postal address is Azcuenaga 1090, 1663 San Miguel, Argentina; his electronic address is philonis@fastmail.fm.

Olivier Munnich is Professor of Greek language and literature at Paris-Sorbonne University (Paris IV), where his chair is devoted to the Religious literature of the Greek language in late Antiquity. His postal address is 108bis Boulevard Auguste Blanqui, 75013 Paris, France; his electronic address is olivier.munnich@paris-sorbonne.fr.

Maren R. Niehoff is Professor in the Department of Jewish Thought at the Hebrew University, Jerusalem. Her postal address is Department of Jewish Thought, Hebrew University, Mt. Scopus, Jerusalem 91905, Israel; her electronic address is msmaren@mscc.huji.ac.il.

Jennifer Otto is a Ph.D. student in Church History at McGill University in Montreal, Canada. Her postal address is Birks Building, 3520 University Street, Montreal, Quebec, H3A 2A7, Canada; her electronic address is jennifer.otto@mail.mcgill.ca.

Sarah J. K. Pearce is Ian Karten Professor of Jewish Studies at the University of Southampton. Her postal address is Department of History, Faculty of Humanities, Avenue Campus, Highfield, Southampton SO17 1BF, United Kingdom; her electronic address is sjp2@soton.ac.uk.

M. Jason Reddoch is Assistant Professor of Language, Literature, and Mass Communication, Colorado Mesa University. His postal address is Dept. of Lang., Lit, and Mass Comm., Colorado Mesa University, 1100 North Ave, Grand Junction, CO 81501-3122, USA; his electronic address is jreddoch@coloradomesa.edu.

James R. Royse is a Visiting Scholar at the Claremont School of Theology. His postal address is P.O. Box 567, Claremont, CA 91711-0567, USA; his electronic address is jamesrroyse@hotmail.com.

David T. Runia is Master of Queen's College and Professorial Fellow in the School of Historical and Philosophical Studies at the University of Melbourne. His postal address is Queen's College, 1–17 College Crescent, Parkville 3052, Australia; his electronic address is runia@queens.unimelb.edu.au.

Torrey Seland is Dean of Studies and Professor in New Testament Studies at the School of Mission and Theology, Stavanger, Norway. His postal address is MHS, Misjonsmarka 12, 4024 Stavanger, Norway; his electronic mail address is torreys@gmail.com.

Karl Shuve is Assistant Professor in the Department of Religious Studies, University of Virginia. His postal address is Department of Religious Studies, P.O. Box 400126, Charlottesville, VA 22904-4126, USA; his electronic address is karl.shuve@virginia.edu.

Gregory E. Sterling is the Lillian Claus Professor of New Testament and the Reverend Henry L. Slack Dean of the Yale Divinity School. His postal address is 409 Prospect Street, New Haven, CT 06511, USA; his electronic address is gregory.sterling@yale.edu.

Nicole L. Tilford is a Visiting Lecturer in the Department of Religious Studies at Georgia State University. Her postal address is Department of Religious Studies, Georgia State University, P.O. Pox 3994, Atlanta, GA 30302-3994, USA. Her electronic address is ntilford@gsu.edu.

Thomas H. Tobin, S.J. is Professor of New Testament and Early Christianity at Loyola University Chicago. His postal address is Department of Theology, Loyola University Chicago, 1032 West Sheridan Road, Chicago, IL 60660-1537, USA; his electronic address is ttobin@luc.edu.

Walter T. Wilson is Professor of New Testament at Emory University. His postal address is Candler School of Theology, Emory University, Atlanta GA 30322, USA; his electronic address is wtwilso@emory.edu.

The Studia Philonica Annual 25 (2013) 254–260

INSTRUCTIONS TO CONTRIBUTORS

Articles and Book reviews can only be considered for publication in *The Studia Philonica Annual* if they rigorously conform to the guidelines established by the editorial board. For further information see also the website of the Annual:

http://www.nd.edu/~philojud

1. *The Studia Philonica Annual* accepts articles for publication in the area of Hellenistic Judaism, with special emphasis on Philo and his *Umwelt*. Articles on Josephus will be given consideration if they focus on his relation to Judaism and classical culture (and not on primarily historical subjects). The languages in which the articles may be published are English, French and German. Translations from Italian or Dutch into English can be arranged at a modest cost to the author.

2. Articles and reviews are to be sent to the editors in electronic form as email attachments. The preferred word processor is Microsoft Word. Users of other word processors are requested to submit a copy exported in a format compatible with Word, e.g. in RTF format. Manuscripts should be double-spaced, including the notes. Words should be italicized when required, not underlined. Quotes five lines or longer should be indented and may be single-spaced. For texts in Greek only Unicode fonts can be accepted. For Hebrew the font provided on the SBL website is recommended. In all cases it is **imperative** that authors give **full details** about the word processor (if it is not Word) and foreign language fonts used. Moreover, if the manuscript contains Greek or Hebrew material, a PDF version of the document must be sent together with the word processing file. If this proves difficult, a hard copy can be sent by mail or by fax. No handwritten Greek or Hebrew can be accepted. Authors are requested not to vocalize their Hebrew (except when necessary) and to keep their use of this language to a reasonable minimum. It should always be borne in mind that not all readers of the Annual can be expected to read Greek or Hebrew. Transliteration is encouraged for incidental terms.

3. Authors are encouraged to use inclusive language wherever possible, avoiding terms such as "man" and "mankind" when referring to humanity in general.

4. For the preparation of articles and book reviews the Annual follows the guidelines of *The SBL Handbook of Style for Ancient Near Eastern, Biblical, and Early Christian Studies*, Hendrickson: Peabody Mass., 1999. For members of the Society of Biblical Literature, a downloadable PDF version of this guide is available on the SBL website, www.sbl-site.org (if non-members need a copy, they are asked to contact the editors). Here are examples of how a monograph, a monograph in a series, an edited volume, an article in an edited volume and a journal article are to be cited in notes (different conventions apply for bibliographies):

> Joan E. Taylor, *Jewish Women Philosophers of First-Century Alexandria—Philo's 'Therapeutae' Reconsidered* (Oxford: Oxford University Press, 2003), 123.
> Ellen Birnbaum, *The Place of Judaism in Philo's Thought: Israel, Jews, and Proselytes* (BJS 290; SPhM 2; Atlanta: Scholars Press, 1996), 134.
> Gerard P. Luttikhuizen, ed., *Eve's Children: The Biblical Stories Retold and Interpreted in Jewish and Christian Traditions* (Themes in Biblical Narrative 5; Leiden: Brill, 2003), 145.
> Gregory E. Sterling, "The Bond of Humanity: Friendship in Philo of Alexandria," in *Greco-Roman Perspectives on Friendship*, (ed. John T. Fitzgerald; SBLRBS 34; Atlanta: Scholars Press, 1997), 203–23.
> James R. Royse, "Jeremiah Markland's Contribution to the Textual Criticism of Philo." *SPhA* 16 (2004): 50–60.

Note that abbreviations are used in the notes, but not in a bibliography. Numbers should be given in full for texts, e.g. *Aet.* 107–110; in references to modern publications the conventions of the *SBL Handbook of Style* should be followed (see p. 16). When joining up numbers in all textual and bibliographical references, the n-dash should be used and not the hyphen, i.e. 50–60, not 50-60. For publishing houses only the first location is given. Submissions which do not conform to these guidelines will be returned to the authors for re-submission.

5. The following abbreviations are to be used in both articles and book reviews.

(a) Philonic treatises are to be abbreviated according to the following list. Numbering follows the edition of Cohn and Wendland, using Arabic numbers only and full stops rather than colons (e.g. *Spec.* 4.123). Note that *De Providentia* should be cited according to Aucher's edition, and not the LCL translation of the fragments by F. H. Colson.

Abr.	*De Abrahamo*
Aet.	*De aeternitate mundi*
Agr.	*De agricultura*
Anim.	*De animalibus*
Cher.	*De Cherubim*
Contempl.	*De vita contemplativa*
Conf.	*De confusione linguarum*
Congr.	*De congressu eruditionis gratia*

Decal.	*De Decalogo*
Deo	*De Deo*
Det.	*Quod deterius potiori insidiari soleat*
Deus	*Quod Deus sit immutabilis*
Ebr.	*De ebrietate*
Flacc.	*In Flaccum*
Fug.	*De fuga et inventione*
Gig.	*De gigantibus*
Her.	*Quis rerum divinarum heres sit*
Hypoth.	*Hypothetica*
Ios.	*De Iosepho*
Leg. 1–3	*Legum allegoriae* I, II, III
Legat.	*Legatio ad Gaium*
Migr.	*De migratione Abrahami*
Mos. 1–2	*De vita Moysis* I, II
Mut.	*De mutatione nominum*
Opif.	*De opificio mundi*
Plant.	*De plantatione*
Post.	*De posteritate Caini*
Praem.	*De praemiis et poenis, De exsecrationibus*
Prob.	*Quod omnis probus liber sit*
Prov. 1–2	*De Providentia* I, II
QE 1–2	*Quaestiones et solutiones·in Exodum* I, II
QG 1–4	*Quaestiones et solutiones in Genesim* I, II, III, IV
Sacr.	*De sacrificiis Abelis et Caini*
Sobr.	*De sobrietate*
Somn. 1–2	*De somniis* I, II
Spec. 1–4	*De specialibus legibus* I, II, III, IV
Virt.	*De virtutibus*

(b) Standard works of Philonic scholarship are abbreviated as follows:

G-G   Howard L. Goodhart and Erwin R. Goodenough, "A General Bibliography of Philo Judaeus." In *The Politics of Philo Judaeus: Practice and Theory* (ed. Erwin R. Goodenough; New Haven: Yale University Press, 1938; repr. Georg Olms: Hildesheim, 1967), 125–321.

PCH   *Philo von Alexandria: die Werke in deutscher Übersetzung*, ed. Leopold Cohn, Isaac Heinemann *et al.*, 7 vols. (Breslau: M & H Marcus Verlag, Berlin: Walter de Gruyter, 1909–64).

PCW   *Philonis Alexandrini opera quae supersunt*, ed. Leopoldus Cohn, Paulus Wendland et Sigismundus Reiter, 6 vols. (Berlin: Georg Reimer, 1896–1915).

PLCL   *Philo in Ten Volumes (and Two Supplementary Volumes)*, English translation by F. H. Colson, G. H. Whitaker (and R. Marcus), 12 vols. (Loeb Classical Library; London: William Heinemann, Cambridge, Mass.: Harvard University Press, 1929–62).

PACS	Philo of Alexandria Commentary Series
PAPM	*Les œuvres de Philon d'Alexandrie*, French translation under the general editorship of Roger Arnaldez, Jean Pouilloux, and Claude Mondésert (Paris: Cerf, 1961–92).
R-R	Roberto Radice and David T. Runia, *Philo of Alexandria: an Annotated Bibliography 1937–1986* (VCSup 8; Leiden: Brill 1988).
RRS	David T. Runia, *Philo of Alexandria: an Annotated Bibliography 1987–1996* (VCSup 57; Leiden: Brill 2000).
RRS2	David T. Runia, *Philo of Alexandria: an Annotated Bibliography 1997–2006* (VCSup 109; Leiden: Brill 2012).
SPh	*Studia Philonica*
SPhA	*The Studia Philonica Annual*
SPhM	Studia Philonica Monographs

(c) References to biblical authors and texts and to ancient authors and writings are to be abbreviated as recommended in the *SBL Handbook of Style* §8.2–3. Note that biblical books are not italicized and that between chapter and verse a colon is placed (but for non-biblical references colons should not be used). Abbreviations should be used for biblical books when they are followed by chapter or chapter and verse unless the book is the first word in a sentence. Authors writing in German or French should follow their own conventions for biblical citations.

(d) For giving dates the abbreviations B.C.E. and C.E. are preferred and should be printed in small caps.

(e) Journals, monograph series, source collections, and standard reference works are to be be abbreviated in accordance with the recommendations listed in *The SBL Handbook of Style* §8.4. The following list contains a selection of the more important abbreviations, along with a few abbreviations of classical and philosophical journals and standard reference books not furnished in the list.

ABD	*The Anchor Bible Dictionary*, 6 vols. New York, 1992
AC	*L'Antiquité Classique*
ACW	Ancient Christian Writers
AGJU	Arbeiten zur Geschichte des antiken Judentums und des Urchristentums
AJPh	*American Journal of Philology*
AJSL	*American Journal of Semitic Languages*
ALGHJ	Arbeiten zur Literatur und Geschichte des hellenistischen Judentums
ANRW	*Aufstieg und Niedergang der römischen Welt*
APh	*L'Année Philologique*
BDAG	Bauer, W., F. W. Danker, W. F. Arndt, and F. W. Gingrich. *A Greek-English Lexicon of the New Testament and Other Early Christian literature.* 3^d ed. Chicago: University of Chicago Press, 1999
BibOr	Bibliotheca Orientalis

BJRL	*Bulletin of the John Rylands Library*
BJS	Brown Judaic Studies
BMCR	*Bryn Mawr Classical Review* (electronic)
BZAW	Beihefte zur Zeitschrift für die alttestamentliche Wissenschaft
BZNW	Beihefte zur Zeitschrift für die neutestamentliche Wissenschaft
BZRGG	Beihefte zur Zeitschrift für Religions- und Geistesgeschichte
CBQ	*The Catholic Biblical Quarterly*
CBQMS	The Catholic Biblical Quarterly. Monograph Series
CC	Corpus Christianorum, Turnhout
CIG	*Corpus Inscriptionum Graecarum*. Edited by A. Boeckh, 4 vols. in 8. Berlin, 1828–77
CIJ	*Corpus Inscriptionum Judaicarum*. Edited by J. B. Frey, 2 vols. Rome, 1936–52
CIL	*Corpus Inscriptionum Latinarum*. Berlin, 1862–
CIS	*Corpus Inscriptionum Semiticarum*. Paris, 1881–1962
CPh	*Classical Philology*
CPJ	*Corpus Papyrorum Judaicarum*. Edited by V. Tcherikover and A. Fuks, 3 vols. Cambrige Mass., 1957–64
CQ	*The Classical Quarterly*
CR	*The Classical Review*
CRINT	Compendia Rerum Iudaicarum ad Novum Testamentum
CPG	*Clavis Patrum Graecorum*. Edited by M. Geerard, 5 vols. and suppl. vol. Turnhout, 1974–98
CPL	*Clavis Patrum Latinorum*. Edited by E. Dekkers. 3rd ed. Turnhout, 1995
CSCO	Corpus Scriptorum Christianorum Orientalium
CWS	Classics of Western Spirituality
DA	Dissertation Abstracts
DBSup	*Dictionnaire de la Bible*, Supplément. Paris, 1928–
DPhA	R. Goulet (ed.), *Dictionnaire des philosophes antiques*, Paris, 1989–
DSpir	*Dictionnaire de Spiritualité*, 17 vols. Paris, 1932–95
EncJud	*Encyclopaedia Judaica*, 16 vols. Jerusalem, 1972
EPRO	Études préliminaires aux religions orientales dans l'Empire romain
FrGH	*Fragmente der Griechische Historiker*. Edited by F. Jacoby et al. Leiden, 1954–
FRLANT	Forschungen zur Religion und Literatur des Alten und Neuen Testaments
GCS	Die griechischen christlichen Schriftsteller, Leipzig
GLAJJ	M. Stern, *Greek and Latin Authors on Jews and Judaism*, 3 vols. Jerusalem, 1974–84
GRBS	*Greek, Roman and Byzantine Studies*
HKNT	Handkommentar zum Neuen Testament, Tübingen
HNT	Handbuch zum Neuen Testament, Tübingen
HR	*History of Religions*
HThR	*Harvard Theological Review*
HUCA	*Hebrew Union College Annual*
JAAR	*Journal of the American Academy of Religion*
JAOS	*Journal of the American Oriental Society*
JAC	*Jahrbuch für Antike und Christentum*
JBL	*Journal of Biblical Literature*
JHI	*Journal of the History of Ideas*
JHS	*The Journal of Hellenic Studies*

JJS	*The Journal of Jewish Studies*
JQR	*The Jewish Quarterly Review*
JR	*The Journal of Religion*
JRS	*The Journal of Roman Studies*
JSHRZ	Jüdische Schriften aus hellenistisch-römischer Zeit
JSJ	*Journal for the Study of Judaism in the Persian, Hellenistic and Roman Periods*
JSJSup	Supplements to the Journal for the Study of Judaism
JSNT	*Journal for the Study of the New Testament*
JSNTSup	Journal for the Study of the New Testament. Supplement Series
JSOT	*Journal for the Study of the Old Testament*
JSOTSup	Journal for the Study of the Old Testament. Supplement Series
JSP	*Journal for the Study of the Pseudepigrapha and Related Literature*
JSSt	*Journal of Semitic Studies*
JThS	*The Journal of Theological Studies*
KBL	L. Koehler and W. Baumgartner, *Lexicon in Veteris Testamenti libros*, 3 vols. 3rd ed. Leiden, 1967–83
KJ	*Kirjath Sepher*
LCL	Loeb Classical Library
LSJ	*A Greek-English Lexicon*. Edited by H. G. Liddell, R. Scott, H. S. Jones. 9th ed. with revised suppl. Oxford, 1996
MGWJ	*Monatsschrift für Geschichte und Wissenschaft des Judentums*
Mnem	*Mnemosyne*
NCE	*New Catholic Encyclopedia*, 15 vols. New York, 1967
NETS	New English Translation of the Septuagint. Edited by Albert Pietersma and Ben Wright, New York: Oxford University Press, 2007
NHS	Nag Hammadi Studies
NT	*Novum Testamentum*
NTSup	Supplements to Novum Testamentum
NTA	*New Testament Abstracts*
NTOA	Novum Testamentum et Orbis Antiquus
NTS	*New Testament Studies*
ODJ	*The Oxford Dictionary of Judaism*. Edited by R.J.Z. Werblowsky and G. Wigoder, New York 1997
OGIS	*Orientis Graeci inscriptiones selectae*
OLD	*The Oxford Latin Dictionary*. Edited by P. G. W. Glare. Oxford, 1982
OTP	*The Old Testament Pseudepigrapha*. Edited by J. H. Charlesworth. 2 vols. New York–London, 1983–85
PAAJR	*Proceedings of the American Academy for Jewish Research*
PAL	*Philon d'Alexandrie: Lyon 11–15 Septembre 1966*. Éditions du CNRS, Paris, 1967
PG	Patrologiae cursus completus: series Graeca. Edited by J. P. Migne. 162 vols. Paris, 1857–1912
PGL	*A Patristic Greek Lexicon*. Edited by G. W. H. Lampe. Oxford, 1961
PhilAnt	Philosophia Antiqua
PL	Patrologiae cursus completus: series Latina. Edited by J. P. Migne. 221 vols. Paris, 1844–64
PW	Pauly-Wissowa-Kroll, *Real-Encyclopaedie der classischen Altertumswissenschaft*. 49 vols. Munich, 1980
PWSup	Supplement to PW
RAC	*Reallexikon für Antike und Christentum*

RB	*Revue Biblique*
REA	*Revue des Études Anciennes*
REArm	*Revue des Études Arméniennes*
REAug	*Revue des Études Augustiniennes*
REG	*Revue des Études Grecques*
REJ	*Revue des Études Juives*
REL	*Revue des Études Latines*
RGG	*Die Religion in Geschichte und Gegenwart*, 7 vols. 3rd edition Tübingen, 1957–65
RhM	*Rheinisches Museum für Philologie*
RHR	*Revue de l'histoire des religions*
RQ	*Revue de Qumran*
RSR	*Revue des Sciences Religieuses*
Str-B	H. L. Strack and P. Billerbeck, *Kommentar zum Neuen Testament aus Talmud und Midrasch*, 6 vols. Munich, 1922–61
SBLDS	Society of Biblical Literature Dissertation Series
SBLMS	Society of Biblical Literature Monograph Series
SBLSCS	Society of Biblical Studies Septuagint and Cognate Studies
SBLSPS	Society of Biblical Literature Seminar Papers Series
SC	Sources Chrétiennes
Sem	*Semitica*
SHJP	E. Schürer, *The History of the Jewish People in the Age of Jesus Christ*. Revised edition, 3 vols. in 4. Edinburgh, 1973–87
SJLA	Studies in Judaism in Late Antiquity
SNTSMS	Society for New Testament Studies. Monograph Series
SR	*Studies in Religion*
STAC	Studies and Texts in Antiquity and Judaism
SUNT	Studien zur Umwelt des Neuen Testaments
SVF	*Stoicorum veterum fragmenta*. Edited by J. von Arnim. 4 vols. Leipzig, 1903–24
TDNT	*Theological Dictionary of the New Testament*. 10 vols. Grand Rapids, 1964–76
THKNT	Theologischer Handkommentar zum Neuen Testament, Berlin
TRE	*Theologische Realenzyklopädie*, Berlin
TSAJ	Texte und Studien zum Antike Judentum
TU	Texte und Untersuchungen zur Geschichte der altchristlichen Literatur, Berlin
TWNT	*Theologisches Wörterbuch zum Neuen Testament*, 10 vols. Stuttgart 1933–79.
TZ	*Theologische Zeitschrift*
VC	*Vigiliae Christianae*
VCSup	Supplements to Vigiliae Christianae
VT	*Vetus Testamentum*
WMANT	Wissenschaftliche Monographien zum Alten und Neuen Testament
WUNT	Wissenschaftliche Untersuchungen zum Neuen Testament
YJS	*Yale Jewish Studies*
ZAW	*Zeitschrift für die alttestamentliche Wissenschaft*
ZKG	*Zeitschrift für Kirchengeschichte*
ZKTh	*Zeitschrift für Katholische Theologie*
ZNW	*Zeitschrift für die neutestamentliche Wissenschaft*
ZRGG	*Zeitschrift für Religions- und Geistesgeschichte*